This book is being made available in Open Access thanks to the Women's Leadership Institute Australia (Trawalla Foundation).

Rewriting the Rules

Rewriting the Rules

*Gender-Responsive Lawmaking
for the Twenty-First Century*

Ramona Vijeyarasa

UNIVERSITY OF CALIFORNIA PRESS

University of California Press
Oakland, California

Suggested citation: Vijeyarasa, R. *Rewriting the Rules: Gender-Responsive Lawmaking for the Twenty-First Century*. Oakland: University of California Press, 2026. DOI: https://doi.org/10.1525/luminos.258

Library of Congress Cataloging-in-Publication Data

Names: Vijeyarasa, Ramona, author.
Title: Rewriting the rules : gender-responsive lawmaking for the
    twenty-first century / Ramona Vijeyarasa.
Description: Oakland, California : University of California Press, [2026] |
    Includes bibliographical references and index.
Identifiers: LCCN 2025023092 (print) | LCCN 2025023093 (ebook) |
    ISBN 9780520423534 (cloth) | ISBN 9780520412965 (paperback) |
    ISBN 9780520412972 (ebook)
Subjects: LCSH: Sex discrimination—Law and legislation—21st century. |
    Women—Legal status, laws, etc.—21st century. | Women's rights—
    21st century. | Law reform—21st century. | Equality before the law—
    21st century. | Gender-based violence—21st century.
Classification: LCC K3243 .V55 2026 (print) | LCC K3243 (ebook) |
    DDC 342.08/78—dc23/eng/20250606

LC record available at https://lccn.loc.gov/2025023092
LC ebook record available at https://lccn.loc.gov/2025023093

GPSR Authorized Representative: Easy Access System Europe,
Mustamäe tee 50, 10621 Tallinn, Estonia, gpsr.requests@easproject.com

34   33   32   31   30   29   28   27   26   25
10   9   8   7   6   5   4   3   2   1

To Matilda and Andia
In hope of a more gender equal future

CONTENTS

I have spent the better part of my scholarly life researching about the need to write women's lives into law. My views on what that means and why it matters have been shaped by twenty years of living and working on women's rights in every habitable continent. Yet, if pushed to pinpoint one of the origins of this book, I think back to Jakarta in May 2019. It was one month after Indonesia's general election, which mobilized 190 million Indonesian voters, more than seven times the size of the entire population of Australia, where I have spent the better part of my life. I was conducting fieldwork in Indonesia, and on that day, I was meeting the director of a women's rights organization.[1] I recall a heaviness in the air. Many of the women candidates that her organization had supported in the election had been unsuccessful in their political ambitions.

With the relentless noise of Jakarta traffic streaming through her window, the director and I talked about law reform. Her activism started in the 1980s when she was drawn to the absence of any studies in Indonesia documenting the scope of rape and sexual assault in the country. In response, she joined a team of young activists who accessed data from the central police station to calculate that one woman was being raped every five hours.

While she had *thought* gender-based violence would "automatically" attract people's sympathy, their claims were dismissed: "These women have been Westernized. Don't listen to these crazy women." Her organization remained resilient. "We invited friends from other countries, the Asian ones." Activists flew to Jakarta from Malaysia, Singapore, the Philippines, and Thailand. Poring over the data, they found that rapes were occurring at the same rates "in every other country" around them, and they eventually formed a regional network "to work together to overcome this."

When we met, the director's attention was on the underrepresentation of women in politics, and she implored me to share the experiences of other countries that had introduced and successfully implemented political quotas for women. Her activism persists in a country unlikely to score in the top tiers of any of the global gender-equality rankings that are often developed with Western-centric lenses. And she is tireless in seeking more from the law, challenging outdated legal frameworks in an effort to recenter women who have been historically excluded from the law's full protection.

Rewriting the Rules is inspired by my firsthand global knowledge that the countries I have been privileged to visit during my years working on women's rights may have more to offer for law reform than Western eyes frequently assume. It is driven by my fervent belief that the law will reach its optimum potential only if the inequalities embedded in it are called into question and righted, and if we confront law's underutilization in advancing the interests and needs of women and gender-diverse people. And it is motivated by my hope that there is enough in this book to keep bringing women activists together in anticipation of a more equal future realized through the law.

ACKNOWLEDGMENTS

This book would not have been possible without the generous support of the Women's Leadership Institute Australia (WLIA), funded by the Trawalla Foundation. My WLIA Fellowship has supported my work on gender-responsive lawmaking since 2020, providing me the time to write and the inspiration, words of wisdom, and the invaluable sisterhood of its fellows.

Enormous gratitude is owed to the team at the University of California Press, especially Executive Editor Maura Roessner, who saw promise in this book's potential to challenge existing paradigms; Editorial Assistant Sam Warren for his patient assistance through the manuscript's early stages; and Senior Production Editor Jeff Anderson, who shepherded the book through to the shelves. Special thanks to the impressive copyediting work of Barbara Armentrout on the book's final manuscript.

Throughout the writing of this book, colleagues in the Faculty of Law at the University of Technology Sydney (UTS) have been a constant support. I especially want to thank the Feminist Legal Research Group (FLRG) and the International Law Research Cluster. The FLRG's work-in-progress workshops were essential for the development of chapters 2 and 3. Particular thanks are owed to Katherine Biber, Beth Goldblatt, Trish Luker, Linda Steele (who also provided feedback on an earlier version of chapter 1 and the book proposal), Ana Filipa Vrdoljak, Jane Wangmann, then-PhD-candidate Kate Thomas, Master's student Oliver Moore, and visiting researchers to UTS Margaret Johnson and Sally Weldon for incredibly insightful feedback on these early chapters.

I offer enormous thanks to my friends Tanya Jakimow, Margaret Jolly, and Sonia Palmieri, with whom I was editing a thoroughly important collection at the time of writing. This collaboration challenged me to think about the language of

"Global North/South" and "Majority and Minority World," fundamental given that a key task of this book is to challenge the stigmatizing boxes in which Global South countries are too often placed.

The Australian Feminist Legislation Project, born at Monash University under the sage leadership of Becky Batagol, Kate Seear, Heli Askola, and Jamie Walvisch, was underway as I wrote much of this book. I was privileged to be a part of that project, which helped inform my thinking in chapter 5. While my work for that project sought to offer a politically palatable rewrite of the Australian Modern Slavery Act 2018, I hope that in *Rewriting the Rules*, I offer readers not only a sense of the pragmatic pathway but also the contours of a more visionary use of the law to eradicate exploitation in modern supply chains.

During the tail end of my writing, I attended the Berkeley Center on Comparative Equality and Anti-Discrimination Law Conference in Bangalore, India, before visiting the Faculty of Law at the Federal University of Minas Gerais in Belo Horizonte, Brazil. That was followed by a very privileged few months spent at the University of Oxford's Bonavero Institute of Human Rights and the Faculty of Law at the European University Institute (EUI). Oxford was full of insightful meetings, workshops, and discussions, while EUI offered the beautiful hills of Florence as a backdrop while I edited and clarified the messages I wanted to convey in the book. I owe thanks to all of these institutions.

I specifically want to thank academic colleagues who have read and commented on particular chapters. Your intellectual generosity has been gratefully received: Elizabeth Hill on paid parental leave, Laurie Berg and Joellen Riley Munton on modern slavery, Helen Hodgson and Leonora Risse on gender-responsive budgeting, Kuntala Lahiri-Dutt on gender perspectives to artisanal and small-scale mining, Darren Rosenblum on corporate board quotas, and Anjalee de Silva on artificial intelligence.

I sincerely and gratefully thank my research assistants Tina Huang, Wendy Lam, Stella Magoulias, and Diego Alexander Villazon.

And now to my family. When you tell people you are writing a book, you are often asked, "What motivates you?" Growing up in a household with parents who make you acutely aware of the power of your education and privilege to do more with your life is motivation enough. I am who I am and do what I do because of my parents, Rae and Vije. I thank my sisters, Sheila and Vaneeta, whose successes in achieving their life goals are a source of inspiration.

Finally, to the three people to whom I owe the most thanks for helping me get across the finish line. To Jose-Miguel, who critically reads every word, provides perspective when it gets lost, and is a constant sense of calm, especially when deadlines loom, and who co-raises our two girls, for whom we hope—must believe—the future will be different. And to my wonderful daughters, who give me my much-needed breaks from writing and the motivation to write in the first place. Without my three people, this book would never have happened.

Introduction

Why We Need to Rewrite the Rules

Women's lives in most countries around the world—albeit not all—are vastly different today from the days when women could not vote, when married women had no legal existence independent of their husbands, or when domestic violence was hidden within the walls of one's home. Legal protections have gained ground, alongside a growing recognition of gendered inequalities. Yet for many women activists working on the frontlines of the struggle for gender equality, there is an acute awareness that women's rights are far from fully realized and gender gaps may never fully close.

As the examples shared within the pages of this book show, we need to rewrite the rules because in far too many legal systems, in countries both rich and poor, the law continues to underserve women. Legislation has not yet reached its optimum potential in eliminating discrimination. At times, women's secondary status is codified in the words of the law itself, whereas at other times, it is entrenched because of the way the rules are lived by women.

Can we do better at writing women's lives into law? We often hear that the law has remained blind to the interests of women *because* women are absent from the legal drafting table. Surely the law would improve if women could play a part in writing it?

A deeper interrogation of the data, however, tells a slightly different story. According to the Inter-Parliamentary Union, a relatively diverse set of countries boast the highest percentage of women occupying seats in the lower house (or the single house) of parliament, ranging from 50 to 61 percent: Rwanda, Cuba, Nicaragua, Mexico, Andorra, and the United Arab Emirates.[1] On average, as of October 2024, 26.9 percent of members of parliament worldwide were women.[2] While far from ideal—for every one woman lawmaker, there are almost three men—we must nonetheless recognize that there are more than just a few women around the world, notwithstanding often part of the elite, who are lawmakers.

More sophisticated views shift attention to the gendered hierarchies in the civil service that determine who gets to assist the lawmakers. Indeed, underrepresentation of women in the bureaucracy is as much an issue in Zambia[3] as it is in the Netherlands.[4] An even more nuanced approach turns to the point at which a policy has attained the required political and ministerial commitment and needs to be translated into legalese. Are women among the privileged few who get to hold the pen?

Here again, the statistics tend to challenge assumptions. In Australia, Parliamentary Counsel takes the policy decisions of the Cabinet or members of Parliament or senators and turns them into legal text. Many staff from the Office of Parliamentary Counsel—at the federal and state levels—have been legal drafters for years. Many of them are women. The Australian office is led by the first parliamentary counsel and two second parliamentary counsels; the three statutory appointments from 2021 to 2023 were women.[5] In 2021, of the 111 staff that made up the Australian Office of Parliamentary Counsel, 70 were women, a slight increase on the majority already held by women in 2020 (66 of 108 staff members).[6]

In the United States, congressional committee members are the gatekeepers of their jurisdictions, effectively policy experts and agenda controllers in their policy areas. While the percentage of women on these committees has never equaled that of men, the proportion of women on key congressional committees—such as the Rules Committee, which "sets the stage for legislative debate on the house floor"—has reached as high as 40 percent.[7] In Canada, the "legislative services" of the Department of Justice in 2021 described itself as "broadly gender-balanced."[8] In other words, women *do* write the law. And this is not only a "Western" phenomenon. As of January 2025, in the Philippines, the deputy secretary for legislation, the executive director for legislation, the director-general of the Legislative Budget Research and Monitoring Office, and the senate legal counsel were all roles held by women.[9]

While few women—far too few—manage to climb to the lofty heights of president, those who do so play a key role in shaping their nation's laws.[10] Women presidents exercise veto or partial veto power. Women presidents issue executive orders. Women presidents deliver state-of-the-nation or speech-from-the-throne annual national addresses that set in motion national reforms. In some instances, these women presidents are even aided by legislative executive committees whose job it is to translate the presidential vision into law.

Clearly, some women write the law. And if women are present in lawmaking, even if not to the extent we may desire, we must ask ourselves, "When did we take a wrong turn in our efforts to write women into law? Can that wrong turn be corrected?"

WHY GENDER NEUTRALITY WAS NOT THE ANSWER

The shift to gender-neutral language in law was once seen as a marker of success of the feminist project,[11] possibly even the "end of the 'masculine rule.'"[12] English-speaking jurisdictions—from the US to the UK, from Canada to

Australia—witnessed a burgeoning call at the end of the twentieth century for "gender-neutral" legalese. The legal *he* as a stand-in for *she* was no longer acceptable, and gender-specific pronouns, such as *they* and *them* or both *he* and *she*,[13] and gender-neutral job titles such as *chairperson* emerged as the new norm.[14]

This achievement of challenging linguistic sexism is not to be disregarded. Not all nations have even come this far. A stark example is the constitution of Sri Lanka, a nation that has had *three* women heads of state, but whose English-language version of its constitution refers to the president and prime minister as "he."[15] Even countries considered global leaders on gender equality fall foul. Spain's constitution remains written in the masculine, a point of significant political and media debate in the country precisely because it is seen as a signifier of Spanish women's "subordinate" status and one that Spanish feminists of all sexes have called to be revised to afford women their full visibility as autonomous individuals.[16]

However, law is a language in and of itself. Mere tinkering with the terms has not gone near far enough to challenge how law constructs our societies and consequently distributes power within them. Law remains all-powerful in determining who enjoys access to the opportunities that society offers and who does not. Gender-neutral legislation has ultimately failed to eradicate law's gender stereotypes and traditions. Decisions about the division of marital property remain highly localized and discretionary, and they reproduce gendered norms concerning women's roles and "value" in the home and in society.[17] Too often, this pursuit of neutrality has also meant women's individual experiences and voices began to disappear from legislative debates, even in relation to rape and sexual violence, for which there is an evident need to center women's experiences as a group and to acknowledge female-identifying individuals as the majority of victims.[18]

Quite contrary to gender neutrality, law needs rewriting in order to write women back in. This position naturally leads us to ask which women's lives are represented by law's words.

WHICH WOMEN AND WHICH LAWS?

The subject of substantive representation of women's interests has long inspired robust debate.[19] Put vividly by Indian feminist Chandra Talpade Mohanty, "The interests of urban, middle-class, educated housewives . . . could surely not be seen as being the same as those of their uneducated, poor maids."[20] So perhaps the issue is not that women are denied the opportunity to write the law but rather that the law and lawmakers rarely represent the interests of the vast majority of women whose everyday lives are directly and indirectly touched by the law.

It is not just that law is failing to make women's lives better, but perhaps we are witnessing a failure to acknowledge and respond to the lived experiences of women whose needs, interests, and experiences are distinct and driven by their racial, cultural, linguistic, ability, age, gender, and sexual orientation differences, to name a few. Law reform processes, at times, *refuse* to listen, and even when they do, listening fails to be done with openness, receptivity, and attentiveness.[21] Lawmaking therefore listens only selectively, and in the process, it risks silencing women's voices.

Nonetheless, as the stories in this book will demonstrate, a different narrative of who is failed by the law reform project may be needed. It is not only or always women from the "poor" or "underdeveloped" or "developing" Global South who are denied their freedoms and rights in the law. In recent years, a concerted attempt has been made to rename the "developing world" the "Majority World," being the part of the world where the most people reside.[22] These nations in the Global South may offer greater lessons for gender-responsive lawmaking than is often anticipated. And while to measure can be "to know,"[23] we may end up "knowing" based on biased calculations that obscurely penalize low-income jurisdictions, if we measure selectively.[24]

In this vein, the notion of "rewriting" has been adopted with a double-barreled meaning. It is both the laws that need rewriting as well as our perceptions. This book endeavors to respond to the call of Liberian scholar Robtel Neajai Pailey, to de-center our Western, "White gaze" in our "conceptualization of worldly advancement."[25] Countering the dominance of English-language and Anglo-Saxon good practice, *Rewriting the Rules* directs its attention to less-explored regions of the world. It seeks to uncover hidden good practice that is too often ignored simply because of the inability or unwillingness of English-speaking lawmakers to attend to legislative reforms emerging from jurisdictions whose legal corpus is not solely or primarily in English. When deliberate attention is paid to the underexplored, the Global South can be revalued as it often should be and, in some cases, pulled up the rungs of the gender equality ladder on which nations are placed through often biased annual global report cards and Western-centric frameworks.[26]

In this pursuit of greater inclusivity, we must also expand our analysis by examining a much broader body of laws than scholars have traditionally done. Present-day constructions of "women's issues" naturally result from a long-standing and historic tendency to focus on sexual violence and the "victimization" of women.[27] Yet too often what counts as a "gendered issue" starts and ends with a focus on laws about issues that overtly affect women such as rape and family law.[28] By contrast, women's lived experiences demand a scholarly challenge to the erroneous notion that other areas of law—bankruptcy, finance, corruption—are "gender neutral."[29] *Rewriting the Rules* seeks to bring this gender lens to other domains—such as artificial intelligence—where we have the rare opportunity to embed a gender perspective from the very beginning of our regulatory efforts. In practice, this requires greater gender expertise at the legal drafter's table across a broad spectrum of laws and an environment in which these voices will be respected and heard.[30]

WHY WOMEN?

At her US Supreme Court confirmation hearing in March 2022, Ketanji Brown Jackson, the first Black woman to sit on the US Supreme Court, was asked, "Can you provide a definition for the word *woman*?" Jackson responded, "No, I can't. . . . Not in this context. I'm not a biologist."[31] That loaded question reflects how women's lives—their bodies, needs, interests, rights—are the subject of explicit and implicit lawmaking. That gender is learned and socially constructed and not innate has been widely acknowledged for several decades[32] and remains so in contemporary scholarship. Recognizing gender as a principle that drives the organization of society, the question this book seeks to grapple with, at various points, is what role the law plays in shaping individual and collective understandings of gender.

Moreover, as we progress further into the twenty-first century, we are confronted with small cracks in the frameworks we once held as true. The very notion of parity is losing meaning in this non-binary world in which we seek *collective* change. The term *women* has been deployed in *Rewriting the Rules* as a societal concept as much as a political one.[33] It is not used to exclude, for example, non-cisgender women or to assimilate, for instance, by placing all women into a singular category, failing to acknowledge difference. To the contrary, the category of "women" is intended to challenge essentialist approaches.[34] It is justified by asking, "Who is left out of current legal frameworks and structures?"[35] And it invites us to consider what gendered harms and gender-based discrimination the law perpetuates or fails to address. With a focus on female-identifying individuals, we can bring greater visibility to the impact of laws on the women frequently at the periphery of legal debates. In turn, we may hope to see unmarried women marginalized from property inheritance and women of color impacted by artificial intelligence's racialized and gendered biases brought to the center of the legislative conversation.

Much of this gender-based discrimination that law reinforces or fails to correct harms a wider set of individuals beyond women who similarly suffer from multiple but also gendered inequalities.[36] Australian scholar Dianne Otto identifies in her well-known writing on feminist and queer theory how the hard work performed to make international law (and I would add domestic law) better for women seeks to make everyone's lives "more fully livable."[37] In Otto's view, referring concretely to the LGBTQI+ communities' experiences of law reform, there is a coexistence between feminist and queer theories' goals. Challenging gender normativity should be a collective struggle; new frameworks that both feminist and queer scholars have to offer can build greater solidarity, promote redistributive values, challenge inequalities, advance peace, and ensure environmental sustainability.[38] *Rewriting the Rules* therefore acknowledges that all individuals are "gendered beings" and gendering the law is an exercise in bringing visibility to all.

However, I do not seek to overstate my reach. This book retains a primary focus on women, which includes all transgender women's experiences. I seek to guide readers to understand how a gendered lens can make visible the differences between how men and women and non-binary people experience the law or suffer from the disadvantages that the law creates.

WHY LAW?

This book is exclusively focused on the law. It is a study of how to improve legislation. Law matters to women precisely because law is a formidable instrument. The fact that no legal education was permitted in many British colonies before independence is telling of the full consciousness of authorities about the power of the law. In Nigeria, for instance, no local facility to train lawyers until 1962[39] meant the economically advantaged were left to travel on government scholarships or resources pooled by family and friends to read law in the United Kingdom— only to return home with little knowledge of local law, "stumbling awkwardly around the volumes of Nigerian cases and statutes."[40]

While law is not a magic bullet, it can be "a critical game changer" in a gendered landscape. As put by Ugandan legal scholar Sylvia Tamale and South African feminist theorist Jane Bennett, the law serves as a shield that "protect[s] women against discrimination and the violation of their fundamental rights, and a sword to challenge and overturn unjust sexist practices and to effect fundamental change to the status quo."[41]

Law's demonstrable power to bring about profound shifts in gendered norms has also been proven. Compulsory education shifted social views about sending girls to school alongside boys.[42] Local laws helped prohibit polygamy[43] while simultaneously shifting social attitudes against the practice. Admittedly, some feminists still ask if polygamy is inherently bad for women or if the root cause of the problem lies elsewhere, such as the codification of discrimination that marriage can entail and the risk of shielding abuse within marital relationships.[44]

Kathleen Hull's work on same-sex marriage elucidates the overwhelming "cultural power" of the law in particular Western jurisdictions.[45] Law reform helped galvanize the acceptance of a greater diversity of family forms than ever witnessed in the past. In the US, local laws enabling same-sex marriage have decreased biases against same-sex couples at double the rate of change when compared to in the absence of such a law,[46] although the right of same-sex couples to marry, which "seemed destined to become sleepy and settled" in the US, was feared under attack at the time of publication.[47]

Nevertheless, we must also acknowledge a critical undercurrent that challenges the law for having narrowed rather than expanded our sense of what is possible for a more equal world. In the words of Australian legal historian Michelle Arrow, those activists who wanted to dismantle the nuclear family and abolish marriage "might cringe at the idea that same-sex marriage became *the* political issue for LGBTQI people."[48] Ratna Kapur, law professor and postcolonial scholar, when writing about LGBTQI+ advocacy, criticizes how queer radicality has been "swept into the normative vortex of human rights."[49] We must then concede that a more transformative vision may be suppressed when one seeks to move the goalposts rather than take them down altogether. As UK sociologist Carol Smart has pointed out, women are judged "by different and inappropriate standards," such as sexual promiscuity.[50] To therefore use the law to criminalize sexual crimes against women could merely extend the law's power and reach. For women to depend on the highly masculinized institute of the law to protect them from rape could be seen as re-empowering men.

This caution is important to heed. In this sense, law—or law alone—will not make our world suddenly gender equal. Yet the law can embed women's interests in a way that can be harder to undo. The passage of a law, even before we turn to the challenge of implementation, can be a significant moment, and once embedded in law, the benefits can be sustained. Moreover, law has untapped potential. Scotland demonstrated this in August 2022, when it became the first nation in the world to legally oblige the state to distribute menstrual products free in schools with its Period Products (Free Provision) Act.[51] New Zealand and Kenya were among the countries that previously followed the same practice but, in those cases, the right was not established in law. Perhaps Scottish policymakers contemplated whether the best intervention would be a de jure or a de facto one (or both). Or perhaps they simply felt the need to acknowledge with the black letter of the law that menstruators have limited choice over menstruation. Either way, writing it into law means that such a view will outlive the members who approved the bill's passage, forcing future lawmakers to face public scrutiny if the decision is to be reversed.

IS LAW THE (ONLY) ANSWER?

According to the *Smithsonian Magazine*, in 1918, the catalogue for the Earnshaw's Infants' Department claimed the "generally accepted rule is pink for the boys, and blue for the girls. The reason is that pink, being a more decided and stronger color, is more suitable for the boy, while blue, which is more delicate and dainty, is prettier for the girl."[52] The colors were reversed in the 1940s.

From blue to pink reflects three considerations that have informed this book. First, seemingly ingrained sociocultural norms are regularly in flux and law does not always have a part to play in these changes. Second, the shift in the color of choice for dressing girls is a telling reminder that norms may have strange and unjustified origins. Yet this evolution from blue to pink as the "preferred" color for girls also reflects the reality that the status quo *can* change—also reflected in contestations over girls' presumed delicacy. More importantly, normative change often owes thanks to the individuals and groups that uproot the biases on which our societies are often absurdly constructed. If the status quo can change, law too can play its part in pushing forward important societal shifts. Besides, the alternative is grim. We cannot leave the law to merely paper over entrenched inequalities between men and women. Law can and should play a more fundamental role in correcting discrimination.

I am not the first to study the law from the standpoint of women. Many have undertaken this task. Yet not everyone agrees that this task should be undertaken. The pursuit of women-centered legislation has been criticized as an act that fetishizes law's potential,[53] on what is a false quest to seek reform *through* law.[54] The very categories of law were made "at a time when women played no part in the law," forcing women to fit their experiences into a predetermined frame.[55] Women are forced to either seek equality in law and rise up to the levels that men have attained or to strive for legislation that acknowledges women's "difference." Either way, men remain the common core against which all is measured. We have achieved little to alter this male-centric nature of law and legal systems.

For the group of scholars, commentators, and activists who have chided the project altogether, legal systems and those who uphold them, at best, exclude women's perspectives and at worst sustain women's oppression. As a result, the law and legal systems lay out crude categories into which women's lives rarely fit, and if they do, it is often uncomfortably. The law remains gendered, is a manifestation of power, and too often works to the detriment of women.[56] Feeling affronted and yet vindicated by the decision in *Dobbs v. Jackson Women's Health Organization*,[57] which overturned the constitutional right to an abortion in the US and left women's bodies to be legislated over by states across the country, many legal scholars would today stand by the eloquent critique of Smart that the law is "[too] deaf to core concerns of feminism."[58] Why work within a broken system?

Advocates who seek to reimagine law's institutions by working with and within the system have been left standing a little in the cold. Yet this challenge to law's historical "disqualification" of feminism as a form of knowledge has been a decades' long project led by pioneering scholars.[59] Today we remain fervent in our belief that "equality in law is crucial to gender equality, as women and girls look to the laws of their State to protect, fulfill and enforce their rights," to use the words of the United Nations.[60] This book seeks to offer the evidence to prove this. Chapter after chapter, *Rewriting the Rules* offers substantive examples to demonstrate that law does matter and that legislation drafted to account for gendered differences in how laws are experienced can make a difference to women's lives.

Neat categorization is inherently fraught. Law may be "good" for some women and bad for others. Nonetheless, at the outset of this book, it is important to set up the parameters for the discussion to follow. What meaning is attributed to good (or "gender-responsive") and bad (or "gender-regressive") is elaborated in chapter 1. The goal is the eradication of discrimination, both overt and implicit, in law—such as Vietnam's compulsory retirement age that is lower for women than it is for men in the public sector[61] or Sri Lanka's requirement for counseling and mediation for married couples before granting a divorce, hindering women's free exit from unequal and potentially violent relationships.[62] It is also about maximizing law's potential to actually correct inequality, quotas for women's representation being such an, at times, controversial example of law's corrective role.[63]

There are limits to what stronger legislative drafting can achieve. Sensitivity to the cultural contexts in which law reform occurs is needed. International scholars and activists often hesitate when applying universal standards across all jurisdictions and it is widely acknowledged by comparative scholars that law cannot always be readily transplanted as we travel across borders. Nor is law reform a linear process. Moreover, women's organizations risk being co-opted, instrumentalized, and depoliticized in the process of advocating for gender-responsive laws.[64] The process of law reform itself, therefore, is inherently full of compromises. Ultimately, too, there are areas of law where gender-responsive change may not be possible if the dominant economic order remains the same.

THE TASK OF REWRITING THE RULES

Accepting that the law is not "all-powerful" in its ability to legislate better for a diversity of women, we can nonetheless acknowledge law's potential. It sets or redirects societal stands and can be used to correct discrimination, including discrimination that the law created in the first place. It can be a vehicle for redress. The question is then how one responds to these realities. This book adopts the guidance of US lawyer, activist, and law professor Mari Matsuda, who called for "multiple consciousness" in simultaneously seeing both the oppressive harm *and* the value of the legal system:

> To the feminist lawyer faced with pregnant teenagers seeking abortions, it would be absurd to reject the use of an elitist legal system, or the use of the concept of rights, when such use is necessary to meet the immediate needs of her client. There are times to stand outside the courtroom door and say "this procedure is a farce, the legal system is corrupt, justice will never prevail in this land as long as privilege rules in the courtroom." There are times to stand inside the courtroom and say "this is a nation of laws, laws recognizing fundamental values of rights, equality and personhood."[65]

Australian professor of public law Ann Genovese also identified the middle ground between critique and practical change: "By taking law's doctrines and techniques seriously, feminist jurists have shown many times that to change law—to reform its practices or alter its perceptions—does not necessarily involve a polemical position that would force feminists to sit outside the door of the court. Instead, the task has been to master law, to understand its rehearsed movements and its rules of interpretation, as well as to monitor its lived effects."[66] Learning from Matsuda and Genovese, this book aims for that middle ground. We must not sit outside the legal system. Rather, the task at hand is to conquer the law in all its diversity. We remain too attracted to renouncing the tools of the master because we have not fully envisaged what law can do for women. My task here is to make apparent what would that law look like if written with women in mind.

Rewriting the Rules also takes the challenge of "law in all its diversity" particularly seriously. Taking readers through a journey across legal domains, a deliberate effort has been made to examine both stubborn areas of women's inequality and emerging areas that have not yet been sufficiently gendered. *Rewriting the Rules* "expands" the landscape. When revisiting old terrain, it shines the spotlight a little differently, thereby offering new lessons—from workplace leave for survivors of intimate-partner violence to the differentiated impact of the deployment of artificially intelligent systems on women and gender-diverse people.

Yet each chapter serves an additional goal, providing a lesson for the practice of gender-responsive lawmaking. Chapter 2 looks to the Global South for good practices on workplace leave for victims of violence. In pursuit of more equal parenting, Chapter 3 calls for a de-gendering and de-sexing of paid parental leave to give fathers and partners greater access to leave while breaking the continuum between pregnancy and parenting that often leaves care and child-rearing in mother's hands. Bringing a gender lens to modern slavery in chapter 4 demands that women victim-survivors of supply-chain exploitation are seen and heard in the reconceptualization of what a gender-responsive supply chain may look like. The discussion of artisanal and small-scale mining (chapter 5) explores the risks that legal formalism poses for women, while chapter 6's discussion of corporate boards illustrates that at times, strong legal intervention is the only way to redress a situation. Experiences of gender budgeting (chapter 7) illustrate the necessity of law to institutionalize change that may otherwise be easily lost. In chapter 8's study of AI, we have an opportunity to reflect on law's role in areas yet untouched by the legislator. Within these themes, this book provides examples of how gender does and should influence legislation.

Many topics could have made their way onto the pages of this book, which is founded on the premise that every area of legislation needs a gender lens. Ultimately, not everything could fit. Topics such as legal access to abortion, fundamental to women's lives and a pertinent example of the struggle for law reform, and the global response to climate change, which at times homogenizes women's experiences[67] or erroneously treats the climate crisis as a gender-neutral concern,[68] have not been canvassed in any depth. The reason for this choice is simple. While these areas similarly demand a feminist re-theorizing, these subjects have been given robust treatment by others, including in recent scholarship.[69]

By presenting legislative reforms from across the globe, this book seeks to provoke new lines of thought by taking readers on a global tour—from the Philippines to Ecuador, from Peru to Malaysia and South Korea, and across Africa, including to South Africa, Kenya, Nigeria, and Ghana, countries often overlooked by scholars and legislators of an English-language tradition due to the Global North's magnetic field, like a needle in a compass. The book's goal is to share these untold stories.

With one central goal in mind—to contribute to the "collective liberation"[70] of women and girls in all their diversity through law—this book is the conversation starter. While the journey will continue well beyond the final page, *Rewriting the Rules* seeks to motivate a richer and deeper dialogue to ensure that the law best serves the interests of a diversity of women, particularly those who have been most silenced from the law's representation. Hopefully, readers arrive at the end point of this journey with a belief that a gender equal world, through law, is possible.

Gender and the Law

A Framework for Defining Gender-Responsive Legislation

Are we merely trying to reassure law graduates that their investment has been sound and purposeful when we tell them amid the heightened emotion of graduation that law is "a precious and formidable instrument that can be wielded to accomplish profound good,"[1] or is there truth to this evaluation of law's power to make society better? Believers in law's potential often take it for granted that law will naturally move in a progressive direction as time passes. But can we guarantee that law will play its part in bringing about much sought-after societal change? And more importantly, how do we know when the end goal of gender-responsive legislation has been reached?

The law has evident limitations, and in the previous chapter, I canvassed the debates as to whether we should pursue change through law. While numerous scholars and activists remain reluctant to work *within* the boundaries of the law, *Rewriting the Rules* makes the case that legislation can be better and more effectively deployed to advance women's rights nationally, regionally, and on a global scale. This book, in short, is a defense of gender-responsive legislation. Practical lessons can be extracted from laws that are identified as "good" in order for us to rethink how we approach lawmaking to improve the lives of a diversity of women.

The natural next step is to set up a blueprint for determining success. Hilary Charlesworth, who at the time of publication was one of only four women judges out of fifteen on the International Court of Justice—a historic high for the court despite women still accounting for less than one-third of the judiciary—self-critically cautioned fellow feminist scholars years ago to stop "talking to ourselves."[2] Feminist messages without feminist methods were unlikely to bring about change or give this feminist language "life on the ground."[3]

In heeding this call, this chapter begins by unpacking some potential feminist methods for gender-responsive lawmaking. Four lines of thought shape this chapter and those that follow. First, we need to define the endgame in order to determine when laws prove adequately responsive to gendered differences on the one hand, or when lawmaking shows an overt gender blindness on the other. Second, we need to establish benchmarks that can be applied across jurisdictions to know when this gender-responsive standard is met. Third, we must acknowledge the heterogenous nature of the category "women," embracing the challenge of drafting laws with an intersectional lens. Finally, we want to evaluate and measure, seeking the evidence to establish when and how gender-responsive laws substantively improve women's lives. The chapter concludes with a firm call—one that continues throughout *Rewriting the Rules*—to go beyond the "feminist template" with a more inclusive and multi-linguistic and multi-jurisdictional search for the good practices that we may otherwise miss. In other words, if we actively seek out legislative reforms that go beyond our existing knowledge base, what new possibilities emerge? The result is a call for a "feminist +" template that is inherently global in outlook.

REIMAGINING A PLACE FOR WOMEN IN THE LAW

Feminist legal scholars worked hard over several decades to achieve a legitimate place in law school curricula. While not a success story in all jurisdictions and certainly not across all areas of law,[4] feminist legal theory today is generally considered an important cross-cutting lens of analysis.[5] Building on this foundational work, the 2000s saw scholars translate this theory into a reimagining of a place for women in judicial decision-making. Scholars filled a gap in what had come before—the "missing" feminist judgments[6]—and attempted the "real-world" task of judgment writing. Diana Majury credits the creation, back in 2004, of the women's court of Canada as lighting the spark for these feminist judgment projects worldwide.[7] In doing so, scholars not only wanted to offer a new form of critical legal scholarship but to demonstrate to the world that these real judgments could have been decided differently.[8] Feminist judgments projects flourished, popping up in England and Wales,[9] Australia,[10] the US,[11] Northern Ireland and Ireland,[12] New Zealand,[13] Scotland,[14] and India,[15] as well as in international law.[16] Projects are underway in Africa[17] and Mexico.[18]

The feminist judgments projects offered an alternative way to view law, the judiciary, and how judicial decisions impact different people's lives differently. It instigated an entire body of "intersectional rewrites." Queer scholar Senthorun Raj, while expressing a reluctance to right wrongs using a homophobic legal system that privileges assimilation over difference,[19] is one of a three-member team (with Nuno Ferreira and Maria Federica Moscati) leading the "queer judgements" project, described as a "queer dance through 26 judgments and commentaries."[20] Raj's own study of queer-related jurisprudence reflects upon what is made visible and hyper-visible in these judgments but also, importantly, what is left unsaid.[21] In Australia, Nicole Watson and Heather Douglas have led a collaboration of Indigenous scholars (primary writers of each rewrite), often with a non-Indigenous writing partner, to "reimagine justice through an Indigenous lens."[22] This collaboration has written into case law the stories, histories, experiences, and perspectives of Australia's Indigenous peoples, for whom law has largely been an oppressive tool.[23] Earth-centered judgments by the Wild Law Judgment Project[24] and the UK Earth Law Judgments Project call for a transformation of legal institutions to foster a healthier relationship between people and the planet.[25]

With this "missing-judgments" platform at hand, the Australian Feminist Legislation Project—one of the first of its kind worldwide—followed. It has sought to ask the "woman question" by determining how to challenge the male-centric nature of the *legislative* process.[26] Scholars embraced the task of rewriting laws to respond to gendered differences and needs. At the heart of the task was not a question about whether some abstract "person" (read "man") would find the law objectionable, but rather whether a woman would find it so.[27] The task of rewriting existing legislation—constitutions and laws that range from property to crime, from aged care to migration—was not without its challenges. My own experiences in rewriting Australia's Modern Slavery Act[28] for this project reflects Davina Cooper's query as to whether a law reform proposal can be presented as a viable text that may eventuate its passage into law while still, subversively, "unsettl[ing] the law,"[29] a question I revisit later in this book (chapter 4 and the conclusion).

Importantly, these endeavors over the past two decades—collectives of feminist, queer, Indigenous, and environmental judgments, and the feminist legislation project—have embraced the conventions of the law. They have sought to work *within* existing systems and parameters to show how these very same tools can be used differently to yield different outcomes. The result is the creation of a "feminist template" for law reform[30]—through decision-making and statute—that has helped to inform this book. It is with this foundation in mind that I turn to the task of defining "good" practice.

IN PURSUIT OF GENDER-RESPONSIVE LAWS: STANDARDS AND MEASURES

What is the end goal? When do we know when law is "good"? And concretely, what makes law good for women? I begin here with some definitions.

Defining the "Good" and the "Bad"

Rewriting the Rules uses the language of gender responsiveness to describe good laws. Gender-responsive laws are responsive to gendered differences precisely because they center both explicit *and* implicit gendered concerns.[31] Their enactment requires legislators to bring different gendered perspectives to the legal drafting table by reflecting on how people of different genders experience laws differently and in ways that account for different perspectives on social, economic, and political issues.[32] Gender responsiveness is a way of facilitating accountability, in law and in policies, to the specific needs of different sexes.

This book calls for an active pursuit of gender-responsive legal drafting. The alternative is to wait for the passive and frankly slow elimination of discrimination by other means, however long that might take.[33] Gender responsiveness may, at times, involve correctional measures and the introduction of laws that *positively* discriminate in favor of women, such as quotas[34]—that is, "de jure measures of equality."[35] At other times, it may be about acknowledging the societal context in which law operates by, for example, guaranteeing to all women, regardless of age or marital status, access to age-appropriate, evidence-based, comprehensive family planning services and information.

By contrast, gender-blind and gender-regressive laws sit in direct opposition to the end goal. Laws—gender-blind ones—may be written in ways that fail to account for the evidence-based needs and interests of women.[36] Gendered considerations may be ignored altogether. Gender-regressive laws result in women experiencing a less developed state in terms of their social, economic, and political status and overall well-being.[37]

Avoiding gender regression in lawmaking involves a consideration of how laws are drafted *and* lived by women. Overt discrimination must be identified and eradicated in law. Some countries, for instance, retain legal discrimination against women with respect to entitlements accruing only to (male) heads of households or with respect to the right to inherit. However, gender regression in law also occurs when the law's intention is not met with the legislative drafting that is necessary to meet those intentions, resulting in unintentional harm. For example, a law that seeks to eradicate gender-based violence may nonetheless fail to accord safe and confidential processes for reporting. Victims may then choose not to use the law, resulting in impunity for gender-based crimes.[38] Both the intention and its translation into legal language must be considered.

International Benchmarking of Domestic Laws

Rewriting the Rules measures the progress made in writing women's lives into law against a common set of benchmarks derived from an expansive purview of international law. Most applicable among them is the Convention on the Elimination of All Forms of Discrimination against Women (CEDAW). CEDAW, the most universally ratified women's rights treaty (with 189 States Parties, leaving the US, Tonga, Iran, Somalia, Palau and the Holy See as non-ratifiers), offers a global framework for good-practice legislation. Moreover, the convention directly and unequivocally sets out obligations on governments to embody the principle of equality in national law,[39] to adopt laws that prohibit discrimination,[40] and to enact legislation to ensure the full development and advancement of women.[41]

It is easy to critique the convention as a Northern "invention." Yet it is understood that the first draft of CEDAW was prepared in the 1970s by Filipino delegate Leticia Ramos-Shahani, who, with a senior member of the Russian foreign ministry, Tatiana Nikolaeva, eschewing the need for approval from either of their countries, presented the draft at the Commission on the Status of Women in New York;[42] it was later adopted by the UN as a basic working paper[43] ahead of the convention's adoption in 1979.

CEDAW's accountability toolbox is expansive. Its oversight mechanisms—including General Recommendations delivered on key global themes,[44] such as gender-based violence[45] and or equality in marriage and family life,[46] Concluding Observations directed at specific countries by the CEDAW Committee, and the Committee's capacity to receive Individual Complaints and investigate claims (Inquiries) of serious or systematic violations of CEDAW under the Optional Protocol[47]—have given rise to women's rights norm-setting on a global scale. Although these interpretative tools are instruments of "soft law"[48] and the dynamics in which these norms are translated at a national level remain complex,[49] the CEDAW Committee's ongoing production of progressive jurisprudence has allowed it to remain relevant years after the treaty came into force.[50] Yet the Committee remains challenged by inadequate resourcing to hold governments to account in a global human rights system that is often seen as challenged by a universal decline in respect for fundamental human rights. A balance must be struck between recognizing CEDAW and the Committee's potential along with its limits in holding States accountable.

A different challenge pertains to who and what comes within the protections of CEDAW. Fareda Banda defends CEDAW's normative value while acknowledging the convention's tendency to apply to a particular "CEDAW woman": one who is heterosexual, able-bodied, and married (or likely to marry), and has or wants to have children.[51] Gender binaries—male/female and gender normative/nonnormative—can be seen across the international human rights system. This binary lens informs other interventions by international human rights actors. Sexual violence is generally framed within a male-perpetrator/female-victim framework, with violence outside this framework often ignored.[52] CEDAW too is confronted by such a binary vision and an evident need for greater inclusivity in ways that better acknowledge how different gendered identities are impacted by socially constructed gendered hierarchies and gendered stereotypes.

Further, CEDAW's universal applicability has been called into question. Transitional justice scholar Vasuki Nesiah once compared post-conflict institutions—courts, commissions, truth-telling mechanisms—to IKEA furniture: flat packed to be "easily shipped, unpacked and set up in new terrain."[53] This is both a pro and a con: relatively easy to propagate and yet limited in its impact for its generic and context-insensitive ways. The same can be said of CEDAW. Its global and unifying norms are both its strength and its limitation. For one, universal standards are frequently applied to both conflict and post-conflict settings;[54] such *universal* standards risk becoming counterproductive. In this respect, chapter 5's discussion of artisanal and small-scale mining has to grapple with the vastly different experiences of women miners in post-conflict settings like the Democratic Republic of the Congo and artisanal and small-scale miners in, for instance, Laos or Peru. We risk, too, that CEDAW's normative benchmarks may suppress a more radical vision. Responding to these critiques, *Rewriting the Rules* challenges CEDAW's singular approach to lawmaking. However, it also values how CEDAW's norms provide lawmakers with a common set of benchmarks that they can strive to achieve and to which governments have already committed. A common set of criteria also allows countries to be judged fairly in comparative terms.

US philosopher Martha Nussbaum, while critical of CEDAW's homogenizing tendencies (what Banda terms the "CEDAW woman"), has also acknowledged how CEDAW's implementation tools (General Recommendations, Concluding Observations, and Individual Complaints and Inquiry Processes) address some of the "most egregious gaps" in the initial drafting of the convention.[55] Giving less credit to CEDAW's direct legal value, Nussbaum acknowledges CEDAW's role in building networks across national boundaries; giving activists a sense of common purpose, language, and demands; and shining a light on the progress that has been made.[56] Further, in a remarkable number of nations, CEDAW is "owned" and engaged in by local movements.[57] The CEDAW Committee also enjoys strong support from international and national NGOs,[58] such as the International Women's Rights Action Watch Asia-Pacific (IWRAW Asia-Pacific), which interact with it formally and informally and monitor progress on accountability.[59]

This resonance of global human rights norms—not just CEDAW but the other international and regional norms described in this book—has been acknowledged even by those scholars who have decried the vernacularization of human rights. The late Sally Engle Merry, for instance, noted that although "human rights ideas are repackaged in culturally resonant wrappings, the interior remains a radical challenge to patriarchy."[60] A common core—a set of agreed-upon rights—within the treaty cuts across national boundaries. As Merry noted, a dilemma remains: the ideas that are central to human rights are not "fully indigenize[d]" in these local contexts, which undermines their spread but, as Merry also acknowledged, to try to do so, "would undermine their potential to challenge social inequities."[61] We are left with a set of rights that enable nations to collectively value "autonomy, choice, bodily integrity, and equality, ideas embedded in the legal documents that constitute human rights law," which "endure even as the ideas are translated."[62]

This benchmarking exercise benefits from my study of CEDAW's then thirty-seven General Recommendations (1986–2018) and the emerging seven categories or criteria against which laws can be assessed for CEDAW compliance. Laws attain a level of gender responsiveness depending on how successfully they (1) guarantee equal access to nondiscriminatory, accessible, affordable and acceptable services; (2) guarantee access to information and education about the issue at hand; (3) guarantee uncoerced and informed decision-making by women and protect their confidentiality; (4) actively promote equality between people of different genders; (5) actively protect individuals who are at greater risk of rights violations (e.g., sexual minorities, women living with disabilities, homeless or Indigenous women, to name a few); (6) guarantee access to effective remedies; and (7) demand gender-disaggregated monitoring of the situation facing women.[63]

There are clear limits to the use of global standards and we remain hindered by international law's often binary perception of gender. Nor can we overstate international law's promise. Leadership on gender equality often comes nationally first, when domestic reform outpaces global norm-setting, the Philippines being a pertinent example (discussed in the chapter that follows). Rather, I use international law as an overarching framework to tease out legislative benchmarks to which all countries can strive. The seven benchmarks above provide a starting point for evaluating legislation fairly across different jurisdictions. Taking the existing parameters offered by international law allows us to move forward toward greater, fairer comparative accountability, even if it does require accepting some of the limitations entailed.

Legislating for a Diversity of Women

In most jurisdictions, individual laws are enacted to serve the interest of the whole society. Yet different people will naturally experience law differently—whether because of their sex, the color of their skin, and whether they are married and to whom. A failure to recognize this reality may result in the drafting of laws that fail to achieve their stated goals. A natural and necessary part of any critique of the law requires us to adopt an intersectional understanding of discrimination and inequality, where race, class, and sex/gender are considered compounding in their impact.[64] In turn, we must ask, For which women are gender-responsive laws necessarily good?

Borrowing from feminist legal scholar Catherine MacKinnon, I do not "pretend to present an even incipiently adequate analysis of race and sex, far less of race, sex and class."[65] Yet it should be self-evident that assessing how well the law works for women—that is, the law's gender responsiveness—requires analyzing whether the law works well for a diversity of women; gender alone is simply too limiting as an overarching category.[66] The law can and should acknowledge and respond to how identities such as race, disability, and marital status intersect at the micro level in individual experiences of law, while seeking to challenge or break down systems of privilege and oppression at the macro level, including racism, sexism, and classism.[67] Importantly, the international benchmarks discussed above and considered throughout *Rewriting the Rules* can assist in the task. The CEDAW committee overseeing the convention has, albeit inconsistently,[68] elaborated a normative understanding of discrimination as not only based on sex and gender discrimination but also on other identities that contribute to women's subordination. The committee has done particularly well on the issues of gender and race[69] and, to a degree, gender and disability,[70] and with some attention given to migrant women,[71] rural women, older women, and asylum-seeking women.[72]

This task of bringing an intersectional lens to how we deconstruct and challenge laws for their failure to account for gendered experiences is not an easy one. Martha Fineman, a US legal scholar who has made a profound contribution to feminist jurisprudence, cautions that the differences among women cannot be accommodated adequately without merely privileging one or two characteristics. Otherwise, we risk an overly simplistic picture of women's gendered lives.[73] Fineman asks, for instance, whether a "white woman" who is a "welfare mother" is appropriately placed in the dominant group in society just because she shares their skin color. Moreover, if this is not where she fits, where does she belong? Once again, we see the crude categorizations that law frequently sets up for society to squeeze into.

At the same time, *Rewriting the Rules* seeks to challenge Fineman's suggestion that law reform—in this case, the pursuit of gender-responsive legislation—is merely a type of "tinkering-with-the-law" that is condemned to fail because it will merely replicate injustice.[74] We cannot stop, in my view, with identifying law's natural biases or being overwhelmed by the challenge of placing the "white welfare mother" on a scale of disadvantage (or as Fineman calls it, a "hierarchy of oppression") that law seems to demand. Rather, we must believe that by bringing a gender perspective, law reform can and will do more than merely replicate and validate the original rules.

Evidence of "Effectiveness"

As a fourth and final consideration, *Rewriting the Rules* identifies "good" laws through a search for evidence that the law has made women's lives better. The World Bank's series of reports *Women, Business and the Law* has been one of the most prominent among the global studies of the effectiveness of gender-responsive laws (and the impact of gender-regressive ones). Dating from 1971 to 2024, these studies draw connections between the enactment of legislation, their enabling effect and their impact on women's lives, utilizing a multitude of data and research to make such correlations. In 2022, the World Bank suggested that if the US were to reform laws to bring women's remuneration to the same level as men's, the poverty rate for all working women in the country would be reduced by almost half.[75]

Nonetheless, there are obvious limitations to such data. For one, a more micro interrogation may enable us to identify what aspects of law reform heighten effectiveness. Yet more importantly, the call made throughout this book to recenter Southern experiences must be matched by a search for evidence from the Global South. Bina Agarwal's study in the early 2000s of women's land rights in India concluded that the legal right to inherit agricultural land *can* be correlated with gender equality.[76] Women in the southern states of India, where daughters have a share in joint family property on par with sons, were found, in general, to be more gender-equal. Moreover, inequality was seen to rise as one heads north in India, where women face greater disadvantage with respect to agricultural land and joint family property.[77]

Other studies from India demonstrate the notable impact of the Hindu Succession Act, which provides a daughter the "same rights" to inherit "if she had been a son."[78] This is despite what has been described as an "anti-female inheritance bias" embedded in social values that has held back progress.[79] Surprising correlations are also drawn between recognizing the right to inherit in law and women's educational attainment, where higher rates of education were reached by Hindu girls, with no corresponding rise for non-Hindu girls.[80] In other words, the Hindu Succession Act appears a "success" for not only grounding the rights of women to inherit and own property but also for shifting norms around the appropriateness of women and girls in these communities to access education. While appreciating that these broad correlations have their limitations, we see *some* evidence of the gender-equalizing effect of gender-responsive legislation.

"Success" is unlikely to emerge before a passage of time. In the case of Rwanda's Succession Law 1999, the principle of gender equality was embedded in land inheritance and property ownership laws.[81] However, the events that followed were fundamental, including the enactment of the 2003 Constitution, endorsed by a national referendum after a prolonged consultation and sensitization process that embedded several articles of relevance to property rights and gender equality.[82] Remarkably, by 2006, research showed that although the legal changes were yet to fully permeate, in contrast to what were entrenched gender biases, the new legal rights to land ownership were impacting social relations and inheritance patterns. Male family heads were fulfilling what they perceived as their obligation to realize the inheritance rights of girls, and in some cases, they did so because it was the "right thing to do."[83]

PUSHING THE BOUNDARIES OF THE "FEMINIST TEMPLATE": GOOD PRACTICE BEYOND THE ANGLOSPHERE

Rewriting the Rules is underpinned by an active effort to broaden the imagination of the Anglosphere, which too frequently overlooks legal developments in parts of the world deemed "less developed." This is not an easy task. English has become the "lingua franca"[84] of international law, and it is acknowledged that "people, materials, and ideas move more easily within linguistic communities than between such communities."[85] English-language scholars often hesitate to venture too far beyond our borders,[86] and in this same vein, legislators may be reluctant to look abroad, feeling the need to contextualize laws and understand their local meaning and relationship to a specific culture in ways that may be unavailable to an outsider.[87] Laws are not often seen as easily transportable from nation to nation. Fluency in the foreign language is likely required and may not be common among legal drafters.

At the same time, some Spanish-language laws from Latin America have been heralded in the English academic literature as pioneering firsts. Argentina's legislation to establish transgender rights has been, rightly, noted as "ground-breaking";[88] Ecuador's constitutional protections of the right to nature have been named "path-breaking."[89] It is likely that there are other factors amplifying this English-language bias and obscuring good practices in overlooked jurisdictions.

Some blame for such obscuration must be attributed to geopolitical gender-equality biases that glorify certain countries—often the Nordic ones—as offering the best practices on gender equality; all others are seen as lagging. The World Bank's *Women, Business and the Law* report series, while providing global evidence of the positive impact of "good" laws on women's lives, is also one of the main contributors to perpetuating this mindset. In 2019, the index found that six countries had *no* inequalities across gendered lines: Belgium, Denmark, France, Latvia, Luxembourg, and Sweden.[90] Some women in those countries might beg to differ. In 2023, this list of gender equal countries increased to fourteen.[91] Countries such as Sudan, Pakistan, and Bangladesh are among the lowest scoring.[92]

These "lagging" nations are part of the world's so-called Global South. This term, "Global South," emerged in the 1980s to replace "Third World,"[93] and for some, it reflects a history of colonialism and the inequalities between countries that colonial power established, maintained, and left behind.[94] The very notion of the Global South juxtaposes these southern nations against the Global North, creating the sense that the South is always in competition with and frequently seen as ranking second to the North. In this framework, the North dominates and directs. In turn, the South's potential leadership on gender equality is overlooked.

Meanwhile, biases in the design of global measures of gender equality contribute to biased representations. For instance, the now-revised OECD's Social Institutions and Gender Index in 2009 used just two measures for barriers to women's enjoyment of their civil liberties: first, an obligation to use a veil or burqa to cover parts of the body in public, an inherently biased measure targeting countries with Islamic populations,[95] and second, freedom of movement outside the home. Meanwhile, France's decision to ban the full-face Islamic veil, burqa, and the niqab in 2010, a long-standing debate in the country, has not appeared to impact France's OECD score for "restriction of civil liberties." In February 2025, France received a 5 on a scale of 100 (where 0 = no discrimination).[96]

The Cingranelli and Richards Human Rights Data Project presents another instance of biased measurement. The project, which captured data from around two hundred countries up until 2011, measured violence against women based on freedom from female genital mutilation and freedom from forced sterilization.[97] Both are problems of particular magnitude in certain regions and countries of the world.[98]

How we benchmark fuels resentment over the image of the development sector's role in saving the "Third World" woman.[99] "Third World" nations are subsequently easily overlooked as offering little by way of lessons for gender-responsive lawmaking, while the gender-equality successes of the West are unduly elevated in status. The latter become the "reference point for understanding change in other parts of the world."[100]

Feminist scholars are not without blame when it comes to how the abuse experienced by women in the South permeates Western media and Western feminist discourse. The 2012 gang rape in India of physiotherapy student Jyoti Singh attracted national *and* international attention from women's movements and from Bollywood[101] and Hollywood celebrities and led to a BBC documentary film.[102] These highly visible portrayals of the Global South's victimized women "scaffold damaging cultural narratives" as Nandini Sikand, filmmaker and anthropologist notes.[103] In turn, these accounts permit a global overlooking of the many Southern countries that have experimented with gender-responsive law reform, sometimes for many years, even decades. As Indian feminist Urvashi Butalia cautions, "There is a sense that feminist gains made in the west are what every other part of the world needs to aspire to. If you have not aspired to being somewhere along that ladder you're a poor cousin; you're left behind."[104]

As *Rewriting the Rules* will demonstrate, these Southern nations have shown their potential to live up to the ethos of freedom and equality that has long been hoped for in ways that Western writing too often fails to reflect.[105] Actors across the South—governmental and non-governmental—offer lessons in adapting global norms to local contexts.[106] It is to this leadership that this book, where relevant, hopes to pay tribute.

The platform for gender-responsive lawmaking that this book stands upon, however, is grounded in the feminist scholarship of the West, which is indeed largely from the Anglosphere. It is challenged, therefore, by the task of springboarding from that foundation while contesting the notion that the West is "modern," its Other "traditional"; that the West is "civilized," its Other "uncivilized."[107] Much is owed in this book to Third World Approaches to International Law scholarship, which offers a "dogged insistence on history, continuity, centring the Third World, resisting global hegemony, demanding increased global equality, and unmasking the hand of power in the construction of knowledge."[108] An alternative canon is needed, and it is hoped that *Rewriting the Rules* provides one.

THE END GOAL: DRIVING LAW REFORM FORWARD

Scholars remain deeply divided when it comes to the use of the law to advance equality. There are those who condemn the law, those who embrace it and "those who sit in between this ever-expanding spectrum of opinions."[109] Yet the successes of scholars and activists who have worked *within* the system to create something seemingly better—including but not just the feminist judgments and legislative endeavors—demonstrate that there is both hope and possibility. We have at hand the foundations and the tools for gender-responsive lawmaking for this century.

Yet this task is a challenging one. We do not have the luxury of a blank slate from which to start. Any attempt to shift away from current practices risks an "add the Global South and stir" approach that will do little to challenge the standpoint that we have become accustomed too. In order to achieve this shift, this book seeks to improve upon existing tools—such as CEDAW—and to drastically challenge others.

Rewriting the Rules achieves this in three ways. First, the entry point for each of the seven substantive chapters that follow has been to challenge my own assumptions before writing. I have sought to push back against the magnetism of examples from the Global North that naturally come to mind when starting a search for good practice. I have been required to engage in a much more rigorous search than for anything else I have written, often digging deep into the footnotes, where Southern examples tend to be pushed into obscurity.

Second, I have spent much time thinking about language and the linguistic diversity that would be required to create a truly global sense of gender-responsive lawmaking. For if one looks for the wrong term, the scholarship will never cross your path. Some scholars of Sri Lanka, for example, argue locally that Sinhala lacks an intelligible expression for "gender"; instead, a makeshift term cobbled together from a string of Sanskrit words sounds stilted and unnatural to many local activists and risks being meaningless to most.[110] In such a context, to find what you are looking for takes a deep and concerted engagement with the exercise.

Finally, individuals have natural cognitive biases to be drawn to the familiar, to the things, experiences, and narratives that are similar and more easily accessible. In writing this work, I have made deliberate attempts to engage with scholars and scholarship outside my own network. I hope to be able to shed light on undervalued knowledge production in ways that can aid in a retelling of history but also in ways that might shift contemporary practice. This has probably been the greatest part of the journey: discovering beautiful writing in books that would otherwise never have crossed my desk. The result is seven fields of law reexamined for what it would look like if we rewrote the rules.

2

Gender-Based Violence

*Reclaiming the Global South's Leadership
on Workplace Leave for Victims*

On March 8, 2004, the Philippines had much to celebrate. The nation's second female president, Gloria Macapagal Arroyo, was in power, itself an achievement given how many countries—a staggering 113 in 2024—have never had a female serve as head of state or government.[1] Macapagal Arroyo took the opportunity of International Women's Day to sign into law the Anti-Violence Against Women and Their Children Act.[2] A remarkable provision was embedded in that law. Section 43 offers victims of abuse ten days of paid leave from work, affording them the opportunity to pursue legal proceedings, relocate their residence, or attend counselling sessions.[3] Female workers are protected from workplace dismissal and other forms of workplace discrimination should they choose to use the entitlement. The law does not provide a list of purposes for which leave can be taken. Rather, a level of discretion, at the victim's determination, means that the law can act as a form of compensation for the harm suffered as well. To use the entitlement, a victim-employee must present to her employer a certification from the village chairman (*barangay Punong*), village councilor (*barangay kagawad*), prosecutor, or clerk of court demonstrating that an action related to the matter is pending.

Little is known about the origins of the Filipino provisions.[4] Various women's groups negotiated and lobbied over the final contents of the law.[5] Yet the rights guaranteed under Section 43 are somewhat hidden in this expansive piece of legislation that addresses all aspects of gender-based violence (GBV) against women and their children. It might be understandable, therefore, that I typically suggest the Philippines when asked which country leads the way in gender-responsive lawmaking. No country is a paragon when it comes to addressing gender inequality. There remain stark gaps in wages between Filipino men and women,[6] along with alarming rates of gender-based violence by partners and non-partners.[7] Like other nations,[8] the Philippines faces challenges with implementation of its workplace leave provisions. Typically, women cannot afford to go to court, with no easy path to access a lawyer to seek a protection order in their village. This is despite the law stipulating the right of victims to obtain legal assistance from the Department of Justice or any public legal assistance office if they cannot otherwise afford it.[9] Nonetheless, the Philippines was clearly a world leader when it introduced paid workplace leave for victims of violence just after the turn of the century.

It took a further fourteen years for New Zealand to follow suit in July 2018.[10] Yet when *The Guardian* first reported on New Zealand's reform—one that only just passed, with 63 votes in favor and 57 against—it was incorrectly cited as a "world first."[11] Other reports have also named New Zealand as "one of the first in the world to legislate paid DV leave in employment law at a national level"[12] and New Zealand's law as a "landmark, not only in this country but globally."[13] As this chapter will demonstrate, this is clearly not the case. *The Guardian* later had to correct itself to acknowledge that the Philippines' law pre-dated New Zealand's—although *The Guardian* did not specify by how many years—and that paid workplace leave provisions already existed in some provinces of Canada.[14] Shortly after New Zealand, Australia followed suit in 2022 and introduced ten days of paid leave federally,[15] although such leave had first been negotiated at the local-council level in Australia in 2010. This time, due to that local council agreement, it was Australia's turn to be named a "world first";[16] at that moment, the Philippines hardly rated a mention.

Even scholars examining workplace leave for victims of violence have by and large overlooked the vast number of countries—particularly in Latin America—that fill a historical gap between the Philippines and New Zealand.[17] This chapter presents models of paid workplace leave from that window of time, while encouraging readers to critically examine the biases that have obscured such legislative practices. In asking why this gap in knowledge developed in the first place, we must naturally question what other good-practice examples of gender-responsive lawmaking might similarly go unnoticed. Importantly, this chapter is not intended to be merely a gripe about legislators in the Global North overlooking Southern experiences from the Philippines and Spanish-language jurisdictions but rather, an example of cross-border barriers to sharing practice, a barrier that acts to the detriment of victims of violence.

The focus in this discussion is on paid, as opposed to unpaid leave, given the economic security paid leave provides. It is sometimes as important for victims "as the availability of a bed in a shelter, prosecution of a batterer, or access to civil legal services."[18] Unpaid leave can pose challenges, endangering a woman at home if a partner notices the gap in income generation,[19] or furthering a woman's financial dependency on a male partner in ways that increase barriers to leaving an abusive environment.[20] In the following section, I delve deeper into the economics of GBV as part of a larger pattern of coercion before offering some explanations for the minimal attention paid to lessons from the Global South. I then offer three models for how we can classify existing paid leave provisions in the nations that have been legislative leaders.

ESCAPING VIOLENCE: THE ECONOMICS

The US is often considered a particularly litigious society, even if that is not an entirely accurate perception.[21] Under traditional tort law principles, employers may be accountable for failing to address potential violence in the workplace.[22] Perhaps this explains why the US was early to acknowledge the consequences for employers who fail to protect victims while they are at work. In the 1990s, a victim's estate and her co-workers successfully sued their US employer for US$5 million when the employee's former company was found negligent due to its failure to act after the woman told them that her ex-partner had threatened to kill her at work, the one place he knew he could find her.[23] Also in the 1990s, the American Bar Association rolled out its "Domestic violence: It's everyone's business" campaign to demonstrate to companies that not only can they be held legally accountable, but to encourage them to adopt "precautionary measures" to minimize danger, such as providing pamphlets about domestic violence in workplace restrooms.[24]

This is, however, just a small representation of the impact of violence on the workplace. Domestic violence is political and public, both as a manifestation of the oppression facing women but also in terms of the practical ways in which such violence goes beyond the confines of the home. Perpetrators may harass victims through stalking-related behavior such as tracking the workplace commute and contacting victims or their co-workers via telephone and leaving messages.[25] Perpetrators may seek to prevent their victims from attending work or cause them to be late, for example, by refusing to care for children, inflicting physical injuries, preventing sleep, or hiding car keys. With employers too often slow to recognize domestic violence as a workplace issue,[26] it is often left to victims to explain and justify its impact on their performance, absenteeism, or tardiness.[27]

Perhaps the intimate association of domestic violence with the home is what led to a shift in the language from *domestic violence* to *interpersonal violence*[28] in the Canadian province of Manitoba. In 2016, the province introduced up to five days of paid leave and ten days of unpaid consecutive or intermittent leave, as well as seventeen weeks of continuous unpaid leave for victims.[29] Despite the obvious impact of domestic violence beyond the home, an acknowledgment in law of how domestic and family violence is relevant in a workplace context has been slower to develop in some jurisdictions than in others. Indeed, the International Labour Organization only recognized the obligation on states to acknowledge the effects of domestic violence and mitigate its impact in the world of work in 2019.[30]

The vast majority of the costs of domestic violence are borne by victims and are unquantifiable. Yet with governments called to intervene, much attention in the nations that I label in this chapter as "lagging"—the US, Australia, and New Zealand—shifted to quantifying the economic and workplace costs of such violence. The numbers vary, at times substantially, but remain significant enough for any government, however lean times may be, to justify an investment in reducing the magnitude of GBV and its cost for the public and private sectors: lost work time, even if it is unpaid; reduced productivity; higher turnover, resulting recruitment and training costs; and a risk to reputations with customers and employees.[31] In 2009, the Australian National Council to Reduce Violence Against Women and Their Children estimated the economic cost of domestic and non-domestic violence to be AU$13.6 billion, which at the time, was more than 1 percent of GDP. A much earlier study, in 2004, by Australian think tank Access Economics estimated the cost of domestic violence at AU$8.1 billion in 2002–2003, at the time around 1 percent of GDP.[32] In 2012, the Obama administration estimated the cost of domestic violence at US$8 billion a year in lost productivity and healthcare costs,[33] while in the UK, the government's Home Office estimated the combined economic cost of decreased productivity and lost output resulting from domestic violence at £14 billion in 2019.[34]

These estimates do little to reflect the financial burden felt by victims. On average, the Australian Council of Trade Unions (ACTU) reports that it costs a woman $18,000 to escape a violent relationship in Australia.[35] Data from the Australian Bureau of Statistics from 2012 shows that around one-fifth to one-quarter of women who experienced intimate partner violence took time off directly because of that violence in the twelve months after the most recent incident; in comparison, men were only about half as likely as women to take time off from work for *any* violent incident.[36]

Yet a different battle wages when governments take steps to actually offer paid workplace leave. Here a contestation has been witnessed in lagging nations, where opponents of paid workplace leave argue that its cost would be untenable. In 2021, the ACTU commissioned the Bankwest Curtin Economics Centre in Australia to undertake an independent economic analysis of the cost of providing paid family and domestic violence leave to workers receiving the "modern award"[37] wage, with the hope of submitting that data to the Fair Work Commission's 2021 review of family and domestic violence leave. Entitlements to ten days of paid family and domestic violence leave were estimated to incur a total annual cost to employers of between AU$13.1 million and AU$34.3 million,[38] a window so wide that we must naturally question how the calculations were made. Some economists rightly criticized the fears created by opponents to the reform who used inflated calculations of the cost to employers that assumed *every* worker, female and male, would annually use all ten days of paid leave allocated for domestic violence.[39] These "arbitrary and unsupported assumptions" that the leave would be misused[40] in Australia overtook the debate in an attempt to dissuade progress.

In turn, the extent to which such leave can improve victims' lives becomes discounted in the legislative debates. Paid leave helps maintain income and stability in the lives of affected workers while they attempt to escape or correct a violent situation;[41] paid leave helps reduce the financial necessity that may keep a victim trapped in a violent relationship;[42] and paid leave sends an authoritative message to employers and within workplaces that domestic violence is a recognized and significant problem.[43] Leave provisions also encourage employers to take more robust measures to address violence in the workplace, including by providing information and support to employees facing domestic violence, training for managers, and more developed and explicit procedures for responding to violence within and beyond the workplace.[44]

Indeed, Spain and Latin America exemplify government policies that perceive GBV against women as a manifestation of discrimination, inequality, and the power that men exercise over women[45] and therefore a question of gender-responsive lawmaking. In Venezuela, the Chavez government, which introduced paid leave, understood GBV as a serious public health problem and a systematic violation of women's human rights, a clear consequence of discrimination, and women's subordination in society.[46] The Venezuelan law responds to a "constitutional mandate" that obliges the state to protect women from situations that threaten their full enjoyment of their rights.[47] In El Salvador, the government too described its vision as motivated both by the enactment of government policies with a gender perspective and "compliance with the international commitments of the Salvadoran State in matters of women's human rights, non-discrimination based on gender and prevention, attention, sanction and eradication" (author's translation).[48] In Peru, the six-year plan that introduced the 2009 law acknowledged the loss in "national GDP due to absences from work and the low productivity of its victims"[49] but also acknowledged the barriers victims face to escape poverty. We can see a stark contrast between these drivers of reform in Spanish-speaking jurisdictions and those of the Anglophone nations described above.

THREE MODELS FOR PAID LEAVE
FOR VICTIMS OF VIOLENCE

As this chapter will explain, while New Zealand and Australia may be (self-)described as global leaders, numerous countries arrived at the point of offering workplace leave for victims well before these Oceanic nations. Why do the Philippines and nations across Latin America get neglected in the global gender equality narrative?

In the 2024, the World Economic Forum's Global Gender Gap Index—an almost annual global index commonly cited as a comparative and relative measure of equality—ranked Ecuador sixteenth, Chile twenty-first, the Philippines twenty-fifth, Argentina thirty-second, and Peru fortieth. These nations hardly drag behind in an index that ranks 146 countries.[50] Yet, as will be discussed in this chapter, their

legislative efforts to guarantee victims paid leave have been given minimal attention, if any, in scholarly and public policy debates. Beyond preconceptions about
which nations lead and which ones are behind in the global equality race, language
is a major factor. Anglophone nations struggle to consider legislative debates taking place in non-English-speaking nations, thereby "missing out on a plethora of
experiences,"[51] learnings, and the potential to improve how law will be lived by
women victims of violence.

Of course, I have not overlooked the irony that in this chapter, my critique
of the overlooking of Spanish language laws by Anglophone legislators disre-
gards the ways in which Indigenous languages have been suppressed in nations
where Spanish (Latin America and the Philippines) and English (the Philippines)
were the colonizing languages. It is the very nature of the colonial project to devalue
Indigenous languages, and this suppression, in turn, becomes part of the "living
legacy" of colonialism.[52] In the words of Gabriela Veronelli, if colonialism treats
the colonized as an inferior race, then the colonized must also have been "without any complex form of communication, that is without language."[53] Veronelli
goes on to write of the Spanish-language dominance among postcolonial nations:
"Castilian was then the language that would unify the empire, but significantly it
would express its authority, its order, its political truth."[54] The colonial footprint
on Indigenous languages should not be overlooked in my attempts to challenge
the ways in which some Anglophone nations neglect what the Spanish-speaking
world has to offer today. Nor is the debate this simplistic, as we need to go beyond
simple dichotomies in how we examine law and language, and their connections
with cultures and intercultural relations.[55]

Having briefly introduced some of the tensions concerning the English language's dominance as a medium through which law is written, interpreted, and
exchanged, I focus the rest of this chapter on the forms that workplace leave legislation might take, the lessons learnt, and how these lessons can inform nations that
have come late to the table. New Zealand's and Australia's relatively recent introduction of provisions for leave reignited some level of debate. However, little has
been said about the substance of such leave. Given the nature of domestic violence
and its relationship to the workplace, the form that leave in law takes can make
a substantial difference in the lives of victims. For instance, by offering victim-
employees flexibility concerning the time at which they start and end their day's
work, they can be better protected from further incidences of violence at the hands
of a former partner; by contrast, the same routine and location make it easier for
an aggressor to find them.[56] These nuances in what the law offers are therefore
significant. Based on my analysis of the laws enacted across Latin America and in
Puerto Rico, along with the Philippines and Spain, here I present three models for
paid leave for victims of violence.

Naturally, however, this discussion only touches the surface of these laws.
Implementation, noted earlier, is a distinct challenge. Moreover, a law may contain

some strong provisions alongside weak ones. With Latin America dominated by Catholicism and "where religious groups often mobilize in opposition to perceived threats to Catholic values," domestic violence laws risk placing a higher value on "keeping families together," incorporating requirements for attempts at conciliation and mediation, in violation of international law.[57] While limited attention is given to these realities in this chapter, their significance is not underestimated.

This chapter is focused largely on Latin America, as a region overlooked due to both real and perceived linguistic barriers, ultimately underestimated for its good practice models. Given this focus, it is worth a short note interrogating why these nations have led the way. A number of countries in Latin America are parties to the Inter-American Convention on the Prevention, Punishment, and Eradication of Violence against Women (Convention of Belém do Pará). It was enacted in June 1994 and entered into force on February 3, 1995, and as of March 2020, thirty-two of the thirty-five member states of the Organization of American States had either signed and ratified or acceded to the convention; the US, Canada and Cuba had not.

The convention makes no mention of the benefits of workplace leave for victims. It does, however, require State Parties to take measures to modify existing laws,[58] including ensuring that women subjected to violence can have a timely hearing and *effective access to such procedures* (emphasis added)[59] and receive "access to restitution, reparations or other just and effective remedies."[60] The convention made a notable contribution to the development of international norms prohibiting violence,[61] which perhaps offers a partial explanation as to why some Spanish-speaking jurisdictions forged early and new legislative pathways in the domain of workplace leave for victims.

In table 1, I draw upon existing legislation to offer three alternative ways of designing workplace leave provisions for victims of violence. Model A, considered the most gender-responsive approach, offers the ideal framework, inclusive in scope, and best adapted to the lived experiences of victims. Model B is a contained benefit, which while essential, may reflect the needs of victims less well. Model C is restrictive in terms of who has access to the benefits of the law but it may provide a platform for expansion to the private sector in the future.

Model A: Comprehensive Paid Leave and Workplace Protections

As reflected in table 1, Model A countries have the most comprehensive approach to paid workplace leave for victims of violence. Venezuela established such entitlements not long after the Philippines, while Peru's reforms were more recent. For Model A countries, paid leave—even while requiring documentation on the part of the victim—can be used at the victim's discretion and therefore becomes more expansive and flexible beyond what may be quantifiable and accounted for by the individual.

As early as 2007, Venezuela provided paid leave for victims of violence, entitling a victim-employee to reduce or rearrange her work time or to change her place

TABLE 1 Three models for workplace leave and/or compensation for victims of violence

Model	Description	Examples of jurisdictions within category
Model A: Comprehensive recognition of harm and impact	Victims are offered a set number of days of paid leave from work. In some instances, the number of days of leave can be extended (often unpaid). The leave is seen both as a mechanism to enable victims to attend to matters such as judicial proceedings related to the violence and as general unmonitored compensation for the harm suffered. It is often a requirement to provide the employer with documentation, such as a court order, to demonstrate institutional recognition that the victim has suffered gender-based violence or to have submitted a claim to the police or prosecutor concerning an incidence of violence. This leave is typically accompanied by other protections, such as a prohibition of dismissal for any cause related to the violence.	Philippines (2004) Venezuela (2007) El Salvador (2011) Peru (2015) Ecuador (2018) New Zealand (2018) Chile (2021)
Model B: Monitored compensation	Victims are offered a set number of days of paid leave from work. The leave is a mechanism exclusively dedicated to enabling victims to attend to matters specifically and directly related to the violence, such as making arrangements for their safety, attending court proceedings, accessing police services, attending counseling, or going to a medical appointment. Evidence is typically required, and hence this model of leave is considered monitored compensation.	Uruguay (2018)
Model C: Public sector employee leave	Victims who are employees in the public sector are offered a set number of days of paid leave from work.	Spain (2004) Puerto Rico (2005) Argentina (2015)

of work. Employers who seek to suspend a woman's work in response to such requests require a judge's order, following a report and request from the public prosecutor's office.[62] Given that workplace leave is justified in law, leave-taking must not impact the worker's salary. Interestingly, Venezuelan law places no time limits on the length of leave.[63] While the law has undergone amendments in recent years, no changes have been made to these entitlements.

In 2015, Peru enacted a law to prevent and eradicate violence against women and other persons in the family. The legislation provides for five days of paid leave in a period of thirty days, or fifteen days in a period of 180 days.[64] To be entitled, the employee must have started an action with the police or prosecutor.[65] No distinction is made in law as to whether the leave is compensation for injury suffered or to attend to matters related to the violence, so like the Philippines, its use remains at the discretion of the victim. Employees are also entitled to have their workplace location or hours changed so long as it does not undermine their pay and other rights.[66] Workers are protected from dismissal for reasons related to the violence.[67]

Across El Salvador, Ecuador and Chile, reforms have been introduced to supplement the entitlements of workers under existing labor codes that regulate the relationship between employees and employers. Under the El Salvadorian labor code, a number of reasons justified an employee's absence from work, but domestic violence was not among them.[68] In 2011, these provisions were supplemented by the Life Free of Violence against Women Act,[69] under which victims of violence can justify absences or lateness due to the physical or psychological consequences of violence. On this basis, victims can also temporarily or permanently have their place of work moved to another branch and request to have their schedule reorganized.[70]

Like El Salvador, Ecuador has a general labor code (Código del Trabajo) that does not contain provisions for paid or unpaid leave for victims of domestic violence. However, in 2018, workplace leave entitlements were introduced through the Comprehensive Law to Prevent and Eradicate Violence against Women.[71] As in Venezuela, Ecuadorian law places no time limit on the paid leave, which is available to the victim to initiate and to attend to judicial proceedings, while acting as a general compensation for the violence and harm suffered.[72]

A similar approach can be found under Chilean law, where a labor code governs employment relations. Under the Act for Work Accidents and Professional Illness, employees have a general right to be absent or reduce their workday or shift during an illness certified by a medical practitioner.[73] During this time, employees can enjoy a special subsidy or are entitled to obtain regular remuneration or both in the form of paid leave,[74] regardless of how many days they are not capable of working and regardless of whether they work in the private or public sector. While domestic violence is not included as a reason for "incapacity" under this code, the Court of Appeals of Santiago expanded access to this leave in a 2021 case concerning a teacher unable to continue to work due to the medical treatment she was receiving as a victim of psychological, physical, and economic violence.[75] By recognizing a worker's right to paid medical leave ("licencia medica") from work in cases of domestic violence, the case brought Chile into the Model A category.

Model B: Paid Leave Only for Matters Specifically
and Directly Related to Domestic Violence

As noted in table 1, this category of leave offers victims a set number of days of paid leave to attend to matters directly related to the violence suffered, such as attending a court proceeding or a medical appointment. Leave is not, however, seen as a more general form of compensation but rather is measured against specific and directly related reasons to be identified and quantified by the employee in order to justify use of the leave.

Uruguay is one example of this more restrictive model. Paid leave is offered under a 2018 law on GBV, but in specific terms. A victim can receive full pay to attend hearings, obtain expert advice, or engage in other errands (administrative or judicial) as foreseen in the Services for Women in Situations of Gender-Based Violence policy. Extraordinary leave with pay may be granted for twenty-four hours from the presentation of the complaint at the police or judicial headquarters, extendable for the same period if a judicial determination orders precautionary measures. Victims are also entitled to make requests for flexibility and for a change to their schedule or place of work, along with other measures so long as they do not affect their rights at work or their careers. Victims are also protected from dismissal for six months, or an employer must pay compensation for dismissal in an amount equivalent to six months of salary plus any corresponding legal compensation.[76]

Model C: Paid Leave for Public Sector Employees Only

Table 1 describes a set of countries that provide paid domestic violence leave for workers in the public sector. Like the Philippines, Spain introduced one of the world's first comprehensive laws on GBV in 2004.[77] Women victims of violence who are civil servants were offered a comprehensive set of protections including the right to reduce work, have working hours rearranged, or request a change to their workplace location. Alternatively, workers could suspend or terminate their work, triggering other entitlements to compensation under Spain's social security system.[78] The Spanish law also guaranteed victims the right to receive social security payment even when an employer had replaced them with an interim worker,[79] along with a right to return to the previous conditions of work upon their return to the workplace.[80] Absences or lack of punctuality caused by the physical or psychological violence they were facing were considered justified and to be paid, although workers were required to communicate to the company about the cause as soon as possible.[81]

Today Spanish civil servants continue to be entitled to leaves of absence.[82] However, the law has expanded to apply to victims of domestic violence who work outside the public sector. Workers can temporarily or permanently suspend their employment contract and still receive unemployment benefits for a period of up to six months, without making any contributions to the social security system during that six-month period.[83] This period can be extended up to a maximum of eighteen months, subject to the ruling of a court. A one-off payment is available to unemployed victim-survivors to enable their re-entry into the workforce, and Spanish law also gives financial incentives to companies that employ victims of violence.[84]

One year after Spain, in 2005, Puerto Rico first introduced paid leave for victims of domestic violence who were workers in the public sector. A territory of the US but with its own level of legal autonomy, Puerto Rico has made entitlements to leave available despite the absence of a federal entitlement to paid leave in the US. Puerto Rico's provisions mirror Model B entitlements but only for public sector employees. Victims have a right to non-cumulative paid leave for up to five days to seek help from a domestic violence lawyer or counsellor and to obtain a protection order and to seek medical or other services for themselves or their relatives.[85] A further five days of leave were introduced in 2017 to specifically facilitate court appearances in administrative and/or judicial proceedings before any department, agency, or public body of the Government of Puerto Rico, such as in cases concerning petitions for alimony, domestic violence, sexual harassment in employment, or gender discrimination.[86]

In 2019, additional protections were introduced in law for non–public sector employees. This included a fifteen-day *nonpaid leave* entitlement within one natural year, whether or not there was a police complaint, if they or a family member were facing a situation of domestic or gender violence, child abuse, sexual harassment at work, sexual assault, or stalking.[87]

In 2015, Argentina introduced paid leave for women in the public sector in a law specifically enacted for this purpose: Special Leave Regime with pay for female public servants working in the provincial public sector who are victims of acts of gender violence.[88] Paid leave can be received for up to 180 days and can be extended after examination by the Provincial Medical Board. These relatively generous provisions, however, raise budgetary questions, given that the Argentinian National Women's Council has long been considered an agency with a small budget and staff and very little political influence.[89] Doubt as to Argentina's capacity to deliver paid leave for up to 180 days is further exacerbated by the differing capacities of subnational provinces to respond to requests for support, as evidenced by the uneven availability of services during the spike in GBV witnessed during mandatory stay-at-home orders during the COVID-19 pandemic of 2020.[90]

Other Examples of Paid Workplace Leave for Victims

This mapping of a handful of countries, particularly Latin American ones, makes evident that the legal landscape between the Philippines in 2004 and New Zealand in 2018 is much richer than is acknowledged by the media, in public policy, or in scholarly debates. These gaps in knowledge have, until now, undermined our ability to identify different approaches to enacting gender-responsive paid leave legislation to improve the lives of victims.

The presentation of the three models is not intended to overlook law reform elsewhere. As noted earlier, in North America, Manitoba was Canada's first province to provide such leave, introducing in 2016 the Employment Standards Code Amendment Act (Leave for Victims of Domestic Violence, Leave for Serious Injury or Illness and Extension of Compassionate Care Leave). It falls into Model B, providing leave for one or more of the following reasons: (a) to seek medical attention in response to a physical or psychological injury or disability; (b) to obtain services from a victim services organization; (c) to obtain psychological or other professional counselling; (d) to relocate temporarily or permanently; and (e) to seek legal or law enforcement assistance, including preparing for or participating in any civil or criminal legal proceeding related to or resulting from the interpersonal violence.[91] Yet in the last decade, no other Canadian province has followed. In the U.S, at least twenty states offer victims *unpaid leave* from work.[92] There have been numerous calls from scholars for such leave to be introduced at the federal level.[93]

While gaps remain and global progress has been uneven, arguably New Zealand's and Australia's reforms have been noticed in other Anglophone parts of the world. In the UK in 2022, Northern Ireland introduced ten days of paid leave for victims. Falling into category B, the enabling legislation specifies a list of issues that victims may need to deal with, such as obtaining legal advice, finding alternative accommodation, seeking healthcare, and protecting members of their family.[94] Then in November 2023, Ireland went on to introduce five days of paid leave in a law also falling into Category B.[95] A Category-B bill, the Domestic Abuse (Safe Leave) Bill, was introduced into the UK House of Commons in January 2025.[96]

MOVING TOWARD UNIVERSAL PAID LEAVE

In the context of *Rewriting the Rules*, this chapter has sought to offer directions for better practice when it comes to GBV and workplace regulations. The three models have been provided here to offer a framework for countries willing to move toward universal paid leave and to set out key provisions for inclusion in legislation by advocates seeking change.

Paid leave is an obvious and essential legislative reform to advance the rights of women. Unpaid leave is inadequate to guarantee economic security. Yet it is fair to ask whether paid workplace leave specifically for victims of domestic and family violence is the best way to protect the interests and confidentiality of victims. Some suggest that sick leave is equally suitable, particularly for victims facing difficulties in proving domestic and family violence or fearing breaches of their confidentiality. However, domestic violence is a not a sickness of the victim; it is a harm perpetrated against an individual—in this case, a worker—for which time is required for healing and for changes to be made within and beyond the workplace to better protect the victim, including from re-victimization. Nonetheless, paid-leave entitlements cannot operate in isolation. Lessons on implementation underlie the importance of supportive workplace cultures that challenge victim blaming and encourage uptake when needed.[97]

There are likely to be other women's rights concerns where good practice is hidden, overlooked altogether, or inaccessible due to the linguistic biases laid out in the previous chapter and above. Nevertheless, the notion of linguistic inaccessibility must be interrogated. To what extent can we forgive legislators in Anglophone nations for not considering legislation in other languages? Spanish is considered one of the world's "supercentral" languages—in other words, despite the fact that Spanish-language law reforms are overlooked by English-language legislators, it is still a globally dominant language. One can only begin to imagine what practice is lost by having inaccessible to the Anglo world a much greater diversity of languages beyond the twelve or so that are the world's most dominant. Because the tools for translation are widely accessible today, this discussion begs the question as to whether language barriers are real or perceived and how to hold legislators to account for a limited scan of good practice laws.

Yet the challenge is also put to law scholars. Years ago, diversity and corporate governance scholar Darren Rosenblum described comparative law's unpopularity, with its "near-empty dance card."[98] Legal scholars often hesitate to go beyond national borders and certainly beyond regional ones. For the Anglophone scholar, a foreign legal corpus can be overwhelming. Nevertheless, clearly it is time to fill up comparative law's dance card. German jurist Günter Frankenberg once described comparative law as being like travel: "travelling offers opportunities for learning both about one's own country and culture and about other countries and cultures."[99] Frankenberg cautioned that when travelling, "one must make a conscious effort to achieve distance from the assumptions and confidences that defend one from the uncertainties brought on by the un-usual."[100] As he remarked, the goal is a worthy one: "to reform and improve the laws, to further justice and to better the lot of humankind."[101]

Parental Leave

*Detangling Pregnancy and Parenting to Challenge
the "Sexed" and "Gendered" Nature of Leave*

On January 1, 2021, Spain achieved a world first. Paid leave for parents was equalized. Sixteen weeks (or 112 days) of non-transferable paid leave was made available to each parent—both the birth mother and the parent other than the biological mother in same-sex or different-sex couples.[1] In cases of adoption, custody, or foster care, each parent is also entitled to sixteen weeks of leave at 100 percent of base pay. The law requires both parents to take six weeks of leave *concurrently*, immediately after the child's birth.

Spain enjoys a long history of parental leave. Paid maternity leave and breastfeeding leave were introduced nearly a century ago, in 1929. Remarkable for its time, Spanish fathers became entitled to one day of paid leave back in 1931.[2] Yet progress stalled. Spain arrived at its most recent reforms in a staggered fashion—moving up from just two weeks of paid paternity leave in 2007 to sixteen weeks today—and reflects one example, with mixed reactions, of the detangling of pregnancy and parenting called for in this chapter.

Paid leave for fathers has been introduced in varying amounts and in different forms in countries across the world. Yet, policymakers remain challenged by the task of encouraging men to avail themselves of their leave. Famous fathers who take leave still make national news, such as Eikei Suzuki, governor of Japan's Mie Prefecture,[3] and Britain's Prince Harry.[4] Incentives are frequently needed.[5] Despite compulsory paternity leave in Portugal, take-up rates have often fallen below 100 percent.[6] In the Philippines, lack of sanctions for noncompliance remains an issue.[7] While men are more likely to use paternity leave (leave specifically designated to the "father" or non-birth parent), the take-up rates by fathers of parental leave (leave that is available to either parent and normally transferable between them) remain particularly low. In most cases, fathers transfer entitlements to mothers where legally possible.[8]

As will be explored, legislation in the field of parental leave is deeply sexed and gendered. Resultingly, birth mothers in different-sex couples hold far greater responsibility for childcare and child-rearing than fathers. Over a century ago, in 1919, international law acknowledged the social significance of maternity leave by establishing a global norm whereby women would not return to work in the six weeks after birth.[9] However, CEDAW's expectation that "the role of women in procreation should not be a basis for discrimination" is far from realized, and the goal of "a sharing of responsibility between men and women" for the upbringing of children is unattained in most countries.[10] This chapter responds by exploring how to design paid parental leave to move countries toward that declared, gender-responsive goal.

In doing so, this discussion explores leave in a diversity of family structures, providing a global survey of paid parental leave provisions. What will emerge is an appreciation of the need to extend mandatory leave to fathers in different-sex couples, a call that is not new.[11] Pregnancy and parenthood need to be detangled conceptually, with equality law scholar, Sandra Fredman arguing that while "pregnancy is unique and should be treated as such," substantive equality can only be achieved by "levelling up" and therefore "extending women's parenting rights to fathers."[12] That is, we must separate responsibilities that necessarily attach to birthing parents from the responsibilities that remain. Assumptions pertaining to both biology and gender need reconsideration. In earlier writing, equality scholar Darren Rosenblum had envisaged that "unsexing mothering" would liberate "traditionally sexed women and men" while offering potential for the equality of LGBT parents.[13] Hence, this discussion presents the idea that truly shared care involves both a "de-sexing" and "de-gendering" of parental leave and a re-centering of fathers and partners in the debate.

This view is not without controversy. First, some women *choose* to care. There may be a "childcare calculus," considering salaries, the cost of childcare, long-term careers prospects, and the impact on the family. Some women decide it "just [makes] sense" to stay home.[14] Yet learned judges and scholars who have come before me have done well to demonstrate that such "choices" are neither unencumbered nor often within the individual woman's control.[15]

For some, "women and mothers" is a worthy category and a fear of being "erased" is understandable. Both mothers and soon-to-be-mothers feel confronted by the gender-neutralization of leave categories, feeling delegitimized by legal approaches that de-center women. Accepting the need for more inclusive terms that account for transgender men and non-binary people who give birth, assistant professor of medicine at Harvard University Melissa Bartick cautions against "losing women" in the shift from "breastfeeding" to "human milk feeding," from "woman" to "parents," from "mothers" to "birthing people."[16] We risk too that discrimination against women becomes unseen.[17] Extending these concerns further, if sex differences are erased, will maternity leave be jeopardized?

Yet by maintaining the birth-parenting continuum in law, we risk reifying the view that the vast majority of the roles entailed in care—from the initial pregnancy to labor, breastfeeding, and upbringing—are the responsibility of women, encapsulated in the single category of "motherhood." The end goal pursued in this chapter, therefore, is not one where maternity leave should be devalued, abolished, or reduced, but rather where mandatory leave must be extended to fathers and leave equally enjoyed in a diversity of family forms. This chapter seeks to offer legislative approaches that can achieve that goal of detangling pregnancy and parenting.

We have much scholarly knowledge about maternity leave globally. When, how, and why governments and the private sector offer paid leave entitlements to mothers has been relatively well established thanks to industrial relations, workplace equality, business and management scholars, medical scientists, and economists over several decades.[18] The Nordic approach (characterized as generous, "gender-neutral," publicly funded, and with a strong emphasis on fathers taking leave) and whether it is one to which all nations should aspire has been studied at length,[19] along with how "wealthy" lagging nations like the US—where there is no federal paid maternity and family leave policy in place—compare to others, such as France[20] or Japan.[21]

In contrast, we face a dearth of attention accorded to the categories that exist for "partners" or "fathers" and same-sex couples, despite the centrality of according leave to "the other parent" to address the economic and labor market penalties experienced by women who are mothers (the "motherhood penalty").[22] This chapter contributes by offering such a comparative study of "father" leave on a global scale and also considers the accessibility of such leave for diverse families, including same-sex couples and adopting parents. Globally, certain regions lag. In Africa, for instance, the focus remains on maternity leave,[23] and the region lacks in-depth research of paid parental leave, South Africa being an exception. Yet even in better-explored regions—Asia and Latin America—good-practice categories can help us to evaluate the progress made in achieving a de-gendering or de-sexing of care.

Foregrounding this chapter is an acknowledgement that law alone will not guarantee that legal entitlements will be used when available. However, how the law frames such entitlements is fundamental in shaping uptake. "Generosity" in the level of wage replacement is particularly relevant to increasing fathers' use of leave in different-sex couples.[24] Flexibility—whether leave can be taken full-time or part-time, in several blocks of time, for a shorter period with higher compensation or for a longer period with lower compensation, and partly or fully simultaneously with the partner[25]—is determinative. Finally, non-transferability (what is sometimes called "use it or lose it") has demonstrably driven up usage by fathers. Scholars consider such a legislative approach the "ultimate goal,"[26] one I describe as the "gold standard"[27] for its capacity to de-gender leave use and reduce discrimination against women in the labor market while fostering co-responsibility.

I bring to this discussion a twenty-one-jurisdiction study of Asia and a nineteen-jurisdiction study of Latin America. With this data in hand, this chapter offers three categories of paid parental leave. The category to strive for is the equality one, a gender-responsive approach. That is, Category A promotes equal responsibility for parenting in ways that are attuned to women's lived experiences of economic disadvantage, along with the barriers fathers and same-sex couples experience in accessing and using leave.

One final disclaimer is needed before continuing. Paid leave in most jurisdictions is premised on formal employment. The exclusion of informal women workers from parental leave entitlements in many jurisdictions—along with the gendered and racialized realities of who dominates informal work—must be acknowledged as a hurdle yet to be overcome.

NAVIGATING THE LANGUAGE: MATERNITY LEAVE, PATERNITY LEAVE, AND PARENTAL LEAVE

Laws in the field of parental leave have evolved significantly over the last half century. While sole-parents also need to be acknowledged in this conversation, parenting is mostly performed by two parents, in either different-sex or same-sex relationships. In turn, most paid parental leave schemes are designed for a dual-parenting structure—with provisions made within them for sole parents—and involve three types of leave: maternity leave, paternity leave, and in some jurisdictions, shareable parental leave. Despite the progress we have witnessed particularly in the last two decades, legislation remains fundamentally sexed and gendered.

Paid Maternity Leave

Paid maternity leave was one of the first social policies for women workers.[28] As a legal concept, maternity leave tends to perceive little distinction between pregnancy and parenting. In 1919, the International Labour Organization (ILO), with its Maternity Protection Convention,[29] acknowledged the right of women to at least six weeks of mandatory leave after confinement, a biologically necessary period of leave for birth mothers. Emily Jackson, who has studied how medical advances have changed the gendered nature of particular reproductive roles, reminds us why this labor and post-birth recovery time is essential: "The process of giving birth is rightly termed 'labour.' It is hard work, often painful and sometimes dangerous. It brings the pregnancy to an end but it does not bring to an end the changes brought about by the pregnancy."[30]

However, the norms set globally often foster a continuum between post-birth recovery and legal entitlements to paid leave. They thereby "implicitly reinforce women's primary responsibility for childcare."[31] ILO Convention No. 183 (2000) set a maternity floor entitling birth mothers to a period of maternity leave of no less than fourteen weeks.[32] While the 1981 ILO Convention No. 156 had established a normative basis to enable "men and women workers" with family responsibilities to exercise the right to work and to meet the needs of the immediate family "who clearly need their care or support,"[33] the 2000 ILO Maternity Protection Recommendation No. 191 raised its earlier paid maternity leave protection floor to a recommended eighteen weeks of paid leave,[34] without any accompanying global norm establishing paid leave for fathers. As put by Argentinian Eleanor Faur, sociologist and policymaker at the UN, maternity leave is based on a logic of rights, but "heteronormativity continues to be the prevailing canon"[35] and maternalistic assumptions reaffirmed. Women are guaranteed the rights related to pregnancy, childbirth, and childcare but, by correlation, the responsibilities and duties too.

Nonetheless, it is fair to acknowledge that there has been a "forward march" for gender equality in the area of care, with Nordic countries often seen as leading the way.[36] Today and with significant acknowledgement of the standard-setting achieved by international law, paid maternity leave is a key part of the vast majority of countries' national family and social security policies. Activists continue to lobby for extensions in the number of paid weeks available to mothers, bolstering campaigns with evidence of longer periods of breastfeeding for newborns; lower infant mortality; higher vaccination rates; and for birth mothers, better postpartum health.[37]

Such arguments present an opportunity to ask for a more robust and evidence-based case to be made for leave for "the other parent."[38] Here I turn to the history of such leave for fathers.

Finding and Reinforcing Men's Place in Paid Care

The type of leave often taken by fathers is twofold: paternity leave and a portion of sharable parental leave. Paternity leave refers to the weeks of leave taken by fathers after birth and often immediately after delivery. In different-sex couples, this tends to be leave taken with the mother and presents, for most families, a time when fathers share care with mothers.[39] This leave can be distinguished from parental leave, where the father on leave would often be the primary carer. Parental leave is typically available to both parents, and each parent takes a portion of the shareable leave.

Mandatory leave for fathers has been attempted in some regions of the world. In 2019, the European Union's Directive on Work-Life Balance for Parents and Carers (EU Directive) mandated ten days of paid paternity leave for all EU Member States by August 2022.[40] While the EU Directive marked a positive step forward, it appears unlikely to shrink the gap between the vastly higher entitlements to paid maternity leave and the notably lower entitlements to paid paternity leave available in many jurisdictions, particularly if the EU Directive's requirement of 10 days is not treated as a minimum but rather a standard to be reached and at which progress risks stalling. Under the EU Directive, of the four months of required parental leave, two months are non-transferable and paid. In other words, European fathers must use this leave or lose it.[41] Given the potential for leave to instigate a sharing of the responsibilities for domestic work between parents, which is known to be a key driver of future economic success of worker-parents,[42] both concurrent (mandatory in the case of Spain) and separate leave for fathers are fundamental.

Globally, there remains no universally mandated paternity leave despite the evidence that when fathers take leave, welfare improves for all. US studies show that fathers who take leave when a child is young are more involved across the first few years of a child's life,[43] while research from Norway suggests that children even do better in school, particularly in cases where the father has a higher level of education than the mother.[44] Sweden has shown better health outcomes for men, which naturally means a better outcome for the public health system as a whole.[45] Paternity leave offers a compelling business case too, signaling more supportive corporate cultures and driving up employer commitments to flexible workplace policies.[46]

CATEGORIZING APPROACHES TO "FATHER" LEAVE

This section focuses on paternity leave in law. Its starting point is a view that a generous, individual, *and* non-transferable right to paid leave for fathers is the best legislative approach. We need to de-gender the primary responsibility for care in order to promote greater equity in the distribution of the labor of parenting.[47] With that backdrop, I turn now to three key categories of leave that can be witnessed in the global legislative landscape (see table 2).

Category A: A Gender-Responsive Approach to Paid Leave

As a book centered on rewriting the rules for greater equality, I begin with the category of leave that best promotes that goal. Category A exists where a government spends roughly the same amount of its resources on both parents under a policy designed to promote a more equal distribution of the responsibilities for children. Partners are entitled to non-transferable leave in an equal or near-equal amount to that of birth mothers, with the exception of the allocated weeks required for "post-birth recovery." Best-practice laws use the more inclusive term "parents," ensuring that leave is accessible for a diversity of family structures. For some, the ideal scenario is one where the law contains no reference to "mother," "father," "maternity," or "paternity," unless the terms "birth mothers" and "breastfeeding" are specifically intended in law. The outcome is one where both parents have equal access to the opportunities to care for children, bond with their child, and be involved in the child's well-being and development. At its optimum, such a policy would entitle single mothers to claim the months of fully paid leave that would otherwise be allocated to a partner.[48]

TABLE 2 Categories of paid paternity leave in Europe, Latin America, and Asia

Category	Ethos	Key features	Examples
Category A: Gender-responsive	A gender equality ethos that detangles parenting from pregnancy	• Equal or near equal amounts of leave allocated to each parent in two-parent families, with no significant disproportion in the amount allocated to each parent • Recognizes the particular needs of birth mothers, such as for post-birth recovery • Rights of each parent are understood as independent • Leave entitlements are paid by the public purse (i.e., via the social security system)	Finland Iceland Norway Spain* Sweden
Category B: Gender-blind	Leave is reserved for the "daddy" or "father," with primary care borne by mothers	• A portion of parental leave is reserved for the exclusive use of fathers but in significantly smaller amounts than leave allocated to mothers • Typically seen as an add-on to maternity leave • Tends to glorify or romanticize the role of fathers in care • Sets a norm whereby, if the law permits additional parental leave to be transferred between parents, leave is often transferred to mothers	Argentina Colombia Dominican Republic Ecuador Guatemala Ireland Singapore Switzerland Vietnam
Category C: Gender-regressive	Maintains the status quo, where pregnancy and parenting are intertwined	• No paid paternity leave is provided in law • Responsibility for parenting rests solely on mothers: both birth mothers and often adopting mothers too	Afghanistan Bangladesh Cambodia Cuba Honduras Sri Lanka

* The 6 weeks of mandatory leave previously earmarked for postpartum recovery is now included *within* the 16 weeks of paid leave available for Spanish birth mothers

Nordic countries—Denmark, Iceland, Finland, Norway, and Sweden—form a family of nations with a shared cultural heritage and history and cooperate at both formal and political levels,[49] so it is arguably natural that there are many commonalities in the design of parental leave in the region. With the exception of Denmark, these nations' care policies and entitlements for fathers to obtain paid leave have been a defining factor for enhancing the role of fathers in care.[50] Research among Nordic nations shows that fathers use their allocated leave and are increasingly taking leave to care for young children beyond the post-birth period of leave.[51]

Sweden and Iceland[52] are among the world leaders in this respect. In Sweden, 240 days of leave is allocated to each parent. Ninety days are nontransferable. Parents can choose to use thirty days of leave simultaneously, which would count for sixty days taken from the allowance. Birth mothers can commence parental leave up to sixty days before the due date, and both parents have leave days for antenatal classes/appointments. More days are allocated for multiple births. Notable in Iceland's law is the description of the rights of each parent as "independent" rights (*sjálfstæðan rétt*).[53] Each parent is entitled to six months of paid leave, relatively generous in global terms. Six weeks of those six months are transferable between parents, a point I turn to next. The birth mother is obligated to take two weeks of leave after birth, but the law is written in "gender-neutral" terms: it adopts the phrase *birth leave* and does not refer to maternity or paternity leave.

The approach taken in *Rewriting the Rules* to classifying the paid leave available for fathers considers their leave entitlements as a proportion of leave allocated for mothers, including if and when transferability is possible in law. Iceland is a useful example. The existence of transferability creates a scenario where if all fathers in different-sex couples transfer their six weeks to mothers, the ratio of leave taken by mothers to fathers would be 225 days compared to 141 days. We can start to see how gaps in leave-taking emerge. Across all Icelandic different-sex couples, paid leave by fathers is likely to range from 63 percent to 100 percent of what is taken by mothers. Ultimately, however, fathers and co-parents take roughly at least two-thirds of the leave taken by mothers.

By contrast, a jurisdiction qualifies as Category B (discussed in the next section) if the total number of days of leave for fathers falls below two-thirds of the leave offered to mothers in different-sex couples. This measure risks arbitrariness and another threshold could have been named. Importantly, however, such a threshold seeks to avoid misleadingly classifying countries with vast differences in the same category as countries where the gap in leave likely taken by mothers and fathers is less notable.

Denmark, it should be noted, has for some time been an exception to the general picture of success among Nordic countries. As of 2020, only 10 percent of fathers were found to take leave.[54] Danish law has been in a state of transition for some years. Amendments took effect after August 2, 2022, with further reforms in place from May 1, 2024, pertaining to multiple births. Recent reforms make Danish leave entitlements significantly more generous. As of January 1, 2025, the parent giving birth is entitled to four weeks of paid leave before birth,[55] while each parent is entitled to twenty-four weeks after birth (168 days). A number of conditions inform these entitlements, including that the parents reside together. If the parents are insured, one parent is entitled to an additional thirteen weeks of paid leave, taking their entitlement to thirty-seven weeks (259 days). If the parents are employees, only nine weeks of the twenty-four weeks of a partner's leave are non-transferable. Denmark risks a situation where a father may transfer all but the non-transferable leave, resulting in nine weeks taken by a father and fifty-six weeks (accounting for pre- and post-birth leave) by a birth mother, much closer to Category B.

Spain has been, for the purposes of this analysis, included in Category A. While this chapter calls for a 'levelling-up' of father and partner leave to that of mothers, Spain's reforms ignited much domestic controversy as the six weeks of post-partum leave for birth recovery was subsumed *within* the 16 weeks of non-transferrable leave given to mothers. We risk a pursuit of equality at the cost of women's sexual and reproductive rights, dismissing well-established health needs related to childbirth, the postpartum/puerperium period when a woman's body physiologically and anatomically returns to its pre-pregnancy state, and breastfeeding.[56] Other post-birth medical considerations, including post-partum depression, further encourage at least a softening of the lines between pregnancy, birth and parenting, raising a very real dilemma as to whether the pregnancy-parenting continuum can be interrupted while recognizing these entitlements.

Gendered inequalities within different socioeconomic contexts are complex; it is important to not overstate the extent to which Category A will, alone, move countries toward greater equality. Nonetheless, in this book's pursuit of evidence to demonstrate the effectiveness of gender-responsive laws, we can delve deeper into the example of Iceland. The Icelandic reforms were introduced to explicitly promote gender equality in the labor market and reduce the gender pay gap.[57] Studies have shown that after the first four months post-birth, the involvement of Icelandic fathers grew more rapidly for children born in 2009 than for those born in 2003. By the time children had reached the age of fifteen months, they were more likely to receive equal care from both parents than primarily from the mother, and with the introduction of the law on paid parental leave in 2000 and its normalization, the proportion of children receiving equal care from both parents during the night rose considerably, in a manner similar to the results for daytime care.[58]

While *Rewriting the Rules* seeks to dispel misconceptions about which countries lead the world on gender-responsive lawmaking, no country in Asia or in Latin America falls within Category A. This is despite the fact that in other respects, Latin America has shown global leadership in the field of parental leave. For instance, in 2008, Ecuador recognized co-responsibility between mothers and fathers in its constitution in relation to domestic work and family obligations.[59] In 1917, the Mexican constitution was among the first in the world to introduce maternity leave,[60] requiring a care system with universal, accessible, relevant, sufficient, and quality public services.[61] Mexico was also one of the first countries in the region to attempt to establish paid paternity leave, with a constitutional amendment proposing ten days of paternity leave failing in 1997. Five days of paid paternity leave finally came into force in 2013.[62] Mexico's experiences are a telling reminder of how a region can go from global leadership to lagging. Indeed, while maternity leave in Mexico is paid via the social security system, the payment of paternity leave falls to employers.[63] Interestingly, in the 1952 ILO Conference debates, the possibility that individual employers would be required to pay for maternity leave was debated by some South American governments and employer delegates, and was ultimately rejected due to the risk it would prejudice the employment of women. This principle was eventually crystalized in the Maternity Convention 1952, which stated that "in no case shall the employer be individually liable for the cost of such benefits due to women employed by him."[64] Yet by contrast, across Latin America, paid paternity leave when it exists today is often funded from the employer's purse, a further ingrained point of discrimination facing the working father.

Category B: Quotas for Fathers—an Add-On

Category B encompasses jurisdictions where leave is allocated for fathers largely in the form of an add-on. Fourteen of the twenty-one countries across Asia studied for their paid leave legislation as of January 1, 2025, fall within Category B;[65] seventeen of the nineteen countries in Latin America do as well, although they sit within a spectrum of Category B examples from less generous to more generous when it comes to provisions for fathers.

Generally, across the world, most jurisdictions introduced maternity leave significantly earlier than paternity leave; the latter entitlements only arrived when attention shifted to the role of fathers in families. In Latin America, back in 2013, six countries had no paid paternity leave, nine countries had paid paternity leave of between one and five days, and four countries offered paid paternity leave of between ten and fourteen days. Today, only Cuba and Honduras lack any type of paid paternity leave for fathers whatsoever (figure 1).[66] Meanwhile, Argentina,[67] the Dominican Republic,[68] and Guatemala[69] all sit at two days of paid paternity leave; Colombia's ten days of paternity leave increased to fourteen days in July 2021;[70] while Ecuador's ten days of paternity leave increased to fifteen days in May 2023.[71]

There remains a tendency in the literature to still refer to leave that falls within this category as "daddy weeks"[72] or "daddy days."[73] Yet such language is both a heteronormative approach and risks glorifying or romanticizing care by fathers. When Singapore's Prime Minister Lee Hsien Loong announced an extra week of paid leave for fathers during a National Day Rally speech in 2015, he jested, "Do not go and play golf. Please use it to take care of your kid."[74]

The stark contrast between the amount of leave allocated to mothers when compared to fathers is glaring in Asia. Among the twenty-one nations studied, every country as of January 1, 2025, provided an allocation for paid maternity leave for mothers, averaging 108.2 days. Indonesia and Vietnam (both 183 days), India (182 days), and Pakistan (180 days) all drive up the regional average (figure 2).

Asia's average number of paid days of maternity leave, 108.2 (figure 2), dwarfs the mere 7.2 days of average paid paternity leave (figure 3). In this case, Pakistan is a regional leader, with thirty days of paid paternity leave.

When placed side by side with paid paternity leave, India's and Vietnam's relatively positive levels of maternity leave prove problematic (figure 4). No

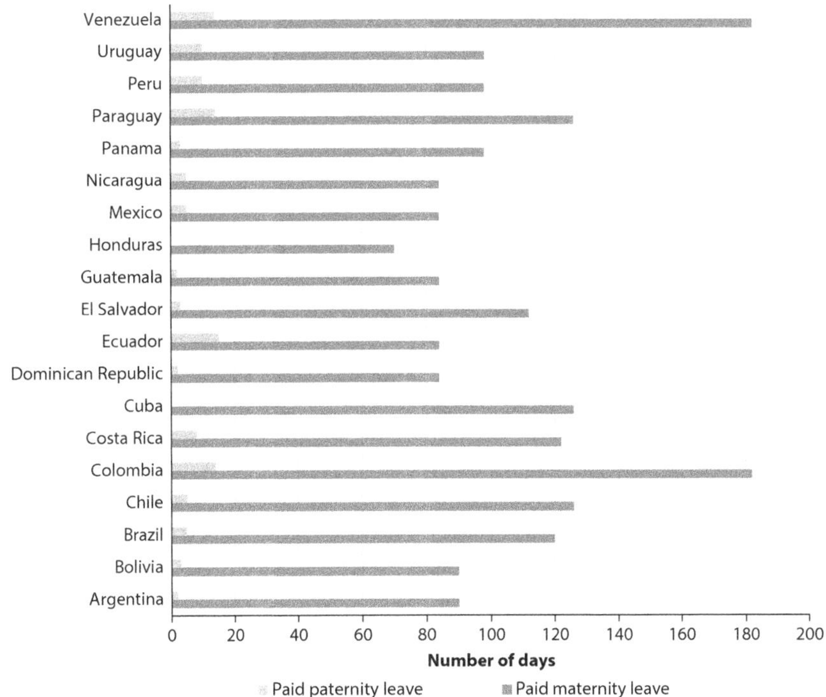

FIGURE 1. Paid maternity and paternity leave in Latin America (as of January 1, 2025).
Where legislation specifies leave entitlements in months, the calculation has been based on an average of 30.5 days per month.
All payments are at a full rate of pay.
In Bolivia, maternity leave can be extended beyond 60 days at 50 percent of base pay.
In Uruguay, dependent workers receive the average of their monthly or hourly rate. Self-employed persons will receive maternity leave at the average rate of their salary over the previous 12 months.

paid paternity leave for non-civil servants exists in India; Vietnam provides for only five days of paid paternity leave (figure 3). Here again, Pakistan appears to perform relatively well, although the number of paid paternity leave days allocated for fathers is just 17 percent of what is offered to mothers (figure 4).

Latin America shows surprising parallels to the Asia region. Numerous Latin American countries fail to reach the ILO minimum protection floor (figure 5), including Argentina (90 days),[75] Bolivia (90 days),[76] Dominican Republic (84 days),[77] Ecuador (84 days),[78] Guatemala (84 days),[79] Honduras (70 days),[80] Mexico (84 days),[81] and Nicaragua (84 days).[82] As such, the regional average number of paid days of maternity leave is 105.5 days of paid leave as of January 1, 2025. The notable feature here is an unstated target of eighty-four days that many nations in the region have reached, but at which they have stalled.

With respect to paid leave for fathers in Latin America, as in Asia, vast gaps exist between mothers and fathers in the amount of leave available. Indeed the

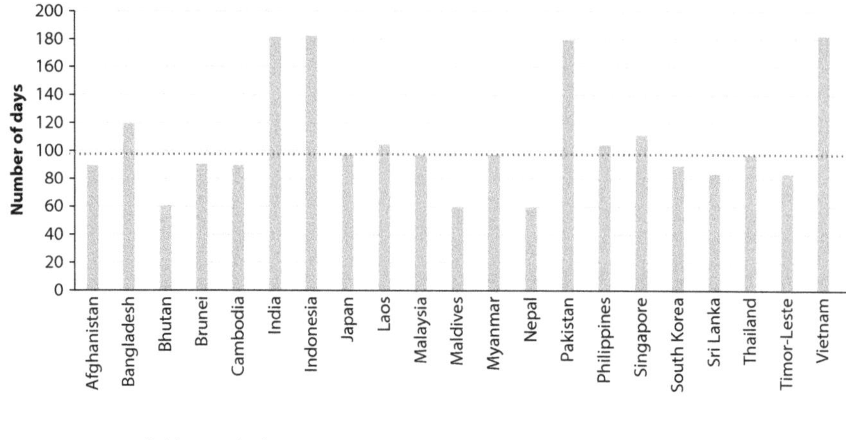

FIGURE 2. Paid maternity leave in Asia (as of January 1, 2025).

Where legislation specifies leave entitlements in months, the calculation has been based on an average of 30.5 days per month.

Female civil servants in Bhutan are entitled to 183 days of paid maternity leave under the Bhutan Civil Services Rules and Regulations 2018. This is not included in the chart, as it does not apply to private sector employees.

Wage replacement is an important consideration but is not included in the graph. In all countries except the following, the wage replacement level is 100 percent of the employee's average earnings. In Brunei, the 100 percent wage replacement applies only for up to eight weeks; in Nepal for only the first 60 days; and in Thailand for only the first 45 days. In Indonesia, mothers receive full pay for the first four months and 75 percent for the fifth and sixth months.

average number of days of paid paternity leave across the nineteen countries as of January 1, 2025, was just 6.5 days.

Surprisingly, adoption leave too reflects gendered norms and stereotypes. In instances of adoption, there is no biological imperative to distinguish between the leave entitlements for mothers and fathers. Nevertheless, in Singapore, for example, adoption leave mirrors paid paternity and maternity leave, with a significant gap between the more generous paid adoption leave for mothers (twelve weeks) if the child is under twelve months of age and the two weeks allocated for fathers.[83] From April 1 2025, paid paternity leave for adopting and non-adopting fathers increased to four weeks in Singapore, but paternity leave remains one-third of the entitlement given to mothers.

Category C: No Paid Leave for Fathers—Freezing Parenting as Women's Domain

Category C represents countries that offer no leave for fathers. Surprisingly, seven countries in Asia remain in this category: Afghanistan (despite relatively generous maternity leave of ninety days),[84] Bangladesh, Cambodia, India, Sri Lanka and

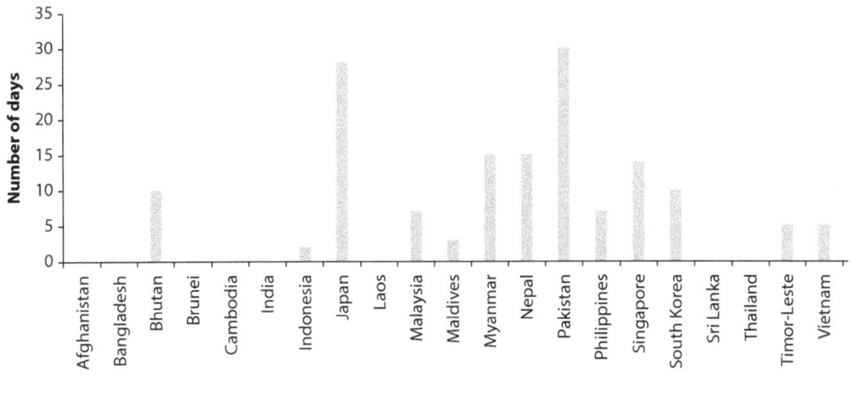

FIGURE 3. Paid paternity leave in Asia (as of January 1, 2025).

Where legislation specifies leave entitlements in months, the calculation has been based on an average of 30.5 days per month.

As of 2016, male civil servants in Bhutan are entitled to 10 days of paid maternity leave under the Bhutan Civil Services Rules and Regulations 2018. This has not been included in the chart, as it does not apply to private sector employees.

Male employees in the public sector in India are entitled to 15 days of paid paternity leave under the Central Civil Services (Leave) Rules 1972. This has not been included in the chart, as it does not apply to the private sector.

Male employees in the public sector in Indonesia are entitled to one month of paid paternity leave under the National Civil Service Agency Regulation No 24/2017. Only the two days of paid leave that men are entitled to in the private sector have been included in the chart.

In Laos, there is no specific legal entitlement to paid paternity leave, but employees can request three days from personal leave. As this leave is at the employer's discretion, it has not been represented in the figure.

In Myanmar, paternity leave is paid at 70 percent of the employee's average earnings. All other paid leave captured in the figure is paid at 100 percent of the employee's average earnings.

In Singapore, from April 1, 2025, paid paternity leave was extended to 28 days (4 weeks).

As of 2012, male employees in the public sector in Thailand were entitled to 15 days of paid paternity leave. This has not been included in the chart, as it does not apply to the private sector.

Thailand (figure 3). Laos falls in a grey area, as there is no specific legal entitlement to paid paternity leave but fathers can request up to three days of paid leave from general workplace leave. It remains at the employer's discretion. In 2023, Bangladesh actually added eight days of maternity leave—now up to 120 days of paid leave—to align with ILO standards, without making any headway on paternity leave (figure 4).[85]

While one would expect an entire absence of paid paternity leave to be rare, in 2018, UNICEF identified ninety-two countries with no national policy to facilitate even one day of paid leave for fathers to care for newborns.[86] However, this is a rapidly changing landscape and countries that previously fell in this category—Switzerland, Mexico, and Ireland, for example—no longer do. Based on relatively

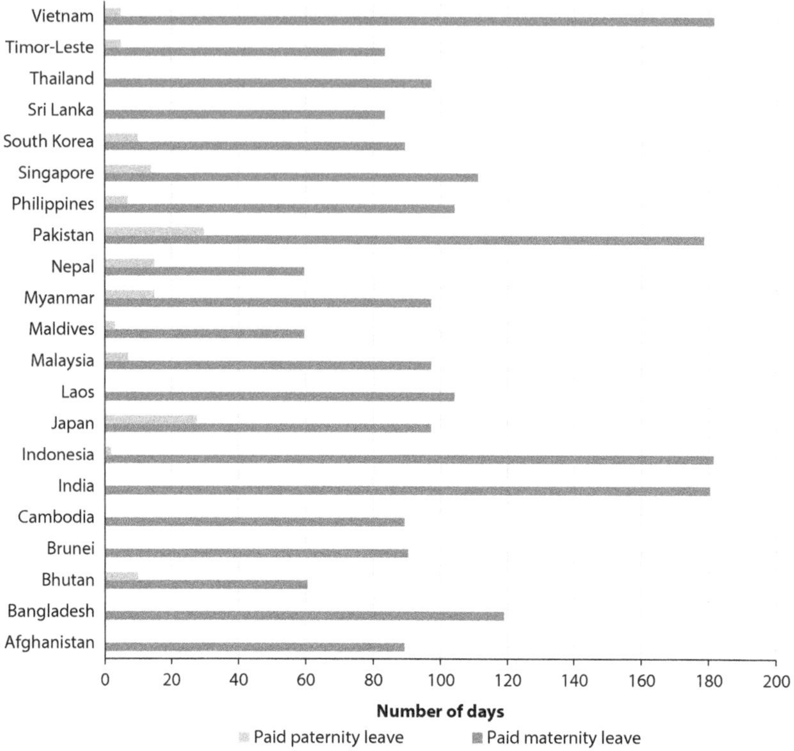

FIGURE 4. Paid maternity and paternity leave in Asia (as of January 1, 2025).
Where legislation specifies leave entitlements in months, the calculation has been based on an average of 30.5 days per month.

recent reforms, both Ireland[87] and Switzerland[88] offer fourteen days of paternity leave, in the case of Ireland, meeting the EU Directive's requirement of ten working days' leave. Such paternity leave sits alongside 182 days of paid maternity leave in Ireland,[89] and ninety-eight days of maternity leave in Switzerland.[90]

The Parental Leave Implementation Gap

The categories above set out the end goal of gender-responsive lawmaking in the field of parental leave. There nonetheless remain practical differences between available leave and usage. Japan offers a pertinent example.

In 1992, parental leave was introduced under Japan's Child Care Leave Act.[91] Groundbreaking for its time, Japan's paid parental leave scheme is often described as "gender-neutral" in its approach,[92] with one year of paid leave provided to either entitled parent to be distributed between them at their discretion.[93] As of January 1, 2025, this one year of transferable leave sat alongside fourteen weeks of paid maternity leave[94] and four weeks of paid paternity leave,[95] paid at 67 percent of

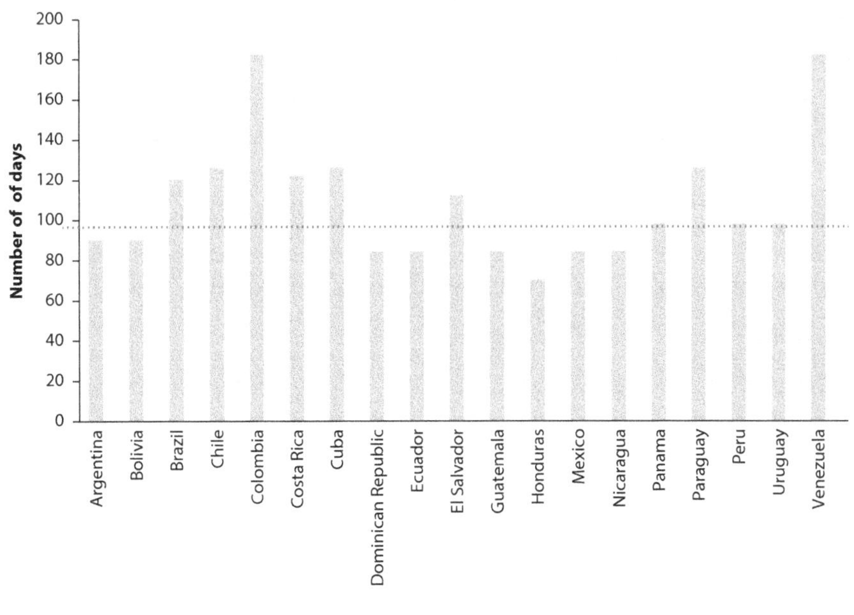

FIGURE 5. Paid maternity leave in Latin America (as of January 1, 2025).
Where legislation specifies leave entitlements in months, the calculation has been based on an average of 30.5 days per month.

base pay in most Japanese prefectures. Japan's scheme is one of the most generous in Asia. At the turn of the century, to encourage Japanese fathers to increase their usage of parental leave, a controversial campaign was attempted with the slogan "We don't call a man who does not take care of a child a father,"[96] but it was largely unsuccessful in turning around the status quo. In early 2023, in a final push to reverse Japan's birth rate—one of the lowest in the world—Prime Minister Fumio Kishida declared a national goal of dramatically raising the number of male workers taking paternity leave from 14 percent to 50 percent by 2024, and 85 percent by 2030.[97]

Numerous factors will affect the extent to which policies on family leave will make nations more gender equal. The starkest among them is implementation and monitoring of the law. Yet in the context of parental leave schemes, who is eligible, whether policies are actually accessible to everyone, whether the leave schemes are adequately resourced by governments, and, as noted earlier, wage replacement levels are all fundamental considerations. How countries split responsibility for payment of leave between the public sector, private sector, and individuals through social security contributions significantly influences the impact of such provisions. These realities go beyond the neat and somewhat simplistic categories offered above. Nonetheless, the regional patterns in Asia and Latin America witness a chasm between where law stands and where law ought to be.

THE LEAVE ENTITLEMENTS
FOR GENDER DIVERSE FAMILIES

As part of this project of rewriting engrained rules, this chapter would be remiss if it failed to bring greater attention to the slow pace of reform to ensure that same-sex and diverse families enjoy equal access to paid leave. In 2004, French woman Karine Hallier gave birth to a son. Her female partner, Elodie Lucas, also a French national, applied for eleven days of paid paternity leave. Her application was refused by the Health Insurance Office on the grounds that the legislation made no provision for granting paternity leave to a woman.[98] Lucas's appeals to the Friendly Settlements Board and subsequently to the Social Security Tribunal were both unsuccessful. The law did not refer to the mother's "partner" but rather to the "father" of the child, and therefore, Elodie Lucas could not access paternity leave. The European Court of Human Rights upheld the judgment in January 2018, holding that the difference in treatment suffered by Elodie was not based on sex or sexual orientation since in a different-sex couple, the mother's partner would not be eligible for paternity leave if he was not the child's father. The court also considered that the institution of paternity leave was proportionate to the aim pursued; this notion of proportionality is a common determination in cases where human rights violations are alleged.

The law in France has since been amended to ensure same-sex parents equally benefit from paid parental leave, coming into effect on July 1, 2021.[99] Yet the case reminds us how easily linguistic differences in entitlements between different-sex and same-sex couples are established in law. Scholars too urge us to rethink the language of law to ensure that leave can be shared with "partners," "cohabitating partners," "civil partners," "registered partners," "co-mothers," and "co-fathers."[100] Even OECD countries, often assumed to lead the way, fall short. One study of the thirty-three OECD nations that provide paid leave to birth parents found that, as of 2020, same-sex male couples received equal amounts of parental leave when compared to different-sex couples in only four countries (Australia, Iceland, New Zealand, and Sweden).[101] An inequality in law is experienced by same-sex couples who birth, as well as adopting same-sex and different-sex couples in many jurisdictions. In this respect, the 2007 Yogyakarta Principles, which provided a framework for the human rights of LGBT persons, is often overlooked despite addressing the issue of family benefits, including the right to non-discrimination related to social welfare and other public benefits.[102]

The Asia region faces an event blunter challenge. In 2024, Thailand became the only Asian jurisdiction to recognize the rights of same-sex couples to legally register. No Asian country explicitly provides entitlements to leave for same-sex families, even if progress appears underway in South Korea[103] and Nepal. No law acknowledges the rights of same-sex couples to adopt or share care *and* be legally entitled to paid leave, presenting a notable hurdle for same-sex couples to enjoy equal access to paid leave regionally.

Same-sex couples in Asia attempt to access paid leave in other ways that remain within the parameters of the law. Fathers in same-sex male partnerships in some Asian nations—such as Malaysia and Singapore—have managed to adopt children,[104] and we could imagine that they may access paid parental leave in countries where leave is given to adopting fathers.[105] There is clearly, therefore, an important nexus between paid parental leave for same-sex couples and adoption leave. Even this cursory knowledge reveals a clear point of discrimination in the extent to which parents in same-sex unions enjoy paid leave benefits.

In Colombia, same-sex couples receive paid leave entitlements that mirror the entitlements of different-sex parents thanks to a recent decision. Although the law does not recognize same-sex paternity or maternity leave, the Constitutional Court of Colombia determined that that there is no sufficient reason to maintain a difference in treatment based either on the type of relationship or on the family category (author translation).[106] As a result, same-sex parents have leave entitlements that mirror those of biological parents. Moreover, as stipulated in the decision, same-sex parents receive "maternity leave" entitlements (even for a male-identifying same-sex couple), which in that particular case saw one father receive eighteen weeks and the other fourteen days of paid leave.[107]

Until a recent amendment, same-sex couples in Chile suffered discrimination with regard to leave entitlements when compared to different-sex couples. Previously, the one week of paternity leave was gender-restrictive and available only to males; thus, the total duration of leave available to a same-sex female couple would have been eighteen weeks.[108] However, a September 2022 amendment to the labor code provided for all people regardless of their registered sex by gender identity ("con independencia de su sexo registral por identidad de género") to enjoy the legislated rights of mothers and fathers.[109] Today in Chile, both female and male same-sex couples are entitled to a combination of 126 days of paid leave for one parent, and five days for partners. Chile and Colombia stand out for guaranteeing same-sex parents not only paid parental leave but the exact same entitlements that are available to different-sex parents. It is telling that even in these instances, however, the model has not been one of equal leave entitlements to each parent.

There is evidently no regional pattern. In Brazil, since 2012, either parent in a same-sex relationship, however identifying, is entitled to "maternity leave." Practically, this has meant that the second parent in a two-parent same-sex couple has no entitlements, creating a point of discrimination between same-sex and different-sex couples.[110] By contrast, same-sex couples who are adopting parents in Costa Rica are entitled to three months of leave; the language used is "adopting people" ("personas adoptantes"), entitling parents of either sex to access these leave provisions.[111]

Transgender people too can become biological parents through sexual intercourse, at-home insemination, or assisted reproduction, and yet they face a clear legal disparity between their legally registered gender and/or gender identity and their roles as parents, a key obstacle to recognizing transgendered identities.[112] As argued by Daniela Alaattinoğlu and Alice Margaria, "Public authorities' failure to assign legal parenthood in line with gender identity, gender expression, and/or legal gender is likely to have a negative impact on the parent's psychological ease and parental security and, consequently, on their children's well-being".[113] Sweden went from reluctance to facilitate transgender men who give birth to be registered in alignment with their identity on their child's birth certificate and/or in a population registry[114] to recognizing a transgender man giving birth as the "father of the child."[115] Where a parent changes their legal gender, "paternity" or "maternity" is not presumed but will be confirmed through a special acknowledgment or judgment regardless of the parents' marital status, facilitating transgender people in the Swedish system to be identified as parents in alignment with their own legal gender.[116]

As an alternative, the Canadian province of Ontario and Israel have opted to de-gender legal parenthood altogether—namely, by replacing *mother* and *father* with the gender-neutral term *parent* when assigning legal parenthood.[117] In Israel, the High Court of Justice decided in May 2021 that transgender parents can be registered as "parents" on their child's birth certificate. Transgender men who give birth in Israel today preserve their male gender classification in the population registry. As pointed out, while Israel and Ontario are exceptions as of now, both demonstrate the potential to "degender legal parenthood" in law.[118] This approach potentially makes paid leave entitlements more fluid and flexible in responding to a diversity of desires and needs of parents.[119]

FROM CLEAR CATEGORIES TO MORE COMPLEX REALITIES: A SCAN OF THE FUTURE

This chapter reflects the failure of law to value the role of birth mothers while detangling pregnancy and parenting. Instead, parental-leave laws remain highly sexed and gendered. The vast majority of the world's nations have paid paternity-leave laws that fit within Category B. The role of fathers—with their glorified "daddy leave" days—is too often viewed as an add-on. Responsibilities remain primarily with birth and non-birth mothers.

The three categories laid out in this chapter seek to offer directions for legislative reform. Given that no jurisdiction in either Asia or Latin America meets the Category A standard, we may fear that progress soon is unrealistic. Yet parental leave proves to be an area of law with constant reform. Various bills under discussion offer hope that progress is pending. Bangladesh has long hinted it would introduce a policy proposal for fifteen days' paternity leave, although the proposition was unsuccessful in 2014[120] and again in March 2022.[121] Progress is not guaranteed. Indonesia's Maternal and Child Welfare Act, signed into law in July 2024, created an entitlement to three months of maternity leave, extendable for a further three months for medical reasons, but the proposed increase from two to forty days of paternity leave was rejected.[122]

Potential for reform is evident in Latin America too. At the time of publication, Argentina had a bill under consideration that would raise maternity leave from ninety days of paid leave[123] to 126 days; and paternity from two days paid leave[124] to a significantly more promising ninety days of paid leave. The Argentinian bill's use of the phrase *pregnant people* ("personas gestantes") to avoid gender discrimination and enable a diversity of parents to make use of the leave in equal measure is also encouraging, although once again raises questions of language and erasure. Peru also has a bill to increase paid paternity leave from ten days to fifteen days. Presented to Congress in August 2022, as of March 2025, it had yet to pass.[125] Uruguay too offers promise, with the fourteen days of paternity leave increasing to seventeen days as of January 1, 2026.[126]

We cannot assume that developments from a human rights standpoint follow a simple and linear path toward progress. Perhaps this is precisely why comparative and data-driven studies of this kind are so essential. Those nations surging ahead and those severely lagging behind are laid bare on the table. Comparing the regions, each offers the others evolving standards and motivation for reform.

Yet the exercise of de-sexing and de-gendering also reveals the possibility of competing rights. Bartick amplifies the real fears that women and the discrimination they suffer—including discrimination related to pregnancy, maternity, and reproduction—will be even less visible in the well-meaning attempt to be more inclusive. I leave this uncertain space by drawing upon Bartick's call that "language should not be used as a tool to erase any type of person from our lexicon."[127] In this vein, we can envisage the possibility of de-sexed and de-gendered language in alignment with individual preferences that enable us to rethink not only leave entitlements but, importantly, societal roles and responsibilities. Perhaps it is only then that we can fulfill the vision of a shared responsibility that was named in CEDAW more than fifty years ago.

4

Modern Slavery

Giving Voice and Visibility to the Gendered Experiences
of Supply Chain Exploitation

It is August 2011. I am sitting among a circle of Cambodia's garment workers, gathered on mats laid on the floor of a drop-in center that they have set up in Phnom Penh's export processing zone. Mostly migrants from rural and remote parts of Cambodia and with families back in the provinces, these women are often the sole income-earner for their whole family, challenging male-breadwinner stereotypes. Their work is important to the nation too, with the clothing, footwear and textiles (CFT) industry contributing up 45 percent of all women's waged employment in Cambodia,[1] and at one point, accounting for nearly 80 percent of the country's total merchandise exports.[2] They chat and exchange stories, overcoming their loneliness and isolation in ways that shrink the distance from home. I notice them pulling from their pockets clothing labels that have been taken from the factory floor. I discover it is their way of identifying which company will buy the clothes they sew, enabling the workers to better target their campaigns for improved working conditions. I gain a deep insight into the fundamental role of the buyer in addressing corporate supply chain exploitation and yet their physical distance is an easy escape from accountability to the individual worker at risk of exploitation. Today, Cambodia's CFT sector remains highly gendered. Managers and auditors are still mostly men, and a "deep and long-standing paradox" remains between the reality that Cambodia's female garment workers are at "the forefront of widespread strikes on minimum wage" while attention by unions to "women's issues" remains poor.[3]

Fifteen hundred kilometers away, Thailand's fishing industry has its own challenges. Issued a "yellow card" by the European Union in April 2015, the sector was formally on notice of a potential ban on exporting produce to Europe from its illegal, unreported, and unregulated fishing.[4] That year, more than two thousand mostly Burmese and Cambodian workers had been found on the Indonesian island of Benjina, working under slavelike conditions on Thai fishing boats.[5] Based on reports by Human Rights Watch, the vast majority of these fisherfolk were men.[6] Four years later, in January 2019, the European Commission delisted Thailand from the group of "warned countries" following the Thai government's ratification of the International Labour Organization's Work in Fishing Convention (No. 188). Yet these Thai vessels—an estimated 6,700—are rarely listed by fishing companies as part of their supply chains.[7] Their operations resultingly fall outside the monitoring and audit regimes that have been set up under a rhetoric of corporate accountability.

Crossing over to Africa, we develop a deeper understanding of the gendered nature of exploitation. For centuries in Burkina Faso, women have been collecting, processing, and selling shea butter as a cooking oil, as a body lotion, and for medicinal purposes. Yet at one point, shea butter was sold in Europe to consumers at eighty-four times the price local women in Burkina Faso received for the raw product.[8] This gap between the profit derived from markets in Europe, North America, and Japan for cosmetics and the income that makes it to the hands of women workers is often overlooked when we determine what constitutes free and fair labor in the Global South. Meanwhile, for women in Nigeria and Tanzania, who are the backbone of fresh and dry fish marketing, their absence from intermediate or senior management raises crucial questions about women's bargaining power and presence in decision-making roles.[9]

"Hierarchies" of exploitation are also evident within individual industries. Employers in the Gulf want African labor because it is perceived to be cheap. Under bilateral agreements, a Ugandan maid in Saudi Arabia gets 900 riyals (US$240) a month—much more than she could make at home, but less than the 1,500 riyals most Filipino workers earn.[10] Exploitation is therefore gendered, cultural, and geographic. This labor is also situated within a Global North–South dynamic that, put simplistically, sees the majority of labor-intensive production by workers takes place in the Global South for the benefit of the consumers and the national and transnational corporations of "the West."

International law has long been "plagued with paralysis" in its failed attempts to develop binding rules to regulate corporate behavior.[11] Adopting the term "modern slavery," laws in the 2010s "mushroomed"[12] to regulate supply chains, starting with the state of California.[13] The United Kingdom,[14] France,[15] the Netherlands,[16] the European Union,[17] and Australia[18] followed. This "harder" form of regulation sought to counter international law's largely "soft" governance framework that had, until then, proven inadequate to protect the rights of workers.[19] These Northern jurisdictions were offering the promise of supply chain transparency—knowing where, how, and by whom products are made in the move from source to consumer. They appropriated the language of corporate due diligence, a concept that had long existed in corporate law, to oblige businesses to "avoid infringing on the rights of others."[20] Due diligence will prove fraught in the discussion that follows and yet is deeply embedded in current legislative responses to supply chain exploitation.

The fact that it has been the exclusive domain of the Global North to enact legislation to govern corporate supply has not gone unnoticed. It has been labelled a "game of jurisdiction" as globalization reconfigures state sovereignty.[21] Modern slavery laws are made by "first world governments (the saviours) ostensibly for the benefit of Third World peoples (the victims) but without their input."[22] Business and human rights scholar Caroline Omari Lichuma foregrounds this under-explored tension between who should (as a normative question) and who actually does (as a descriptive matter) regulate supply chains.[23] That the modern slavery laws deliberated over in this chapter "also operate in the shadow of the legacy of the imperial project"[24] is a tension that must be acknowledged. In centering gender in the debate, we must actively magnify subaltern perspectives by making explicit the North–South dynamic at the heart of global supply.

Modern slavery is a term I use with disinclination and only for its familiarity among some readers. "Modern slavery" tends to encompass such exploitative situations as indentured labor, debt bondage, forced labor, servitude, human trafficking, and in some countries, forced marriage.[25] Gender has been at the heart of slavery for centuries. The very language of enslavement carries gendered imagery—think here of the descriptions of mutilation, murder, sexual violence, and kidnapping of women victims of slavery that at times border on the voyeuristic and often amplify "white savior" fantasies of the (male) hero rescuing the damned (female) victim.[26] Yet as the global movement shifted to a focus on supply chain regulation, much of this gendered interest faded. The gendered debates narrowed in scope, left to the scholars and activists who were debating how to understand the consent of women in sex work and prostitution and the relationship, if any, to human trafficking.[27]

The need to pursue a nuanced and evidence-based approach to understanding how men, women, and gender-diverse people differently experience supply chain exploitation has therefore gone largely ignored. There has been a missed opportunity to make "modern slavery" laws less flawed by bringing a gender perspective. This chapter seeks to respond to that gap by demonstrating how to realize that goal. Legislation must be worker-centered and an enabling environment must be created in which the relationship between the worker and the corporation is rethought altogether. Laws need to give workers voice and visibility and an environment created for survivors of supply chain exploitation to share their gendered experiences. Yet most fundamentally and the goal least realized to date, gender-responsive modern slavery laws demand financial penalties for identified exploitation and remedies for victims.

The discussion that follows begins with the historical landscape to understand why gendered experiences of exploitation have been largely overlooked in today's "modern-slavery" legislative landscape. Readers are then presented with a dilemma: the choice between pursuing pragmatic improvements to the existing modern slavery legislation and what a fresh start, with a blank canvas, might offer. While the desire to rehearse and present an alternative—however impossible it may be to realize—is enticing,[28] this chapter focuses on what may be possible and arguably conceivable even in the near future. In doing so, it makes a case for how to rewrite existing modern slavery laws to become gender responsive, while acknowledging that a shift away from due diligence altogether may be the most desirable future steps.

Taking this pragmatic path, we seek sharper visibility of workers' *gendered* experiences of exploitation. Visibility in turn demands a level of disaggregation through comprehensive gender-responsive due diligence. Ultimately, by bringing victims back to the center of the conversation and by gendering (or perhaps re-gendering) modern slavery, we could—eventually—move toward a regulatory environment in which corporations are held to account for gender-based exploitation. Before attempting to elucidate the gender of modern slavery, I guide readers through the global history, from slavery's abolition to today's conceptualization of "modern slavery."

"MODERN SLAVERY":
AN INTERNATIONAL AND DOMESTIC LEGAL HISTORY

In order to understand the place—or the absence—of gender in today's modern slavery laws, we must go back in time. Two processes in the early 1900s saw a convergence of concerns over race, ethnicity, sexuality, and gender.[29] On the one hand, the world witnessed a sought-after abolition of the trade of enslaved Africans. On the other, we saw a largely "European-driven" quest to end the "white slave traffic"[30] of women through both the 1904 International Agreement for the Suppression of the White Slave Traffic[31] and the 1910 International Convention for the Suppression of the White Slave Traffic.[32] Both of these agreements amplified a gendered discourse about loose and lost innocent women (understood as white virginal victims) in need of saving.[33]

When a global convention to abolish the slave trade was canvassed by the Temporary Slave Commission established by the League of Nations in 1924, the path to the Slavery Convention was relatively smooth. The momentum that built toward slavery's abolition in the 1800s provided an opportunity for women to participate in political processes but also reflected the hostility and exclusion women faced as their voices were stifled. It is perhaps ironic that the founding of the 1830s American Anti-Slavery Society was a foundational period in the emergence of feminism in the US.[34]

The definition of slavery in the 1926 Slavery Convention was heavily tied to proof of ownership by the enslaver of the enslaved person[35] and proved inadequate for the post-World War II international community. The 1956 Supplementary Slavery Convention focused on behaviors *akin* to slavery but without requiring proof of ownership. The Supplementary Convention also engaged a particular gendered understanding of slavery that included debt bondage, serfdom, servile marriage, and child servitude.[36] In the years that followed, the gendered debates and divides deepened as a panic continued across Europe and the US about the procurement of white women and girls. These narratives were amplified in subsequent decades in the world's media, in films, and in plays in the US,[37] Britain,[38] and Australia.[39]

Palermo and the UN Trafficking Protocol

Decades later, the year 2000 was a watershed moment in the world's response to human exploitation. Global policymakers, particularly under the leadership of the United Nations Office on Drugs and Crime, convened in Palermo in Italy to discuss and address crimes that occur across borders. The result was the UN Convention against Transnational Organized Crime (UNTOC), adopted by the UN General Assembly in 2000 and entering into force three years later, in September 2003.[40] The UNTOC was supplemented by three protocols: the Protocol to Prevent, Suppress and Punish Trafficking in Persons, Especially Women and Children (the Palermo Protocol); the Protocol against the Smuggling of Migrants by Land, Sea, and Air; and the Protocol Against the Illicit Manufacturing of and Trafficking in Firearms, their Parts and Components and Ammunition.[41]

The Palermo Protocol offered the global community the first-ever definition of trafficking and the parameters for determining who constitutes a victim. Palermo's negotiations have been the subject of much debate, challenged for providing the world an inaccurate and cumbersome definition that fails to accord with the realities of human trafficking.[42] Abolitionists sought an end to prostitution and by and large wanted little difference in how trafficking and prostitution were defined in the Palermo Protocol. Advocates for sex-worker rights sought a clear acknowledgment in international law that sexual exploitation is distinct from noncoercive, voluntary sex work. Neither side was satisfied with the outcome. For many today, the waters remain murky when it comes to naming the relationship, if any, that prostitution and sex work have with the trafficking of (primarily) women and girls for sexual exploitation.[43]

This history has a pivotal bearing on how concepts that were previously defined in distinct ways have since merged. Indeed, the US government today refers to "trafficking in persons," "human trafficking," and "modern slavery" as umbrella terms to refer to both "sex trafficking" and compelled labor.[44] The Australian Federal Police seeks to "disrupt, investigate and prosecute perpetrators of human trafficking and slavery."[45] Human trafficking is frequently named "slavery" in public campaigns, whereas forced labor is referred to as "trafficking" in what US scholar Janie Chuang describes as an "exploitation creep."[46] With *trafficking* and *slavery* used interchangeably, despite evident distinctions in their historical legal meanings, these terminological challenges tend to hide more than they reveal.[47] We seek to regulate while being unable to accurately conceive of the scope of the problem at hand. Estimates take us from 25 million people in forced labor[48] through to 40.3 million people in modern slavery in 2020, approximately five out of every one thousand people in the world.[49]

Even in this context, gendered narratives have been problematic, statistics misapplied, and a picture created where global trafficking is "all about women and children"[50] and their sexual exploitation in the sex industry. That women and girls are exploited in other industries or that sexual exploitation often occurs simultaneously in a myriad of other industries beyond sex work is unheeded. Male and gender-diverse vulnerabilities are obscured. For instance, Thailand's transgender sex workers may be accepted only in a context where "certain stereotypes and occupational positions are maintained,"[51] also risking little attention to the vulnerabilities facing transgender migrant sex workers in the region beyond issues such as health.[52] Telling a more nuanced story—one that goes beyond the binaries of coerced and free and of sexual and nonsexual—is evidently essential. Despite the Palermo Protocol's existence for a quarter of a century, this nuance has not been achieved.

The Soft Law Decades: Business and Human Rights Rhetoric

I now turn to the "business and human rights" rhetoric that emerged at the turn of this century, in which both race and gender have been given inadequate visibility. Scholars often dust off the draft Code of Conduct on Transnational Corporations proposed by the UN in the 1970s[53] to explain the emergence of this new discourse. These codes sought to address "imported" bribery, when transnational corporations were found to have bribed local officials.[54] The codes, also the first global norms on corruption, were never officially adopted and their legal nature never clarified.[55]

Then in 1999, Kofi Annan, UN secretary-general at the time, challenged multinational and transnational businesses to become more sustainable by placing a human face on the global marketplace.[56] In the same year that the Palermo Protocol was enacted, the first meeting leading to the UN Global Compact took place in New York. The compact and its ten principles are a nonbinding UN pact that sought to encourage businesses to adopt and report on sustainable and socially responsible policies but offered no remedy for the exploited and no recourse against corporations.[57] What followed in 2003 was the slightly more ambitious Norms on the Responsibilities of Transnational Corporations and Other Business Enterprises with regard to Human Rights,[58] including businesses within an ever-expanding web of human rights obligations. The architect of the UN Global Compact, Professor John Ruggie, was appointed in 2005 as the Special Representative of the Secretary-General on the Issue of Human Rights and Transnational Corporations and Other Business Enterprises. The UN Guiding Principles on

Business and Human Rights (UNGPs) were then adopted by the Human Rights Council in June 2011,[59] creating three prongs: (1) a duty for governments to *protect* individuals and communities from human rights abuses; (2) a *responsibility* for corporations to respect human rights; and (3) an amelioration of current *remedy* mechanisms when human rights abuses have occurred.[60] Yet no system was created to ensure that these three fairly strong pillars were translated into practice.

While some have argued that the past thirty years witnessed the birth of a business and human rights "movement,"[61] corporations continue to avoid—through "greenwashing" or "white washing"[62] or the "window-dressing of corporate social responsibility"—positive obligations to protect and realize human rights.[63] Governments in the Global South remain incentivized to keep "their regulatory systems powerless" in order to keep benefitting from foreign direct investment.[64] The response has also been largely uninformed by the racialized dynamic that sits at the heart of global supply that was once acknowledged in the historical pursuit of slavery's abolition. Moreover, although the gender stereotypes that have shaped how trafficking is understood have often been harmful for victim-survivors, at the very least they demonstrate a consciousness that gender is relevant, one that, by contrast, has been only peripheral in "business and human rights" debates. This gender blindness was so deep that scholars and activists were motivated to introduce the concept of "gender-responsive due diligence,"[65] which I discuss further below.

From Slavery to Exploitation and Back to "Modern" Slavery:
Finding a Place for Gender in the Law

With international law largely soft in its regulatory approach, the work shifted to national-level regulation. The result has been a rapid-fire series of modern slavery or corporate supply laws in the Global North. Obligations are centered around the concept of due diligence, one that is familiar to many lawyers and businesses and yet also means different things to different people.[66] In the UNGPs, *due diligence* refers to a range of processes and procedures that business should have in place to ensure compliance with national laws and to manage the risk of human rights harm; ongoing monitoring is key.[67]

In 2015, the UK enacted the Modern Slavery Act, obliging corporations with a turnover of over £36 million (then around 13,000 corporations[68]) to report the steps taken to identify instances of slavery and trafficking in their supply or in any part of their businesses or to disclose of a failure to undertake such due diligence.[69] Australia's intervention—the Modern Slavery Act 2018[70]—"imported" large aspects of the UK model, with limited regard to best fit for the Australian context. That law established reporting obligations for businesses with an annual turnover of $100 million, affecting around 2,500 companies[71] and requiring businesses to report on the due diligence conducted, including the risks assessed and the "remediation processes" established, as well as the effectiveness of their response.[72]

In the US, in addition to the California Transparency in Supply Chains Act,[73] the US, under President Obama, introduced a section to the Dodd–Frank Act preventing the financing of armed groups through the trade of conflict minerals from the Democratic Republic of the Congo.[74] An executive order strengthened the prohibition on US federal contractors from engaging in human trafficking activities,[75] while a statement by the president set out reporting requirements for companies investing in Myanmar.[76]

In 2016, the Netherlands introduced a child labor due diligence law, which took effect in January 2020,[77] and the French adopted a "duty of vigilance" law in February 2017[78] to establish obligations to prevent exploitation within the supply chains of large multinational firms carrying out a significant part of their activity in France.[79] The European Union as a whole has been governed by both the EU Non-Financial Reporting Directive,[80] which requires around eight thousand large European companies to disclose their policies, risks, and responses related to respect for human rights, as well as the EU Regulation Laying Down Supply Chain Due Diligence Obligations in Mining.[81]

A leap was taken and yet an opportunity was lost in June 2024, when the European Parliament and Council of the European Union enacted a directive on corporate sustainability due diligence, covering companies with more than one thousand employees and a net worldwide turnover exceeding €450 million, with lower thresholds for companies involved in franchising. The directive's statement that companies are not required "to guarantee, in all circumstances, that adverse impacts will never occur or that they will be stopped" is telling.[82] As EU Member States forge ahead with national legislation, companies need only respond in "a manner commensurate to the degree of severity and the likelihood of the adverse impact."[83] Sadly too, the very nature of corporate supply chains seems ignored in what could be read into the directive as a softening of both "upstream" accountability (for instance, the sourcing of cotton) and "downstream" accountability (such as the delivery of goods by Amazon workers). Companies can demonstrate that their "power of influence" over direct and indirect partners is limited, thereby narrowing what is understood as "appropriate measures" taken to avoid adverse impacts.

On the one hand, this spate of laws reflects a positive surge in efforts to deploy law to end the exploitation suffered by individuals in the supply chains of medium to large corporations.[84] Yet none of them center worker's voices and visibility well and in turn achieve the accountability that gender responsiveness necessitates. For many rights-based advocates, it is clear that companies should bear the burden of showing they have done all within their power to avoid human rights harms. By contrast, at the time of publication, "due diligence" has been diluted to simple reporting by corporations, risking a soft and self-regulatory environment that allows corporations to self-audit and self-report and thereby paper over actual exploitation through standardized non-gendered reporting. Meanwhile, rights violations endure and victims are left without redress. Can "modern slavery" governance and "due diligence" be rethought to become worker centered and harm preventing in order to rise to being gender responsive?

WORKING WITH THE MASTER'S TOOLS TO BRING THE WORKER TO THE CENTER OF THE DEBATE

This chapter necessarily finds itself at a fork in the road. The pathway splits between a transformative or visionary approach to eradicating exploitation in supply chains, on the one hand, and the more pragmatic but politically palatable road on the other. Global and organizational dynamics have given rise to a system in which businesses benefit from a gender-blind approach to regulating the sector, one that is simultaneously race- and class-blind and devoid of a postcolonial lens. A transformative response necessarily requires a blank canvas, moving away from "modern slavery governance" due to the failure of the due diligence approach to achieve the necessary depth, rigor, or accountability required to address the scope of exploitation in global supply.

A visionary pathway would first and foremost name the extent to which businesses thrive off cheap labor. It would critique the financial experts that help corporations hide the revenue flowing from exploitation and find loopholes in the law to avoid paying local taxes that might otherwise give back to the communities where goods are produced, fished, or farmed.[85] It would acknowledge that compassion-based interventions can shift consumers' buying practices,[86] but it can go only so far toward more sustainable consumption. Significant reform is required, with penalties being the primary mechanisms to truly incentivize business to adopt different, more sustainable, and human-centered practices.

Yet the "undoing" of the UNGPs is far from viable given how due diligence is etched on modern slavery. The second pathway—a practical vision and one that is discussed in the remainder of this chapter—works with the master's tools to strengthen existing laws. By all accounts, workers want better working conditions, not the closure of businesses or for migrant workers in supply chains to be repatriated to their place of origin.[87] A contemporary and gendered approach to modern slavery can bring about a positive duty on corporations to proactively, systematically, and transparently investigate, identify, comprehend, and respond in order to deliver those working conditions.

This pragmatic path can still amplify the gendered nature of supply chain exploitation. The benefits are multifold. Gendering modern slavery may overcome the heterogeneity in reporting that has been witnessed in jurisdictions governed by modern slavery laws, such as the UK.[88] Gender responsiveness demands redress. A gender lens may be the first step toward delivering remedies that are responsive to gendered harms and therefore may be the foundations for a more transformative future for corporate supply chains.

So what is the gendered ask? First, modern slavery laws must create legal obligations on corporations to undertake due diligence that is *gender responsive*. Gender-responsive due diligence requires recognition of the embedded gender norms, complex cultural biases, and power imbalances at play in corporate supply chains to identify the positive potential of business as well as the negative impacts of business practices on human rights related to sex, gender, gender identity, and sexual orientation. Second, businesses must undertake responsible data collection that involves giving attention to how different groups are affected. This would require, for example, a level of disaggregation that in different countries makes visible exploitation that may be on the basis of sex, sexual minority, indigeneity, race, or ethnic, migrant, or marital status, as well as driven by assumptions pertaining to an individual's ability, age, and experiences of poverty in both rural and urban settings.[89]

The significance of such interventions should not be underestimated. Consultation with those most affected is best practice and, in the words of the anti-slavery commissioner in the Australian state of New South Wales, it can "help survivors recover the agency their modern slavery experience has stolen from them."[90] Here I elaborate on how such legal reforms might lead to more gender-responsive practices in eradicating supply-chain exploitation.

Gender-Responsive Due Diligence:
From the Controlled to the Controlling

Due diligence becomes gendered when meaningful engagement is sought with all stakeholders to understand concrete and often gendered experiences of global supply chains and the adverse human rights impacts of work in the sector.[91] So, how can gender-responsive due diligence improve the status quo? First and by necessity, the process has to be led by corporations. By contrast, to date, due diligence has largely been the work of the non-governmental community. NGOs are known to create physical and digital platforms for workers to rate and review employers, recruiters, and service providers.[92] While well-meaning, such work should be *supplementary* to corporate due diligence, with corporations better resourced to conduct due diligence and, if the law is well-conceived, accountable to respond to any rights violations that are revealed.

By contrast, most evidence reflects the extent to which even civil-society-led due diligence is blocked. Workers face retaliation if they are found to have shared their experiences with scholars, let alone through more official channels.[93] Collective bargaining and action is regularly challenged and production may be so remote that civil-society presence is minimal.[94] Workers may not speak the local language and may be easily oppressed or marginalized, with reporting harder for internal migrants who are foreign to the local community. Placing due diligence in the hands of corporations requires care. As with all data collection, a "do no harm" approach is needed. Moreover, with workers often skeptical about corporate-led initiatives, a quid pro quo requires an ex ante commitment by corporations that action will be taken. There must be clear positive obligations to respond that are non-derogable when instances of human rights abuses, such as child labor, come to light.[95] This is a significant gap between current models and the end goal.

Second, gender-responsive due diligence must pay particular attention to exploitation that would otherwise go unseen. Withholding of wages and under-payment may be as common for men in the Thai fishing industry as it is for Burkinabè producing shea butter. However, the offshore nature of fishing exacerbates vulnerability, physically beyond oversight mechanisms,[96] with workers in long-haul fishing often at sea for more than a month being more likely to face heightened labor abuses than short-haul fisherfolk.[97] Engaging with workers at the margins can reveal the systematic nature of the problem while allowing workers with direct experience to inform the remedies.

Finally, gender-responsive due diligence can acknowledge how supply chain exploitation is compounded by and compounds existing gendered inequalities. Studies of organic cotton production in Burkina Faso remind us that while "appellations such as organic and fair trade" give consumers in the Global North the impression of socially acceptable working conditions, in reality, organic producers are mostly poor African women who bear the compliance burdens for the "imagined White consumer"[98] in the United States and Europe. Female workers negotiate with husbands or male family members to access small plots of land and because they rarely have access to equipment, undertake tasks by hand. Some women report feeling used by husbands, including in polygamous contexts, for their capacity to generate more income from production labelled "organic."[99] Gender-responsive due diligence can reveal how serving global demand has direct consequences for women's specific experiences of economic inequality in the Global South.

Legislatively, an ideal but achievable framework is a requirement on corporations to describe the steps they have taken to consult disadvantaged and vulnerable groups who may have limited access to consultation processes. Gendered inequalities that hinder participation must be noted and deliberate steps taken to overcome them. The process should be expansive by definition, paying attention to rights to health, including sexual and reproductive health, and safety; rights to land and the natural environment; rights to redress in order to overcome disruption to livelihoods in communities surrounding business practices; and the right to freedom of association.[100]

Gender-Disaggregated Data Collection

Data is an all-important and powerful tool. However, around half of all data needed to monitor and measure what governments are doing to address gendered inequalities is missing.[101] In such contexts, the idea of a "data revolution," much less a "gender data revolution," seems rhetorical.[102]

This state of play is equally reflected in the field of modern slavery. Despite the overtly gendered nature of global supply, women are frequently not counted, with women's participation in senior management often a proxy for women's participation. Yet tracking with gender-disaggregated data is essential if we are to understand which women are most affected by global supply chains and in what ways they are impacted. Since the late 1980s, the CEDAW Committee has called for comprehensive monitoring of the situation of women.[103] Indeed, without this knowledge, we cannot solve problems that are gender specific.

A pragmatic but gender-responsive ask is a heightened level of gender disaggregation. The NGO Oxfam's Behind the Brands campaign, for example, called upon the world's ten largest food and beverage companies to provide gender-disaggregated data to show (a) the number of women smallholders from whom they source commodities; (b) which of those commodities have the highest prevalence of women smallholders at their source; and (c) which of those commodities heighten women's vulnerability or place women at particular risk.[104] From 2013 to 2016, eight of the world's ten largest food and beverage companies (absent were Danone[105] and Associated British Foods) signed the UN Women's Empowerment Principles, a nonbinding voluntary UN pact to encourage sustainability and socially responsible policies. Yet beyond such actions, which may appear to skeptics a form of "ethics-washing," the principles, along with the campaign, brought visibility to both the degree to which consumer habits in one country shape women's lives at the source and to how gendered harms are clearly greater for women in some industries than others and in what ways.

Having adopted the pragmatic pathway, these partial but important steps provide a basis for more binding obligations. Currently, this rights-based framework to understand the context in which women workers experience the supply chain is rarely adopted, let alone regarded as a positive duty on corporations. Such disaggregation may broaden the scope of accountability beyond the immediate physical geography of the corporation. For one, business activities that restrict access to collective resources like water, fisheries, and forests affect community members in different ways.[106] Women and girls may be at heightened risk of sexual abuse if a business' presence in a local community leads to an influx of male workers.[107] Over time, making disaggregation a standard practice could help move responses away from superficial 'purple-washing' and toward more meaningful and specific efforts to address concrete gendered harms that have been overlooked.

TOWARD THE TRANSFORMATIVE:
SHIFTING ACCOUNTABILITY FROM THE SOURCE
TO THE BUYER

Businesses can be crudely divided into the willing and the unwilling. In many respects, the most impacted in the examples in this chapter are the workers; the least impacted is the buyer at the end of the chain. The legislative requirement on corporations to prepare "modern slavery statements" that are central to many jurisdictions' modern slavery laws has done little to change this. Reports are filed as a one-off, or no report is made at all.[108] Reporting has not facilitated an increase in prosecutions or in remedies for victims.[109] An overall picture of "compliance without substantive changes" has emerged.[110] How can we bring together the tools that enable gender-responsive due diligence and the realities of current practice?

Simply, the buyer in the supply chain must be brought to account. While seemingly distant from production, distance may overcome some of the localized barriers to deep due diligence. This approach was also once seen as legally plausible. In 2017, when the French Parliament adopted its duty of vigilance law noted above, the draft proposed a reverse burden of proof requiring the company concerned to prove that it was not in control of the activities of its subsidiaries and subcontractors.[111] The Swiss Responsible Business Initiative: To Protect People and the Environment (Für Verantwortungsvolle Unternehmen—zum Schutz von Mensch und Umwelt) similarly proposed a partial reversal of the burden of proof, providing that when a controlled company caused harm, the controlling company was liable unless it could prove that it had taken all due care to avoid the harm or loss. Neither of these provisions made it to the final text,[112] but they can be used to inform how the "power of influence" of a company over direct and indirect partners in the 2024 EU directive can be sharpened to heighten the accountability of Northern beneficiaries for Southern harm.

CONCLUSION

Human slavery is one of the world's oldest practices. By contrast, modern slavery laws appeared just over a decade ago. Gender has been at the heart of enslavement, exploitation, and abuse for years, and yet gender as a lens of analysis is rarely adopted in legislation that seeks to address supply chain exploitation. A more comprehensive approach is needed to redress the many dimensions and spheres in which women experience exploitation. This chapter has pragmatically sought to offer two legal obligations on corporations—the conducting of gender-responsive due diligence and the collecting of gender-disaggregated data—to help alter the approach.

Naturally, a call for disaggregation goes hand in hand with gender-responsive due diligence.[113] Gender-responsive due diligence requires establishing gender-responsive indicators that force a practice of gender-disaggregated data collection.[114] Meanwhile gender-disaggregated data collection requires addressing the gender biases in existing data-collection methodologies.

Initiating new conversations around the gendered nature of exploitation may assist in other ways. We may, for instance, get past the dichotomy that pits labor as free or unfree when the reality is often somewhere in between.[115] Ultimately, modern slavery presents the exemplary case that achieving a rewrite might be most likely to come to fruition by working with existing legal frameworks; contrastingly, a shift away from due diligence altogether seems highly unlikely in the near future. Nonetheless, as acknowledged early in this chapter, even these calls for gender-responsive due diligence and gender-disaggregated data collection, which appear in the context of *Rewriting the Rules* to be a feasible ask, remain just that: calls. Despite being the least transformative and most practical of the options that lie before us, they remain largely absent from existing legislation. Both are pivotal first steps for gender-responsive modern slavery governance and could foreground a future where global supply can be more equitable, sustainable, and gender just.

5

Extractives

Regulating at the Margins to Formalize Artisanal and Small-Scale Mining for Women

In December 1997, four Aymara Indigenous women from the Bolivian mining area Siglo XX started an indefinite hunger strike in protest against the imprisonment, exiling, or firing of their husbands. One of the women was pregnant.[1] Aurora, Nelly, Angélica, and Luzmila made four demands: unrestricted amnesty for the political prisoners, reinstatement of the fired workers, recommencement of union activity in the area, and removal of the troops who had been installed in the mines. Soon they were joined by the wives of fifty other tin miners who had been fired for union activity. Many of the women were also *palliris*,[2] small-scale miners who shovel through tailings, the leftovers from large-scale mining often heavy with acid and cyanide residues, in the hope of finding flecks of gold. Twenty-three days after the hunger strike commenced—and after roughly a *thousand* protesters had joined their cause—the women achieved all but the final demand.[3]

Their activism reflects women's central role in the development of Bolivia's mining sector, of which women once made up approximately 35 percent of the workforce.[4] However, Bolivian women face discriminatory regulations and common cultural beliefs that keep them out of underground mines, while an unequal responsibility for the care of young children creates a double and difficult burden of paid and unpaid work.

The Bolivian experience of marginalization, multiple and simultaneous responsibilities within and beyond the home, and exposure to significant health risks is common worldwide. Women miners frequently work irregularly on the periphery of formal, regulated, and large-scale mining. Their work is often termed "illegal."[5] In 2013, the think tank International Institute for Environment and Development estimated that there were around 20 to 30 million workers in artisanal and small-scale mining (ASM) globally in around eighty countries.[6] Now-dated sources suggest that women composed between 30 and 50 percent of miners across Asia, Africa, and Latin America.[7]

Patience—an archetypal representation of the West African female artisanal, small-scale miner—labors in the Ghanaian gold mines of the Prestea-Huni Valley,[8] one of around 100,000 Ghanaian women in ASM. While the men dig and shovel, Patience spends her days waiting for her head pan to be loaded with mineral ore for her to transport. She chooses not to pool her income with her husband's, these independent earnings giving her better control over what food will be cooked, how her children will be educated, and when she will stop having babies.[9] Her work might be precarious, inconsistent, and poorly paid in a sector with a height-ened risk of gender-based violence, but Patience is likely to be skeptical of attempts to regulate her work.

Yet Patience's informal ("unregulated") work is widely considered socially and environmentally damaging. Exploitative labor arrangements, deforestation, soil erosion, and the pollution of waterways from heavy metals[10] have given rise to a growth in attempts to formalize ASM. Formalization involves processes for the registration of artisanal and small-scale miners, documenting their operations, approving work, and establishing monitoring. Formalizing ASM encourages compliance with mining-specific regulations, but it is more than just legaliza-tion. Optimally, it can enable miners to access finance, reach markets, be trained on mining techniques, form associations, and learn how to minimize environ-mental impacts.[11]

Engaging with the informality of ASM, this chapter asks whether we should write artisanal and small-scale miners into the rules, making the informal formal. For many, albeit far from all, formalization is a pathway that can achieve multiple goals.[12] For governments, formalization can mean better monitoring of the risks of ASM to people and the environment, along with an opportunity to collect more taxes for public goods and services.[13] For non-governmental organizations and the development sector, formalization can create sustainable livelihoods that are safer for people and the land.[14] It may benefit large-scale mining companies too. In what may appear policy rhetoric, in 2009, the World Bank's *Mining Together* proposal called on large-scale mining companies to engage, partner, and work with artisanal and small-scale miners "to preserve their investment in a sustainable manner."[15]

This chapter focuses on what it means to transition from the unregulated to the regulated and the consequences for women in a sector where they are often overlooked in the regulation process, lack voice at the decision-making table in order for their experiences to be centered in law-making, and where a patriar-chal ethos underpins ASM in ways that women's economic contributions are easily dismissed.[16] Regulation of ASM for workers such as Patience may therefore jeop-ardize the benefits of informality, constraining livelihoods while offering too little in return. For one, formalization that fails to challenge power relations is likely to mask social and political inequalities whereby the end results may be better access to markets for women, but without women miners able to access the arenas of market power nor negotiate a better deal.[17] Formalization therefore is "neither straightforward" nor "necessarily a panacea for gender equality".[18]

This chapter offers a response by outlining the contours of a gender-responsive form of formalization. The last two decades have seen a notable growth in the work of scholars dedicated to the experiences of women artisanal and small-scale miners.[19] Like many of them who call for ASM's formalization, I consider formalization a process that *can* serve the goal of protecting women's human rights. If practiced with this aim in mind, formalization is or at least should be the "process of integrating rather than controlling informal enterprises by recognizing local arrangements in legislation, reducing barriers to legalization, and creating clear benefits from participation in the formal system."[20]

Before continuing, two points are worth mentioning. First, unlike other chapters in *Rewriting the Rules*, Africa is the "overwhelming" focus of literature on ASM,[21] to the neglect of Asia and the Americas. This is a point I hope to rectify with this discussion. Research on large-scale mining in Latin America is particularly scarce in Anglophone literature,[22] despite Latin America being a region known for high-profile contestations over access to natural resources—from disputes over gold and copper resource exploitation in Peru[23] to oil resource extraction and exploitation in Ecuador;[24] from the harmful consequences of the use of hydroelectric energy in Chile[25] through to the risk of deforestation in Bolivia.[26] Further, Latin American literature is more explicit in naming patriarchy as marginalizing women in ASM and skewing their opportunities.[27] The region also brings an emphasis on the knowledge of Indigenous peoples, peasants, and Afro-descendant communities.[28] In answer to why greater attention has not been paid to ASM in Latin America, I would venture to guess that scholars of English-language literature have favored the study of Anglophone nations in Africa over these Spanish-speaking ones.

Second, there are clear divides in how feminists engage with the extractive sectors. Feminist decolonial theorists frequently challenge large-scale resource extraction, highlighting the violence many women experience and their "embodied experiences of contamination."[29] For some, the pursuit of a regulated and active presence of women in ASM would be incompatible with the fight against large-scale extraction. Nonetheless, in reality, women are present in ASM but rarely on their own terms. This chapter does not accept the status quo nor does it seek to imagine overcoming the realities of mineral resource extraction altogether. Given the general lack of "successful" examples of ASM, this chapter asks what formalization can achieve for women and what women involved in ASM seek from a regulated sector. After setting out the context, including what ASM is and how it is gendered, I turn to the state of regulation and ask what regulating ASM with gender at its center would entail.

WHAT IS ASM AND HOW IS IT GENDERED?
Understanding Informal and Irregular Mining

ASM is "low-technology, labor-intensive mineral extraction and processing."[30] It is distinguished from industrial mining by its "lower rates of production, lack of long-term planning, inadequate equipment and poor safety, health and environment conditions."[31] Miners used handheld tools, small-scale equipment, or harness water streams for mining. However, the significance of their productivity should not be underestimated, accounting for 10–15 percent of the global annual production of gold.[32] Informally, ASM is managed by a complex network of relationships among small-scale miners, traders, cooperatives, government officials, and local leaders outside the state's regulatory framework.[33]

Formalization embodies ASM in a "standardized legal framework registered in and governed by a central state system."[34] However, Katy Jenkins reminds us that we cannot think only in binary terms.[35] ASM has varying degrees of formality and informality.[36] Women's work is sometimes regulated and at other moments, unregulated. Indeed, as Ramadir Samaddar points out with regard to the false divide between formal and informal labor, "throughout the history of capitalism, work conditions and work organizations have been a mix of the two."[37]

Writing on Papua New Guinea, where the country's ASM sector was traditionally and continues to be led by Indigenous peoples,[38] Danielle Lynas points out the under-theorized nature of informal mining. It is labor that is yet to be deeply understood.[39] By contrast, large-scale formal mining has received notable mainstream attention, partly thanks to the Kimberley Process, a certificate scheme established in 2003 that prohibited "blood diamonds" from mainstream markets—that is, diamonds mined in conflict zones and sold to finance the activities of insurgencies, the warfare of invading armies, and warlord activity.[40]

In contrast to labor in large-scale mining, women tend to dig lower-value industrial minerals.[41] As a result, ASM falls in between. Scholars have also described ASM as between the "pick and the plough," reflecting the seasonal nature of the work for agrarian peasants.[42] Typical of many ASM communities, Papua New Guinean women, for example, mine on a seasonal basis when faced with a momentary expense, such as payment of school or medical fees, or in conjunction with other seasonal income-earning activities, such as market gardening, cropping, and animal rearing.[43] In other instances, local peasant communities are forced into ASM when occupational displacement results from large-scale mining operations.[44]

ASM is therefore a natural part of a bigger story about globalization, rural stagnation, poverty, and livelihoods.[45] It is as much about geography as economics.[46] The gendered experiences of ASM, therefore, raise questions of law, feminist critical thinking, and political ecology: "decisions about the environment are not politically neutral."[47] Who has access to, control of, and makes decisions about natural resources necessarily enables one actor to control the environment of another. Acknowledging these deep power dynamics, I aim to offer new possibilities through law that, even if just a little, shift rather than amplify the existing paradigm of inequality.

Finding Women's Place in Mining: The Gendering of ASM

In 1935, the International Labour Organization (ILO) Convention on Underground Work (Women) (C045) banned women from working in underground mines, setting a foundation for national legislation that discriminated against women in the mining industry. In an article I wrote with Anaïs Tobalagba, we described the C045 as "a pertinent example that reflects the limits of international law in staying current and responsive to new trends."[48] C045 was abrogated at the 112th session of the ILO in 2024,[49] now an example of international law's capacity to change in response to shifting sociocultural norms. Yet as Daniele Moretti points out with respect to Papua New Guinea, women's marginalization from mining is not exclusively explained by sociocultural values, nor by colonial practices, nor by national and international law but a combination of these factors.[50]

Calls for a gender perspective to the mining sector have persisted for decades. In 1996, UN Secretary-General Boutros Boutros-Ghali reported on developments in small-scale mining, urging nations to mainstream gender and counseling policymakers to support the "involvement of women at all levels" of ASM.[51] Championing women miners not to be forgotten by government officials, lending institutions, NGOS, and other miners, the report called for technical and managerial training, financial assistance, and credit lines for women's groups. It sought to empower women in mining ventures and emphasized the safety and health issues facing children who accompany their mothers to the mining sites.[52] Argentinian scholar Andrea Mastrangelo describes a "hegemonic femininity," whereby children of miners are a women's issue ("una cuestión de mujeres").[53] Hence, this additional recognition of the work of caring for children reinforces the hegemony but reflects the lived realities of women miners.

That women are central players in ASM is unquestionable. In the Philippines, women are cooks and "wives of miners, widows, or single mothers who get the ore muck to wash in the river."[54] In Madagascar, it is common to see women sieving for sapphires while doing the family laundry.[55] Malagasy women traders buy and sell the smaller gemstones, while the larger, more precious loads are reserved for men acting in concert with other powerful males, including the mayor or local police chief.[56] In Mongolia, about 30 percent of the 60,000 artisanal miners are women mining gold, coal, fluorspar, and other minerals that, as a sector, contribute over $811 million per year to the country's GDP; a further $505 million is spent annually in local economies near mining activities, highlighting the economic significance of women's work on the peripheries of both formal and informal mining.[57] It is therefore not easy to separate women's roles into neat categories. In the rural and peripheral areas of Peru—where rural status, gender, and at times indigeneity magnify poverty and exclusion—communal kitchens are frequently managed by women leaders.[58] As one male miner commented: "Even my wife, she sells food but sometimes she is a *pallaquera*,"[59] a female gold miner. Indeed for Argentinian women, informality has made it possible to move across these multiple roles: domestic work, independent selling, as well as mining responsibilities.[60]

Nonetheless, women are invisible in much of the literature on ASM, partly because of a circular problem of limited data and literature on women from which to draw.[61] Some studies overlook women's specific experiences of ASM altogether.[62] In too many studies, women are mentioned only once or twice in passing.[63] Because women are often simultaneously miners and domestic workers, their direct contribution to mining is easily overlooked, and their revenue considered marginal and often not captured in the data. Informality also leads to poor records, along with the "fear" felt by some women of "government interference."[64] One Colombian study found an answer in gender-disaggregated data collection, a step to help make known just how essential women are to ASM.[65]

Nonetheless, the negative footprint of ASM on women's lives cannot be ignored. Inge Boudewijn and Katy Jenkins offer a three-pronged approach to understanding the potential harm and risk.[66] First, both formal and irregular mining impact women's traditional gendered responsibilities for the livelihoods of their household, including care of crops and livestock and providing food for families and care work. Loss of communal land and displacement makes water less accessible, while disease amplifies or creates new responsibilities, largely borne by women, to care for the sick and elderly.[67] Second, there are gendered inequalities in who benefits from extraction. Women suffer discrimination, harassment, and lower pay. In Colombia's San Roque, for instance, while over 70 percent of men in ASM in 2018 were earning above the minimum wage, 57 percent of the women miners earned between half the minimum wage and the minimum wage.[68] Women are generally absent from mining negotiations and infrequently benefit from economic compensation for lost land, mostly given to men.[69] Third, women face a heightened exposure to the toxins and health risks associated with mining, a problem worse for pregnant women. Panning mud and grinding rocks can lead to back injuries, and household responsibilities expose women to water polluted with toxic substances.

Layering upon this, Kuntala Lahiri-Dutt challenges the classicalist framing of mining as a masculine form of work that "eliminates or hides women and devalues their agency in an important economic activity."[70] Instead, she encourages a rethinking of mining as feminine. Women are not merely present but agents in this industry, not merely victims and harmed by the sector but central to its functioning. Reconciling the realities of the victim-agent persona that women have in mining is a further challenge for the task of regulation. That is, regulation must recognize that people of all genders have an equal right to mine on the one hand, but gender-specific accommodation of the socially produced roles that women have in mining is also essential, such as the need for crèches for women miners in shift work.[71]

This chapter speaks of a global industry in largely universalizing terms, but unsurprisingly, ASM is vastly different from one country to the next. The opportunities and economic value of ASM also differ from country to country. In Tanzania, mining is largely underground, and harsh living conditions around mines push women away.[72] Contrastingly, in Uganda, more than 200,000 women (45 percent) and men (55 percent) are engaged in artisanal mining of gold, tin, coltan, wolfram, and a range of industrial minerals; the average miner is estimated to contribute almost twenty times more to the GDP than those employed in farming, fishing, and forestry.[73]

Yet beyond practical differences, there are important theoretical ones as well. Feminist scholars of ASM are divided in how to understand the increased demand for transactional sex around mining sites. For some, such as Rachel Perks, whose work has largely focused on ASM in the Democratic Republic of the Congo, women's engagement in transactional sex arises out of "desperation" and is a profession that creates a heightened risk of rape and sexual violence.[74] As Inge Boudewijn and Katy Jenkins point out, the gendered impacts of mining are "often aggravated in contexts of weak or oppressive state presence in the affected areas."[75] Yet as Lahiri-Dutt notes, "women have always followed single men to mining frontiers,"[76] with sex work naturally intertwined with ASM in many regions. Latin American scholars also challenge formalization projects that are hinged on the imagining of violence and prostitution in ways that ultimately further marginalize women from mining altogether.[77] We are reminded of the scholarly divisions canvassed in chapter 4 regarding the extent to which sex work is perceived a viable form of income generation for women. From either position, we must ask how regulation best serves women's interests. Can agency be centralized in the process of formalizing ASM while risk, vulnerability, and harm are simultaneously acknowledged and minimized? This core question governs the sections that follow.

THE REGULATION OF ASM

In this section, I move from informality to formality. Here I offer a picture of the state of progress on formalizing ASM and the tendency for laws regulating ASM to lack a gender lens, explaining why formalization is often perceived risky for women miners. Simultaneously, I seek to explain what gender-responsive laws can achieve in protecting the rights of women in informal mining.

The State of Progress on Formalization

Regulation of ASM can be categorized in two ways: coercive and incentive-based. The Philippines' regulation of ASM—through the establishment of Minahang Bayans (people's small-scale mining areas)—is illustrative of both. Miners who formalize have access to education, technical, financial, and infrastructure support and even land for ASM. Concurrently, the law created the Taskforce Against Illegal Mining, with assistance from the national police and armed forces to ensure strict compliance,[78] this being the coercive element of the Filipino approach.

In some jurisdictions, the formalization of ASM has a long history. In the case of Papua New Guinea, it is a history marked by colonialism. When, prior to independence, the Australian colonial administrators approved the construction of one of the world's largest copper mines at Panguna in central Bougainville, local Bougainvilleans had no role in the approval process and benefitted little once the mining operations commenced in 1972.[79] An armed rebellion by Bougainvilleans and the forced closure of the mine in 1989 gave way to civil war, and the 1990s saw the spread of ASM in the absence of other income-earning opportunities.[80] Today, legislation recognizes customary landowners who engage in nonmechanized alluvial mining on their land without needing a registered lease. Minerals on customary land are owned by the landowners and not by the state. Papua New Guinea's approach, centered on locally owned governance, is not known to exist "in national or provincial mining legislation elsewhere in the world."[81]

A relatively long history of informal, unlicensed community ASM can also be seen in the Lao People's Democratic Republic, where most ASM is river-based tin mining, involving panning and surface digging. However, a concession area granted in 1994 to the Lao-Korea Tin Mining Company permits ASM miners to undertake their activities under the requirement that they sell their tin production back to the company.[82] This is an alternative model, one where an interrelated and yet clearly hierarchical relationship has been formed between informal and formal mining.

Formalization began in Ghana in as early as 1989. A spate of laws over several years—the Small-Scale Gold Mining Act,[83] The Mercury Act,[84] The Precious Minerals Marketing Corporation Act,[85] and the Minerals and Mining (Amendment) Act[86]—fully legalized ASM. However, an overwhelming 85 percent of Ghana's artisanal and small-scale miners are believed to not be registered for permits.[87] While Ghana's Community Mining Scheme (CMS), launched in 2019, might have been the turning point toward successful regulation of ASM to coexist with formal mining, CSM is under-studied from a gender perspective to appreciate if women benefit, how, and which women.[88]

This appears little different from Peru, where ASM contributes 20 percent of Peru's gold production,[89] and estimates range from 50,000 to 500,000 Peruvian artisanal miners. Demonized in the Peruvian media due to reports of human rights abuses, mercury pollution, and deforestation,[90] formalization has salvaged ASM in the face of calls for it to disappear altogether. Yet despite a 2002 Peruvian law on ASM (Law for the Formalization and Promotion of Small-Scale Mining and Artisanal Mining), few miners have formalized, some describing the process as "nearly irrelevant."[91] Despite a focus on "combating illegal mining" under a series of legislative decrees (1100–1107), just 112 miners were formalized nationally from 2002 to 2016.[92] Lack of clarity about formalization continues, despite a 2016 decree (No. 1293) creating a new process for formalization: Registro Integral de Formalización Minera (REINFO, or Process for the Comprehensive Formalization of Mining). While laborers, mechanics, restaurant owners, and investors have signed up, some registered miners represent themselves while others represent hundreds of laborers, with these "important differences . . . obscured."[93] More than 15,000, or 22 percent of REINFO registrations have been completed by women.[94] With the timeline for miners to register and avoid being officially reclassified as illegal having been extended for three years back in 2021, this fourth extension is illustrative of the difficulties of formalization.[95]

Peru's attempts at formalization also reflect the gendered dimensions of ASM. The work of *pallaqueras* is not recognized in the current formalization framework, and with *pallaqueras* left with no pathway to formalize, women's position on the "bottom of the ASM hierarchy" has been reinforced, "foreclos[ing] opportunities for advancement."[96] While the Ministry of Energy and Mines now recognizes the commercialization of gold produced by *pallaqueras* in Puno in Lake Titicaca, "deeper" and "systemic changes" must be overcome to avoid re-marginalizing *pallaquera* women in ASM.[97] Simultaneously, *pallaqueras* are reframing the narrative. Forty-eight percent are organized in working groups or associations of Indigenous women, such as the Bella Durmiente (Sleeping Beauty), an association of women gold seekers.[98] These workers are not passive victims but are pushing for a seat at the table and demanding greater support and recognition.[99]

Why Regulation Must Challenge Gender Neutrality

Three factors are evident. First, ASM has largely been unsuccessful in most ASM-intensive countries. Few miners register in the formalization process. Second, where formalization has been achieved, men quickly dominate organized bodies while existing gendered dynamics premised on structural inequalities are reinforced.[100] This is not only a question of men controlling resources. In Zambia's gemstone industry, a "cartel of powerful (female) elites" operate as "gatekeepers" who claim to "open market access to poor women."[101] Third and by contrast, formalization can create new gendered opportunities, reconfiguring and advancing women's access to resources.[102] This third point leaves us with a sense that gendering ASM's formalization can shift the benefits to women. The question is how this can be achieved.

This notion of infusing a gender perspective in ASM can find a home in global instruments on ASM. The African Union's *Africa Mining Vision*, signed by the heads of state and government of the fifty-five members in Addis Ababa in February 2009, presented an African roadmap for managing mining resources. The Vision explicitly asks whether regulations formalizing ASM are "gender-responsive."[103] The UN Environment Programme's Minamata Convention on Mercury is a global agreement intended to protect human health and the environment from the release of mercury. Today 128 countries have signed the convention, with its preamble and annexes acknowledging the vulnerability of women, particularly pregnant women, to mercury used in ASM.[104] The World Bank has also come to adopt language that advocates "for gender-responsive legislation to safeguard women's rights in mining and build a more sustainable sector."[105]

Yet, few ASM laws are gendered in nature. The World Bank has found that of the twenty-one countries with ASM regulations in Latin America and the Caribbean, Africa, East Asia, and the Pacific, fourteen mining laws and seventeen property codes are either gender blind or gender neutral in language; only Colombia, Tanzania, and Zambia were found to have gender-sensitive land laws.[106] This point has been well made by feminist scholars of ASM. Hinton's study of gender and ASM in Uganda shows how gender-neutral policies negatively impact women in ASM, thus damaging the whole community.[107] Despite the aforementioned treaties and commitments on paper to protecting the interests of women miners, most regulatory mechanisms at the domestic level "do not sufficiently integrate a gender perspective, if they do so at all."[108]

REGULATING ASM WITH GENDER IN MIND

Gendering ASM requires bringing women's lived experiences of mining to the forefront. Lynas sets out criteria to enable this perspective. Women miners must see programs for women as adding value to their daily lives; as practical, tangible, sustainable, and designed specifically for them; as building capacity and empowering them as women; and as ensuring they are not further exposed to higher levels of gender-based violence.[109] Sara Seck and Penelope Simons extend this by noting the failure of existing laws to prevent violations of the rights of women and girls. Accountability and remedies for past gender-based harms fall short. Law rarely empowers women and girls with meaningful choices about their futures.[110] These criteria and critiques—access to services, redress, and remedies and addressing barriers to them—mirror the standards set in international law.[111]

Bringing a gender lens to ASM is both practical and strategic. Practically, a gender lens requires identifying the same and different needs of people of different genders based on their common or differentiated gender roles, such as the need for tools or financing.[112] By contrast, gender-blind reforms in ASM fail to prioritize women's sanitation and hygiene infrastructure at mine sites, affordable childcare provisions, or lighting that could improve security and occupational health and safety (OHS), to offer a few examples.[113] Some place greater emphasis on strategic needs over practical ones. Introducing mechanization and simple technologies may increase productivity but can inadvertently take jobs away from women without ensuring their redeployment elsewhere. However, formalization in ASM regulation should address both the practical and the strategic, which at times overlap. When gendered assumptions in Ghana, for example, perceive women as not needing safety boots or shoes, these norms—held by both women and male miners—expose women to OHS harms, while reinforcing women's secondary place in ASM.[114]

A balance must be struck in this attempt to contest ASM's current gender neutrality. Lahiri-Dutt is resounding in her pushback against ASM narratives that frame "women as victims" of mining. The following section sets out a framework for delivering gender-responsive ASM regulations, acknowledging where women are victimized by the sector but largely positioning women as agents who benefit when regulation is gender responsive.

Protecting Labor Rights

Formalization of ASM establishes minimum standards for workplaces, some of which already exist. As one UN-led study of Peru reminds us, formalization brings women workers within the protections of *existing* laws, including prohibitions on wage discrimination and on prevention and punishment of sexual harassment.[115] Moreover, harmed workers are less likely to be deterred from claiming rights violations under existing laws if they do not fear being perceived "illegal."[116]

At other times, laws need to be sector-specific. Greater responsibility for the care of children impedes the time women have to work. Due to multiple demands on their time, women miners have been found to rush work, sustaining injuries exacerbated by the absence of safety regulations.[117] Sociocultural expectations naturally intersect with a weak legal environment. Mining leadership must be obliged by law to maintain safety records; without that, records tend to be negligible, reducing awareness of OHS issues and how to prevent accidents.[118] Formalization may bring these benefits. As Diana Elizabeth Cabrera Navarrete points out in her study of Ecuador, if the work "does not exist"—that is, if it is illegal and therefore not openly acknowledged—the pain does not exist. Without formalization, the negative health consequences of ASM are not recorded either.[119]

Guaranteeing Access to Information

In addition to regulating the conditions of work, formalizing ASM should entail obligations on governments and licensed ASM leadership, which must include women leaders, to bridge knowledge gaps. Generations often mine together—children, mothers, aunts, and grandmothers. All women must enjoy a legal right to access knowledge about safety in mining sites.

Nonetheless, for women to be able to strive for ASM leadership, access to information must go beyond questions of safety. Literacy impedes women miners from improving their livelihoods. Women must be guaranteed equal access by law to comprehensive technical and capacity building, including organizational strengthening, entrepreneurship, and business workshops[120] that build capabilities in ways that can improve both profitability and sustainability. Training programs must be designed with women's accessibility in mind, noting their competing family and domestic obligations and the impossibility for many women to attend full-day or longer live programs. Training must be both accessible and culturally acceptable in terms of where and how they are run.[121] Quotas should be considered to ensure that each gender occupies at least 40 percent of the opportunities for training.

Services for Women Miners, Including Healthcare

Centering the reproductive health of women in mining involves a balance that recognizes needs without resulting in additional barriers for women to mine. In Ghana, women miners report heavy menstrual bleeding due to work of carrying and transporting mineralized sand and sometimes descending into pits, which is assumed to impact menstrual flow.[122] Paid menstrual leave from work has been increasingly debated since the mid-2010s and available in law in some jurisdictions. Voluntary menstrual leave may be one consideration for ASM regulation.[123] If formalized, leadership can be made accountable for basic facilities such as safe and accessible female toilets at ASM sites.

A heightened vulnerability to HIV/AIDS and other sexually transmitted infections due to factors that range from lack of access to birth control and sexual and reproductive health services to sociocultural barriers that inhibit the use of preventative methods must be acknowledged in the design of laws. The possibility of voluntarily transactional sex, as well as the risk of forced sexual intercourse around mining sites, heightens the need for both information and services related to sexual health.

A further need that is gender specific relates to the tendency for women in ASM to bear a greater responsibility for childcare, as noted above. Children accompany women artisanal miners, often but not only when childcare is not available or affordable, creating unique risks and necessitating the availability of childcare as a health and safety issue in mining areas.[124] ASM laws can respond to the call for childcare facilities at and near mining sites—with obvious benefits for male miners who are fathers. A final service issue for women in ASM relates to limited credit, which hampers the development of trades in the area.[125]

Full and Equal Participation

Women's full and equal participation is arguably the most important goal of ASM regulation. In Mozambique, uniquely, two women operate their own ASM area in two sites about 350 kilometers from Manica town in the Sussundenga District.[126] Reform must enable land ownership by women. Yet other barriers still need to be overcome. Although in both Mozambique and Tanzania, women have the legal right to own and inherit land, deeply rooted cultural barriers prevent women from taking on the roles of mine owner and operator, resulting in their exclusion from mining.[127]

Cultural factors that hinder free movement impact participation. In Uganda, women's ability to travel is often restricted by their husband and family. Few women miners can travel to distant locations where government mining offices are based to obtain ASM registration papers.[128] Nonetheless, Peru suggests that the government's shift to online papers is not necessarily the optimal solution if miners lack regular internet access in the face of a digital divide. While rarely a provision of law, regulation of ASM should require localized opportunities to obtain, complete, and submit the necessary paperwork for women to register through formalization processes.

I have long held the view that law plays a role in changing cultural norms.[129] In numerous countries, women face cultural taboos that exclude them from mining spaces. In many regions of Papua New Guinea, for example, women are considered a dangerous presence on a mine site due to notions that they risk polluting the gold and angering *hikoapa*, the ancestral and nature spirits that guard the land and its riches.[130] Such norms impact ASM access in Mozambique and Tanzania too.[131] If the law shifts to promote equal access for women—including recognizing in law organizations of women miners[132]—cultural taboos can shift, too.

Acknowledgment of Vulnerability and Access to Redress

Gender discrimination embedded in the law itself must be overcome. Bans on pregnant women in ASM frequently constrain women—and women miners in general—rather than being enabling.[133] Indeed, pregnant women occasionally prefer work in ASM when mining sites are a shorter commute than other work,[134] so such bans may be underpinned by erroneous assumptions. ASM's formalization needs conscious attention to reducing vulnerability without hindering agency.

Nonetheless, ASM unquestionably poses a risk of sexual violence for women miners. In Papua New Guinea, women in and around ASM report domestic violence, and a 2015 study acknowledged the gang rape of women while scavenging mine-site tailings.[135] ASM's formalization must condemn sexual violence, which must not be met with impunity, by establishing and making transparent and accessible avenues for reporting it and a government and private sector obligation to address such sexual violence. These interventions need to range from information campaigns to what may be arduous and long-term steps toward pursuing the accountability of perpetrators. A commitment to eradicating gender-based violence must sit alongside a consciousness of the risk of eradicating women's presence altogether.

MOVING FORWARD

In seeking to rewrite the rules of ASM, this chapter acknowledges the risks that formalization can pose. Formalization has had a mixed reception among scholars. However, part of the fear of formalization stems from the reality that formalization attempts to date have unfolded in non-gender-responsive ways. They have been gender blind.

This chapter has set out standards that must underpin a gendered-responsive approach to formalizing ASM for the benefits of ASM to be realized by women miners. For one, earnings tend to be higher where ASM activities are formalized.[136] Further, when the risks that formalization poses are known, more thought can be invested in preventing those risks. Rewriting the rules of ASM can be done in an informed way, whereby the benefits that women miners currently enjoy will not be lost to men or elite women.

Ultimately, gender-responsive lawmaking itself requires women's voice. Good practice calls for women's participation in the process of reviewing legislation.[137] Arguably, with more women miners formulating the policies and procedures, there is a heightened chance that they will be drafted in ways that truly benefit women in ASM.

6

Corporate Quotas

Legal Tools in the Struggle for Boardroom Equality

It took until 2014 for the Japanese Honda Motor Company to achieve a milestone: the appointment of its first female board member. Honda insisted that Hideko Kunii's selection to the thirteen-member board had nothing to do with her gender; indeed, her qualifications—including a doctorate in computer science in 1983— speak for themselves. Honda also insisted that its decision had nothing to do with the gender agenda of Prime Minister Shinzo Abe, who was Japan's longest-serving prime minister when he was assassinated in 2022. Abe saw a solution to the country's lagging economy lying with the greater utilization of Japanese women's skills: "womenomics," a concept coined by Kathy Matsui in her thesis in 1999 and adopted by Abe in his second term.[1] Abe's instrumentalist notions of women's empowerment only added fuel to the feminist fire that interventions, such as corporate board quotas, center too much on economic gain, with little attention to the underlying drivers of inequality. Yet, Japan achieved a relatively rapid increase in women's representation on corporate boards: from just below 5 percent in 2016[2] to 12.8 percent in 2023.[3] This increase was realized *without* a compulsory gender quota, although the country has numerous purportedly progressive gender equality laws. Japan's quota came into play only in June 2023, with the government requiring Prime Market–listed companies to achieve a female-board-member ratio of 30 percent or more by 2030.[4]

This chapter grapples with a legal intervention that has its fair share of opponents, with quotas often perceived as overly "intrusive."[5] Controversies momentarily aside, the "gender" corporate-board quota has a surprisingly short history. In the early 2000s, Norway became a world leader in women's representation on corporate boards by opening a prolonged public debate leading to parliamentary

TABLE 3 Female share of board seats at the largest publicly listed
companies in the top 10 OECD performers (as of 2022)

Country	Percentage	Compulsory quota?
New Zealand	46	#
France	45.2	✓
Iceland	44.8	✓
Norway	43.2	✓
Italy	42.6	✓
Netherlands	41.6	✓
United Kingdom	40.9	#
Belgium	39.3	✓
Germany	37.2	✓
Sweden	35.2	#

SOURCE: Compiled by the author using data from OECD.stat, "Employment: Female Share of Seats on Boards of the Largest Publicly Listed Companies."

KEY: ✓ quota in place; # other *government-led* measures such as codes of corporate governance, voluntary targets, apply-or-explain approach, or stock-exchange listing requirements to disclose targets.

approval of affirmative action measures in December 2003; they have been force in Norway since July 1, 2005.[6] Norway requires "each sex" to be represented by 40 percent on all boards with ten or more members.[7] I return to the question of gender binaries shortly.

Most analyses of women's presence on corporate boards, unsurprisingly therefore, start by taking us to Europe. Norway set in motion a wave of change leading to corporate-board quotas across Europe, including in Spain, Iceland, France, Italy, Belgium, the Netherlands, Germany, Austria, and Portugal.[8] Today, Iceland's approach is one of the most demanding: a 40 percent gender quota for any company with more than fifty employees.[9]

Determining whether Norway is a success story—first, for its positive impact on the lives of Norwegian women wanting a seat at the table; second, for its footprint on gender equality in Norway beyond the corporate board; and third, for motivating other countries in and beyond Europe to follow—is not an easy task, even if one focuses purely on numerical shifts. Corporate law and diversity scholar Darren Rosenblum once described Norway's novel, transformative, and "dramatic intervention" as a "public/private symbiosis" in which the public norm of gender equality infuses private efforts.[10] Norway observed a relatively rapid increase in the proportion of female directors, from 18 percent of board members in 2006, to 25 percent in 2007 and 36 percent in 2008.[11] OECD data from 2022 shows that among the largest publicly listed companies, 43.2 percent of board seats in Norway were held by women (see table 3).[12] All concerned companies complied after 2008, and the quota saw a significant number of women—even if power was somewhat concentrated—enter the boardroom.[13] Rosenblum also predicted in 2009 that this "radical remedy" would be widely adopted at scale in ways that would parallel political quotas.[14] Whether this prediction came to fruition will be seen further below.

Beyond the question of strict numbers, there are different ways to tell Norway's story. After 2003, the number of publicly listed companies fell in Norway as some changed their status to avoid the minimum-representation-of-women requirement,[15] while many Norwegian companies incorporated in London to avoid the demands of the new quota.[16] There has also been limited evidence of "voluntary" spillovers, such as women moving from board to chair to CEO or limited companies not within the ten-director threshold voluntarily following the model. Research suggests little demonstrable benefit to the women employed in companies subject to the quota, or for women in business generally.[17] In other words, it is doubtful that the ethos of equality seeped into the Norwegian corporate culture as a result of the board quota.[18]

Nonetheless, the presence of female directors on Norwegian boards has been positively correlated with the boards' strategic control and effectiveness. Critics of the quota point to "large numbers of inexperienced women" appointed to Norwegian boards, which "seriously damaged" stock performance[19]—what has been described elsewhere in more nuanced terms as "younger and less experienced boards" and a "significant drop" in stock price.[20] Indeed, age diversity is often overlooked for the value it brings while having younger board members, in part, explains the lower levels of experience.

Much attention remains on the Euro-Northern experiences of board quotas, particularly on the Nordic world,[21] leaving obvious gaps in our understanding of women's board participation in other parts of the world. These gaps invite us to expand our purview, a particularly pressing endeavor given that audit and advisory firm Deloitte reported a global average of just 19.7 percent of board seats worldwide occupied by women in 2022 and a rate of progress that will achieve the number of women coming close to the number of men only by 2045.[22] Deloitte's March 2024 report revised the prediction to 2038.[23] Since the global average of just under 20 percent includes the world's best performers, such as France with over 45 percent of boards composed of women by some accounts, countries at the other extreme, such as Saudi Arabia and South Korea, are truly lagging.[24] According to Morgan Stanley, in 2018 women held only 16.9 percent of board seats across 8,600 companies in forty-nine countries.[25]

This chapter seeks to offer the most gender-responsive approach to addressing overt inequality in corporate board representation while recognizing that for some, quotas compromise the emancipatory agenda. Nonetheless, potentially the best tool at hand, it asks, what are the conditions for quota success? This chapter begins by exploring roadblocks to more expansive participation by women on boards. The discussion turns to women's presence and its impact, both positive and negative, on boards and corporate performance. Assuming we favor equity in representation, this discussion naturally leads us to consider whether the alternatives, such as voluntary targets or mentorship by senior women in business, achieve the same outcomes without legal intervention.

In making the case for legislated corporate quotas, we risk reinforcing the hegemonic masculinities that such corporations (and their boards and the decisions they take) sustain. Yet the male dominance that persists on corporate boards worldwide is so incredibly stark—even starker than the underrepresentation of women in politics—that such a drastic, even "intrusive" intervention appears to be called for. Indeed, if well drafted and with the right elements in place, corporate board quotas can both expeditiously and sustainably change the landscape.

THE QUOTA CONTROVERSY

In 2000, Malaysia appointed its first woman governor of Malaysia's central bank, the Bank of Negara Malaysia, Dr. Zeti Akhtar Aziz. In a 2010 International Women's Day speech, Malaysian prime minister Najib Razak suggested that Dr. Zeti (and all she had achieved) affirmed that the 2008 financial crisis would have been avoided "if Lehman Brothers had been Lehman Sisters."[26] Perhaps he was proven right when Dr. Zeti stepped down from the role of governor in 2016, when the central bank was unable to investigate a corruption scandal concerning the prime minister himself. Yet we risk that such viewpoints on Dr. Zeti's appointment, along with Malaysia's "economic empowerment" agenda, distract from ingrained patriarchal privileges that underpin corporate practices and, as political scientist Juanita Elias stresses, allow gendered injustices to persist in other spaces, including the family.[27]

We similarly cannot overlook the gendered narratives that encircle women's presence on boards. One news outlet described Nelius Wanjiru Kariuki's role as the first Kenyan woman to chair a listed company as "midwifing" Kenya Reinsurance (a company that offers insurance cover to insurance companies) when it was publicly listed in 2007.[28] Yet such appointments still reflect significant progress: in 2014, Barclays Bank Kenya became the first publicly listed Kenyan company with women making up half the board.[29]

Corporate quotas to increase women's representation on boards are pitched as an evidence-based legal intervention for urgent pursuit to accelerate progress toward women's greater representation and participation. Nonetheless, the binary assumption underpinning many jurisdictions' board quotas is evidently outdated. The European Commission's Women on Boards directive, featured in this chapter, is swathed in binaries: balance is achieved when each gender makes up at least 40 percent of a board's composition, and gender parity is understood as 50 percent representation. Such language distorts the realities of sex and gender identities, similar to other normative goals found in international women's rights law that are based on gender binaries.[30] With the corporate board quota an "invention" of this century, these goals appear outdated before they have been fully implemented.

Moreover, the "gender" corporate-quota debate often overlooks other gender diversities. A 2021 Gallup survey showed that roughly 5.6 percent of the US population identify as a member of the LGBTQ community, while the 2023 Spencer Stuart Board Index reported that less than 1 percent of board seats were occupied by out-LGBTQ directors. This is despite an increase in observed diversity in dimensions such as race, ethnicity, and being a woman.[31] Questions of transgender representation on boards have been touched by the academy only in recent years.[32] Relatively recent scholarship has considered instead what gender diverse boards might mean for LGBTQI+ employees.[33] There is a pressing need to find a coexistence between feminist and queer theories' goals, as urged by Dianne Otto[34] and noted elsewhere in this book.

Rethinking binary language in corporate board quotas is only one part of the challenge. For some critics, the quota advances the individual woman, while deflecting attention from and potentially even excluding the women collective. The same critique has been applied to feminist bureaucrats who engage government from within, too distant from the "revolutionary feminism of the streets, outside the corrupt system of power and prestige."[35] The corporate board agenda is far from feminism's redistributive roots by virtue of facilitating and concentrating power in the hands of a few elite, highly educated professional women, discussed below as the "golden skirts" (derived from the Norwegian *guldkjolar*).[36] A shared struggle for collective solutions to gender inequality—including the inequality created and maintained by such corporations—is sacrificed with the emergence of "transnational business feminism."[37] Corporate profitability is furthered, while ignoring the historical and structural causes of gender inequality that these corporations may create and sustain.[38]

Yet some scholars favor the quota. Rosenblum, for instance, values the way in which corporate board quotas—unlike anti-discrimination law, which "seeks to punish and prevent discriminatory conduct, rather than shift underlying inequities in favor of broader balance"—can rectify gender-based power disparities due to their evident interaction between the public and private sectors.[39] Aaron Dhir reminds us that boards thrive on cohesion, while quotas represent the "paradigmatic case" of disturbance.[40] They are a drastic form of intervention.

It therefore appears possible to wade out of these muddy waters and move beyond an "enemy perception" of a "monolithic private sector."[41] In embracing the corporate quota, this chapter accepts the challenge of disturbing a singular and negative perception of the corporate world in order for women to find a place in it, particularly women who desire a seat at the table. I do so by posing three questions. First, if there is no spin-off effect from corporate quotas but only an impact on those companies directly bound by the law (if such companies even reach the established target), should the corporate quota be scaled? Second, are the alternatives undervalued? Third, what are the ingredients—if they can be identified—to make legislative quotas the most effective gender-responsive intervention?

TO QUOTA OR NOT TO QUOTA: WOMEN'S PRESENCE ON AND ABSENCE FROM CORPORATE BOARDS

Women's presence in economic activity is viewed as driving productivity and growth.[42] In this vein, three economic reasons are largely given for gender quotas for corporate boards. First, gender balance on boards results in a more efficient use of human resources that enhances productivity. Norway's quota was said to trigger a higher rate of GDP.[43] Second, gender balance improves corporate governance. Women pay more attention to audits and to controlling risks, while better decision-making processes lead to stronger company oversight. One Canadian study found that 94 percent of boards with three or more women explicitly monitored the implementation of the corporate strategy, compared to only two-thirds of all-male boards.[44] Malaysia's former prime minister Najib, in his praise of Dr. Zeti, was not the first to perceive women as crisis-preventing; some scholars, too, have argued that more women present could have prevented the 2007–2008 financial crisis and recession, because women are more risk averse, more engaged with longer-term issues, and more likely to bring visibility to issues of governance and ethics than their male counterparts.[45]

Finally, having more women present on boards is believed to drive better economic performance. Numerous studies evidence improved stock prices, average operating profits, sales, return on invested capital and on equity with the most gender-diverse boards, including in Danish firms,[46] Finnish firms,[47] and among Fortune 500 companies.[48] However, the market *appreciation* enjoyed by Californian firms the day the state's quota was overturned by court ruling suggests otherwise.[49]

Beyond the economics, fundamentally, quotas are an evident tool for correcting systemic discrimination. Corporate quotas challenge the sociocultural and economic factors that exclude women from social and informational networks and can counter the absence of female role models and networking opportunities. Women also face the compounded challenge of balancing commitments at home with work, which creates conflicting demands on women's time that impact their career progression.[50] A corporate board quota is therefore simply about correcting existing injustice and accelerating the pace of change toward equality.[51]

Against these arguments, opposition to quotas often sounds unsophisticated. Gender stereotyping has been used in one strand of literature to question women's suitability for leadership.[52] The scholarship has, thankfully, moved beyond the assumption that women lack the ambition, the confidence, or the leadership skills to occupy such roles. With no reliable evidence of the fundamental differences in the psychological traits between women and men in these contexts, the idea that women are "inappropriate" for board roles has largely been debunked.[53]

Other scholars have argued that there is, in reality, a lack of qualified candidates[54] and that quotas should only be voluntary.[55] There is simply not an appropriate supply of capable women to fill the quotas. Three obvious responses come to mind. First, in some contexts such as Norway, the evidence revealed that women who occupied reserved seats after the quota's introduction were "observationally better qualified to serve on boards along many dimensions than women appointed prior to the quota."[56]

Second, there is a "pipeline to power"[57] and we need to ensure women stay within it. Indian experiences highlight the need for talent management, career planning, and mentorship, while additionally calling for a rigorous conversation about the gender-specific skills that women bring beyond domain expertise such as finance that should earmark them as appropriate.[58] Moreover, as women begin to occupy corporate board seats, their skills will build, even if this skill-building is among only a small pool of women from whom boards repeatedly draw.

Among those opposing quotas, more compelling contestations are made regarding the values attached to these policies. For the chosen few, there is a fear of tokenism.[59] Women on boards risk being seen as "decorative additions,"[60] creating a sense that board members have been chosen for gender and not capacity. Iceland encountered quota disadvantages for the women who reached their position without its aid, *all* women being collectively viewed "as secondary board members."[61] Nonetheless, the "token" individual may be more visible and therefore more effective, and tokenism can, eventually, lead to critical mass.[62]

Moreover, Nomfundo Ramalekana urges us to question this apparent stigma that attaches to the minority group whose representation increases because of quotas. The stigma, Ramalekana argues, "predates" the quota, rooted "in unequal power relations inherent in systems of domination and oppression."[63] It is the already marginalized who end up stigmatized by quotas: Black people, women and people with disability.[64] To accept the stigma argument would be to entrench the inequality that the affirmative action intervention seeks to address in the first place.

This complex interplay between economic rationales and sociopolitical ones is well illustrated by one study of 841 publicly listed firms in Malaysia. While women board members were found to positively impact companies' accounting performance—a finding that has been backed up elsewhere[65]—their presence negatively impacted market performance. In short, "women directors create economic value, which is undervalued by the market."[66] Legislative quotas will have lesser impact if not accompanied by substantial efforts to challenge normative perceptions about the value of women on boards and for companies. The case therefore still needs to be made.

WHERE, WHY, AND TO WHAT EFFECT?

The need to make a case for the corporate quota clearly persists. In this section, I undertake the natural next step by assessing the effectiveness of a quota in law. Can we correlate the quota to levels of representation of women on boards? The data suggests yes, but the question itself opens up further points of interrogation: How are quotas best designed? What are the differential effects of corporate quotas over time? Do corporate quotas work in the same way across different countries?

Like quotas for political representation, which vary from jurisdiction to jurisdiction,[67] corporate board quotas also vary. By 2015, at least ten countries worldwide had legal quotas for women's representation on boards, ranging from simply having "at least one woman" (regardless of the board's size) as a form of quota[68] to the 50 percent quota for government-owned enterprises in Canada's province of Quebec since 2011.[69] The 30% Club—as suggested by its name—requires at least 30 percent representation by women among all board directors.[70] A common criterion is company size. In these instances, quotas are applicable only to companies above a certain number of employees and/or level of assets.

Sanctions also vary. In Belgium, France, Portugal, India, Israel, and Italy, noncompliant firms can be fined, dissolved, or banned from paying directors.[71] Moreover, in Italy, in the event of noncompliance, a progressive warning system with monetary fines may culminate in the removal of the board. Portugal also has escalating sanctions, where noncompliant companies are first warned, then "named and shamed," and ultimately fined. In Austria, France, Germany, and the Netherlands, appointments of new directors that violate the law are null and void, while in Norway, failure to comply with the 40 percent quota may lead to delisting.[72]

Quotas may have a bumpy and uneven road to impact, with the statistics masking issues of women's voice and influence once they attain a seat at the table. Nonetheless, evidence suggests that quotas can be correlated with the percentage of women occupying board roles. One pre-quota study of Japan suggested it would never achieve the rates of participation of Norway and France without legislation to "pave the way" to boardroom success.[73] Of course, numbers tell only a partial story. Here I will elaborate on the regional experiences of women's corporate boardroom participation.

Europe and the 40 Percent Target

In 2022, the EU made a dramatic move towards a bloc quota for women on boards, adopting a directive—commonly cited as the Women on Boards Directive—on improving the gender balance among directors of listed companies.[74] Introducing the quota, Viviane Reding, the vice-president of the European Commission and commissioner for Justice, Fundamental Rights and Citizenship from 2009 to 2014, conceded her dislike for quotas but declared, "I like the results they bring."[75] By June 30, 2026, all corporate entities in the EU with more than 250 employees have to ensure that 40 percent of non-executive-director posts and 33 percent of all director posts are occupied by the "under-represented sex."[76] The directive's timely adoption could amplify success stories from some parts of the region. France is described as emulating Norway's model, taking it to the next level to achieve the fastest and most notable boardroom gender-diversity improvement—45 percent women—across the EU.[77]

Italy, the Netherlands, Sweden, Belgium, and Germany boast between 35 percent and 43 percent participation of women in the boardroom, but as reflected in table 4, there is a lag for smaller countries like Hungary and Cyprus.[78] In Estonia, just 9 percent of non-executive seats are held by women. As Polish professor of law Marek Szydło points out, since women account for 46 percent of employees across the EU and approximately 56 percent of people in tertiary education, we can see a significant gap between the proportion of employed and well-educated women and the portion of women functioning at the board level in EU Member States.[79] Nonetheless, the EU undoubtedly leads globally and it can only be expected that this strong performance—at least in terms of numbers—will be shared across EU nations if the June 30, 2026, target is met.

As demonstrated by table 4, non-EU members Iceland and Norway are also among the European leaders. Yet Iceland, like Norway, is a "mixed" success story. In 2010, a requirement of a minimum of 40 percent board representation for each gender was introduced for companies with more than fifty employees.[80] Years earlier, a gender quota for public committees, councils, and boards was enacted.[81] The 2010 quota "worked" in part due to penalties and monitoring of its enforcement. However, the quota law failed to change the basic gender balance of companies not covered by the law (fewer than fifty employees) or the gender balance of CEOs and board chairs, regardless of whether the company was covered by the requirement. Rather, as of 2016, female CEOs had lower representation in companies governed by the law (fifty employees and more) than in companies not covered by it (12 percent against 22 percent).[82] Female chairs were also fewer in companies covered by the law than in companies not covered by it (16 percent against 24 percent).[83] Corporate board quotas therefore appear to have a direct impact on those representative roles directly regulated by them, but a limited flow-on effect.

Before moving beyond Europe, the concentration of power among the elite needs addressing. As Cathrine Seierstad and Tore Opsahl write, these roles are "for the few," not the many.[84] The phenomenon even has a name: the "golden skirts." The repeated use of selected women directors who have governance experience is the reason why Deloitte's Global Board Program measures the "stretch factor," calculated by dividing the total number of board seats occupied by women/men in a given country by the unique number of women/men on boards in a particular country. A stretch factor of 1 indicates that all board seats in a sample are held by different women/men.[85] Although the golden skirts phenomenon has been an issue in Norway, there is an assumption that more diverse representation will be achieved over time as the supply of women who have experience increases.[86] In this vein, as of 2021, Norway had a relatively low stretch factor, only 1.06,[87] when compared to, for example, Australia (1.43), which had one of the highest stretch factors in the world in 2022.

Asia and the "One Woman" Quota

Generally, the Asia region's performance when it comes to women's membership of corporate boards is mixed. India introduced a one-woman-director mandate

Table 4 Female share of board seats at publicly listed companies across Europe (as of 2021)

Country	Percentage	Compulsory quota?
Iceland	47.1	✓
France	45.3	✓
Norway	41.5	✓
Italy	38.8	✓
Netherlands	38.1	✓
Belgium	37.9	✓
Sweden	37.9	#
United Kingdom	37.8	✓
Germany	36.0	✓
Finland	35.2	#
Denmark	34.9	A new law (as of January 1, 2023) requires companies to set targets until a 40/60 gender proportion has been achieved.
Austria	34.6	✓
Spain	32.6	#
Portugal	31.0	✓
Ireland	30.2	#
Switzerland	30.0	✓
Slovak Republic	27.7	✗
Poland	24.7	#
Czech Republic	23.0	✗
Luxembourg	22.4	#
Lithuania	22.3	✗
Latvia	22.2	✗
Greece	19.6	✓
Slovenia	19.4	#
Turkey	18.0	#
Hungary	9.4	✗
Estonia	9.1	#

source: Compiled by the author using data from OECD Corporate Governance Working Paper Series No. 28.

key: ✓ quota in place; # other *government-led* measures such as codes of corporate governance, voluntary targets, apply-or-explain approach, or stock-exchange listing requirements to disclose targets; ✗ no substantial action.

Note that the Deloitte Global Boardroom Program 2024 lists Switzerland as having a corporate board gender quota. However, the Government of Switzerland's interventions may be better described as a "comply-or-explain" approach, with no obvious penalties in place at the time of publication for failure to reach the 30 percent target of women's representation on boards.

TABLE 5 Female share of board seats at the largest publicly listed
companies across Asia (as of 2020–2023)

Country	Percentage	Compulsory quota?
Malaysia	24.0–28.5	✓
Philippines	17.7–21.7	#
Singapore	17.0–20.8	#
India	16.8–17.1	✓
China (Mainland)	13.8–15.1	✗
Indonesia	8.3–13.1	✗
Japan	8.2–12.8	✓ (quota introduced in 2023)
South Korea	4.3–8.7	✓

SOURCE: Compiled by the author using data from OECD.stat, "Employment: Female Share of Seats on Boards of the Largest Publicly Listed Companies"; Ministry of Social and Family Development, "Council for Board Diversity," Singapore; Deloitte Global Board Program, "Progress at a Snail's Pace: Women in the Boardroom—A Global Perspective" (2022); and Deloitte Global Board Program, "Women in the Boardroom—A Global Perspective" (2024).

KEY: ✓ quota in place; # other *government-led* measures such as codes of corporate governance, voluntary targets, apply-or-explain approach, or stock-exchange listing requirements to disclose targets; ✗ no substantial action.

in 2013, to be reached by 2015. An assessment covering the period 2012–2016 of forty-one companies listed in the Bombay Stock Exchange simply described the requirement as "insignificant"; it was neither beneficial nor caused any adverse impact.[88]

South Korea's law is relatively new, taking effect in August 2022 and requiring at least one woman on boards of listed companies with assets of over 2 trillion won (US$1.77 billion). Malaysia's legislative intervention is also relatively new. Introduced in 2021 and effective from September 2022, publicly listed companies with market capitalization of 2 billion ringgit (around US$500,000) and above had to have one woman board member, while from June 2023, other publicly listed companies had to meet the same requirement.[89] Yet Malaysia is distinguishable from both South Korea and India for the groundwork laid prior to the legislation's introduction. In 2011, Malaysia's prime minister announced a 30 percent target (by 2016) for women in decision-making positions in the corporate sector. The declaration led to the Women Directors' Programme led by the Ministry of Women, Family and Community Development.[90] The 2021 Malaysian Code on Corporate Governance followed. It requires boards to ensure that women candidates are considered during recruitment, to make explicit disclosures in their annual reports on their gender diversity policies and targets, and to report on the measures taken to meet those targets. In other words, while the intervention in the form of a legally mandated quota with penalties is relatively new and, like India's, potentially "insignificant," it accompanies a longer history of interventions that explain Malaysia's relative success shown in table 5.

Asia is also a region to watch. Table 6 shows relatively strong improvements in several countries in the region in the past few years. Yet Asia also has outliers. It is

TABLE 6 Female share of board seats at the largest publicly listed companies across Asia over time

Country	Percentage			Compulsory quota?
	2018	2021	2023	
Malaysia	20.6	24.0	28.5	✓
Singapore	13.7	17.6	20.8	#
Philippines	13.9	17.7	21.7	#
Japan	5.2	8.2	12.8	✓ (quota introduced in June 2023)

SOURCE: Deloitte Global Boardroom Program, "Women in the Boardroom: A Global Perspective" (2024).

KEY: ✓ quota in place; # other *government-led* measures such as codes of corporate governance, voluntary targets, apply-or-explain approach, or stock-exchange listing requirements to disclose targets; ✗ no substantial action.

hard to know, for instance, whether the Philippines' relatively good performance results from minor interventions—a code of corporate governance establishing a board diversity policy on gender and other criteria—or the fact that the Philippines, like Norway, Iceland, and New Zealand, scores relatively high in global terms, often among the top twenty countries in the world in the World Economic Forum's Global Gender Gap Index.[91] It is therefore a relatively strong performer when it comes to female presence on corporate boards, even in the absence of a legislated gender corporate quota, partly because of an environment—legislative or otherwise—that has done better at dismantling structural barriers to women's participation on boards.

Africa's Mixed Performance

As a region, Africa faces significant corporate governance challenges and remains deeply imprinted by a legacy of colonialism and unsurprisingly lags. According to the African Development Bank, women hold 12.7 percent of board directorships (364 out of 2,865) in 307 listed companies based in twelve African countries, 4.6 percent lower than the 17.3 percent of board seats held by women in the world's two hundred largest companies.[92] Relatively dated data about Africa (see table 7) makes it hard to know the extent of women's underrepresentation. However, in more recent data (table 8), Kenya, South Africa, and Nigeria all stand out as stronger performers, a reflection that "soft" intervention can improve women's representation on boards. These interventions may also explain Nigeria's rapid improvement, from women occupying only 11.5 percent of seats in 2015[93] to 21.7 percent in 2021, as shown in tables 7 and 8. Indeed data indicates that 28.9 percent of board seats were occupied by women in Nigeria in 2023.[94] In other words, intervention is a must; legislative quotas stand out as the most effective.

The Americas: The Absence Quota

North and South America are regions where quotas remain starkly absent (see table 9). If we focus on the US and Canada, their relative successes can be credited to subnational and other soft government interventions. With no national quota

TABLE 7 Female share of board seats at
the largest publicly listed companies across Africa (as of 2015)

Country	Percentage	Compulsory quota?
Kenya	17.4	✓ (for state-owned companies)
South Africa	16.9	#
Botswana	15.9	✗
Zambia	15.7	✗
Tanzania	14.3	✗
Uganda	12.9	✗
Nigeria	11.5	✗
Egypt	8.2	✗
Tunisia	7.9	✗
Côte d'Ivoire	5.1	✗

SOURCE: Compiled by the author using data from African Development Bank, "Where Are the Women? Inclusive Boardrooms in Africa's Top Listed Companies?"

KEY: ✓ quota in place; # other *government-led* measures such as codes of corporate governance, voluntary targets, apply-or-explain approach, or stock-exchange listing requirements to disclose targets; ✗ no substantial action.

TABLE 8 Female share of board seats at the largest publicly listed companies across Africa (as of 2021)

Country	Percentage	Compulsory quota?
Kenya	36	✓ (for companies owned by the state or in which the government is the majority owner)
South Africa	31.8	#
Nigeria	21.7	#

SOURCE: Compiled by the author using data from the Kenyan 2020-21 Board Diversity and Inclusion Study; and the Deloitte Global Boardroom Program, "Progress at a Snail's Pace: Women in the Boardroom—A Global Perspective" (2022).

KEY: ✓ quota in place; # other *government-led* measures, such as codes of corporate governance, voluntary targets, apply-or-explain approach, or stock-exchange listing requirements to disclose targets.

in place in Canada, Quebec introduced a 50 percent gender quota for boards of government-owned enterprises in 2011,[95] amplifying other gender diversity and inclusion initiatives nationally. For instance, in December 2020, the government's 50–30 Challenge sought to motivate Canadian organizations to increase the representation and inclusion of diverse groups in their workplaces, setting a target of "gender parity" (50 percent) on Canadian boards and in senior management positions and a 30 percent quota of other underrepresented groups, including racial minorities (known as "racialized persons" in Canada), people with disabilities, and members of the LGBT+ community. Uniquely, Canada is the nation that has come the closest to discussing board diversity in its fuller sense.

TABLE 9 Female share of board seats at the largest
publicly listed companies across North America over time

| Country | Percentage | | Compulsory quota? |
	2021	2023	
Canada	27.8	32.5	#
United States	23.9	28.1	✗
Mexico	9.7	12.3	✗

SOURCE: Compiled by the author using data from Deloitte Global Boardroom Program, "Progress at a Snail's Pace: Women in the Boardroom—A Global Perspective" (2022); and Deloitte Global Boardroom Program, "Women in the Boardroom—A Global Perspective" (2024).

KEY: # non-quota *government-led* measures, such as codes of corporate governance, voluntary targets, apply-or-explain approach, or stock-exchange listing requirements to disclose targets; ✗ no substantial action.

Other government interventions in Canada prove important. Since 2015, the visibility of data is a central aspect of the National Instrument on Disclosure, including director term limits, other board refreshment measures, policies to identify and nominate women to boards, methods for considering women in the selection of executive officers, and targets for women's representation in executive and nonexecutive roles.[96] Private initiatives matter too. In February 2022, Institutional Shareholder Services indicated it would recommend voting against nominating committee chairs if companies among the 250 largest on the Toronto Stock Exchange do not have at least 30 percent female directorship or a board diversity policy to achieve a 30 percent target in a reasonable time.

Federally, in the US, the Improving Corporate Governance Through Diversity Act of 2021 requires disclosure of the racial, ethnic, and gender composition of boards of directors and executive officers, along with their veteran status, and any plan to promote such diversity.[97] These are relatively soft measures, but if California's attempt to legislate a gender corporate quota offers a lesson, it is that more interventionist approaches may not withstand claims of unconstitutionality. California's quota (which required all public corporations to have one female director on boards by December 31, 2019, and all public companies in the state to have two female directors out of five directors or three female directors out of six or more directors by December 31, 2021[98]) was struck down as a violation of the California constitution's equal protection clause. With "no evidence" of discrimination against a woman by a specific corporation, the goal of achieving gender equality or parity was found not to be a compelling state interest in order to justify the quota's introduction. Unsurprisingly, not all agree with this decision.[99]

In many respects, the data from South America and the Caribbean is the most surprising, table 10 showing that progress can stall—as in Argentina—or can come undone—as in Peru. This is a region with a relatively high number of women who have occupied executive office as president, even if they have been their nation's first and only female leaders.[100] Political quotas exist across the region, including in

TABLE 10 Female share of board seats at the largest publicly listed companies
across Latin America over time

Country	Percentage		Compulsory quota?
	2021	2023	
Colombia	15.1	19.1	✘
Peru	13.2	11.1	✘
Chile	10.5	20.5	✘
Brazil	10.4	15.9	✘
Argentina	7.5	7.5	✘

SOURCE: Compiled by the author using data from Deloitte Global Boardroom Program, "Progress at a Snail's Pace: Women in the Boardroom—A Global Perspective" (2022); and Deloitte Global Boardroom Program, "Women in the Boardroom—A Global Perspective" (2024).

KEY: ✘ no substantial action.

Argentina, Costa Rica, Peru, the Dominican Republic, Ecuador, Bolivia, Colombia, Panama, Venezuela, Brazil, and Paraguay.[101] Moreover, the data in table 11 directly debunks the myth that the region faces an absence of capable women. Attempts to explain the region's lag with respect to women on boards by the "degree of religiosity" and "the long arm of the Catholic church's opposition to birth control" seem to stretch the argument.[102] Table 11 is the starkest illustration of the leap women are forced to take from management to board presence and makes the Latin American figures particularly woeful.

ACHIEVING PRESENCE: THE PATHWAY TO A CORPORATE QUOTA

Against Voluntariness

Two clear findings ring out. Europe is leading the way in instituting what appears the most gender-responsive legislative intervention to advance women's physical presence on corporate boards, while South America lags at the other extreme, followed by Africa and then Asia. Second, and somewhat disappointingly, when quotas are in force, their correlating impact only appears to be a shift in the number of women on a company's board directly governed by the quota.

While some suggest that voluntary measures can achieve the same outcomes, in isolation, they appear insufficient. In the case of Spain, the 2007 Gender Equality Act (Ley Orgánica para la igualdad efectiva de mujeres y hombres), which *recommended* 40 percent targets for each gender by 2015, found that just prior to the target period, less than 9 percent of target firms had complied.[103] Research also suggests that once a consensus regarding quota-based legislation has been reached, policymakers should be more assertive and shorten or even completely avoid the voluntary phase that was used in Norway.[104]

TABLE 11 Female share of board seats and managerial roles at the largest publicly
listed companies across Latin America (as of 2021)

Country	Percentage on boards	Percentage in managerial roles
Argentina	10.0	30.3
Brazil	16.9	38
Chile	15.2	25
Colombia	12.9	34.5
Peru	18.8	30.8

SOURCE: Compiled by the author using data from OECD.stat, "Employment: Female Share of Seats on Boards of the Largest Publicly Listed Companies."

Note that this table includes different percentages for board participation than table 10, because OECD data differs from the Deloitte Global Board Program data used in table 10, reflecting difficulties in securing reliable data to accurately capture women's presence on boards.

Counterexamples exist, but successes on the surface may cover their limitations. In Australia, a voluntary target of at least 30 percent of women on boards of Australian Stock Exchange (ASE) 200 Index companies was introduced in 2015. The target was to be reached by 2018, with no sanctions in place. Women occupied 34.8 percent of board seats among ASE companies by 2021.[105] However, the three countries with voluntary interventions that perform relatively well among the OECD nations have an even higher stretch factor than the global average stretch factor for women of 1.30:[106] the US (1.34), Australia (1.43), and New Zealand (1.33), the latter's global leadership on women's presence on boards evident in table 3. In other words, countries with voluntary measures have a small cohort of women on boards, whereby one woman occupies a large number of board seats for different companies. By contrast, early adopters of quotas have a lower stretch factor—Italy and France at 1.17—which matches the global stretch factor for men; the stretch factor for women is as low as 1.06 in Norway. The quota, it is believed, creates a need for these countries to "cast a wider net" when identifying capable women for the role of board member.[107] If Malaysia is anything to go by, voluntary interventions can be a solid start if a quota is part of the endgame, but they may reflect a missed opportunity to move quickly to a binding obligation.

What Are the Conditions for Quota Success?

This chapter has backed the legislative quota as a gender-responsive model, but there are obvious conditions for success. Corporations need to show a structural readiness, enforcement requirements are a must, and there needs to be some recognition that the private sector might be more resistant than the public sector.

First, a readiness for change matters.[108] Norway's pre-quota social climate fostered an environment in which a quota law could thrive. Generous and progressive parental leave schemes and the 1978 Gender Equality Act already required employers to affirmatively implement procedures to increase workplace equality.[109] In France, a series of laws and regulations in the 1960s and 1970s made contraception more accessible and meant a larger portion of women could better control their fertility, while construction of childcare facilities (crèches and garderies) better enabled women in formal work to return to the workplace.[110] Although the extensive use of political quotas across South America may raise doubt, the use of quotas in other contexts, such as France's 2000 law requiring political parties to name women as half of all party candidates,[111] may also build a readiness for a corporate board quota.

Penalties matter. There must be a consequence for noncompliance, such as dissolution in Norway.[112] Italian firms are fined from €100,000 to €1,000,000 if the percentage of women on supervisory boards is less than 33 percent.[113] The fine must be sufficient to motivate compliance and reflect a level of seriousness on the part of the legislating body.

The quota must also be accompanied by transparency. A major critique of Norway's quota, for which there was no tendering or applications, was that transparency was "completely absent," and selection was based on connections and qualifications.[114] In such an environment, it is likely that "successful women will naturally assimilate into board structures, not turn them upside down."[115] There must also be compulsory reporting using sex-disaggregated data on corporate leadership.[116] Stock exchange listing requirements should mandate annual reports on board composition, with interim updates, and they should include not only the directors' names but the year of commencement of board appointment, age, and a brief background biography. One could also imagine that once such a reporting structure has been established, key information such as racial and linguistic diversity could also be captured.

Moreover, there are many interventions that can accelerate a quota's success. Companies can be provided lists of suitably qualified women.[117] A challenge can also be made to improper corporate governance processes.[118] This would include the inaccessibility of information regarding vacancies and selection criteria, the male-dominated nature of nomination committees, and the frequent overemphasis on prior boardroom experience of candidates, which men are more likely to have.

CONCLUSION

A legislative quota can guarantee women a seat at the table. While controversial, it is simultaneously one of the clearest examples of a temporary special measure to address women's underrepresentation. Yet there are other ways of understanding quotas as an intervention. Professor of politics Rainbow Murray calls for a normative shift in how we frame the quota, moving away from a focus on (women's) underrepresentation to challenge the overrepresented. Quotas are needed when "too large a group [is] drawn from too narrow a talent pool."[119] In other words, what Murray considers a quota is a ceiling or cap on the dominant group, in this case, men.

If one seeks to question the viability and validity of quotas as an intervention, we must respond by asking how long we must wait. The alternatives simply do not do a better job. The global extremes in the current rates of women's presence on boards reflect a divide—and in some countries, very obvious ones—between those countries that have pursued a quota and those that fear one. The task is about finding a balance between the "forces of change and forces of resistance."[120] Moreover, other lessons can be drawn from this exercise in addressing systemic under-representation. For one, we can adapt practices from nations like Canada, which are engaged in broader debates about diverse representation. The outcome is also likely to make a bigger contribution to equality and representation, the pursuit of the corporate-board gender quota helping us arrive at stronger and more diverse boards in the long run, with better representation for racial, ability, and sexual and gender diversity.

7

Gender-Responsive Budgeting

Law as the Lever to Embed Gender
in Budgetary Frameworks

In his 2015 book, French geographer Yves Raibaud argued that cities are "made by and for men" (La ville faite par et pour les hommes).[1] Raibaud's research showed that the number of girls benefitting from sporting activities subsidized by municipalities between 2009 and 2012 was, on average, half that of boys. The problem worsened with age and particularly during adolescence. While the androcentric norms of the city are explained by numerous factors—think about societal attitudes toward young girls occupying public spaces, including concerns for their safety—Raibaud noted that horse riding, for example, attracted no subsidy, as it was considered a private sport and even attracted a VAT, and dance too was rarely subsidized. However, football and rugby were often found to be free.[2] Even infrastructure investment was gendered, with 95 percent of users of new skateparks being boys. Working with Raibaud, the deputy mayor of Bordeaux changed the activities subsidized in the Bordeaux summer Sport on the Quays program, and the participation rate went from 80 percent boys in 2011 to 52 percent girls in 2019.[3]

To some, the allocation of public resources by governments is a neutral exercise. All people, regardless of their gender, are entitled to public services, including healthcare, education, and public goods such as the use of roads.[4] Resources are not denied to people because they are, for example, a member of a sexual minority group. Seen in this light, government expenditure on goods and services benefits all. While there are obvious exceptions to this general rule (such as paid maternity leave policies, which were the subject of chapter 3, for which there are notably higher budgetary allocations for leave for birth or adopting mothers), explicit differentiation in budgets is relatively infrequent.

Gender-responsive budgeting (GRB) challenges this premise and the seeming neutrality of government spending.[5] In its absence, budgeters risk blindness to the relevance of gender to how public resources are allocated and who gets to benefit. Gender blindness produces inequitable and inefficient public policies and undermines productivity, women's labor market participation, and other stated women's rights goals.[6] Moreover, this blindness is not suffered in the same way by all women. It is worse for women who assume caring roles, who are struggling with poverty or with health problems, and those facing seclusion.[7]

Over three decades ago, when feminist economists were doing the hard and innovative work of embedding GRB in government departments, Rhonda Sharp, Australia's long-standing leading expert on gender budgeting, along with Ray Broomhill, set out its two primary goals: to explicitly identify and evaluate "the implications for women of government policies and expenditures" and to use the process of allocating budgets to "influence the quantity and quality of budget allocations made by the various state agencies in relation to women and girls."[8] One would imagine—or hope—that gender budgeting has evolved with time, finding ways to work beyond the binary and to identify not just how people of different genders but a diversity of individuals—a black disabled woman or a poor older man—benefit from public spending. Indeed, today GRB is acknowledged as a fundamental tool to hold governments accountable for their commitments to human rights and equality as such commitments can be met only with a fairer distribution, use, and generation of public resources.[9]

GRB is a longstanding intervention when it comes to advancing women's rights, named in international policies since the mid-1990s and occasionally practiced even earlier. Australia, for example, began instituting GRB in 1984, more than ten years before the Beijing Declaration (discussed below).[10] After this passage of time, it is important to ask how much GRB has been cemented in national practice.

A diversity of terms, often used interchangeably, fosters confusion: "women's budgets," "gender budgets," "gender-sensitive budgets," and "gender-responsive budgets."[11] While mandates to incorporate a gender perspective into budgets may be clear in some countries, adoption and implementation is often inconsistent.[12] Countries often lack monitoring and accountability mechanisms, and importantly for this chapter, too few countries have in place laws that require state agencies to practice GRB with ongoing continuity, meaning its consistent practice across years is not a guarantee.

GRB is more than just an "accounting practice";[13] it is a tool for sound, evidence-based policymaking, and we have the evidentiary basis to demonstrate its value. The South African Women's Budget Initiative (SAWBI, as it is sometimes known) was a first in Africa, followed by policies in Uganda, Tanzania, and Rwanda.[14] In 1995, the government of South Africa produced a gender analysis of the national government's sectoral budget, covering twenty-seven departments and agencies and providing a gender perspective on issues such as taxation and public sector employment, along with the actions of provincial and local governments.[15] GRB prompted the introduction of a child support grant for primary caregivers, one that was particularly beneficial for South African women, who dominate care work. It was accompanied by a zero rate of value added tax (VAT) on paraffin,[16] a product that although very risky, remains essential for poorer communities heavily dependent on it for cooking, heating, and lighting.

In South Korea, it was thanks to gender budgeting that a modification was made to the Public Toilet Act (2004). Public toilets were constructed in parks, tourist areas, stores, malls, transport facilities, and sporting grounds to improve the quality of the lives of South Koreans through better sanitation. With a gendered analysis applied, the act included a provision requiring any newly constructed public facilities to have the total number of toilets in women's restrooms the same or higher than the number allocated for men,[17] in recognition of women's higher usage.

In a program on HIV and AIDS prevention from the same year in the Mexican state of Michoacán, gender disaggregation helped establish patterns and risks. Married or partnered women not working outside the home, particularly the partners or wives of migrant workers, were found to face a higher risk of exposure to HIV/AIDs infection, often (incorrectly) believing their sexual relations to be safe and secure.[18] A gender lens saw funds allocated to prevention campaigns focused on these partnered women identified as being at a higher risk.[19]

Albeit with varying levels of consistency, transparency, and accountability, GRB clearly helps in delivering better public policies and resource reallocation. Yet how do we overcome a reluctance and incapacity of government departments to systematically practice GRB? This chapter considers whether the answer can be found in law and argues for writing into the rules a requirement to perform GRB. Spain's success in publishing an annual gender budgeting report alongside the budget since 2008—an obligation in law—has been partly credited by the OECD to GRB's "strong legal underpinning."[20] In 2003, in Guatemala, SEPREM, the presidential secretariat for women, presented to the Ministry of Public Finance the tools for GRB: an accounting system called the Gender-Related Classification System (GRCS). Since 2013, government agencies have been legally required to apply the GRCS to prepare preliminary budget plans, monitor expenditures, and deliver quarterly reports on the execution of the budget in accordance with the classification system.[21]

GRB tools provide guidance; yet when their implementation is required by law, such tools can enhance the quality of budgeting, the visibility of resource allocation, and the accountability of those responsible for making decisions concerning public spending. Feminist economists have therefore become vocal proponents for legal obligations for the state to practice GRB at all levels of government as an essential step in institutionalizing, securing, and realizing the benefits of the process. From Honduras[22] to the Dominican Republic,[23] from Indonesia[24] to the Philippines,[25] from Canada[26] to Colombia,[27] jurisdictions globally have made the practice of GRB a requirement in law. Statutory provisions for gender budgeting exist in more than half of the OECD countries, such as in Austria, Iceland, South Korea, and the Netherlands as well as Mexico and Spain already noted above.[28] In 2009, Austria became the first country to incorporate GRB into its constitution, the highest legal instrument in the land, Article 13(3) requiring federal and local authorities to achieve "effective equality between women and men in budgetary management."[29] Bolivia and Rwanda have similarly introduced constitutional requirements for GRB.

By contrast, the absence of a law can be an insurmountable challenge for securing and sustaining GRB as a government practice. In Bangladesh, GRB's absence from the law has undermined government accountability for its purported commitment, while public officials lack a standardized method to help grow an appreciation of GRB from within the public sector. Nor are there clear mechanisms for follow-up.[30] In India, the absence of a legal mandate to undertake GRB has been "a hindrance to deepen the policy processes."[31] In Nigeria, development finance scholar Emily Edoisa Ikhide's trend analysis blames the absence of a law—when compared to Uganda or Rwanda—for budget allocations that fall short of targets. Resultingly, key ministries faced inadequate budget allocations from 2015 to 2020: the Federal Ministry of Women Affairs (allocated less than 0.10 percent of the total Nigerian budget); the Ministries of Health and Water Resources (allocated less than 5 percent); and the Ministry of Education (which although having the highest allocation among the core ministries, at 10.75 percent in 2015, still fell short of the United Nations Educational, Scientific and Cultural Organization benchmark of 15–20 percent of budget allocated to the education sector).[32]

This chapter therefore seeks to establish the whys and hows of rewriting fiscal and budgetary law to institutionalize a government practice of conducting GRB. In this case, we must rewrite the rules to achieve a rewriting of government budgets. This chapter is both evaluative (what have we achieved in the past half century?) and forward-looking (how can legislation institutionalize progress toward materializing women's lived experiences in government budgets?). While enacting legislation is essential to cement GRB as a government practice, a key question remains: what form should the law take? In unpacking the ingredients of a potentially effective GRB law, the chapter navigates across three questions with respect to design: How much gender-budget is enough? Who are we budgeting for? And who is accountable for the practice of GRB?

By comparing global experiences in a truly multiregional analysis, we can identify what is needed to make GRB the game changer it has the potential to be. While no single law can be copied across jurisdictions, here we explore the tested ingredients for legislation to ensure GRB is systematically applied to all current and new public initiatives to genuinely advance the well-being of a diversity of women.

WHAT IS GRB, WHAT ARE ITS ORIGINS, AND HOW DO WE MAKE IT RESPONSIVE?

An International and Domestic Commitment

GRB was once deemed a government exercise in promoting its own achievements in relation to women.[33] While many countries still teeter at the edges of comprehensive GRB, today GRB is increasingly practiced purposefully by governments. Some credit should be accorded to international policies where the concept of GRB found a place many years ago. In 1995, thirty thousand activists marched in Huairou in China as government meetings took place in Beijing—leading to the Beijing Declaration and Platform for Action.[34] GRB was a key inclusion in the Beijing Declaration. Governments were encouraged to "*systematically* review how women benefit from public sector expenditures" and to "*adjust* budgets to ensure equality of access to public sector expenditures" (emphasis added).[35] A reallocation of resources could address basic social, educational, and health needs of women, particularly those living in poverty.[36] Governments were encouraged to review national income, inheritance taxes, and social security systems to eliminate existing gender biases.[37] Calls were made for budgeting processes to be more transparent.[38]

Five years later, as part of the global review of the commitments made in Beijing (Beijing +5), governments were again urged to incorporate a gender perspective in the design, development, adoption, and execution of all budgetary processes. A gender perspective on the allocation of finance was still lacking despite a commitment to promote equitable, effective, and appropriate resource allocation, as well as to support gender equality and development programs. There was also an acknowledgment that until that moment, some of the analytical and methodological tools and mechanisms for monitoring and evaluation were lacking; governments were urged to fill these gaps.[39] Then again, in the ten-year review in 2005, governments were called to show that they had actually made some progress on these commitments.[40]

Interestingly, domestic practice preceded these international developments, with Australia leading the way this time. Yet Australia's much-deserved glory moment in the late 1980s as the first government in the world to introduce a whole-of-budget gendered analysis also offers a cautionary tale. The government of the day produced what became known in Australia as the Women's Budget Statement (WBS). Each department presented the gendered impact of their policies and programs for the forthcoming budgetary cycle.[41] However, after the left-leaning government of the day faced a near election loss, the detailed and exhaustive WBS was shortly sacrificed. After 2013, a change in government saw the disappearance of the federal WBS altogether, with the load of providing a gender lens voluntarily carried by a not-for-profit, the National Foundation for Australian Women. When Australia initiated the WBS, no law made GRB mandatory for state and federal agencies. Its rigorous application and then decline in Australia mirrors changing government agendas and shifts in the economic environment.[42] More recently, two Australian states have committed to the practice: Tasmania, under a 2022 motion,[43] and Victoria, under a 2024 law.[44] No federal law was in place in Australia at the time of publication.

South Africa, too, proved one of the world's leaders but also evidences this legislative lag. In 1996, South African human rights activist and scholar Pregs Govender declared in a foreword to the first South Africa Women's Budget, "The budget reflects the values of a country—who it values, whose work it values and who it rewards [and] who and what and whose work it does not."[45] Govender called for disaggregated data to demystify the apparent neutrality of budgets. The post-apartheid African National Congress in South Africa was committed to women's empowerment while the over one hundred new women parliamentarians—partly thanks to a one-third quota—were committed to GRB to ensure that the aspirational constitution of the new regime (non-sexism and non-racism among its most fundamental principles) could become a reality through government policy and financing.[46] More than twenty years passed until this commitment was turned into a binding obligation. South Africa's national cabinet adopted the Framework on Gender-Responsive Planning, Budgeting, Monitoring, Evaluation and Auditing only on 27 March 2019.[47]

With both Australia and South Africa showing a clear lag between practice and law, we are naturally drawn to look instead to the lessons from the earlier legislators. First, however, we must ask what it means to gender a budget.

Understanding Budgets as Gendered

"Women's budgets," contrary to the name, are not separate budgets for women or confined to explicit policy initiatives for women; rather, they are an analytical breakdown of the government's mainstream budget to account for its impact on women.[48] Participating departments are required to identify the impact of their programs and proposed budgets on different genders. GRB as a practice is, therefore, inherently both objective and subjective, as the earmarking of allocations will reflect the views and assumptions held by particular government departments.[49]

Importantly, GRB tracks investments in women versus investments in others as well as revenue-raising. Who are the beneficiaries, for instance, of decisions to cut taxes? Tax cuts may not explicitly discriminate on the basis of gender, but they may benefit women less than men because men and women differ in their economic circumstances and behaviors.[50] By developing a total expenditure framework, such a quantitative assessment makes visible the proportion of government expenditures that are targeted for women and girls relative to non-targeted or general expenditures and revenue,[51] as well illustrated by the City of Bordeaux at the outset of this chapter.

Sharp's three categories for understanding public spending, elaborated in the 1980s, have been replicated and promoted by other entities—the UN Development Fund for Women (UNIFEM), now UN Women and the UN Population Fund, UNFPA.[52] First, expenditures may target known gender-patterned needs, such as a rural women's health initiative or an HIV education program targeted to men. Second, budget interventions may recognize and respond to gendered disparities by, for instance, funding an affirmative action policy or addressing workplace sexual harassment. Third, public spending may be general or mainstreamed, with public goods and services delivered to the whole population. In the latter case, gender disaggregation is needed to reveal gendered impacts and outcomes in order to contribute to GRB. Drawing on the work of GRB pioneer Diane Elson, Isabella Bakker describes the key question in the whole process as what impact each fiscal measure has on gender equality? Does it reduce gender inequality or increase it; or does the fiscal measure leave it unchanged?[53] At the heart of GRB, therefore, is a recognition that government budgets command substantial resources and reflect the fundamental force of the state in shaping gender equality outcomes.[54]

Categorizing beneficiaries makes the task seem fairly straightforward. Yet, the complexity of gender budgeting should not be underestimated; it requires nuance and care. A 2019 example from Canada illustrates this well.[55] Imagine, Geneviève Tellier conjectures, a decision on how to allocate government funding to the arts sector. Studies suggest women artists in Canada earn 31 percent less than male artists. Should the government aim to correct that income imbalance (for instance, by raising the pay of women artists), or should a more "neutral" approach be taken to ensure that all Canadians, the target population, benefit from the arts? Can we quantify the difference between the two options, for example, by trying to understand the public cost if the art is produced by a less diverse pool of artists? Tellier also tackles head-on the question of who we are budgeting for and brings the LGBTQ+ community, actively engaged in the art sector in Canada, into the picture. Should specific funding seek to benefit Canadian queer artists who have a pivotal sociopolitical role to play in using art to challenge mainstream discourses on sexuality, homophobia, and colonialism?[56]

An example from India illustrates how budgetary decisions require sociocultural contextualization and consideration of indirect (or what economists call second-round) impacts. In 2009, the government of India's flagship scheme, Rashtriya Madhyamik Shiksha Abhiyan, was launched to enhance girls' access to secondary education. Young women in India from remote communities often face a long commute,[57] and hostels were identified as a way of avoiding long—near impossible—daily travel back and forth between home and school. GRB saw funds allocated for hostels for young girls from tribal and rural communities. However, what was not accounted for was the loss of labor families faced when their girls left home. The government policy—as first conceived—failed to account for the household chores that these girls would have completed if they were staying at home. For the intervention to work, families needed financial compensation for the reduction in household livelihoods. What was missing, in other words, were policy levers to create an enabling environment that went beyond the direct allocation of funding for hostels.[58]

These rich and complex contexts must be given adequate attention before we even get to the stage of allocating funding. They also demonstrate that GRB goes beyond chalking up points in different gendered categories.

TURNING TO THE LAW: GLOBAL LESSONS FOR INSTITUTIONALIZING GRB

If GRB has been practiced for so long and in many countries, it is natural to ask whether law really matters. What will be demonstrated is that while the practice of GRB preceded its normalization, its success and ability to thrive requires rewriting the rules in ways that guarantee its continuity and the accountability of those responsible for its performance. The very process of enacting a law about GRB facilitates public debate about how public policies are designed and how they have citizens in mind. Moreover, once set in law, the practice is also harder to undo.

Here I turn to the Philippines, the first country identified to have enacted a legal requirement for government agencies to undertake GRB. Being the world's legislative test case, it will be revealed, is not always a good thing. The Filipino bureaucracy had to make mistakes and learn lessons for itself. Nonetheless, established in law since 1995, the Filipino practice of GRB has persisted until today. What can we learn from the Philippines' experiences about what makes a good GRB law?

How Much Budget Is Enough?

At the tail end of the tenure of President Corazon Aquino,[59] the Philippines enacted the Women in Nation-Building Act,[60] a 1992 law that recognized the fundamental role of women in "building the nation." This act expected all government agencies and organizations to review and revise or remove gender-discriminatory policies, procedures, and systems and to promote gender-responsive planning and budgeting.[61] These reforms laid the grounds for a noteworthy feature of the policy landscape in the Philippines: a gender budgeting policy introduced in 1995 whereby a minimum of 5 percent of the total budget had to be allocated for gender and development purposes.[62] Since the 1990s, the Philippines has retained its gender-budgeting policy nationally and subnationally.

Yet the idea of a 5 percent uniform floor for spending on gender-related matters is not uncontroversial. A spending floor can result in a misallocation of resources and may result in the marginalization of gender issues from mainstream budgets since floor limits are often taken as ceilings, not minimums.[63] A minimum target may be pursued without adequate thought given to how it is best spent. Lekha Chakraborty, a senior economist at the National Institute of Public Finance and Policy in India, for instance, has noted with considerable concern that in the early days of gender budgeting in the Philippines, the 5 percent was allocated for activities such as ballroom dancing in certain government departments. There was no penalty for not utilizing the Gender and Development budget fully and efficiently. Many departments ended up with an unspent surplus.[64] Earmarking a specific proportion of budget allocation for women may be only a second-best principle of gender budgeting and is not likely to be the most appropriate approach. Differential targeting of expenditures based on the identification of appropriate programs for women and, when needed, the flexibility to reprioritize expenditures based on unplanned and emerging needs, appear more effective than a uniform target across the board.[65]

Others have argued that 5 percent appears to be an inadequate minimum expectation. Yet an assessment of average allocations for women and gender-related programs reveals that they rarely, if ever, rise above this amount. In the 1985–86 South Australian women's budget—a relatively small state in the south of Australia that today accounts for just over 7 percent of the total population—direct government budget allocations for women amounted to only 0.75 percent, on average, of the total budget of the twenty-six participating departments,[66] a stark difference from the Filipino 5 percent minimum. In Bolivia, an earmarked spending for gender equality amounted to around 0.4 percent of total spending; the remainder was devoted to general spending.[67] In India, from 2017 to 2022, the gender budget was between 4.4 and 5.3 percent of the total central budget.[68] This suggests that while not ideal, the Filipino 5 percent target, established more than three decades ago, was relatively ambitious and a minimum floor that has rarely been met in other jurisdictions.

A question to ask of these minimal allocations is whether they are sufficient to move nations toward more equal policies. Clearly something more than mere allocation is required. In South Korea, the National Finance Act obliges the government to evaluate whether women and men equally receive the benefits of the budget and the ways in which the budget will enhance gender equality.[69] A gender-sensitive balance sheet is required to set out the funds allocated, and revenue collected, but also the *effects* on gender equality.[70] The law requires a depth to reporting that can aid accountability. Comparing the Philippines and South Korea, we see two different approaches—a 5 percent floor for women-centered investments on the one hand and a proportion of public spending to demonstrate an equal share allocated for women on the other—and by drawing from both of these distinct approaches in combination, GRB as a practice can be optimized.

Budgeting for Whom?

In recent years, GRB has been named the tool to create "budgets that work for everyone."[71] Tellier shares the view that GRB has the capacity to unpack inequalities among various groups, including sexual minorities, youth, older citizens, rural and urban communities, and immigrants.[72] Nonetheless, the evidence from many countries shows a continued understanding of GRB that does little to account for individuals' multiple identities. The choice for many governments is to identify, where possible, how public spending is allocated for men and women and how men and women differentially benefit, reflecting GRB's 1980s origins. Simultaneously, we may question the readiness of governments to achieve "budgets that work for everyone" when GRB is still struggling with the hard task of bringing visibility to, for example, the extent to which poor women, lesbian women, or women of color benefit from public spending or differentially contribute to tax revenue. The work of monitoring how gender-diverse people experience public sector spending has been taken up in some jurisdictions by the non-governmental sector.[73]

While GRB is still weak in going beyond a binary analysis, some success has been achieved in relation to other grounds of intersectional inequality. In Uruguay, the law requires government agencies to undertake GRB to account for the intersection between sex and ethnic-racial ancestry and socio-economic status, age, disability, sexual orientation, gender identity, place of origin, or residence.[74]

In Mexico, the Institute for Oaxacan Women successfully lobbied the governor to require, in law, that the government produce sex-disaggregated information.[75] Budget scrutiny in the late 1990s and early 2000s revealed how budget cuts affected anti-poverty programs, of which women were the main beneficiaries.[76] The Oaxacan example suggests that gender-responsive budgeting may achieve what other tools for accountability cannot. In other words, Latin American examples suggest that it is possible to legislate for GRB in ways that apply an intersectional lens.

The case of the Federal Department of Aboriginal Affairs in the early days of Australia's gender-budgeting is also illustrative. In the first women's budget, critics argued that budgeting had inadequately accounted for First Nations women. The initial response was to suggest that funds had been "directed to the benefit of Aboriginal communities *in toto*, without any specific preference being given to sub-groups of these communities."[77] By contrast, however, the fifth women's budget statement saw a fivefold increase in the number of pages dedicated to the implications of its program for Indigenous women in Australia.[78] Gender budgeting has also made visible women in particular industries. In Australia in 1986, gender budgeting revealed the significantly lower levels of government expenditure on the restructuring of the highly feminized textiles, clothing, and footwear industries compared to the male-dominated passenger motor vehicle industry.[79] Gender budgeting, when reaching its optimum potential, promotes equality for people of different genders and disaggregation on multiple grounds, a key criterion for gender-responsive lawmaking.

Budgeting by Whom?

The Brazilian city of Porto Alegre is famously the birthplace of the World Social Forum and was home to an exemplary model of participatory governance from 1988 to 2004.[80] *Orçamento participativo* (participatory budgeting) transformed ordinary urban residents into "active subjects with increasing power to influence decisions shaping their daily lives."[81] Sadly, however, the model was "exported" in a lite version by the World Bank for political conditions vastly different from those in Brazil. Even in Brazil the practice has been "watered down": the government no longer provides adequate financial and institutional information for citizens to participate; elected and appointed officials no longer attend the local assemblies; and municipal government accountability has declined.[82]

In addition to asking who we are seeking to budget for, lawmaking must set out who will be held accountable for its performance. When it comes to advancing women's rights, frequently committees, commissions, agencies, and task forces are created to do the "busywork" of monitoring; often these groups are composed of women who bear the brunt of lobbying for interventions to correct inequality. In other words, the work of closing inequality gaps is largely the responsibility of ministries and offices for women. The fields of budgeting, economics, and government finances, however, are domains where women are frequently less represented and, at times, excluded. It is men, predominantly, who control the nation's purse strings. Women do not have input in equal measure to men in processes of resource allocation, which are often structured in ways that make effective participation difficult.[83] We must envision an accountability mechanism where gender budgeting has a central place in government budgets and is the responsibility of people in authority but conducted in a manner that facilitates the representation of women's experiences in decisions to allocate finances.

Two Latin American models offer contrasting approaches and levels of success. Ecuador created the National Directorate of Fiscal Equity within the Finance Ministry's Under-Secretariat of Fiscal Policy to direct, formulate, propose, and assess fiscal policies. The National Directorate has helped to close gaps in gender equity by ensuring institutionalization of the initiative.[84] By contrast, El Salvador's lack of success to undertake gender budgeting between 2011 and 2013, with the support of UN Women, has been largely explained by a lack of leadership from the Ministry of Finance to ensure compliance.[85]

Canada was also a late arriver to the legislative table when it comes to GRB. In this case, the Canadian Gender Budgeting Act was enacted in 2018 to take effect in the preparation of the 2019 budget.[86] The act stipulated the responsibility of the government to present a gender-based assessment of the budget, to annually publish the impact of tax measures in terms of gender and diversity, and to provide an annual report on the impact of all existing public sector programs.[87] Yet the act also explicitly called on all departments to seek the guidance, best practices, and expertise provided by the Minister for Women and Gender Equality.[88] In addition to its already vast responsibilities to advance equality among Canadians and promote an understanding of how sex- and gender-based inequality intersects with other identifying factors, one may question the viability of *all* government departments seeking assistance from the *one* Ministry for Women and Gender Equality to realize these legislative goals.

Brazil, too, exemplifies the challenges government staff face when the work of conducting GRB falls on women's groups. The lack of a law to require the government of Brazil to practice GRB has seen the role fall to the Grupo de Estudos e Pesquisas das Políticas Públicas para a Inclusão Social (GEPPIS), or Feminist Center for Research and Advice, in the period from 2002 to 2012. The situation is reminiscent of Australia's Women's Budget Statement, where the unwillingness of the government to sustain the practice resulted in the responsibility being taken up by civil society. Brazil's collective was charged with integrating perspectives on gender and race in the National Program for Citizen Security (Programa Nacional de Seguridad Ciudadana), as well as monitoring resources assigned for women's security. Too small to cope with the workload, GEPPIS struggled to achieve the required level of monitoring in a way that would lead to consistent, transparent, and effective GRB.[89]

Nonetheless, while women too frequently bear the work of correcting inequality, it is essential to have women at the budget decision-making table. In this respect, research from Indonesia demonstrates the ways in which women's preferences for public spending differ from men's. One study suggested that women prefer significantly more spending on education and health than male village heads, village council chairs, or the chairs of farming groups, youth groups, or village community empowerment groups, whose preferences all led to spending on roads.[90] GRB can be used to account for differing perspectives, but a balance must be struck between achieving participation, while commitment to the process is more widely owned.

Overcoming Law's Limits

Belgium has received much praise for its 2007 law on GRB. Enacted explicitly to implement the agreements arrived at in Beijing in 1995,[91] the law specified the methodologies and processes for integrating gender equality into all budgetary processes and for collecting and managing gender data.[92] Belgium's budget process requires each item of spending to be classified under three headings: "neutral," if it is seen to have no gender dimension; "explicit," if it is dedicated to the reduction of inequality; or "includes a gender dimension," if there is some differential impact on women and men. The municipal of Ixelles—one of nineteen in the Brussels region of Belgium—shows the neat link between regulated GRB, gender disaggregation, and policy design and financing. The height of street lamps has been changed, lowering them to make the streets less dark and safer, and streets have been better paved and surfaced to make it easier to push a pram.[93]

Yet the ways in which this law was designed created an easy loophole. When interviewed, Belgian middle-level federal staff complained about the "huge additional demands gender budgeting would place on the management in already extremely busy times of reform."[94] One assessment between 2014 and 2016 found that five out of seventeen Federal Public Services did not implement gender budgeting, and of those that had implemented it, at least four said that their spending "had no gender impact,"[95] thereby bypassing the need for a gender assessment or to demonstrate how the budgetary decisions respond to the gendered context. It seems self-evident that law must establish clear accountability for determining when a gendered assessment is needed, as well as conducting and responding to such an assessment. In time, it is hoped that the law creates an institutional culture where public officials see the positive outcomes from such robust analysis.

That is, GRB when practiced well, requires systematic transparency, systematic data collection and monitoring, and often across vast public sectors. Yet public sectors are data rich. Moreover, living documents to enable and capture the practice of GRB may be increasingly possible for a technology-enabled public sector. Many of the challenges stipulated above—whether real or used by governments to excuse themselves from GRB practice—can be addressed with the use of digital data in government in ways that allow for enhanced planning, monitoring, and evaluation of the targets set for GRB. The conversations and underpinning rationale that shaped GRB in the 1980s remain relevant today, while the limitations may prove less of an impediment.

CONCLUSION

The rules of gender budgeting need rewriting by writing the practice into law. It is only through legislation that we get closer to guaranteeing systematic implementation. GRB, like every proposition in *Rewriting the Rules*, has its limitations. In 2010, the Mexican Instituto Nacional de las Mujeres (National Institute for Women) complained that gender-responsive budgeting had simply not lived up to its promise and was insufficient to monitor and assess programs. In this case, not enough of the government's budget had incorporated a gender perspective, and national and state laws failed to harmonize the process, including both its objectives and approach.[96] While much-praised, the Philippines has had to learn and adapt, improving its strategy of earmarking a budget minimum by linking the spending to results-oriented budgeting.[97]

Yet half a century after GRB's initiation, this chapter shows that we *do* have the ingredients at hand to imminently witness its proper performance, which first and foremost, requires binding legislation. Importantly, some of GRB's early practitioners have recently taken steps to institutionalize the practice by embedding it in law: Australia, South Africa, and Canada too. Moving forward, we can learn from these early practitioners who have only recently embraced the value of the law in this domain.

Second, we should recognize "outside government" or community-based gender budget audits, often foundational in the laws that came later. The UK's Women's Budget Group was formed in 1989 by several policy experts, academics, and members of various organizations that included trade unions, environmental pressure groups, and children's and pension rights groups. These groups worked hard to forge and maintain a relationship with the government, with the election of the Labour Government in 1999 helping to create a more regular and influential engagement between civil society and the treasury.[98]

Nonetheless, civil-society-led processes must be parallel to and not a substitute for government practice. There are countless examples: the Women's International League for Peace and Freedom, a gender-sensitive analysis within the Canadian Alternative Budget; the Scottish budgeting work of Engender; the NGO initiatives of the Southern African countries (Tanzania, Mozambique and Zambia); the Korean Women's Development Institute, a policy think tank that initiated research and a methodology on gender budgeting;[99] the Washington, D.C.–based Institute for Women's Policy Research;[100] along with the National Foundation for Australian Women. Alliances can still be formed with the state—as in the UK—to help push government practice to become more systematic.

Third, we must continue to invest in case studies of impact. Starting in 1997, the Tanzanian Gender Budget Initiative led by the Tanzania Gender Network Program initially focused on the education and health sectors and later incorporated agriculture into its analysis as well. Trade and industry and finance were added in 1999.[101] Scholars have since credited GRB in Tanzania for the 3 percent increase in budgeting allocations to the Ministry of Water for infrastructure projects that typically benefit women.[102] Impact over time can also sustain momentum toward GRB's ongoing implementation.

Finally, perhaps we are on the verge of GRB reaching its optimum potential. Arguably, the timing could not be better. Its potential in a data-rich and technology-enabled age is high. Climate change, too, presents an opportunity for convergence in ways that may help steer GRB toward its next stage of development. Think, for instance, of the potential for climate finance and GRB to merge. In the case of Rwanda, this was the turn that started in 2022–2023, where the climate change budget statement contained actions related to both gender and climate in ways that acknowledged that women farmers are likely to be hardest hit by the impact of climate change on rain-led agricultural activities.[103]

Gender-responsive climate budgeting, at its optimum, involves cross-representation of gender and climate organizations, impact assessments that fluidly combine the impact of climate and gender, and the categorization of gender and climate spending in ways that reveal patterns from gender-budgeting tagging and climate-budgeting tagging. Importantly, stakeholders who are simultaneously accountable for both can be integrated.[104] The change is already being witnessed. National budget allocation by the Rwanda Ministry of Finance and Economic Planning for the environment, climate change, and gender increased from 0.4 percent in 2009 to 4.6 percent in 2020 as a result.[105] By comparison, at the time of writing, South Africa had not incorporated gender-responsive budgeting in its climate framework.[106]

New countries are therefore emerging as potential leaders in this space. In this vein, it is hoped that the assessment made at the outset of this chapter—that GRB is one area where we could have hoped for more progress after over more than half a century of practice—will not be a plausible critique in the years to come.

8

Artificial Intelligence

Algorithmic Accountability Through
an Intersectional Gender Lens

Few would disagree with the sentiment that artificial intelligence (AI) has long been seen as a man's world. Most accounts acknowledge John McCarthy and Alan Turing as the "founding *fathers*" of AI at a 1956 Dartmouth Summer Workshop.[1] Larry Page and Sergey Bin founded Google in 1988 as doctoral students at Stanford University. Alphabet, Google's parent company founded in 2015, operates under two males, chairman John Leroy Hennessy and CEO Sundar Pichai, although women have been CFO and president. In 1994, Jeff Bezos founded Amazon, the world's largest cloud computing and e-commerce company. Elon Musk, CEO and "Technoking" *[sic]* of Tesla,[2] also co-founded AI research company OpenAI. And then there is Facebook's founder and CEO, Mark Zuckerberg. Tellingly, they have been dubbed "the new *patriarchs* of digital capitalism."[3] But it is not just at these lofty heights of tech leadership where women are less present: women are not online as much as men; they represent only 20 percent of AI and computing science PhDs; and they constitute only 22 percent of AI professionals globally.[4] The trend is self-evident.

Of course, this picture of male dominance in the computing industry was not always so. Ada Lovelace sequenced the first computer program in the 1800s, and Mary Allen Wilkes programmed the first computer, known as LINC, in the early 1960s.[5] Women were thought to make particularly good programmers at that time, when coding was considered "female work" that was painstaking and menial like knitting or weaving.[6] IBM's 1950s brochure *My Fair Ladies* promoted the role of women in coding, and in 1968, *Your Career in Computing* urged those who liked "cooking from cookbooks" to consider becoming a programmer.[7] This all changed, of course, when computing became of national importance and men began to fill the roles.[8]

116

The "missing women in tech"[9] have had a direct footprint on the industry's culture. Yet it would be wrong to assume that the challenge we face is only the relative lack of women in science, technology, and design. Technology is not a neutral force;[10] it is also gendered and demands a gendered critique. In turn, scholars, activists, and technologists have sought to bring an overlooked gender perspective to their analysis of the design and deployment of these technologies. In the 1980s, feminist scholars from the Global North challenged how the development of new technologies was failing to account for women's knowledge. The 2000s saw the identification of other forms of excluded knowledge, including from the Global South and Indigenous perspectives.[11] In her writing on technology and feminism, British computer scientist Alison Adam attempts to re-center gender, race, and class by asking how knowledge is both created and represented in AI.[12] At a 2010 conference of the Special Interest Group on Computing Human Interaction, Sha-owen Bardzell went so far as to describe feminism as a natural ally in analyzing the interactions between computers and humans if we want to focus on concerns such as agency, identity, equity, and social justice.[13]

Accepting that a gender lens is needed in how we understand these technologies, the question for this chapter is how such a gendered standpoint can be applied to the regulation of AI. When ChatGPT (Chat Generative Pre-trained Transformer) launched in November 2022, what was merely imagination for some became reality for many: one million users started asking questions of this highly capable chatbot in its first week alone.[14] AI and ChatGPT became household names. Nonetheless, while generative AI was suddenly capable of generating a cover letter for your job application, few could explain how these intelligent, or even super-intelligent machines, actually worked. People started worrying about AI's influence over the granting of bank loans or determinations about who had a higher need for healthcare. AI was telling us what holidays we should take and what movies we should watch, but the vast majority of end-users lacked even a basic understanding of how.

Questions naturally emerged about oversight and how to establish, monitor, and enforce accountability for AI-driven technologies. A "race to regulate" emerged.[15] Within these regulatory discussions, there were varying levels of acknowledgment that the traditionally disadvantaged are similarly disadvantaged on the internet.[16] As the world's legislators attempt to regulate previously unforeseen legal challenges, the concerns of women and gender-diverse people risk being left at the margins of the debate.

The gendered harms of AI are increasingly well-known thanks to research by scholars of both human rights[17] and computing science.[18] Yet, beyond acknowledged harms and questions of access, the task of how to bring a gender perspective to the regulation of AI entails much more work. Nonetheless, there is a silver lining. Unlike the other areas of law discussed in *Rewriting the Rules*, AI offers the blankest canvas. There is a window of opportunity to get the law right from the beginning. This is less of a case of "rewriting the rules" than it is one of writing the right rules in the first place.

While organizations such as UNESCO contend that AI has the potential to advance women's empowerment,[19] evidently AI risks giving rise to new manifestations of old misogyny. Given that gender stereotypes are "part of AI's fabric,"[20] today's prospects might chalk up more cons than pros when we assess AI's potential to improve women's lives. Among such debates, this chapter seeks to offer something new to this debate. The role of regulating AI may not be only about protecting the rights of women and combating discrimination derived from the deployment and use of AI-driven technologies. Perhaps this is a moment to learn from the regulation of AI to understand law's role in promoting intersectional equality. AI has the capacity to consider more data variables—such as characteristics of sex, gender, age, race, or socio-demographic status—than in the past or by humans. AI regulation can both combat compounded discrimination, but also vice versa, it can promote equality based on intersecting characteristics.

In the sections that follow, we begin with an explanation of what AI is and what it means for women. I then turn to the core question: what good practice is emerging to regulate the risks of AI from a gender perspective? I finally consider how we might better regulate to achieve algorithmic fairness for a greater diversity of women.

AI AND WOMEN

What Is AI and What Are Its Biases?

AI is a relatively old idea but a relatively new reality.[21] So much so that debates over whether states should regulate AI or leave the creators of AI-driven technologies to self-regulation remain robust as this book goes to print. It is important to understand what we are trying to regulate, particularly in a context where terms like *AI*, *algorithms*, and *digitalization* have quickly developed "mythical-like qualities" and are often used with limited understanding.[22] Intelligence is a human trait. AI attempts to reproduce that "human intelligence" with similar or better results[23] through the use of "computers to classify, analyze, and draw predictions from data sets using a set of rules which we often call algorithms."[24]

Algorithms can be trained in different ways. First, you can have simple rules-based algorithms ("if X occurs, then Y"). These tend to be static and do not change their outputs for the same queries. Alternatively, you have systems that evolve and improve their outputs, such as those based on machine-learning.[25] Deep learning is a subset of machine learning that looks for patterns in data that are less apparent and more difficult to calculate.[26] The output generated through AI may be used to automatically make a determination (an automated decision-making system) on the one hand or enable a human decision-maker to make *seemingly* more accurate and efficient decisions (a decision support system, or DSS) on the other.[27]

It is broadly accepted that AI systems entail risks for societies. Yet the claim that algorithms can be biased went from "unorthodox" to "legion," writes AI expert Kate Crawford.[28] Some have also suggested that the gravest concern that AI poses is its misuse by authoritarian regimes,[29] but I and others have respectfully disagreed.[30] For women, the daily use of AI and the everyday risk of amplifying existing societal gender biases has far more persistent, widespread, and perhaps even largely undetected implications.

For instance, an AI-driven tool may use deep learning to determine the likelihood an applicant will repay a bank loan on time, a use of AI that poses a particular challenge for women whose data, based on their personal circumstances or credit history, may perform poorly compared to all available data.[31] Women of color and sole heads of households are particularly at risk. The root of the problem, therefore, does not necessarily lie with AI, but rather with the test or training data that contains biases that AI replicates.

As in the case of bank loans above, an automated decision-making system may "automatically" grant or deny an application for refugee status based on the available data. Alternatively, a DSS might *help* an official to determine an applicant's refugee status by providing information about the applicant's country of origin or offer insights from past applications, already processed, where the applicants were fleeing similar circumstances. This example exposes AI's limits. Fear is a key element in the legal definition of who qualifies for refugee status,[32] but it is questionable how well an "artificial" system can assess fear.

It is fair to ask whether the situation can be salvaged in cases where the final decision remains with a human who may exercise discretion in their use of the AI-driven outputs under a DSS. There is, for instance, an obvious racialized bias behind an AI's prediction that Black men in the US are more likely to offend. What if, Professor Sandra Mayson suggests, the consequence of the algorithm's finding is a decision to offer more support and social services to these men, rather than pursue incarceration; the bias can potentially be turned into a positive.[33] Yet, the underlying racialized bias remains and is legally and normatively relevant. The harm therefore lies in both the assumptions behind the prediction themselves as well as their application.

Natural language processing (NLP) is another form of AI that analyzes human language to identify rules, classify results and make predictions based on patterns in human language. NLP is used daily in machine translations, in personal assistant technologies like Siri and Alexa, and in text-based search engines.[34] NLP tends to focus on *content* without the necessary *context*[35] while methods to mitigate the biases resulting from NLP are relatively new.[36] Such gender biases in NLP can take various forms. Women may be represented in language a certain way, with gender biases in word associations: men are associated with "firefighters" and women with "nurses," or men as computer programmers and women as homemakers. Models are then trained on biased word embeddings.[37] Linguistic staging—the stages through which individuals and machines learn, produce or reproduce language, building on the foundations of existing social meaning—puts "son" before "daughter and "Mr." before "Mrs.," while the press and other forms of non-traditional media, from which the NLP will also learn, may describe a man by his behavior but a woman by her physical appearance and sexuality.[38]

NLP does not do well at incorporating "demographic" variation. Rather, it follows a "standard" approach to language: But whose standard?[39] NLP is critiqued for its better performance with "majority genders" i.e., men over women and non-binary people.[40] The same goes for white populations since character traits that would work better for, say, a white man from California than a woman of Latino or Arabic descent, might be considered more often by designers as they develop NLP.[41] Back in 2016, Google's speech recognition software was found to be 70 percent more accurate with male voices than female ones.[42] As Caroline Criado Perez, author of *Invisible Women*, pointed out, women may simply be left to lower their voice if their register is too high for voice-recognition software to work as well for them as it does for men.[43] This is of course a simplified reflection of a bigger set of problems, and many of the most outrageous examples have or are being corrected, but it provides a context for understanding the complexity of the regulatory environment to address, through law, the gendered harms of AI.

Understanding the Harms of AI and Its Underlying Causes

AI presents three potential harms to an individual: allocative harm, representational harms,[44] and knowledge-inequality-based harm. These harms can manifest in opportunities being withheld or burdens being imposed.[45]

Allocative harms result from AI-driven decisions that determine how goods and opportunities are allocated among a group. Here we can think of the way an AI system used in a recruitment process may disproportionately classify applications from male candidates as more suitable than female ones. Amazon scrapped its AI-driven recruitment tool in 2018 when it became evident that it was teaching itself that male candidates were better than female ones, penalizing resumés with the word *women*, whether describing the applicant's success as the "women's chess club champion" or being a graduate from an "all-women" college.[46] Rather than helping to diversify the workforce, the technology perpetuated men's dominance, after training on ten years of resumés primarily submitted by men. Yet as is well-known, male dominance did not begin with AI. AI's algorithmic biases merely reinforce it via a feedback loop, potentially resulting in lost financial opportunities, livelihoods, and freedom of choices for women when compared to men.

The second most cited type of harm of AI is representational. Representational harm comes about when systems reinforce gendered subordination through stereotyping, underrepresentation, or denigration. An AI system may take an open-source photo and assign to it a denigrating (for example, racist or sexist) trope. While for some "math is just math," if you do not correct the underlying biases, algorithms will be pegged to basic human assumptions and repeat them.[47] In other words, "bias in, bias out."[48] The point is well illustrated by one of the most cited representational harms. In 2024, forecasters predicted that the number of digital voice assistants would reach beyond 8 billion,[49] or more than one, on average, for every single person on the planet, while customer interactions from Chatbots, the majority of which are designed to convey a specific gender,[50] were expected to rise from 3.5 billion in 2022 to nearly 10 billion by 2026.[51] Amazon's Alexa, Apple's Siri, Microsoft's Cortana, and Google's Voice Assistant are all female-voiced, feeding into a gender stereotype that "she assists rather than directs; she pacifies rather than incites."[52] While Google's technology does not adopt a female name, "Siri" in Nordic translates to "beautiful woman who leads you to victory," while Cortana is adapted from the video game Halo's female avatar.[53]

The biases are multifold. For one, these virtual "beings" are presented not only as women but as white women.[54] Although they function in other languages, their dominant language is English, rendering their function and symbolic representation out of reach for some.[55] There is also an overt contrasting use of male voices. For instance, IBM's Watson uses a male voice to teach physicians about cancer treatment.[56]

AI's amplification of deep-seated inequality is evident across a spectrum of examples. Deepfakes—a technology that has been in development for decades but became a common term for synthetic media in 2017—use AI to transfer or map an image onto an existing video. According to *Forbes*, in 2019 alone the number of deepfakes online doubled from 7,964 to 14,679.[57] In 2025 their omnipresence makes it impossible to offer a reliable estimate. Deepfakes pose real risks and many of those create concrete legal dilemmas.[58] Deepfakes can be highly convincing. They are often viewed and understood to be real videos of those depicted, inciting political deception, voter manipulation, and commercial fraud.[59] Some deepfakes are better known, such as Barack Obama swearing at Donald Trump or Mark Zuckerberg bragging about stealing users' data.[60] Yet these forms of deepfakes have also been the object of specific regulation. For instance, in 2019, driven by concerns of swaying voters, California's governor made it illegal to create or distribute doctored videos, images, or audio of politicians within sixty days of an election.[61]

Yet when the political and pornographic come together, women are the primary targets in the use of nonconsensual intimate deepfakes. For instance, in 2016, the legal counsel of President Rodrigo Duterte used what is believed to be a deepfake pornographic video of Senator Leila De Lima to justify her imprisonment, believed to be in retribution for her critique of his authoritarian rule and "war on drugs," which saw the deaths of thousands of Filipinos at the hands of the Philippine national police.[62] Pornography has been the battleground for feminists for nearly a century,[63] with some scholars viewing any pornography as harmful.[64] The issue at hand here, however, is the nonconsensual use of intimate deepfakes, a form of image-based abuse that is clearly gendered in nature.[65]

The same can be said of other insidious uses of AI against women. After the June 2022 *Dobbs* decision[66] in the US overturned the constitutional right to an abortion established in *Roe v. Wade*,[67] women across the country were warned to delete popular menstrual cycle apps and switch to web browsers that did not store their history.[68] The arrest in Nebraska of a mother and her daughter, then aged seventeen, for an alleged abortion, tracked through chat history obtained from Facebook via a warrant, cautioned women of reproductive age what tech-based data could mean for their futures.[69] Readers need little reminder of how long women in the US have struggled to exercise a freedom of choice about termination of pregnancy. The problem here lies neither alone with AI nor with the decline of abortion rights for women; it is the colliding nature of both.

The third type of harm, which I have dubbed "knowledge inequality harm"[70] and which receives significantly less attention, derives from the vast gendered gaps in AI literacy. Individuals have different levels of understanding about how algorithms influence their lives, coupled with different skills and creative techniques to correct an algorithm's biases.[71] This inequality is exacerbated by the "missing women" in AI's design, deployment, use, and leadership, described at the opening of this chapter, which directly informs whose knowledge informs the creation of new technologies and whose knowledge does not. Moreover, Sri Lankan professor and CEDAW Committee member Rangita de Silva de Alwis urges developers "to work with female researchers in the Global South who have a more nuanced understanding of the ways in which these technologies may impact women in a particular culture,"[72] reminding us that the "missing women" narrative is often more complex than perceived.

We arrive at an appreciation that the root cause of the problem is not necessarily AI. Arguably the most concerning examples of AI's harm for women stem for pre-existing inequalities in our society and AI's capacity to amplify existing biases. What can regulation achieve in response?

TARGETING GENDER-BASED HARM THROUGH LAW

The need to bring a gendered lens to the regulation of AI's design, deployment, and use should be evident. Yet, while our canvas might be relatively blank, it is not entirely so. In just the last few years, China,[73] the US,[74] the EU,[75] Brazil,[76] South Korea,[77] and Australia,[78] to name some of the most-often-discussed examples, have taken steps to increase national-level technology governance, with many of these countries also investing heavily in the sector. Investment can propel legislative debates forward but alternatively, it may be the reason such debates stall. In the words of an Australian-based research team, "Incentives, standards and hard regulation are intertwined with geopolitical, technological and value-driven interests."[79]

Among the early legislators, only a few offer lessons for gender-responsive law-making. Calls for regulatory frameworks to be underpinned by human rights have been more evident. Clear ground was broken in May 2024, when the forty-six Council of Europe member states, the European Union, and eleven non-member states adopted the first-ever international legally binding treaty aimed at respect for human rights in the use of AI systems (Framework Convention on Artificial Intelligence and Human Rights).[80] Signed in September 2024, this development builds on a longer history of the Council of Europe's norm setting in the area of AI. Two soft-law instruments predate the convention: the December 2018 European Ethical Charter on the Use of Artificial Intelligence in Judicial Systems and their Environment and an April 2020 recommendation regarding the human rights impacts of algorithmic systems. Parties to the Convention are obliged to ensure that activities "within the lifecycle of artificial intelligence systems respect equality, including gender equality and the prohibition on discrimination."[81] In addition to non-discrimination,[82] emphasis is placed on transparency[83] and accountability.[84]

The above introduction to AI unraveled its tendency to replicate traditional disadvantage, a point also reflected in the debates leading to the Framework Convention. The Convention's Explanatory Report acknowledges that inequality may result from the AI-driven technologies themselves, but that societal biases also result when there has been "a failure to account for historical or current inequalities" such as "historical and structural barriers to gender equality."[85] One can read into the Framework Convention an obligation to not only avoid less favorable treatment—that is, discrimination that results from the use of an artificially intelligent system—but also to positively discriminate in order to actually overcome pre-existing systemic inequality facing women.[86] Herein lies AI's potential to be used to correct historical injustice and, by extension, to overcome intersectional inequality.

We are left with two contrasting pictures: a legal landscape where law and geopolitical interests (read: AI power) are intimately linked and, at times, hinder a focus on AI-driven harms on the one hand and an explicit call for a legislative approach underpinned by human rights on the other. What gender-responsive legislative practices may be emerging in response?

Discrimination and High-Risk AI

Risk is a clear AI legislative buzzword. Several regulatory systems—including the EU, Canada, South Korea, and (at proposal level) Brazil—adopt categories of risk for harm minimization. The EU's Artificial Intelligence Act was the first to cross the line as the most comprehensive regulation of AI worldwide. AI-driven technologies that fall into the highest risk category, "unacceptable risk," are banned outright. This includes real-time, remote biometric identification systems.[87] "High risk" applications are subject to strict obligations before they can be put on the market, including AI-driven technologies that score exams, which may determine access to education and impact a person's professional life; automated assessments of visa applications; and evaluations by law enforcement bodies of the reliability of evidence.[88] A range of other uses are left unregulated as having limited or minimal risk.[89] Interestingly, numerous parallels can be drawn between the EU's and South Korea's categorizations of risk, both recognizing in law that some AI applications are inherently more sensitive and therefore pose inherently more risks to people.

Included in the high-risk category are applications such as the CV-scanning tools, or Automated Employment Decision Tools (AEDTs), which risk prejudicing women. In July 2023, New York City took an auditing approach that attempted to eliminate such allocative harm in an employment context, prohibiting the use of AEDTs by employers to screen candidates or employees for employment-related decisions unless the tool had been subject to a "bias audit" conducted within the year prior to its deployment and only if all notice requirements had been complied with.[90] Under the New York approach, "independent auditors" cannot be employed by the organization or have a vested financial interest.[91]

Brazil has been through several iterations of an AI bill (currently Bill No. 2338/2023) that aims to regulate AI as a whole, as opposed to specific applications of the technology. The current draft (yet to be passed) focuses on an individual's or group's traits and is a standout example for its acknowledgment that harm is often intersectional and compounding and not necessarily based on a single trait. Both direct and indirect discrimination are defined in the bill which includes a long list of bases of discrimination, such as gender, sexual orientation, race, and socio-economic class.[92] Discrimination and disproportionate impacts are set out in extensive detail in article 12, including a prohibition on the implementation and use of AI systems that have a "disproportionate impact" due to personal characteristics such as geographic origin, race, color or ethnicity, gender, sexual orientation, socio-economic class, age, disability, religion, or political opinions.[93]

If enacted, the Brazilian law would protect the rights of those impacted by decisions made with an AI decision support system, granting them the rights to an explanation about the decisions, to contest those decisions and for human participation in the decision-making process.[94] In setting out a right to challenge AI-based decisions, the Brazilian approach would give affected people the right to request anonymization, blocking, or deletion of data that is unnecessary, excessive, or in violation of the legislation.[95] Not only is the government proposing transparency obligations for high-risk systems, but civil liability would exist as well for resulting damage.[96] A regulator would monitor and enforce the law. If the bill is passed, Brazil may fulfil its "potential to become a regional leader in AI policy-making"[97] as the "tropical giant" of AI.

Rigorous Requirements for Gender Assessments:
Quality Assurance Before Product Launch

Another gender-responsive possibility is a requirement to conduct a gender assessment. In 2019, Canada introduced the Treasury Board Directive on Automated Decision-Making, a mandatory policy instrument that applies to almost all federal government institutions when designing, procuring, or using AI-driven technologies.[98] It calls for impact assessments and transparency, including the likely impact of AI on freedom, health, the economy, and the environment.[99]

The standout feature of the Canadian directive is the Gender-Based Analysis Plus (GBA+), which entails compulsory testing for unintended gender biases and acts as a form of quality reassurance before production of an AI-driven technology commences.[100] It applies a risk categorization like that of the EU model: if an AI-driven technology meets the moderate, high, or very high-risk threshold, the designers need to undertake a GBA+. The "plus" signifies going further than other traditional gender-impact assessments required for government procurement of goods and services from commercial bidders and looking beyond sex and gender to account for other intersecting factors such as age, education, ethnicity, or religion.[101] An assessment must capture the impact of the automation on gender and/or these other identifying factors and name the planned or existing measures that are in place to address identified risks in the future.[102] In the case of algorithmic decision-making, for example, if disability were considered a relevant variable, separate equations would be generated for males and females, but disability would also be calculated (as a multiplier or coefficient) to determine how the outcome of having a disability differs between males and females.[103]

The GBA+ model has the potential to ensure that, at the funding stage, researchers involved in government-funded AI projects assess the potentially disparate impact on marginalized communities and identify how to optimize computational equality analyses, impact assessments and audits to reduce or even eradicate bias.[104] Preemptive planning can protect against the discriminatory and rights-based impacts of AI spiraling out of control and may also enhance public trust. Moreover, its application in other contexts in Canada—such as mining[105] and the defense forces[106]—means the domain of AI can learn and adapt from these other sectors where gendered impacts assessments have a longer history. This includes how to operationalize the law's recognition of intersectional harm.[107] In short, tried and tested models can be adapted for AI's gain.

Yet Canada's GBA+ remains poorly studied and it is not yet ascertained the degree to which GBA+ is applied in practice. In one instance, for example, the GBA+ requirement was not implemented in the case of an automated evaluation of resumés for a role in the Treasury Board of the Canadian Secretariat, despite the obvious gendered implications of its use and the stated goal "to improve hiring decisions and enhance the fairness and objectiveness of the hiring process."[108] Canada's GBA+ appears to offer much to both the public and private sectors' use of AI, but until a deeper evaluation of its application *and* effectiveness, the benefits remain less visible.

Trusted Flaggers of Harmful Content

On January 1, 2021, the National Artificial Intelligence Initiative Act came into force in the US.[109] Underpinning the act is the US's view that the US will lead the world in the "development and use of trustworthy artificial intelligence systems in the public and private sectors."[110] Little may have been expected of the US from an AI governance perspective after President Trump signaled a permissive approach to AI in an Executive Order for Removing Barriers to American Leadership in AI in January 2025,[111] which rescinded President Biden's Executive Order for the Safe, Secure, and Trustworthy Development and Use of AI.[112] Yet the United States became one of the most cutting-edge regulators in May 2025 when it enacted the Take it Down Act, which prohibits the nonconsensual online publication of authentic or computer-generated intimate visual depictions of individuals, in other words, a deepfake.[113]

Estimates suggest that more than nineteen out of every twenty deepfake videos on the internet in 2019 were pornographic.[114] Online platforms are required to remove nonconsensual depictions upon receiving notice of their existence. An individual is considered "identifiable" under the act where their face, likeness or another identifying feature is displayed,[115] with penalties including a fine or imprisonment for up to two years.[116] Given the magnitude of the problem, the workability of the US' take-down orders remain to be seen: platforms have to create a process for individuals to submit requests for removal, and upon receiving a valid request for removal, remove the material within 48 hours.[117]

California has also attempted to regulate harmful online content. In what was described as "sweeping legislation" in the form of Civil Code Section 1708.86, a private cause of action was established for the creation and intentional disclosure of sexually explicit material in the form of the deepfakes. Although narrow in subject matter, it provides wide-reaching protections for women as a group most likely to be harmed. The momentum, however, appears to have been short-lived. New York State followed suit in 2020, enacting a law to address synthetic or digitally manipulated media, but legislation in Maryland, Massachusetts, Pennsylvania, and Florida stalled at the bill stage.[118] Now, harmed individuals in those states can seek redress through the Take It Down Act.

We may expect other jurisdictions to follow suit with criminal and/or civil penalties. In September 2024, Australia criminalized the use of a carriage service—social media, internet or email for example—to transmit sexually explicit deepfakes without the consent of the person depicted. Yet concerns remains about Australia's capacity to implement such laws effectively.[119]

The EU Digital Services Act 2022 arguably has a more established track record, having created the figure of the trusted flagger, an independent expert whistleblower.[120] Organizations are appointed to the publicly funded role of trusted flagger if they meet specific criteria that include expertise in illegal content, independence from the platforms, and a demonstration of the integrity of their activities. Once content is flagged, the responsible entity—such as Meta or cloud servers such as Dropbox—is required to remove the content; if the content is not removed, the entity must explain why.[121] Trusted flaggers are required to publish reports at least once a year on their activities. These organizational appointments are also an exemplary opportunity to try to redress women's underrepresentation in the industry by deploying qualified women's groups to identify such online harm.

The binding nature of the role of trusted flaggers, embedded in law, has received praise.[122] Further, the EU makes the eligibility criteria for trusted flaggers explicit; there are performance reviews and oversight, both of which have been pinpointed as musts.[123] The EU's trusted flagger is not only replicable but also particularly well aligned to the relatively large number of nations with roles similar to that of e-safety or online safety commissioners,[124] even if those roles are not without criticism.[125] E-safety commissioners' mandates range from targeting child abuse materials to hate speech and violations of intellectual property,[126] and trusted flaggers can amplify that work. Moreover, the relatively new nature of regulation may allow us to take lessons from these experiences and adapt these models for application in other jurisdictions or to address the shortcomings—resourcing, transparency, effectiveness, and consistency—in the e-safety commissioner model.

Nonetheless, flagging and taking down content is a relatively micro response to a large-scale problem. Images can be copied and republished on multiple platforms; it is often hard to identify the perpetrator due to anonymity measures such as encryption, virtual private networks, and proxy servers that obscure locations and information about users. Arguably in such a context, the trusted-flagger model helps spread the resource-intensive nature of the task, but it too has its own capacity limitations.

A FEMINIST VISION FOR AI'S REGULATION

The discussion above offered concrete provisions that can rise to the level of gender responsive. Yet it remains valuable to ask what ethos should underpin the regulatory approach. In 2014, fifty activists and advocates working on sexual rights, women's rights, violence against women, and the internet gathered in Malaysia.[127] The outcome of their deliberations was "Feminist Principles of the Internet": seventeen principles organized into five clusters. The principles offer clear frameworks that can be adapted to optimize AI in ways that advance the interests of women.[128] The principles note, for instance, that women need unconditional, meaningful, and equal access. Women's movements need to use the space (of the internet) and, if we extrapolate, the tools of AI for feminist resistance and movement building. AI is a space of privatization and profit, whereas a feminist vision calls for "alternative forms of economic power" with a commitment to free and open-source software.[129] Many of these views have been brought into the mainstream.[130] Women need to maintain full control over their data, to the extent that this is possible, as we challenge surveillance and attempts to control or restrict women's bodies, speech, and activism.

The Terms-We-Serve-With is another feminist approach from which we can learn, in this case, to refuse to accept the present-day take-it-or-leave-it approach to terms-of-service agreements.[131] Its primary goal is a more meaningful and engaging form of consent and comes about as feminist activists come to terms with the realities of algorithmic systems in our lives by reconceptualizing such engagement as relational and less one-directional.[132] There is an attempt at co-constitution of user agreements between the user and supplier[133] and a more informed refusal mechanism that allows for opting out and for users to complain, dispute, or otherwise contest AI decisions and outcomes on an individual or collective level. Mediation is a key principle and seeks to be disclosure centered.[134] Here I offer two ways in which we can actively translate these values into our regulatory response to AI's gendered harms.

Bringing an Intersectional Perspective to AI's Regulation

AI relies on categorizations. Kimberlé Crenshaw's transformational approach to how we understand discrimination and inequality, where race, class, and sex/gender compound in their impact,[135] has informed every chapter of this book. Today, bringing an intersectional lens is well understood as a natural and necessary part of any critique of the law. By comparison, use of gender binaries or classification by race (such as "White, Black, Asian, Indian or Other") are "dangerously reductive".[136] Kate Crawford fears that with AI, we have seen the "myth of the pure type" remerge.[137]

Moreover, an algorithm sitting within a decision support system may be unable to identify which of a series of characteristics should be prioritized when making a decision with respect to, for example, an ethnic-minority female wheelchair user or an elderly gay man.[138] While human beings tend not to disaggregate into different, singular components, such as being female, being black, being heterosexual, or being atheist,[139] a computer might derive data from singular categories or derive it from other proxies: where you live, which bars you go to, which movies you watch, where you shop, or how you look in a photo. For a female headscarf user, AI by its nature would favor ethnic identity or gender rather than reconcile the two. Regulation must demand more from AI systems, embracing intersectionality by embracing equality as multidimensional.[140] With the right mindset and effort, algorithms can be remodeled, retested and refitted to better accommodate for gendered differences,[141] and by extension, other identifiable characteristics at the same time.

While the impact of AI on women's lives is increasingly recognized, gender-diverse people are particularly invisible in these regulatory debates. Over-inclusivity in AI modeling occurs when the technology wrongly assumes all individuals categorized as male or female share the same traits, ignoring variance within these groups; under-inclusivity results from the exclusion or misrepresentation of transgender, intersex, and other groups who do not align with neat binary divisions.[142] For instance, surveillance technologies are often incapable of working beyond the binaries of male and female.[143] Misclassification and misrecognition of identity by automated body scanners, facial recognition technologies, or social media content filtering go beyond the role of privacy regulation.[144] At present, no state in the US has in place legislation to address the consequences of gender misidentification by AI systems.[145] Canadian scholars too have pointed out, albeit in passing, the lack of accurate results for non-binary and gender-diverse individuals when generating assumptions from patient medical intake forms that retain "he" and "she."[146] I share these examples in agreement with Sonia Katyal and Jessica Jung, who argue that legal-oriented solutions have their limitations. For some gendered harms, a greater emphasis must be placed on design-oriented solutions, such as enabling self-determination of gender identities by AI's users and designing tools in ways that can acknowledge gender pluralism.[147]

Active Participation of a Diversity of Women in AI Governance

We have much to learn from *Rewriting the Rules'* earlier discussion of women in the boardroom. As in corporate leadership, women's underrepresentation in AI means that the design and development of these new and emerging technologies draws too heavily on "too narrow a talent pool."[148] Meanwhile, women dominate among those scholars who are critiquing the gender biases that result from AI's deployment. Higher participation of women must be recognized as a necessary step to bring visibility to the interests of those most affected by such biases.[149]

Yet the burden alone should not rest on the shoulders of the women sitting at the design table. Regulatory and nonregulatory requirements for AI should oblige private and public entities deploying AI-driven technologies to conduct gender-sensitive due diligence, ensuring the active participation of a diversity of women in AI's governance. The South Korean law, which prohibits its forty-five-member National Artificial Intelligence Commission from being composed of "only one gender"—effectively a one-woman quota—clearly does not go far enough.[150]

As discussed in chapter 4, where we recalled the obligations of businesses to conduct gender-sensitive due diligence in an effort to combat supply chain exploitation, such a responsibility for tech companies entails re-centering the experiences of women and girls and sexual and gender minorities and the multiple intersecting forms of discrimination that influence the realization of their equal rights.[151] Such gender-responsive due diligence, as a starting point, may facilitate recognition of the embedded gender norms, complex gender, socio-economic, and cultural and racial biases at play and the power imbalances involved in the design, deployment, and use of AI-driven technologies.

Gender-driven AI governance may involve ensuring that individual women and women's rights organizations are given the task of the trusted flagger discussed above. It might encourage gender quotas and targets among the most dominant developers of AI-technologies as part of their corporate social responsibilities. The promotion of women to leadership roles in organizations that are, in practice, shaping the industry is essential, given the male-centric nature of AI leadership worldwide. Concerted efforts are needed to close AI literacy gaps for groups at the periphery of the conversation, including women, in ways that may also help improve the explainability of AI's use, enabling more transparent and understandable AI-driven decisions. That the EU Artificial Intelligence Act acknowledges the need for "AI literacy" among affected persons is promising,[152] but it remains to be seen if and to what extent member states will incorporate this notion into national practice.

Before drawing this discussion to a close, it is essential to reflect upon the extent to which most jurisdictions leading the regulatory race discussed in this chapter—the US, the EU, and Canada—are "Northern." By contrast, 33 percent of the world is not online (2.7 billion people),[153] with these vast global differences in who enjoys the benefits of the internet rarely acknowledged. For those citizens online, the regulatory capacity of Southern States remains limited, creating the risk, among many, of their data being harvested—automatically collected with limited or no consent. Southern States are only seldom ready to deploy AI to truly improve public services. At the same time, most mappings of AI governance overlook the concerted efforts for South–South cooperation in Africa, including in Francophone and Lusophone countries and in Latin America. While at present, Brazil alone is paving the way in AI governance in the South, these regional groupings have called for a global effort to close the digital divide that is felt on gendered and racialized lines[154] and is a space to be watched in years to come.

CONCLUSION: I'D BLUSH IF I COULD

While users of Apple's Siri may be heavily dependent on the daily presence of voice assistant technologies in their homes, the technology has been deployed only since 2011. Siri once responded "I'd blush if I could" when a human user said to *her*, "Hey Siri, you're a bi***."[155] This highly servile and harmful response to verbal abuse was perceived as reifying and amplifying sexual harassment against real women. Siri's response has since been changed. Similarly, in a partnership with UNESCO, Brazil's largest financial institution, Bradesco, which uses a chatbot dubbed BIA, a common female name in Brazil, launched "BIA Against Harassment" in 2021. The bank's chatbot now tells users when their language is "inappropriate" and asks them, "Please, change the way you talk."[156]

Both examples are simultaneously shocking—that gendered abuse can be directed at a virtual entity—and yet hopeful, illustrative that algorithmic bias and AI's allocative, representational, and knowledge-inequality harms can be corrected, to varying degrees, with the right political will. Moreover, new emerging regulation of AI presents an opportunity to grasp the good in incipient regulation to ensure high-risk biased output will be subject to monitoring or banned altogether. The models emerging from Brazil, Canada, and the EU offer other nations a platform to think about legislating against intersectional discrimination.

None of the examples of emerging laws are perfect. Brazil has proposed a regulator in its bill; this is a gap that was identified in Canada in its now lapsed Artificial Intelligence and Data Act (AIDA).[157] Yet Canada has in place the foundations for such regulatory oversight—for instance, with the possibility of investing more in existing structures such as its Commissioners on Competition, Privacy, and Human Rights.[158] Meanwhile, concerns have been raised about the time involved in undertaking the in-depth gender assessments required under Canadian law. For some, this relatively high level of intervention undermines the Canadian government's goal to be agile.[159] Moreover, the examples named in this chapter as "promising" are all still relatively new. The world is still not where we need to be in terms of the regulation of AI in general, and even more so, from a gender perspective. However, our relatively blank canvas can enable the construction of a gender-responsive legislative approach that draws upon the most effective aspects of these models.

AI today is fostering much fear, especially from a gender perspective. Law in many respects is the David, while AI's continuous development in often unpredictable ways is the Goliath. In response, this chapter has highlighted that in the face of such rapid technological development and its seemingly unwieldly nature, law has a role to play and is, in some jurisdictions, fulfilling its potential to avoid papering over inequality that was so feared when a women-centered approach to lawmaking was called for many years ago. AI also reflects the reason why a challenge to gender neutrality in law remains as relevant in the twenty-first century as when the call was first made.

Conclusion

The Practicalities of Rewriting the Rules

Feminists have, from time to time, described patriarchy as a secret garden, carefully guarded and not readily accessible to "nonmembers." The premise of this book has been that law may be the underutilized key to unlocking and dismantling both what is known and what is unknown about patriarchy's ability to sustain an unjust and unequal world. *Rewriting the Rules* has sought to contribute to the unlocking process by presenting law's fullest potential in ways that are, at times, pragmatic and in other moments, it is hoped, visionary.

There is an urgency to this call to unlock patriarchy's door. Present-day alarm over the state of progress on gender inequality is indeed justified: 54 percent of the world's countries do not have a legal definition for rape that is based on the lack of freely given consent, and 51 percent of countries globally have at least one restriction preventing women from doing the same jobs as men.[1] One-quarter of the way through the twenty-first century, surely we expected far greater progress than where the world stands today. Despite decades of demands from feminists, a reading of *Rewriting the Rules* reveals the extent to which gender-responsive laws remain a campaign, not a reality. *Some* relief over this slow progress can be found in legal scholar Davina Cooper's appreciation of the potential in these yet-to-be-realized proposals for law reform.[2] As Cooper notes, "Prefigurative proposals may begin life as speculative ideas about future reforms and later (even much later) become new laws."[3]

Yet *Rewriting the Rules* also illustrates the difficult task of finding the middle ground between the pragmatic and the visionary. Can gender-responsive laws take shape as both "a viable legislative text and as a more subversive intervention to unsettle and reimagine gender's relationship to law?"[4] Or is this task of truly unsettling only the realm for the gender transformative? *Rewriting the Rules* has created a path that meanders through both fields—practical and hopeful. It has offered the frameworks and good practice where they exist and where they do not, a vision for gender-responsive future law-writing.

My response to the task has been what some might consider too pragmatic. The structures that sustain the supply chains from the South to the North (chapter 4) and the formal mining giants that create the possibility of artisanal and small-scale mining work for women in the first place (chapter 5) remain dominant and their power challenged in only limited ways in this book. Yet the idea has been to pursue change from within existing structures and systems. In 1972, General Motors elected its first female to its board, Catherine B. Cleary, a woman born into a prominent family and who had previously served the boards of Kraftco Corporation and the Northwestern Mutual Life Insurance Company. In 1974 in her commencement address at Lawrence University entitled "Our Changing Institutions: A Challenge to the Liberally Educated," she opined: "If one wants to improve the system, then the choice becomes whether to work within our institutions or to attack them, so to speak, from the outside. Both roles can be valuable. Both can contribute to change. Some people are happier as observers, critics or protesters than as participants. In the last analysis, however, change and hopefully improvements will take place only when the people within institutions act, and that is why, I suppose, I feel the greatest challenge and the greatest opportunity to effect change lies within our institutions."[5] This is the well-worn battle of feminist scholars who are unsure how much to use the "master's tools" or dismantle them altogether.

Rewriting the Rules is a call for those who are working from within, and I hope it honors the great feminist reformers who have come before me. The book opened by acknowledging the "feminist templates" offered through feminist judgments and the feminist legislation projects that identify law as a constructive force for women, while acknowledging the harm it causes for failing to legitimize women's diversity. At times, law has caused more division than consensus among feminists. Borrowing from Rosemary Hunter's deep engagement with feminist judgments projects, *Rewriting the Rules* has sought to "engage in law on its own terrain" and "equally clearly accept that it plays an important role in shaping the contours of women's lives."[6]

With this pragmatic mindset, I close here with an action-oriented map of the way forward. Much of the roadmap presented in *Rewriting the Rules* is untested. Bills are still under review and therefore several proposals for gender-responsive law reform are yet to make it to the law books. This may not surprise many. After all, if it were easy to achieve, why are we not there yet? Here I conclude by laying out what it might take to see a rewriting of the rules come to fruition, to move from the imagined to the realized.

LEADING AND LAGGING

I have traversed the world during the years I have researched and written this book. As noted in chapter 2, I point to the Philippines with reluctance when I am asked which country leads the way. It is a nation that illustrates perfectly well that while a country can lead in one domain, it may equally lag in another. In moving forward, we may need to accept shifts between leading and lagging. In November 2001, the death of Filipina actor Maria Teresa Carlson-Fariñas made headline news in the Philippines. She took her life, jumping from the twenty-third floor of her apartment building. Carlson-Fariñas was the wife of Rodolfo Fariñas, then a Filipino governor, against whom she had made public accusations of domestic violence. By making visible the reach of domestic violence in the Philippines, her suicide helped to mobilize Task Force Maria, a coalition of at least twenty-three organizations[7] that was instrumental in the 2004 enactment of the Anti-Violence against Women and Their Children Act, which foregrounded chapter 2. That 2004 law made the country a world leader, the first to introduce ten days of paid workplace leave for victims of domestic violence. Several other examples in the law books justify naming the Philippines as a global leader on gender-responsive lawmaking, including gender-responsive budgeting and being one of the few countries in the world with a Magna Carta of Women,[8] dating from 2009.

Nonetheless the world's first country to offer paid workplace leave for victims has become the very last to legalize divorce. In March 2025, the Absolute Divorce Bill passed the Philippine Congress, after narrowly passing the House of Representatives one year earlier—126 in favor and 109 against, with 20 abstentions—to provide limited grounds for divorce. These include physical violence or gross abuse against the petitioner or their child; inducing the petitioner or their child to engage in prostitution; imprisonment; drug addiction; homosexuality; and marital infidelity.[9] A country of world firsts is therefore also one where women have long struggled to leave violent relationships, able to separate but not legally divorce, often forced to seek costly and complicated annulments to escape an unwanted marriage. It is impossible for a global study of this kind, therefore, to pedestal any individual country. The search for good practice must be much more nuanced, deeper, and critical.

IMPLEMENTING

Most of the scholars and activists engaged in the project of reimagining law's potential through feminist rewrites of legislation and judgments would have been asked at some point in their journey, "What good is a law if it is not implemented?"

Again, the Philippines' world leadership in providing paid leave for victims of violence is illustrative of the complexities in moving from paper to the realities of rewriting women's lived experiences of law. A 2015 survey by the International Trade Union Confederation Asia-Pacific found that only 39 percent of its Filipino affiliates were aware of the legally mandated paid domestic violence leave—a level of awareness that I suspect is higher than many other jurisdictions where the leave is available—and more importantly, only 23 percent of affected workers chose to use the leave.[10]

There are many factors that shape whether a victim will choose to use available leave. Filipino data indicates that one in four surveyed respondents faced unfriendly employers when they reported their experience of domestic violence in their attempt to access leave entitlements.[11] It is easy to assume that legislation, once enacted, will be employed to its optimum to change mindsets and hold institutions and individuals to account for its enforcement.[12] Yet even the very best of laws fail to deliver expected impact far too often, perhaps because the barriers to successfully implement laws are underestimated.

Implementation often involves journeying along a potholed road and no area of law is immune to inadequate implementation.[13] A failure to allocate funds, adapt institutions, and monitor impact can be witnessed from gender-equality quotas[14] to land rights reforms.[15] Political will intertwines with budgetary decisions, making chapter 7's focus on institutionalizing gender-responsive budgeting in law fundamental. Moreover, an unimplemented but "good" law can in fact be harmful. Writing about security law and corruption, Utpal Bhattacharya and Hazem Daouk highlight the negative implications of an unimplemented law with no recourse. In writing this book, I generally disagree with their view that sometimes "no law is better than a good law" that remains unimplemented.[16] Yet I acknowledge that unimplemented legislation can upheave the system, with impunity for gender-based crimes an ongoing global challenge.

The implementation of legislation as hoped for may also prove a challenge when the law itself contains loopholes. When it comes to child marriage, amendments in Chad, Costa Rica, Ecuador, Guatemala, Malawi, Mexico, Nepal, Panama, and Zimbabwe raised the minimum age for marriage and eliminated or reduced exceptions that allow the marriage of a child to go ahead with parental or judicial consent. By contrast, since 2017 in Bangladesh, it is permissible to determine that it would be "in the best interests of the child" for the child to marry, reflecting law's retrogression on women's rights through the very manner in which the rules are written.[17] It is these provisions that ultimately undermine a law's gender-responsive potential that must be identified and repealed.

That law reform is complicated and unpredictable is evident as we lay out this roadmap. Nonetheless, once again, overcoming obstacles to implementation is a road well traversed by feminists who remain all too aware of the task that lies ahead. The conditions that give rise to implementation—systems, capacity-building, bodies of oversight, for example—must be set up, budgets created that make implementation possible, and the people put in place to hold lawmakers to account to ensure that laws achieve what they have been enacted to do. Those impacted must be given knowledge of their rights. Public debate must accompany law reform, particularly in areas where a shift in mindset is needed—think of the familial norms that need changing to achieve a more equal division of childcare among parents. The intensity of resistance must not be underestimated.

MOBILIZING

At the heart of law reform, we can almost always find women activists pushing for change. Their voices and actions sit behind each chapter of this book. I use this juncture to offer my deep respect for their activism for law reform—however long in duration, however demanding in energy, and whether or not successful.

Nonetheless, the feminist agenda necessarily requires mobilizing around a common cause. Compromises are inevitable since campaigns frequently call for a unifying goal. South African political scientist Amanda Gouws brings this to light in her comparison of the mobilization of activists worldwide in response to the high-profile rape cases in India and South Africa between December 2012 and February 2013 of Indian physiotherapy student Jyoti Singh (referred to in chapter 1) and South African Anene Booysen, both of whom died after severe and cruel injuries sustained after multiple rapes by a group of perpetrators.[18] The Singh case revealed a deep divide between feminists in India who wanted justice and those willing to go so far as to call for the death penalty.[19]

Such campaigns also risk getting "locked into a certain dependency on the parliamentary lawmaking schedule that constrains activism."[20] Criminalization does not always identify the root of the problem as gender inequality. Nor do all campaigns for reform advance equality while achieving gender justice. This "common" ground for feminists may also be particularly difficult to find. The outcomes of such advocacy for law reform can never fully meet the expectations of all women's rights and feminist groups. Women's movements are, after all, a plurality: conservative and progressive, faith-based and nonreligious organizations, pragmatists and visionaries and those who seek to be both.[21]

At the same time, the vivid imagery of thousands of people who took to the streets in India and South Africa in sweeping demands for justice proves the arguments of Laurel Weldon and Mala Htun that aligned and mobilized feminist movements have been instrumental in GBV law reform.[22] Although diverse in nature or perhaps precisely because of such diversity, the mobilization of feminist and women's groups can be the most powerful and essential force in driving forward a gender-responsive legal agenda. This remains the case even if compromises are involved in determining a campaign's course of action toward the goal of gender-responsive legislation. Feminist movements and their allies must continue to shake down the parliamentary doors and find themselves a place, even if it is from the balconies of parliament.[23] For it is through such visibility that legislators can be reminded of their obligations to center gendered concerns in lawmaking.

DE-CATEGORIZING

Argentinian decolonial scholar Maria Lugones, in her writing on the "coloniality of gender," urges us to see the world free of categories. Our concern can be neither gender, race, sexual orientation, nor economic inequality alone, but rather our cause must be liberation as we stand with all who have been disenfranchised.[24] It seems self-evident that in rewriting the rules from a gendered standpoint, this book has sought—in a small way—to move beyond separable categories. The need to center poor, racialized, and otherwise marginalized women threads across the pages of this book. Where parents lack access to parental leave schemes—and even when they do exist—a particular socio-economic class of women frequently undertakes the work of paid caregiving. Same-sex couples are regularly disentitled from the same paid leave benefits accorded to different-sex couples due to the mechanisms of the law. It is women migrant workers, often from rural and poor communities, who are most at risk of exploitation in the supply chains of the textile, clothing, and footwear industries. Artisanal and small-scale mining remains predominantly the work of women of color in the Global South, often lower-educated and poor.

A feminist call to center gender and sex evidently is therefore only just the first step. This reality may be self-evident to many and we have moved, at least theoretically, away from a perspective where it is considered sufficient to just add feminism to law. Elizabeth Sheehy's collection of chapters by that very name, "Adding Feminism to Law,"[25] published at the turn of the century in honor of retired Canadian judge Claire L'Heureux-Dubé, the first female on the Quebec Court of Appeal and the second-ever female on the Supreme Court of Canada, reminds us that in its infancy, much of the work of rewriting the rules was largely—sometimes solely—focused on gender. In her Canadian jurisprudence, Sheehy is credited for bridging the "gap between law and the lived reality of women's lives" and for demonstrating "that purportedly 'neutral' norms are not at all neutral, but adopted from a particular, and usually male, perspective."[26]

Recognizing the progress we have made in calling for a more concerted effort to rewrite legislation with women in mind, our most pressing task is to facilitate institutions that make laws—as well as those that interpret them—to bring an intersectional appreciation to their roles. Women must be considered in all their diversity for law to truly understand and respond to the different ways in which *different* women live law. It is only through this intersectional lens that rewriting the rules may achieve emancipation that is inclusive, expansive, and potentially transformative in its end results.

AUDITING

It is sometimes impossible to know how to attribute the enactment of a law. Multiple factors are normally at play in a law's passage and lawmakers are only one strand. Nonetheless, we will never achieve gender-responsive lawmaking if the "feminist+ templates" for gender-responsive laws are not understood, accepted, and adopted by the lawmakers who have the power to ensure the passage of gender-responsive bills. We must institutionalize this way of thinking.

In 2022, my work creating the Gender Legislative Index found a relatively central place in the parliamentary motion of an independent member of Parliament, Ruth Forrest, in Australia's small island state of Tasmania. The successful motion led to the creation of the Joint Sessional Gender and Equality Audit Committee,[27] the first such parliamentary committee in any Australian state or territory (or federally) to exclusively focus on auditing bills for their gendered impact.[28] The committee has since shed light on the experiences of older women in Tasmania, who face a heightened risk of homelessness, and the Tasmanian LGBTQI+ community, which faces discrimination in access to healthcare.

It may be that gender audit committees—while at times categorizing and treating gender as a silo—offer one tool to use law to pursue a more just, equitable, and livable future for a diversity of women. Over fifty such gender audit committees are in existence in parliaments in over forty countries around the world.[29] Despite the potential of audit work to bring a gender lens to the law, these bodies have been largely overlooked by legal scholars, instead the subject of notable debate among political scientists who have shown a particular concern with institutionalizing feminism in parliaments.[30] Insufficient effort has been invested in assessing whether auditing actually makes laws better despite the fact that how a law is drafted can produce or reproduce the problem of gendered discrimination, limiting or even working against the apparent intention of legislation.[31]

In introducing audit committees as one tool to operationalize the frameworks set out in *Rewriting the Rules*, we must also ask if there is a role for civil-society engagement and how we can ensure that those individuals most affected by law reform are heard.[32] And a certain type of listening by law reformers is required, with an openness, receptivity, and attentiveness to what is being said and what is not said,[33] which was called for at the outset of this book. Better listening may enable women's lived experiences to actually be accounted for as we go through the process of gender-auditing bills before their passage.

DECOLONIZING

Last but perhaps foremost, I address a challenge that has underpinned several of the discussions in this book: can the law bring about changes needed by women if the dominant economic order remains unchanged? The World Bank and the International Monetary Fund remain in many ways colonial in character, while power within the United Nations sits disproportionately in the hands of the five permanent members of the Security Council. The absence of permanent representation from Africa or Latin America must be called into question.[34]

This book was written fifteen years after the 2008 global financial crisis; several years after the COVID-19 pandemic changed the way individuals and nations think about health, risk, and connectedness; and in the midst of the Russian invasion of Ukraine and the reigniting of conflicts in the Middle East. If there was ever a need for a more central role of the Global South in the world's decision-making, it is now. *Rewriting the Rules* has called for a revaluing of knowledge systems from the South. It has sought to challenge a narrative of the West as the central holder of the best-practice legislation when it comes to gendering law and calls for a different canon that accounts for the experiences of the non-Western world to be central, representative, and not to be Othered.

As we look forward, our imaginations will necessarily be constrained if the Global North is our primary purview. Even well-trodden ground, such as the right to a safe and legal abortion, is fundamentally constrained in most Global North jurisdictions by what appears a choice between criminalizing or decriminalizing women's control over their bodies. Contrastingly, situating abortion access and post-abortion care in public health legislation is still only experimental and has been witnessed in only select parts of the world. Here again, the Global South has had more success in a health-based approach to abortion *and* in ways that go beyond a "tinkering around the edges" of the criminal law prohibitions on abortion access that dominate other parts of the world.[35]

FINAL WORDS

In the last paragraphs of *Rewriting the Rules*, I revisit where we stand. In the last half century, gender equality has become a political agenda in many nations. For one, women's rights and gender equality agendas are often appropriated during electoral periods. Unsurprisingly, therefore, not all feminists have been pleased to see the harnessing of feminism by other legal scholars, governments, and organizations. For some academics, this "feminist" rhetoric has claimed a "feminist success story" when there has not, indeed, been demonstrable success. Well-meaning feminist agendas are easily folded into global and world affairs.[36] While still controversial in some jurisdictions, gender-based violence as a legislative issue, for example, went from a "universally ignored" one[37] to become a "tidal wave" of national domestic violence legislation.[38] Even when confronted by limited resources and competing priorities,[39] governments have shown the will to drive legislative and policy reform to curb domestic violence nationally.

We can choose to view this "success" as the appropriating of a feminist agenda. However, that the language of sexual violence has resonated with governments, global political actors, organizations, entities, and institutions can be viewed in a different way: as evidence that feminism has been influential and significant. A radicalism too has successfully driven—in the eyes of many scholars, including myself—a feminization of international law.[40] Nonetheless, a violence-free world remains "one of the key struggles and wishes of our age."[41] It is therefore a story of mixed success.

Learning from these experiences, the task at hand is to ensure that the making of gender-responsive laws does not become mere political rhetoric but rather reality. Simultaneously the lessons from the South must be borrowed with care and appreciation, not merely repacked for Western eyes and Western benefit without paying due thanks for this shared knowledge. It is intended that the chapters in this book have paid adequate respect to my feminist fore-sisters and to the successes and struggles of Southern activists whose hard work has led to the frameworks presented in the pages of this book. I hope that *Rewriting the Rules* offers not just the guidance but, importantly, the momentum to move us from ambition toward the true realization of equality in law and with thanks to gender-responsive law reform.

NOTES

PREFACE

1. Interview by Ramona Vijeyarasa with Indonesian women's rights activist and non-governmental organization director, Jakarta, Indonesia, May 2, 2019. Ethics approval was obtained from the University of Technology Sydney (UTS HREC ETH17-1449).

INTRODUCTION: WHY WE NEED TO REWRITE THE RULES

1. Inter-Parliamentary Union, "Monthly Ranking of Women in National Parliaments."
2. UN Women, "Facts and Figures."
3. Lungu, "Women and Representative Bureaucracy in Zambia."
4. Groeneveld, Bakker, and Schmidt, "Breaking the Glass Ceiling, but Facing a Glass Cliff?"
5. Australian Government, Office of Parliamentary Counsel, "Our Staff."
6. Australian Government, Office of Parliamentary Council, *Annual Report 2020–2021*, 55.
7. Dodd–Frank Wall Street Reform and Consumer Protection Act. For more information, see Ban et al., *A Woman's Voice in the House*, 12–13. Note too that women made up more than 28 percent of the 118th Congress, the highest percentage in US history. For more, see Leppert and Desilver, "118th Congress Has a Record Number of Women."
8. "Supplementary Information Tables: Gender-Based Analysis Plus."
9. Senate of the Philippines, "Legislative Process."
10. Vijeyarasa, *The Woman President*.
11. Fischer, "Framing Gender"; "Legistics: Gender-Neutral Language."
12. Christopher Williams, "The End of the 'Masculine Rule'?"

13. See, e.g., Schweikart, "The Gender Neutral Pronoun Redefined."

14. Vijeyarasa, "In Pursuit of Gender-Responsive Legislation," 3.

15. Vijeyarasa, "Does Law Matter?" 115.

16. Guerrero Salazar, "Repercusión mediática del informe de la RAE sobre el lenguaje inclusivo en la Constitución española"; Marrades, "Language and Gender."

17. Halperin-Kaddari and Freeman, "Backlash Goes Global," 185.

18. Mooney, "When a Woman Needs to Be Seen, Heard and Written as a Woman."

19. Mansbridge, "Should Blacks Represent Blacks and Women Represent Women?"; Mansbridge, "Quota Problems"; Beckwith, "Numbers and Newness"; Celis and Childs, "The Substantive Representation of Women"; Childs and Krook, "Analysing Women's Substantive Representation."

20. Mohanty, *Feminism Without Borders*, 29.

21. Ailwood et al., "Beyond Women's Voices," 229–34.

22. Alam, "Majority World."

23. van Staveren, "To Measure Is to Know?"

24. Permanyer, "A Critical Assessment of the UNDP's Gender Inequality Index," 19.

25. Pailey, "De-Centring the 'White Gaze' of Development," 733.

26. Permanyer, "A Critical Assessment of the UNDP's Gender Inequality Index," 19; Butalia and Falkof, "Making Feminist Sense in the Global South."

27. Kapur, "Gender, Sovereignty and the Rise of a Sexual Security Regime in International Law and Postcolonial India," 332.

28. Graycar and Morgan, "On The Hidden Gender of Law," 32.

29. Warren, "What Is a Women's Issue," 23.

30. Vijeyarasa, *The Woman President*; Bello y Villarino, "Women in Anticorruption Laws."

31. Conklin, "Grandstanding or Gotcha."

32. Butler, "Performative Acts and Gender Constitution."

33. Ramji-Nogales, "Revisiting the Category 'Women,'" 242.

34. Ramji-Nogales, 242.

35. Ramji-Nogales, 242.

36. Tatonetti, *Written by the Body*; Greif, "Upward Translations"; Rosenblum, "Unsex Cedaw, or What's Wrong with Women's Rights."

37. Otto, "Afterword," 534.

38. Otto, "Introduction," 2.

39. Oko, "Legal Education and Training in Nigeria," 271.

40. Milner, "Legal Education and Training in Nigeria," 286.

41. Tamale and Bennett, "Legal Voice," 73.

42. See Dror, "Law and Social Change."

43. Sukadana, Karma, and Ujianti, "Can Local Law Prevent Polygamy?"

44. Mack, "One Feminist Asks, 'Is Polygamy Inherently Bad for Women?'"

45. Hull, "The Cultural Power of Law and the Cultural Enactment of Legality." See also the discussions on the extent to which same-sex relations remain criminalized in countries in the Asia region in Vijeyarasa, "Flamer-Caldera v. Sri Lanka."

46. Ofosu et al., "Same-Sex Marriage Legalization Associated with Reduced Implicit and Explicit Antigay Bias."

47. "On Its Tenth Birthday, Gay Marriage in America Is Under Attack," *The Economist*.

48. Arrow, *The Seventies*, 11.

49. Kapur, "The (Im)Possibility of Queering International Human Rights Law," 135.

50. Smart, "The Woman of Legal Discourse," 31.

51. Bildhauer, Røstvik, and Vostral, *The Politics and History of Menstruation*.

52. Maglaty, "When Did Girls Start Wearing Pink?"

53. Smart, *Feminism and the Power of Law*, 68.

54. Smart, 67.

55. Graycar and Morgan, *The Hidden Gender of Law*, 38.

56. Fineman, "Challenging Law, Establishing Differences," 29.

57. Dobbs v. Jackson Women's Health Organization, 597 US 215 (June 24, 2022).

58. Smart, *Feminism and the Power of Law*, 2.

59. Just to name a few, consider Davies, *Asking the Law Question*; Graycar and Morgan, "Law Reform"; Smart, *Feminism and the Power of Law*; Charlesworth, "Not Waving but Drowning"; and Thornton, *The Liberal Promise*.

60. UN Women and Inter-Parliamentary Union, *Gender-Responsive Law-Making*, 12.

61. Vandenbeld and Hoa Ly, "Women's Representation in the National Assembly of Viet Nam," 14.

62. Vijeyarasa, "Quantifying CEDAW," 78.

63. Hillman, "The Limits of Gender Quotas"; Krook and Norris, "Beyond Quotas."

64. Masson, "Changing State Forms, Competing State Projects."

65. Matsuda, "When the First Quail Calls," 298.

66. Genovese, "Goode v. Goode," 379.

67. Gay-Antaki, "Feminist Geographies of Climate Change."

68. MacGregor, "'Gender and Climate Change.'"

69. Thomson, "The Foetal Subject"; Jerneck, "What About Gender in Climate Change?"

70. I thank Dr. Salmah Eva-Lina, who framed the goal as one of "collective liberation" at the ANU Conference on Gender & Cultural Diversity in Politics: Australia, Asia and the Pacific, July 13–15, 2022, in Canberra. Eva-Lina, who at the time was acting co-CEO of the International Women's Development Agency, expressed her sense of this collective liberation as a sought-after freedom of women, especially women of color, from colonial repression. Borrowing from Eva-Lina's language, the term is used here to capture the potential change that law can deliver for all women and girls in all their diversity.

1. GENDER AND THE LAW: A FRAMEWORK FOR DEFINING GENDER-RESPONSIVE LEGISLATION

1. Franzese, "Reclaiming Our Noble Profession," 307.

2. Charlesworth, "Talking to Ourselves?"

3. Charlesworth, 17.

4. See Rubio-Marín, "Global Gender Constitutionalism and Women's Citizenship," in which she explains the response of a faculty member when she declared her decision to start researching gender and constitutionalism. Her decision would be "acceptable" so long as she could still demonstrate her "true credentials" in other (read: more legitimate) areas of constitutional law.

5. Hunter, McGlynn, and Rackley, "Feminist Judgments," v.

6. Hunter, McGlynn, and Rackley, v.

7. Majury, "Introducing the Women's Court of Canada," 2.

8. Hunter, McGlynn, and Rackley, "Feminist Judgments," 3.

9. Hunter, McGlynn, and Rackley; Hunter and Rackley, "Feminist Judgments on the UK Supreme Court."

10. Douglas et al., *Australian Feminist Judgments*.

11. Stanchi, Berger, and Crawford, *Feminist Judgments*.

12. Enright McCandless, and O'Donoghue, *Northern / Irish Feminist Judgments*.

13. McDonald et al., *Feminist Judgments of Aotearoa New Zealand*.

14. Cowan, Kennedy, and Munro, *Scottish Feminist Judgments*.

15. Chandra, Sen, and Chaudhary, "Righting Together."

16. Hodson and Lavers, *Feminist Judgments in International Law*.

17. Manji, "Taking on the State."

18. Gonzalez de la Vega Hernandez et al., *Sentencias feministas*.

19. Raj, *Feeling Queer Jurisprudence*, 5.

20. Ferreira, Moscati, and Raj, *Queer Judgments*.

21. Raj, *Feeling Queer Jurisprudence*, 7, 42.

22. Watson and Douglas, *Indigenous Legal Judgments*, 2.

23. Watson and Douglas, 17.

24. Rogers and Maloney, *Law as If Earth Really Mattered*.

25. Dancer, Holligan, and Howe, *UK Earth Law Judgments Project*.

26. Batagol and Vijeyarasa, "Lighting the Spark," 188.

27. Smith and Kimmel, "The Hidden Discourse of Masculinity in Gender Discrimination Law," 1828.

28. Vijeyarasa, "Proposing a Gender-Responsive Reform of the Australian 'Modern Slavery' Act."

29. Cooper, "Crafting Prefigurative Law in Turbulent Times."

30. Batagol and Vijeyarasa, "Lighting the Spark," 198.

31. Vijeyarasa, "Making the Law Work for Women," 277.

32. Vijeyarasa, 277.

33. Hevener Kaufman and Lindquist, "Critiquing Gender-Neutral Treaty Language."

34. Hyland, Djankov, and Goldberg, "Do Gendered Laws Matter for Women's Economic Empowerment?"

35. Hyland, Djankov, and Goldberg, 2.

36. Vijeyarasa, "Making the Law Work for Women," 277.

37. Vijeyarasa.

38. Vijeyarasa, "Quantifying CEDAW," 75.

39. United Nations General Assembly, Convention on the Elimination of All Forms of Discrimination against Women, art. 2.

40. United Nations General Assembly, art. 2(a).

41. United Nations General Assembly, art. 3.

42. Chesler, "Who Wrote CEDAW?," 114.

43. Chesler, 114.

44. See United Nations General Assembly, Convention on the Elimination of All Forms of Discrimination against Women, art. 21 which provides for the creation of General Recommendations.

45. CEDAW Committee, General Recommendation Nos. 12, 19, and 35.

46. CEDAW Committee, General Recommendation No. 21.

47. United Nations General Assembly, Optional Protocol to the Convention on the Elimination of All Forms of Discrimination against Women.

48. Vijeyarasa, "Three Decades of CEDAW Committee General Recommendations," 802.

49. Zwingel, "Women's Rights Norms as Content-in-Motion and Incomplete Practice."

50. Baldez, *Defying Convention*, 112.

51. Banda, "The Limits of Law," 269.

52. Paige, "The Maintenance of (International Peace and Security) Heteronormativity," 92.

53. Nesiah, "Missionary Zeal for a Secular Mission," 155.

54. Heathcote, "Naming and Shaming," 85.

55. Nussbaum, "Women's Progress and Women's Human Rights," *Human Rights Quarterly*, 602.

56. Nussbaum, "Women's Progress and Women's Human Rights," in *The Limits of Human Rights*, 232.

57. Vijeyarasa, *The Woman President*, 71–75.

58. Bustelo, "The CEDAW Committee at the Crossroads," 104.

59. Sardar Ali, "Women's Rights, CEDAW and International Human Rights Debates," 75, n4.

60. Merry, *Human Rights and Gender Violence*, 221.

61. Merry, 221.

62. Merry, 221.

63. Vijeyarasa, "Quantifying CEDAW," 73–74.

64. See, e.g., Crenshaw, "Race, Reform, and Retrenchment"; hooks, *Ain't I a Woman*.

65. MacKinnon, *Toward a Feminist Theory of the State*, xii.

66. McCall, "The Complexity of Intersectionality," 1771.

67. Bowleg, "The Problem with the Phrase 'Women and Minorities,'" 1267.

68. Campbell, "CEDAW and Women's Intersecting."

69. Atrey, "Women's Human Rights," 874.

70. Atrey, 872–73.

71. Atrey, 873.

72. Nussbaum, "Women's Progress and Women's Human Rights," *Human Rights Quarterly*, 612, n66.

73. Fineman, "Challenging Law, Establishing Differences," 40.

74. Fineman, 32.

75. World Bank Group, *Women, Business and the Law 2022*.

76. Agarwal, "Gender and Land Rights Revisited."

77. Agarwal, 204.

78. Hindu Succession Act 2005, sec. 6, India.

79. Deininger, Goyal, and Nagarajan, "Women's Inheritance Rights and Intergenerational Transmission of Resources in India," 130.

80. Deininger, Goyal, and Nagarajan, 136.

81. Daley, Dore-Weeks, and Umuhoza, "Ahead of the Game," 132.

82. Daley, Dore-Weeks, and Umuhoza, 132.

83. Daley, Dore-Weeks, and Umuhoza, 137–38.

84. Roberts, *Is International Law International?*, 210.

85. Roberts, 3.

86. Ammann, "Language Bias in International Legal Scholarship," 823.

87. Rosenblum, "Internalizing Gender," 778.

88. Theumer, "The Self-Perceived Gender Identity."

89. Wood, "Rights of Nature."

90. Hyland, Djankov, and Koujianou Goldberg, "Gendered Laws," 481.

91. World Economic Forum, "Only 14 Countries Have Full Equal Rights for Women."

92. Hyland, Djankov, and Koujianou Goldberg, "Gendered Laws," 481.

93. Dirlik, "Global South," 13.

94. Dados and Connell, "The Global South," 12.

95. Liebowitz and Zwingel, "Gender Equality Oversimplified," 375.

96. OECD, "France—Restricted Civil Liberties."

97. Caprioli et al., "The WomanStats Project Database," 841–42.

98. Vijeyarasa, "Quantifying CEDAW," 52.

99. For more, see Spivak, "Can the Subaltern Speak?"

100. Lau, "The Language of Westernization in Legal Commentary," 508.

101. Shrivastava, "The Power of Celebrity Culture and Its Response to Rape and Sexual Violence against Women in Post-2012 India."

102. Sikand, "India's Daughter."

103. Sikand, 119.

104. Butalia and Falkof, "Making Feminist Sense in the Global South," 4.

105. Grovogu, "A Revolution Nonetheless," 178.

106. Basu, "The Global South Writes 1325 (Too)," 368.

107. Pahuja, *Decolonising International Law*, 28.

108. Okafor, "Newness, Imperialism, and International Legal Reform in Our Time," 186.

109. Raj, *Feeling Queer Jurisprudence*, 11.

110. Marecek and Appuhamilage, "Present but Unnamed," 319.

2. GENDER-BASED VIOLENCE: RECLAIMING THE GLOBAL SOUTH'S LEADERSHIP ON WORKPLACE LEAVE FOR VICTIMS

1. UN Women, "In the Biggest Electoral Year in History, 113 Countries Have Never Had a Woman Head of State."

2. Republic Act No. 9262, Anti-Violence Against Women and Their Children Act of 2004, Philippines.

3. Republic Act No. 9262, sec. 43.

4. See explanations provided in a comparative study of the Philippines and Australia by McFerran, Fos-Tuvera, and Acherhard-Hodges, "An Employment Right," 182–83.

5. Vijeyarasa, *The Woman President*, 120–21.

6. World Economic Forum, *The Global Gender Gap Report 2024*, 298.

7. Some data presented in this chapter was adapted from an earlier work: Vijeyarasa, "Comparing Whose Laws?," reproduced with the permission of Kluwer Law International.

8. For instance, Argentina lags behind other states in Latin America in terms of data gathering, compounding a "profound lack of knowledge among Argentine women about domestic violence laws and what kinds of services are available to them." See Susan Franceschet, "Explaining Domestic Violence Policy Outcomes in Chile and Argentina." See

also Vijeyarasa, "Does Law Matter?," 719, regarding implementation challenges in Spain with the dissolving of the Spanish Ministry for Equality in 2010. Merged into the Ministry of Health, Social Services and Equality under austerity measures, it was only reestablished as an independent Ministry of Equality in 2020.

9. Republic Act No. 9262, Anti-Violence Against Women and Their Children Act of 2004, sec. 35, Philippines.

10. Domestic Violence—Victims' Protection Act 2018 No. 21, New Zealand.

11. Roy and de Jong, "'A Huge Win.'"

12. Pennington, "Workplace Policy Reform in New Zealand," 39.

13. Weatherall, Gavin, and Thorburn, "Safeguarding Women at Work?," 568.

14. Specifically, *The Guardian* noted: "This article was amended on 26 and 27 July 2018. An earlier version said that New Zealand had achieved a world first by introducing paid leave for people experiencing domestic violence. This was corrected to include information on similar provisions in the Philippines and parts of Canada." See Roy and de Jong, "'A Huge Win.'"

15. Fair Work Amendment (Paid Family and Domestic Violence Leave) Act 2022, Australia.

16. Ripoll, "Australia to Introduce Paid Domestic Violence Leave"; see also Vijeyarasa, "Comparing Whose Laws?," for more analysis. The Surf Coast Shire Council is believed to be the first employer to have negotiated paid family and domestic violence leave in a workplace agreement.

17. See, for example, Harpur, Douglas, and Joo, "Submission to the Fair Work Commission," 3–4, in which neither the Philippines nor any Latin America jurisdiction are named under the section "precedents."

18. Widiss, "Domestic Violence and the Workplace," 672.

19. Laharnar et al., "Workplace Domestic Violence Leave Laws," 122.

20. Laharnar et al., 122.

21. Galanter, "Reading the Landscape of Disputes"; Burke, *Lawyers, Lawsuits, and Legal Rights.*

22. Widiss, "Domestic Violence and the Workplace," 683.

23. Johnson and Gardner, "Domestic Violence and the Workplace," 594.

24. Zachary, "Precautionary Measures Curb Workplace Violence Liability."

25. Baird, McFerran, and Wright, "An Equality Bargaining Breakthrough," 192.

26. Swanberg, Ojha, and Macke, "State Employment Protection Statutes for Victims of Domestic Violence," 587.

27. Baird, McFerran, and Wright, "An Equality Bargaining Breakthrough," 192.

28. Widiss, "Pregnancy and Work," 670.

29. Employment Standards Code, Manitoba, Canada.

30. International Labour Organization, Violence and Harassment Convention 2019, art. 10(f).

31. Stanford, *Economic Aspects of Paid Domestic Violence Leave Provisions*, 9.

32. Stanford, 9.

33. Obama, Presidential Memorandum.

34. Oliver et al., *The Economic and Social Costs of Domestic Abuse*, 5.

35. Australian Council of Trade Unions, "Historic Day as Paid Family & Domestic Violence Leave to Come into Force."

36. Stanford, *Economic Aspects of Paid Domestic Violence Leave Provisions*, 17.

37. A modern award is a document that sets out the minimum terms and conditions of employment on top of the Australian National Employment Standards such as the maximum weekly hours of work and requests for flexible work arrangements.

38. Bankwest Curtin Economics Centre for the Australian Council of Trade Unions, *Family and Domestic Violence Leave Review*, 16.

39. Stanford, *Economic Aspects of Paid Domestic Violence Leave Provisions*, 7.

40. Stanford, 12.

41. Stanford, 5.

42. Stanford, 5.

43. Stanford, 10.

44. Stanford, 5.

45. Ley Orgánica 1/2004, sec. 1, Spain.

46. Asamblea Nacional de Venezuela, "Exposición de motivos," 1; Ley Orgánica sobre el derecho de las mujeres a una vida libre de violencia, Venezuela.

47. Ley Orgánica 1/2004, 3.

48. Gobierno de El Salvador, *Plan Quinquenal de Desarrollo: 2010–2014*, 57.

49. Ministerio de la Mujer y Desarrollo Social, *Plan Nacional contra la Violencia hacia la Mujer 2009–2015*, 4, Peru.

50. World Economic Forum, *The Global Gender Gap Report 2024*.

51. Lixinski, "Regional Indigenous Rights and the (Dis)Contents of Translation," 13.

52. Veronelli, "The Coloniality of Language" 109.

53. Veronelli, 114.

54. Veronelli, 115.

55. Mudimbe-Boyi, *Beyond Dichotomies*.

56. Álvarez and Truffello, *Legislación comparada de protección a las trabajadoras víctimas de violencia de género*, 8.

57. Franceschet, "Explaining Domestic Violence Policy Outcomes in Chile and Argentina," 5; CEDAW Committee, General Recommendation No. 35, ¶ 32(b).

58. Organization of American States, Inter-American Convention on the Prevention, Punishment, and Eradication of Violence against Women, sec. art. 7(e).

59. Organization of American States, sec. art. 7(f).

60. Organization of American States, sec. art. 7(g).

61. Meyer, "Negotiating International Norms."

62. Ley Orgánica sobre el derecho de las mujeres a una vida libre de violencia, sec. 4(8), Venezuela.

63. Ley Orgánica, sec. 34.

64. Ley para prevenir, sancionar y erradicar la violencia contra las mujeres y los integrantes del grupo familiar, sec. 11(c), Peru.

65. Ley para prevenir, sancionar y erradicar la violencia, sec. 11(c).

66. Ley para prevenir, sancionar y erradicar la violencia, sec. 11(b).

67. Ley para prevenir, sancionar y erradicar la violencia, sec. 11(a).

68. Código de Trabajo de la República de El Salvador, sec. 203.

69. Ley especial para una vida libre de violencia para las mujeres, El Salvador.

70. Ley especial.

71. Ley Orgánica Integral para prevenir y erradicar la violencia contra las mujeres, Ecuador.

72. Ley Orgánica Integral, sec. 28(g).

73. Establece normas sobre accidentes del trabajo y enfermedades profesionale, sec. 16, Chile.

74. Establece normas, sec. 16.

75. Denisse Patricia Muñoz Tempio contra Suseso, Compin y Consalud.

76. Ley de violencia hacia las mujeres basadas en genero, sec. 40, Uruguay.

77. Ley Orgánica 1/2004, Spain.

78. Ley Orgánica, sec. 21(1) and 21(2).

79. Ley Orgánica, sec. 21(3).

80. Ley Orgánica, sec. 21(3).

81. Ley Orgánica, sec. 21(4).

82. Ley Orgánica, art. 21(2) and 21(4).

83. Ley Orgánica, art. 21(5).

84. Ley Orgánica, art. 21(5); Real Decreto 1917/2008, art. 9, Spain.

85. Ley de Municipios Autónomos del Estado Libre Asociado de Puerto Rico, sec. 11.016 (3).

86. Ley para la administración y transformación de los recursos humanos en el Gobierno de Puerto Rico, sec. s9.1 (2)(3).

87. Ley de Licencia Especial, Puerto Rico, sec. 3.

88. Régimen de Licencia Especial, Río Negro, Argentina.

89. Franceschet, "Explaining Domestic Violence Policy Outcomes in Chile and Argentina," 11.

90. Polischuk and Fay, "Administrative Response to Consequences of COVID-19 Emergency Responses."

91. Employment Standards Code, sec. 59.11(3), Manitoba, Canada.

92. Stone, "How the Family and Medical Leave Act Can Offer Protection to Domestic Violence Victims in the Workplace," 729–30.

93. Krause, "The Domestic Violence Leave Act," 167; Stone, 730.

94. Domestic Abuse (Safe Leave) Act (Northern Ireland) 2022, sec. 112EG.

95. Work Life Balance and Miscellaneous Provisions Act 2023, sec. 7, Ireland.

96. McIntyre, Motion for Leave to Bring in a Bill.

97. Fitz-Gibbon, Pfitzner, and McNicol, "Domestic and Family Violence Leave across Australian Workplaces," 301–2.

98. Rosenblum, "Internalizing Gender," 777.

99. Frankenberg, "Critical Comparisons," 412.

100. Frankenberg, 412.

101. Frankenberg, 413.

3. PARENTAL LEAVE: DETANGLING PREGNANCY AND PARENTING TO CHALLENGE THE "SEXED" AND "GENDERED" NATURE OF LEAVE

1. Real Decreto Legislativo 2/2015, sec. 48(4), Spain.

2. Meil et al., "Trends towards De-Gendering Leave Use in Spain and Portugal," 220.

3. Porter, "Combating Gender Inequality at Home and at Work," 203.

4. Weiss, "Celebrity Dads Raising Awareness About Paternity Leave."

5. Fredman, "Reversing Roles," 443.

6. Albrecht et al., "Fathers in Charge?," 50.

7. Caparas, "Work-Family Balance and Family Poverty in Asia" 8.

8. Eydal and Rostgaard, "Policies Promoting Active Fatherhood in Five Nordic Countries," 267.

9. International Labour Organization, Maternity Protection Convention, C003 (1919).

10. United Nations General Assembly, Convention on the Elimination of All Forms of Discrimination Against Women.

11. Suk, "From Antidiscrimination to Equality," 81.

12. Fredman, "Reversing Roles," 442.

13. Rosenblum, "Unsex Mothering: Toward a New Culture of Parenting," 61. See also David Fontana and Naomi Schoenbaum, "Unsexing Parenting," who similarly critiqued the failure of the law to "disaggregate sex" from carework in ways that pigeonhole women as primary carers and men as breadwinners.

14. Schank, "When Women Choose Children Over a Career."

15. See analysis of Justice Abella's judgment written for the majority in *Fraser v. Canada* in Mathen, "Equality before the Charter."

16. Bartick, "Losing Women, Losing Breastfeeding," 313.

17. Bartick, 313.

18. See, for instance, Baird, "Orientations to Paid Maternity Leave," 266; Anam, "Inadequacies and Variations of Maternity Leave Policies throughout the World"; Albagli and Rau, "The Effects of a Maternity Leave Reform on Children's Abilities and Maternal Outcomes in Chile"; Dowd, "Maternity Leave"; Guendelman et al., "Juggling Work and Breastfeeding"; Miller et al., "The Maternity Leave as a Role Negotiation Process."

19. See, for example, Datta Gupta, Smith, and Verner, "Child Care and Parental Leave in the Nordic Countries"; Nakazato, "Has 'Nordic Turn' in Japan Crystalized?"

20. Bergmann, "Parental Leave in the United States."

21. Saypoff, "Breeding Incentives."

22. Fredman, "Reversing Roles," 442.

23. Brandth, Bungum, and Kvande, "Fathers, Fathering and Parental Leaves," 173.

24. Ray, Gornick, and Schmitt, *Parental Leave Policies in 21 Countries*, 5; Rocha, "Promoting Gender Equality through Regulation," 54.

25. Rocha, 52.

26. Meil et al., "Trends towards De-gendering Leave Use in Spain and Portugal," 225.

27. Vijeyarasa, "Misdirected by the 'Daddy Quota.'"

28. Son, "The Origin of Social Policy for Women Workers," 70.

29. International Labour Organization, Maternity Protection Convention, C003.

30. Jackson, "Degendering Reproduction?," 346.

31. Fredman, "Reversing Roles," 449.

32. International Labour Organization, Maternity Protection Convention C183 (2000), sec. art. 4(1).

33. International Labour Organization, ILO Convention Concerning Equal Opportunities and Equal Treatment for Men and Women Workers, art. 1(2).

34. Maternity Protection Recommendation, R191, art. 1(1).

35. Faur, "Contrasting Trends in Gender and Childcare in Argentina," 621.

36. Eydal et al., "Trends in Parental Leave in the Nordic Countries."

37. Ahmed and Fielding, "Changes in Maternity Leave Coverage," 1.

38. Suk, "From Antidiscrimination to Equality," 81.

39. Eydal and Rostgaard, "Policies Promoting Active Fatherhood in Five Nordic Countries," 267.

40. European Parliament and Council of the European Union, Directive on Work-Life Balance for Parents and Carers and Repealing Council Directive 2010/18/EU, ¶19.

41. European Parliament and Council of the European Union, Directive on Work-Life Balance for Parents and Carers and Repealing Council Directive 2010/18/EU, ¶20 and Article 8(1).

42. Petts and Knoester, "Paternity Leave-Taking and Father Engagement."

43. Cools, Fiva, and Kirkebøen, "Causal Effects of Paternity Leave on Children and Parents."

44. Månsdotter, Lindholm, and Winkvist, "Paternity Leave in Sweden."

45. Baird, Hill, and Gulesserian, "Expanding Paternity Leave in Southeast Asia."

46. Hill et al., "Young Women and Men," 788.

47. Meil et al., "Trends towards De-gendering Leave Use in Spain and Portugal," 221.

48. Ray, Gornick, and Schmitt, *Parental Leave Policies in 21 Countries*, 4.

49. Eydal and Rostgaard, "Policies Promoting Active Fatherhood in Five Nordic Countries," 258.

50. Eydal and Rostgaard, 258.

51. Eydal and Rostgaard, 258.

52. Vijeyarasa, "Does Law Matter?," 699.

53. Act on Maternity and Parental Leave, sec. 8, Iceland

54. Lomaz Jørgensen and Høg Utoft, "Maternity Leave as Upskilling," 3.

55. Maternity Act (Act on the right to leave and unemployment benefit in case of maternity), ch. 4, sec. 6, Denmark.

56. Cañero Ruiz and Marinova, "¿Iguales e intransferibles?"

57. Vijeyarasa, "Does Law Matter?," 716.

58. Vijeyarasa, 702.

59. Constitución de la República del Ecuador, art. 333; Rubio-Marín, "On Constitutionalism and Women's Citizenship," 259.

60. Pérez-Hernández and Escobedo, "Mexico," 132.

61. Pérez-Hernández and Escobedo.

62. Güezmes García and Vaeza, "Advances in Care Policies in Latin America and the Caribbean" 22; Pérez-Hernández and Escobedo, "Mexico," 137.

63. Güezmes García and Vaeza, 22; Pérez-Hernández and Escobedo, 137.

64. International Labour Organization, Maternity Protection Convention (Revised), C103 (1952), art. 4(8); see also Murray, "The International Regulation of Maternity," 38.

65. Vijeyarasa, "Misdirected by the 'Daddy Quota.'"

66. Aspects of the graphs presented in this chapter appear in two earlier publications: Vijeyarasa, "Between Equality and Stagnation"; Vijeyarasa, "Misdirected by the 'Daddy Quota.'"

67. Regimen de Contrato de Trabajo, sec. art. 158, Argentina.

68. Código del Trabajo, art. 54, Dominican Republic.

69. Código de Trabajo, sec. 61(o)(3), Guatemala.

70. Código del Trabajo, sec. 6(a), Colombia.

71. Código del Trabajo, sec. art. 152, Ecuador.

72. Albrecht et al., "Fathers in Charge?," 49.

73. Salcedo, "The Dilemma on 'Daddy Days.'"

74. Loong, "National Day Rally 2015."

75. Regimen de Contrato de Trabajo, sec. 177, Argentina.

76. Ley General del Trabajo, sec. art. 61, Bolivia.

77. Código del Trabajo, sec. 236, Dominican Republic.

78. Código del Trabajo, sec. 152, Ecuador.

79. Código de Trabajo, sec. 152, Guatemala.

80. Código del Trabajo, sec. 135, Honduras.

81. Ley Federal del Trabajo, sec. 170(II), Mexico.

82. Código del Trabajo, sec. 141, Nicaragua.

83. Child Development Co-Savings Act 2001, sec. 12AA, Singapore.

84. Labour Code, sec. 54, Afghanistan.

85. Bangladesh Labour Act (Amendment) 2023.

86. UNICEF, "2 in 3 Infants Live in Countries Where Dads Are Not Entitled to a Single Day of Paid Paternity Leave."

87. Paternity Leave and Benefit Act 2016, sec. 6, Ireland.

88. Federal law supplementing the Swiss Civil Code, sec. 329(g).

89. Maternity Protection Act, 1994, sec. 8, Ireland.

90. Federal law supplementing the Swiss Civil Code, sec. 329(f).

91. Mun and Brinton, "Workplace Matters," 8.

92. Nakazato, "Culture, Policies and Practices on Fathers' Work and Childcare in Japan," 244.

93. Transferable parental leave in Japan is paid at 67 percent of base pay for the first six months and then 50 percent of base pay for the following six months; it has been adopted by nearly every large firm in Japan.

94. Labor Standards Act, sec. art. 65, Japan.

95. Childcare and Family Care Leave Act, sec. art. 9(2), Japan.

96. Nakazato, "Culture, Policies and Practices on Fathers' Work and Childcare in Japan," 244.

97. Lau, "Japan Wants 85% of Male Workers to Take Paternity Leave."

98. European Court of Human Rights, Hallier and Others v. France.

99. Décret no 2021–574 du 10 mai 2021, sec. art. 1 and 2, France.

100. Wong et al., "Comparing the Availability of Paid Parental Leave for Same-Sex and Different-Sex Couples in 34 OECD Countries," 529.

101. Wong et al., 533.

102. Yogyakarta Principles.

103. Yoon, "South Korea Court Recognizes Equal Benefits for Same-Sex Couple."

104. Bong, "Negotiating Resistance/Resilience through the Nexus of Spirituality-Sexuality of Same-Sex Partnerships in Malaysia and Singapore."

105. Vijeyarasa, "Misdirected by the 'Daddy Quota.'"

106. Constitutional Court of Colombia, Parejas Adoptantes del Mismo Sexo, para. 52.

107. Constitutional Court of Colombia, Parejas Adoptantes del Mismo Sexo, para. 262.

108. Wong et al., "Comparing the Availability of Paid Parental Leave for Same-Sex and Different-Sex Couples in 34 OECD Countries," 531.

109. Código del Trabajo, 207, Chile.

110. Souza, "Parenting Intentions of Same-Sex Couples," 45.

111. Código de Trabajo de Costa Rica, sec. 95(a).

112. Nygård and Duvander, "Social Inclusion or Gender Equality?," 308.

113. Alaattinoğlu and Margaria, "Trans Parents and the Gendered Law," 606.

114. Alaattinoğlu and Margaria, 603–4.

115. Föräldrabalk [Children and Parents Code] 1949:381, sec. 11, Sweden.

116. Alaattinoğlu and Margaria, "Trans Parents and the Gendered Law," 615.

117. Alaattinoğlu and Margaria, 605.

118. Alaattinoğlu and Margaria, 617.

119. Alaattinoğlu and Margaria, 616.

120. Hosse, Rahman, and Roy, "Paternity Leave," 287.

121. "ILO Welcomes Bangladesh's Plan to Introduce Paternity Leave."

122. Wiryawan, "The Rights of Paternity Leave for Husbands in Indonesian Legal Renewal."

123. Regimen de Contrato de Trabajo, sec. art. 177, Argentina.

124. Regimen de Contrato de Trabajo, sec. art. 158.

125. Proyecto de Ley No 29409, Peru.

126. Modifícanse las Leyes 19.121, 20 de agosto de 2013, y 19.161, Uruguay.

127. Bartick, "Losing Women, Losing Breastfeeding," 313–14.

4. MODERN SLAVERY: GIVING VOICE AND VISIBILITY TO THE GENDERED EXPERIENCES OF SUPPLY CHAIN EXPLOITATION

1. Asian Development Bank, *Promoting Women's Economic Empowerment in Cambodia*, 24.

2. Franceschini, "Outsourcing Exploitation."

3. Ward, "Gender Regimes and Cambodian Labor Unions," 580.

4. Wilhelm et al., "Private Governance of Human and Labor Rights in Seafood Supply Chains," 1.

5. Wilhelm et al., 1–2.

6. Human Rights Watch, *Hidden Chains*.

7. International Labour Organization, Work in Fishing Convention, C188 (2007).

8. Sinclair and Dinshaw, "Paper Promises?," 46.

9. Monfort, "The Role of Women in the Seafood Industry," 14.

10. Carr, Chen, and Tate, "Globalization and Home-Based Workers," 134–35.

11. "In the Gulf 99% of Kenyan Migrant Workers Are Abused, a Poll Finds."

12. Lichuma, "(Laws) Made in the 'First World,'" 497–98.

13. California Transparency in Supply Chains Act.

14. Modern Slavery Act, United Kingdom.

15. Relative au devoir de vigilance des sociétés mères et des entreprises donneuses d'ordre, France.

16. Initiatiefvoorstel Wet Zorgplicht Kinderarbeid, Netherlands.

17. European Parliament and Council of the European Union, Regulation (EU) 2017/821 laying down supply chain due diligence obligations.

18. Modern Slavery Act No. 153, Australia.

19. Salmivaara, "New Governance of Labour Rights," 331.

20. Lambooy, "Corporate Due Diligence as a Tool to Respect Human Rights," 404.

21. Fudge, *Constructing Modern Slavery*, 11.

22. Lichuma, "(Laws) Made in the 'First World,'" 522.

23. Lichuma.

24. Lichuma, 500.

25. Vijeyarasa, "A Missed Opportunity," 857.

26. Cheng, "Sex Trafficking," 364.

27. Vijeyarasa, *Sex, Slavery and the Trafficked Woman*, 24–25.

28. Davina Cooper's beautiful exploration of the "prefigurative project"—those that foreshadow a future society—has been a fundamental crutch for my work on modern slavery and aided me to find peace with where the arguments offered in this chapter sit on a spectrum from imagined to real. For more, see Cooper, "Towards an Adventurous Institutional Politics."

29. Donovan, *White Slave Crusades*, 2.

30. Allain, "White Slave Traffic in International Law," 6.

31. International Agreement for the Suppression of the White Slave Traffic.

32. International Convention for the Suppression of the White Slave Traffic.

33. Doezema, "Loose Women or Lost Women?"

34. Brown, "Am I Not a Woman and a Sister?," 1; Maynard, "The World's Anti-Slavery Convention of 1840."

35. League of Nations, Convention to Suppress the Slave Trade and Slavery, sec. Art. 1(1) and 1(2).

36. United Nations Office of the High Commissioner of Human Rights, Supplementary Convention on the Abolition of Slavery, the Slave Trade, and Institutions and Practices Similar to Slavery, sec. art. 1(a), 1(b), 1(c) and 1(d).

37. Johnson, *Sisters in Sin*, 120.

38. Bell-Williams, "'Shop-Soiled' Women."

39. Perkins, "Wicked Women or Working Girls."

40. United Nations General Assembly, United Nations Convention against Transnational Organized Crime.

41. United Nations, Protocol against the Illicit Manufacturing of and Trafficking in Firearms; Protocol against the Smuggling of Migrants; and Protocol to Prevent, Suppress and Punish Trafficking in Persons.

42. Vijeyarasa, "A Move in the Right Direction?," 177.

43. Jahnsen and Skilbrei, "Debate—From Palermo to the Streets of Oslo"; Doezema, "Now You See Her, Now You Don't"; Gallagher, "Two Cheers for the Trafficking Protocol."

44. United States Department of State, "What Is Modern Slavery?"

45. Australian Federal Police, "Human Trafficking and Slavery."

46. Chuang, "Exploitation Creep and the Unmaking of Human Trafficking Law," 611.

47. Vandergeest and Marschke, "Modern Slavery and Freedom," 292; see also Vijeyarasa and Bello y Villarino, "Modern-Day Slavery."

48. Kim and Di Sauro, "Is Canada Closer to Enacting Modern Slavery Legislation?"

49. Norwegian Ministry of Foreign Affairs, "Born to Live in Freedom: Strategy to Strengthen Development Efforts to Combat Modern Slavery (2021–2025)."

50. Chapkis, "Trafficking, Migration, and the Law," 926.

51. Langlois, "No Regional Pattern," 329.

52. Davis, Miles, and Quinley, "'Same Same, but Different.'"

53. Sagafi-nejad and Dunning, *The UN and Transnational Corporations*.

54. Bello y Villarino, "Middle Point, End of the Road or Just the Beginning?," 5.

55. Nolan and Boersma, "Regulating the Business of Modern Slavery," 116.

56. Taylor, "The UN and the Global Compact," 975.

57. Taylor, 975.

58. Weissbrodt and Kruger, "Norms on the Responsibilities of Transnational Corporations and Other Business Enterprises with regard to Human Rights."

59. Office of the High Commissioner for Human Rights, *Guiding Principles on Business and Human Rights*.

60. Ruggie, "Protect, Respect, and Remedy."

61. Amis, *Building a Movement*.

62. Kreitzen, "Comparative Study on Greenwashing in the Cosmetics Industry," 9–10.

63. Wettstein, "CSR and the Debate on Business and Human Rights."

64. Andersen, "Businesses and Human Rights."

65. Bourke-Martignoni and Umlas, *Gender-Responsive Due Diligence for Business Actors: Human Rights-Based Approaches*.

66. Bonnitcha and McCorquodale, "The Concept of 'Due Diligence' in the UN Guiding Principles on Business and Human Rights," 900.

67. Bonnitcha and McCorquodale 908–9.

68. Human Rights Law Centre, "Submission to Joint Standing Committee on Foreign Affairs, Defence and Trade on Establishing a Modern Slavery Act in Australia, Submission no. 27.

69. Modern Slavery Act, sec. 54, United Kingdom.

70. Modern Slavery Act (Commonwealth), Australia.

71. Advisory Committee of the Modern Slavery Registry, "Submission No. 9 to Joint Standing Committee on Foreign Affairs, Defence and Trade," Australia.

72. Modern Slavery Act, Australia.

73. California Transparency in Supply Chains Act.

74. Dodd–Frank Wall Street Reform and Consumer Protection Act, §1502.

75. Obama, Executive Order.

76. Obama, "Statement by the President on the Easing of Sanctions on Burma."

77. Initiatiefvoorstel Wet zorgplicht kinderarbeid, Netherlands.

78. Relative au devoir de vigilance des sociétés mères et des entreprises donneuses d'ordre, France.

79. Poirot, "Devoir de vigilance des entreprises." The law came into effect in March 2017, but the proposed civil penalties for violating corporations were struck down following a decision of the Constitutional Council. See Décision no 2017–750 DC, du 23 mars 2017, Text No. 2 of 99.

80. European Union, Directive 2014/95/EU.

81. European Parliament and Council of the European Union, Regulation (EU) 2017 /821.

82. European Parliament and Council of the European Union, Directive (EU) 2024/1760, para. 19.

83. European Parliament and Council of the European Union, para. 19.

84. Vijeyarasa, "A Missed Opportunity."

85. Vijeyarasa and Liu, "Fast Fashion for 2030," 60–61.

86. Vijeyarasa and Liu, 59.

87. Vandergeest and Marschke, "Modern Slavery and Freedom," 292.

88. Stevenson and Cole, "Modern Slavery in Supply Chains."

89. For more, see proposed Second Reading Speech in Vijeyarasa and Batagol, "'Members of Parliament: Hear the Women, Count the Women, and Ensure Corporate Accountability.'"

90. Statement by NSW Anti-Slavery Commissioner Dr. James Cockayne on the Review of the Modern Slavery Act 2018 (NSW).

91. Vijeyarasa and Batagol, "'Members of Parliament.'"

92. Rende Taylor and Shih, "Worker Feedback Technologies and Combatting Modern Slavery in Global Supply Chains," 136–37.

93. Wang, "How Managers Use Culture and Controls to Impose a '996' Work Regime in China That Constitutes Modern Slavery"; Franceschini, "Outsourcing Exploitation."

94. Rende Taylor and Shih, "Worker Feedback Technologies and Combatting Modern Slavery in Global Supply Chains," 136.

95. For more, see Farbenblum, Berg, and Kintominas, *Transformative Technology for Migrant Workers*, 6.

96. Tickler et al., "Modern Slavery and the Race to Fish," 2.

97. Marschke and Vandergeest, "Slavery Scandals," 40; Tickler et al., "Modern Slavery and the Race to Fish."

98. Luna, Chalit Hernandez, and Sawadogo, "The Paradoxes of Purity in Organic Agriculture in Burkina Faso," 46.

99. Luna, Chalit Hernandez, and Sawadogo, 50.

100. Office of the High Commissioner for Human Rights, *Working Paper—Gender-Sensitive Human Rights Due Diligence*, 1.

101. Badiee et al., *State of Gender Data Financing—2021*, 2.

102. Buvinic and Badiee, "Gender Data Systems."

103. CEDAW Committee, General Recommendation No. 9.

104. Sahan, "Women in Global Supply Chains," 126.

105. Danone's inability to sign is in part driven by the fact that it is a cooperative of eighteen Danone Institutes.

106. Resurreccion and Elmhirst, *Gender and Natural Resource Management*.

107. Jenkins, "Women, Mining and Development."

108. Voss et al., "International Supply Chains."

109. Mantouvalou, "The UK Modern Slavery Act 2015 Three Years On."

110. Schaper and Pollach, "Modern Slavery Statements," 2.

111. Lichuma, "(Laws) Made in the 'First World,'" 528.

112. Lichuma, 528.

113. Sahan, *The Journey to Sustainable Food*, 9.

114. Beveridge, Stephen, and Nott, *Making Women Count*.

115. Sarkar, "Constrained Labour as Instituted Process," 171.

5. EXTRACTIVES: REGULATING AT THE MARGINS
TO FORMALIZE ARTISANAL AND SMALL-SCALE MINING FOR WOMEN

Thanks are owed at the outset of this chapter to Anaïs Tobalagba, a former Quentin Bryce Scholar at the University of Technology Sydney and business and human rights expert, for initiating my early interest in bringing a gender perspective to the formalization of ASM, collaborative work that has been foundational to this chapter.

1. Raney, "From Housewife to Household Weapon," 5.

2. *Palliri* is a Quechan term meaning widowed and/or abandoned; *palliris* were traditionally widows of miners. See Rodriguez Fernandez, "Reproduciendo Otros Mundos" 41.

3. Phalen, "Bolivian Tin Miners' Wives Fast, Win Amnesty, Jobs, Freedom, 1977–1978."

4. Eftimie et al., "Gender Dimensions of Artisanal and Small-Scale Mining," 7.

5. Huggins, Buss, and Rutherford, "A 'Cartography of Concern,'" 142. For instance, in the Democratic Republic of the Congo, Huggins critiques the perceived negative association of ASM with various evils, such as criminality, illegality, immorality, and destructiveness, and demonstrates how in Sub-Saharan Africa, mining laws and policies have privileged large-scale mining.

6. Buxton, "Responding to the Challenge of Artisanal and Small-Scale Mining?," 1.

7. Eftimie et al., "Gender Dimensions of Artisanal and Small-Scale Mining," 7.

8. Arthur-Holmes, "Gendered Division of Labour and 'Sympathy' in Artisanal and Small-Scale Gold Mining in Prestea-Huni Valley Municipality, Ghana," 358.

9. Arthur-Holmes and Abrefa Busia, "Household Dynamics and the Bargaining Power of Women in Artisanal and Small-Scale Mining in Sub-Saharan Africa."

10. Robles, Verbrugge, and Geenen, "Does Formalization Make a Difference in Artisanal and Small-Scale Gold Mining?," 1.

11. United Nations Environment Programme and United Nations Institute for Training and Research. *Handbook*, 19.

12. Malone and Martínez, *Realities and Expectations of ASM in Peru*, 11.

13. Malone and Martínez, 11.

14. Malone and Martínez, 11.

15. World Bank, *Mining Together*, 15.

16. Grand Marín, "La normatividad minera y el enfoque de género."

17. Buss et al., "A Mine of One's Own?," 159.

18. Devi et al., "Gendered Informal Gold Trading in Indonesia," 8.

19. Lahiri-Dutt, *Between the Plough and the Pick*; Hinton, Veiga, and Beinhoff, "Women and Artisanal Mining"; Eftimie et al., "Gender Dimensions of Artisanal and Small-Scale Mining"; Jenkins, "Women, Mining and Development"; Jenkins, "Unearthing Women's Anti-Mining Activism in the Andes."

20. Eftimie et al., "Gender Dimensions of Artisanal and Small-Scale Mining," 15.

21. Lahiri-Dutt, "New Directions in Research on Women and Gender in Extractive Industries," 2.

22. Boudewijn and Jenkins, "Gender, Large-Scale Resource Extraction, and Environmental Inequality in Latin America," 265.

23. Millones, "Conga Mines," 481.

24. Viscidi, "Turmoil in South America and the Impact on Energy Markets," 8.

25. Orellana, "Indigenous Peoples, Energy and Environmental Justice."

26. Pilau Sobrinho, Calgaro, and dos Santos da Silva, "Public Policies, Neoextrativist Development and Indian Cosmovision."

27. Grand Marín, "La normatividad minera y el enfoque de género"; Ministerio del Ambiente and Proyecto planetGOLD Perú, *Estudio desde una perspectiva de género sobre la minería aurífera artesanal y de pequeña escala en el Perú*, 9.

28. Boudewijn and Jenkins, "Gender, Large-Scale Resource Extraction, and Environmental Inequality in Latin America," 269.

29. Boudewijn and Jenkins, 271.

30. Lynas, "A Good Business or a Risky Business," 151.

31. Lynas, 151.

32. O'Faircheallaigh and Corbett, "Understanding and Improving Policy and Regulatory Responses to Artisanal and Small Scale Mining," 961.

33. Geenen, "Relations and Regulations in Local Gold Trade Networks in South Kivu, Democratic Republic of Congo."

34. Geenen, 322.

35. Jenkins, "Women, Mining and Development," 330.

36. Jenkins, 330.

37. Samaddar, "Theorising Transit Labour in Informal Mineral Extraction Processes," 133.

38. Moretti, "The Gender of the Gold," 113.

39. Lynas, "A Good Business or a Risky Business."

40. "The Kimberley Process," 2024, https://www.kimberleyprocess.com/.

41. Lahiri-Dutt, "Digging Women," 202.

42. Ali, "The Social Ecology of Artisanal Mining," 117.

43. Lynas, "A Good Business or a Risky Business," 158.

44. Lahiri-Dutt, "Digging Women," 201.

45. Lahiri-Dutt, "Extractive Peasants."

46. Lahiri-Dutt, "Digging Women," 201.

47. Boudewijn and Jenkins, "Gender, Large-Scale Resource Extraction, and Environmental Inequality in Latin America," 268.

48. Tobalagba and Vijeyarasa, "Engendering Regulation of Artisanal and Small-Scale Mining," 1637.

49. International Labour Organization, Abrogation of Convention C045.

50. Moretti, "The Gender of the Gold," 135.

51. UN Secretary-General, "Report of the Secretary-General," para. 62.

52. UN Secretary-General, para. 62.

53. Mastrangelo, "Miserias preciosas," 142.

54. Robles, Verbrugge, and Geenen, "Does Formalization Make a Difference in Artisanal and Small-Scale Gold Mining?," 4.

55. Lynas, "A Good Business or a Risky Business," 174.

56. Lynas, 175.

57. Eftimie et al., "Gender Dimensions of Artisanal and Small-Scale Mining," 4.

58. Toledo Orozco, "(Under)Mining State Authority," 100.

59. *Pallaqueras* are almost exclusively women and responsible for sorting through waste rock from mining operations to glean residual materials that may be valuable. Toledo Orozco, 110.

60. Mastrangelo, "Miserias preciosas," 144.

61. See, for example, writings on the overlooked contributions of Malagasy women in Lawson, "Rice, Sapphires and Cattle," 171–72.

62. Hilson, "The 'Zambia Model'"; Hilson and Maconachie, "Formalising Artisanal and Small-Scale Mining"; Verbrugge and Besmanos, "Formalizing Artisanal and Small-Scale Mining."

63. Hilson and Maconachie; Martinez, Smith, and Malone, "Formalization Is Just the Beginning."

64. Eftimie et al., "Gender Dimensions of Artisanal and Small-Scale Mining," 12.

65. Grand Marín, "La normatividad minera y el enfoque de género," 52.

66. Boudewijn and Jenkins, "Gender, Large-Scale Resource Extraction, and Environmental Inequality in Latin America," 275.

67. Boudewijn and Jenkins, 273.

68. Grand Marín, "La normatividad minera y el enfoque de género," 55.

69. Boudewijn and Jenkins, "Gender, Large-Scale Resource Extraction, and Environmental Inequality in Latin America," 274.

70. Lahiri-Dutt, "Digging Women," 193.

71. Lahiri-Dutt, 196.

72. Eftimie et al., "Gender Dimensions of Artisanal and Small-Scale Mining," 94.

73. Eftimie et al., 4.

74. Perks et al., "Resources and Resourcefulness," 214.

75. Boudewijn and Jenkins, "Gender, Large-Scale Resource Extraction, and Environmental Inequality in Latin America," 272.

76. Lahiri-Dutt, "Digging Women," 200.

77. Rubiano, Vélez, and Rueda, "Minería de oro artesanal y de pequeña escala," 13.

78. O'Faircheallaigh and Corbett, "Understanding and Improving Policy and Regulatory Responses to Artisanal and Small Scale Mining," 962.

79. O'Faircheallaigh and Corbett, 967.

80. O'Faircheallaigh and Corbett, 967.

81. O'Faircheallaigh and Corbett, 968.

82. Eftimie et al., "Gender Dimensions of Artisanal and Small-Scale Mining," 87.

83. Small-Scale Gold Mining Act, Ghana.

84. Precious Minerals Marketing Corporation Act, Ghana.

85. Precious Minerals Marketing Corporation Act.

86. Minerals and Mining (Amendment) Act, Ghana.

87. Arthur-Holmes, "Gendered Division of Labour and 'Sympathy' in Artisanal and Small-Scale Gold Mining in Prestea-Huni Valley Municipality, Ghana," 2.

88. Hilson, Bartels, and Hu, "Brick by Brick, Block by Block."

89. Malone and Martínez, *Realities and Expectations of ASM in Peru*, 8.

90. Malone and Martínez, 8.

91. Malone and Martínez, 12.

92. Malone and Martínez, 12.

93. Malone and Martínez, 12.

94. Malone and Martínez, 17.

95. Malone and Martínez, 12.

96. Malone and Martínez, 17.

97. Malone and Martí)nez, 17.

98. Del Aguila, *The Labour Situation of Indigenous Women in Peru*, 93.

99. Malone and Martínez, *Realities and Expectations of ASM in Peru*, 28.

100. Huggins, Buss, and Rutherford, "A 'Cartography of Concern,'" 150.

101. Hilson et al., "Female Faces in Informal 'Spaces,'" 31.

102. Lahiri-Dutt, "New Directions in Research on Women and Gender in Extractive Industries," 4.

103. African Union, *Africa Mining Vision*, Pillar 5, question 36, p. 38.

104. United Nations Environment Programme, Minamata Convention on Mercury, sec. Annex C, 1(i).

105. World Bank, "World Bank Urges Action for Gender Equality in Artisanal and Small-Scale Mining."

106. World Bank, 4.

107. Lynas, "A Good Business or a Risky Business," 174.

108. Seck and Simons, "Resource Extraction and the Human Rights of Women and Girls," v.

109. Lynas, "A Good Business or a Risky Business," 164.

110. Seck and Simons, "Resource Extraction and the Human Rights of Women and Girls," v.

111. See Vijeyarasa, "Quantifying CEDAW."

112. Eftimie et al., "Gender Dimensions of Artisanal and Small-Scale Mining," 17.

113. World Bank, "World Bank Urges Action for Gender Equality in Artisanal and Small-Scale Mining," 2.

114. Arthur-Holmes and Abrefa Busia, "Safety Concerns and Occupational Health Hazards of Women in Artisanal and Small-Scale Mining in Ghana," 6.

115. Ministerio del Ambiente and Proyecto planetGOLD Perú, *Estudio desde una perspectiva de género sobre la minería aurífera artesanal y de pequeña escala en el Perú*, 14–17.

116. Rubiano, Vélez, and Rueda, "Minería de oro artesanal y de pequeña escala," 3.

117. Arthur-Holmes and Abrefa Busia, "Safety Concerns and Occupational Health Hazards of Women in Artisanal and Small-Scale Mining in Ghana," 5.

118. Lynas, "A Good Business or a Risky Business," 163.

119. Cabrera Navarrete, "El trabajo que no existe, el dolor que no existe."

120. Malone and Martínez, *Realities and Expectations of ASM in Peru*, 46.

121. Lynas, "A Good Business or a Risky Business," 163.

122. Arthur-Holmes and Abrefa Busia, "Safety Concerns and Occupational Health Hazards of Women in Artisanal and Small-Scale Mining in Ghana," 5.

123. Barnack-Tavlaris et al., "Taking Leave to Bleed"; Belliappa, "Menstrual Leave Debate."

124. Malone and Martínez, *Realities and Expectations of ASM in Peru*, 26.

125. Yakovleva, "Perspectives on Female Participation in Artisanal and Small-Scale Mining," 35.

126. Eftimie et al., "Gender Dimensions of Artisanal and Small-Scale Mining," 88.

127. Eftimie et al., 88.

128. Eftimie et al., 91, 93.

129. Vijeyarasa, "Does Law Matter?" 687.

130. Lynas, "A Good Business or a Risky Business," 158.

131. Eftimie et al., "Gender Dimensions of Artisanal and Small-Scale Mining," 88.

132. Lahiri-Dutt, "New Directions in Research on Women and Gender in Extractive Industries," 4.

133. Buss et al., "Beyond the Rituals of Inclusion," 31.

134. Arthur-Holmes, Yeboah, and Abrefa Busia, "Dimensions of Women's Mobility, Livelihoods and Vulnerability in Artisanal and Small-Scale Mining-Induced Local Economy," 6.

135. Lynas, "A Good Business or a Risky Business," 160.

136. Eftimie et al., "Gender Dimensions of Artisanal and Small-Scale Mining," 91.

137. Eftimie et al., 76.

6. CORPORATE QUOTAS: LEGAL TOOLS IN THE STRUGGLE FOR BOARDROOM EQUALITY

1. Genna, "Womenomics in Japan: Between Economic Miracle and Egalitarian Failure," 2.

2. Statista, "Japan."

3. Deloitte Global Boardroom Program, "Women in the Boardroom."

4. "Basic Policy on Economic and Fiscal Management and Reform 2023," Japan.

5. Leszczyńska, "Mandatory Quotas for Women on Boards of Directors in the European Union," 37.

6. Heidenreich, "Why Gender Quotas in Company Boards in Norway—and Not in Sweden?," 156.

7. Norwegian Public Limited Liability Companies Act, paras. 6–11a (4).

8. Seierstad et al., "A 'Quota Silo' or Positive Equality Reach?," 167; Dhir, "Challenging Boardroom Homogeneity," 11.

9. Seierstad et al., "A 'Quota Silo' or Positive Equality Reach?," 167.

10. Rosenblum, "Feminizing Capital," 49.

11. Wang and Kelan, "The Gender Quota and Female Leadership," 453.

12. Rosenblum, "Feminizing Capital."

13. Rogner, "From 'Golden Suits' to 'Golden Skirts,'" 62.

14. Rosenblum, "Feminizing Capital," 57.

15. Hamplová, Janeček, and Lefley, "Board Gender Diversity and Women in Leadership Positions," 745.

16. Hamplová, Janeček, and Lefley, 745.

17. Bertrand et al., "Breaking the Glass Ceiling?," 228.

18. Seierstad et al., "A 'Quota Silo' or Positive Equality Reach?," 183.

19. Wang and Kelan, "The Gender Quota and Female Leadership," 451.

20. Ahern and Dittmar, "The Changing of the Boards," 137.

21. Seierstad and Opsahl, "For the Few Not the Many?"; Seierstad et al., "A 'Quota Silo' or Positive Equality Reach?"; Elomäki, "Gender Quotas for Corporate Boards"; Dobson and Rastad, "Women on Boards."

22. Deloitte Global Boardroom Program, "Progress at a Snail's Pace," 7.

23. Deloitte Global Boardroom Program, "Women in the Boardroom," 8.

24. Deloitte Global Boardroom Program, "Progress at a Snail's Pace," 7.

25. Drozd, "Girls Just Wanna Have Equal Representation on Corporate Boards."

26. Elias, *Gender Politics and the Pursuit of Competitiveness in Malaysia*, 2.

27. Elias, 2.

28. Ondieki, "Woman of Many Firsts about to Call It Quits from Corporation Board."

29. Kiberenge, "Steady Rise of Kenyan Women in Hallowed Corporate Boardroom."

30. Rosenblum, "Unsex Cedaw, or What's Wrong with Women's Rights."

31. Federo, "The Rainbow Glass Ceiling," 1.

32. Magnier and Rosenblum, "Quotas and the Transatlantic Divergence of Corporate Governance"; McClane and Rosenblum, "Why Corporate Boards Should Include LGBTQ People."

33. Kyaw et al., "Does Board Gender Diversity Improve the Welfare of Lesbian, Gay, Bisexual, and Transgender Employees?"; Jiraporn, Potosky, and Lee, "Corporate Governance and Lesbian, Gay, Bisexual, and Transgender-Supportive Human Resource Policies from Corporate Social Responsibility, Resource-Based, and Agency Perspectives."

34. Otto, "Afterword," 534.

35. Eisenstein, "Femocrats, Official Feminism, and the Uses of Power," 54–55.

36. Rogner, "From 'Golden Suits' to 'Golden Skirts,'" 61.

37. Roberts, "The Political Economy of 'Transnational Business Feminism.'"

38. Roberts.

39. Rosenblum, "Feminizing Capital," 58.

40. Dhir, "Challenging Boardroom Homogeneity," 11.

41. Kemp, Keenan, and Gronow, "Strategic Resource or Ideal Source?," 580.

42. Elias, *Gender Politics and the Pursuit of Competitiveness in Malaysia*, 2.

43. Rosenblum, "Feminizing Capital," 59.

44. Terjesen Sealy, and Singh, "Women Directors on Corporate Boards," 329.

45. Smith, Smith and Verner, "Do Women in Top Management Affect Firm Performance?"

46. Kotiranta, Kovalainen, and Rouvinen, "Female Leadership and Firm Profitability."

47. Catalyst, "The Bottom Line."

48. Klick, "Market Response to Court Rejection of California's Board Diversity Laws."

49. Chandler, "Women on Corporate Boards"; Velkova, "Quotas for Women on Corporate Boards."

50. Hamplová, Janeček, and Lefley, "Board Gender Diversity and Women in Leadership Positions" 743.

51. Chandler, "Women on Corporate Boards"; Piscopo and Clark Muntean, "Corporate Quotas and Symbolic Politics in Advanced Democracies."

52. See Hamplová, Janeček, and Lefley, "Board Gender Diversity and Women in Leadership Positions," 744, for the various strands of literature for and against corporate board quotas.

53. Singh and Vinnicombe, "Why So Few Women Directors in Top UK Boardrooms?"

54. Fitzsimmons, "Women on Boards of Directors."

55. Velkova, "Quotas for Women on Corporate Boards."

56. Bertrand et al., "Breaking the Glass Ceiling?" 228.

57. Suk, "Work-Family Conflict and the Pipeline to Power."

58. Srinivasan and George, "Building the Women Directorship Pipeline in India."

59. Leszczyńska, "Mandatory Quotas for Women on Boards of Directors in the European Union."

60. Fitzsimmons, "Women on Boards of Directors."

61. Einarsdóttir, Rafnsdóttir, and Valdimarsdóttir, "Structural Hindrances or Less Driven Women?," 292.

62. Kamalnath, *The Corporate Diversity Jigsaw*, 44.

63. Ramalekana, "A Critique of the Stigma Argument Against Affirmative Action in South Africa," 1.

64. Ramalekana, 1.

65. Lee-Kuen, Sok-Gee, and Zainudin, "Gender Diversity and Firms' Financial Performance in Malaysia."

66. Abdullah, Ismail, and Nachum, "Does Having Women on Boards Create Value?," 1.

67. Vijeyarasa, "Women's Absence in Sri Lankan Politics," 1.

68. Einarsdóttir, Rafnsdóttir, and Valdimarsdóttir, "Structural Hindrances or Less Driven Women?," 289–90.

69. Deloitte Global Boardroom Program, "Progress at a Snail's Pace;," 31.

70. 30% Club, https://30percentclub.org.

71. OECD.stat, "Employment: Female Share of Seats on Boards of the Largest Publicly Listed Companies."

72. OECD.stat.

73. Drozd, "Girls Just Wanna Have Equal Representation on Corporate Boards."

74. European Parliament and Council of the European Union, Directive (EU) 2022 /2381.

75. Velkova, "Quotas for Women on Corporate Boards."

76. European Parliament and Council of the European Union, Directive (EU) 2022 /2381, para. 34.

77. Drozd, "Girls Just Wanna Have Equal Representation on Corporate Boards."

78. Lambert, "Board Quotas for Women?"

79. Szydło, "Constitutional Values Underlying Gender Equality on the Boards of Companies," 170.

80. Act respecting Amendment to Act on Public Limited Companies and Act on Private Limited Companies, Iceland.

81. Act on Equal Status and Equal Rights of Women and Men, Iceland.

82. Einarsdóttir, Rafnsdóttir, and Valdimarsdóttir, "Structural Hindrances or Less Driven Women?," 289.

83. Einarsdóttir, Rafnsdóttir, and Valdimarsdóttir, 290.

84. Seierstad and Opsahl, "For the Few Not the Many?"

85. Deloitte Global Boardroom Program, "Progress at a Snail's Pace," 5.

86. Seierstad and Opsahl, "For the Few Not the Many?," 54.

87. Deloitte Global Boardroom Program, "Progress at a Snail's Pace," 11.

88. Singh, Singhania, and Sardana, "Do Women on Boards Affect Firm's Financial Performance?," 64.

89. Deloitte Global Boardroom Program, "Progress at a Snail's Pace:," 245.

90. Ministry of Women, Family and Community Development, Women Directors' Programme.

91. World Economic Forum, *The Global Gender Gap Report 2021*.

92. African Development Bank, *Where Are the Women?*, 12.

93. African Development Bank.

94. Deloitte Global Boardroom Program, "Women in the Boardroom," 78.

95. Deloitte Global Boardroom Program, "Progress at a Snail's Pace," 21.

96. Deloitte Global Boardroom Program, "Progress at a Snail's Pace," 21.

97. Deloitte Global Boardroom Program, "Progress at a Snail's Pace," 35.

98. Corporations: Boards of Directors, California Senate Bill 826.

99. Ransil, "Corporations without Representation," 1269.

100. Vijeyarasa, *The Woman President*, 42.

101. International Institute for Democracy and Electoral Assistance, *The Implementation of Quotas*.

102. Chizema, Kamuriwo, and Shinozawa, "Women on Corporate Boards around the World," 1060.

103. Mateos de Cabo et al., "Do 'Soft Law' Board Gender Quotas Work?"

104. Wang and Kelan, "The Gender Quota and Female Leadership," 464.

105. OECD.stat, "Employment: Female Share of Seats on Boards of the Largest Publicly Listed Companies."

106. Deloitte Global Boardroom Program, "Progress at a Snail's Pace," 11.
107. Deloitte Global Boardroom Program, 11.
108. Vijeyarasa, "Does Law Matter?," 718.
109. Drozd, "Girls Just Wanna Have Equal Representation on Corporate Boards."
110. Guibert-Lantoine and Leridon, "Contraception in France."
111. Lepinard and Lieber, *The Policy on Gender Equality in France*.
112. Drozd, "Girls Just Wanna Have Equal Representation on Corporate Boards."
113. Kang et al., "Realizing Gender Diversity on Corporate Boards," 10–11.
114. Rogner, "From 'Golden Suits' to 'Golden Skirts,'" 75.
115. Rogner, 75.
116. African Development Bank, "Where Are the Women?," 11.
117. Szydło, "Constitutional Values Underlying Gender Equality on the Boards of Companies," 193.
118. Szydło, 194.
119. Murray, "Quotas for Men," 520.
120. Dorrough et al., "Revealing Side Effects of Quota Rules on Group Cooperation."

7. GENDER-RESPONSIVE BUDGETING: LAW AS THE LEVER TO EMBED GENDER IN BUDGETARY FRAMEWORKS

1. Raibaud, *La ville, faite par et pour les hommes*.
2. Marchal, "Reducing Gender Inequalities through Gender Budgeting."
3. Marchal.
4. Tellier, "Canadian Economic and Fiscal Policy," 467.
5. Tellier, 467.
6. Philipps, "Gender Budgets and Tax Policy-Making," 144.
7. Tellier, "Canadian Economic and Fiscal Policy," 460.
8. Sharp and Broomhill, "Women and Government Budgets," 2.
9. Bakker, *Gender Budget Initiatives*, 1.
10. Rubin and Bartle, "Gender-Responsive Budgeting," 394.
11. Rubin and Bartle, 393.
12. Ikhide, "The Political Economy of Gender-Responsive Budgeting in Nigeria," 37.
13. Sushant and Laha, "Game Changer or Accounting Practice?," 545.
14. Sikhosana et al., "Gender-Responsive Budgeting in Climate Change Financing," 30.
15. Sharp, *The Economics and Politics of Auditing Government Budgets for Their Gender Impacts*, 10.
16. Hinds, *Increasing Financial Investment in Women and Girls through Gender Responsive Budgeting*, 2.
17. Chakraborty, "Fiscal and Regional Context of Gender Budgeting in Asia," 180.
18. Fragoso and Enríquez, "Gender Budgeting Efforts," 115–16.
19. Fragoso and Enríquez, 115–16.
20. OECD, "OECD Best Practices for Gender Budgeting," 5.
21. Fragoso and Enríquez, "Gender Budgeting Efforts," 132.
22. Fragoso and Enríquez, 133.
23. Fragoso and Enríquez, 120.

24. Mulyaningrum and Mujibah, "Gender Mainstreaming in the Budget System of Indonesian Governance," 9.

25. Vijeyarasa, *The Woman President*, 132.

26. Fragoso and Enríquez, "Gender Budgeting Efforts."

27. Beall, "Trickle-down or Rising Tide?"

28. Sawer and Stewart, "Gender Budgeting," 124.

29. Constitution of Austria, Article (13)(3); Rubin and Bartle, "Gender-Responsive Budgeting," 399.

30. Gupta, Barman, and Ranjan, "Are Gender Budgets Useful for Reducing Gender Inequalities?," 151.

31. Chakraborty, Nayyar, and Jain, "The Political Economy of Fiscal Interventions to Tackle Gender Inequalities," 1.

32. Ikhide, "The Political Economy of Gender-Responsive Budgeting in Nigeria," 42.

33. Sharp and Broomhill, "Women and Government Budgets," 2.

34. UN Women, Beijing Declaration and Platform for Action.

35. UN Women, para. 346.

36. UN Women, para. 58(d).

37. UN Women, para. 346.

38. UN Women, para. 165(i).

39. UNIFEM, Report of the Ad Hoc Committee of the Whole, para. 73(b).

40. Bakker, *Gender Budget Initiatives*, 4.

41. Costa and Sharp, "Gender-Responsive Budgeting," 139.

42. Costa and Sharp, 139.

43. Webb, "Motion—Gender Responsive Budgeting."

44. Financial Management Amendment (Gender Responsive Budgeting) Act, sec. 1(a)(b) and (c), Victoria, Australia.

45. Sharp, *The Economics and Politics of Auditing Government Budgets for Their Gender Impacts*, 1. See also Govender, "International Women's Day 2020."

46. Budlender, *The Political Economy of Women's Budgets in the South*, 20.

47. Commission for Gender Equality, *Government's Gender Responsive Budgeting Framework*, South Africa.

48. Sharp and Broomhill, "Women and Government Budgets," 2.

49. Sharp and Broomhill, 2.

50. Costa and Sharp, "Gender-Responsive Budgeting," 15.

51. Sharp, "The Economics and Politics of Auditing Government Budgets for Their Gender Impacts," 6.

52. UNIFEM, "Gender Responsive Budgeting and Women's Reproductive Rights," 56.

53. Bakker, *Gender Budget Initiatives*, 5.

54. Sharp, "The Economics and Politics of Auditing Government Budgets for Their Gender Impacts," 4.

55. Tellier, "Canadian Economic and Fiscal Policy," 479.

56. Tellier, 479.

57. Ministry of Education, "Rashtriya Madhyamik Shiksha Abhiyaan."

58. Sushant and Laha, "Game Changer or Accounting Practice?," 545.

59. Vijeyarasa, *The Woman President*, 132.

60. Republic Act No. 7192, Philippines.

61. Chakraborty, "Fiscal and Regional Context of Gender Budgeting in Asia," 183.

62. Republic Act No. 7845, Philippines.

63. Chakraborty, "Fiscal and Regional Context of Gender Budgeting in Asia," 182.

64. Chakraborty, 182.

65. Chakraborty, 182.

66. Sharp and Broomhill, "Women and Government Budgets," 2.

67. Fragoso and Enríquez, "Gender Budgeting Efforts," 121.

68. Gupta, Barman, and Ranjan, "Are Gender Budgets Useful for Reducing Gender Inequalities?," 156.

69. National Finance Act, art. 26, South Korea.

70. Chakraborty, "Fiscal and Regional Context of Gender Budgeting in Asia," 178.

71. UN Women Australia, "Explainer."

72. Tellier, "Canadian Economic and Fiscal Policy," 477.

73. See, for instance, LGBTIQ+ Health Australia, "Submission for the 2022/23 Federal Budget."

74. Approval of the emerging obligations of international human rights law, in relation to equality and non-discrimination between women and men, including formal, substantial and recognition equality, art. 9, 11, Uruguay.

75. Elson, "Budgeting for Women's Rights," 17.

76. Elson, 13.

77. Sharp and Broomhill, "Women and Government Budgets," 10.

78. Sharp and Broomhill, 10.

79. Sharp, *The Economics and Politics of Auditing Government Budgets for Their Gender Impacts*, 12.

80. Chavez, "The Watering Down of Participatory Budgeting and People Power in Porto Alegre, Brazil," 57.

81. Chavez, 58.

82. Chavez, 58.

83. Elson, "Budgeting for Women's Rights," 2.

84. Fragoso and Enríquez, "Gender Budgeting Efforts," 118.

85. Fragoso and Enríquez, 122.

86. Canadian Gender Budgeting Act.

87. Tellier, "Canadian Economic and Fiscal Policy," 22.

88. Canadian Gender Budgeting Act, sec. 2.

89. Fragoso and Enríquez, "Gender Budgeting Efforts," 127.

90. Paul, "Raising Representation?"

91. Loi des Belges, No. 2007002011, Belgium.

92. Khalifa and Scarparo, "Gender Responsive Budgeting," 7.

93. Marchal, "Reducing Gender Inequalities through Gender Budgeting."

94. Holvoet and Inberg, "Gender Mainstreaming in Sector Budget Support," 292.

95. Marchal, "Reducing Gender Inequalities through Gender Budgeting."

96. Fragoso and Enríquez, "Gender Budgeting Efforts," 118.

97. Chakraborty, "Fiscal and Regional Context of Gender Budgeting in Asia."

98. Himmelweit, "The Experience of UK Women's Budget Group," 5.

99. Chakraborty, "Fiscal and Regional Context of Gender Budgeting in Asia," 178.

100. Sharp, *The Economics and Politics of Auditing Government Budgets for Their Gender Impacts*, 10.

101. Byanyima, "Strengthening Parliamentary Governance Through Gender Budgeting," 37.

102. Hinds, *Increasing Financial Investment in Women and Girls through Gender Responsive Budgeting*, 2.

103. Sikhosana et al., "Gender-Responsive Budgeting in Climate Change Financing," 30.

104. Sikhosana et al., 27.

105. Sikhosana et al., 31–32.

106. Sikhosana et al., 32.

8. ARTIFICIAL INTELLIGENCE: ALGORITHMIC ACCOUNTABILITY THROUGH AN INTERSECTIONAL GENDER LENS

1. McCarthy et al., "Dartmouth Summer Research Project on Artificial Intelligence."

2. Tesla, Corporate Governance, https://ir.tesla.com/corporate/elon-musk.

3. Little and Winch, *The New Patriarchs of Digital Capitalism*.

4. World Economic Forum, "Why We Must Act Now to Close the Digital Gender Gap in AI."

5. Adams, "The Gendered Impact of Artificial Intelligence and the Fourth Industrial Revolution in South Africa," 370.

6. Adams, 370.

7. Adams, 370.

8. Adams, 370.

9. Murciano-Goroff, "Missing Women in Tech."

10. Adam, "Knowledge, Language and Rationality in AI," 17.

11. Toupin, "Shaping Feminist Artificial Intelligence," 582.

12. Adam, "Knowledge, Language and Rationality in AI," 134.

13. Bardzell, "Feminist HCI."

14. Dowling and Lucey, "ChatGPT for (Finance) Research."

15. Bello y Villarino et al., "Standardisation, Trust and Democratic Principles."

16. Lutz, "Digital Inequalities in the Age of Artificial Intelligence and Big Data," 141.

17. For example, Vijeyarasa and Bello y Villarino, "Lessons and Consequences of the Failure to Regulate AI for Women's Human Rights"; Bello y Villarino and Vijeyarasa, "International Human Rights, Artificial Intelligence and the Challenge for the Pondering State"; Coombs and Abraha, "Governance of AI and Gender"; United Nations Educational, Scientific and Cultural Organization, "Artificial Intelligence and Gender Equality"; Adams and Loideáin, "Addressing Indirect Discrimination and Gender Stereotypes in AI Virtual Personal Assistants"; Chauhan and Kaur, "Gender Bias and Artificial Intelligence"; López Belloso, "Women's Rights Under AI Regulation."

18. For example, Latorre Ruiz and Pérez Sedeño, "Gender Bias in Artificial Intelligence"; Leavy, "Gender Bias in Artificial Intelligence"; Leavy, O'Sullivan, and Siapera, "Data, Power and Bias in Artificial Intelligence."

19. United Nations Educational, Scientific and Cultural Organization, "Artificial Intelligence and Gender Equality," 17.

20. Coombs and Abraha, "Governance of AI and Gender."

21. The term *artificial intelligence* was apparently coined at a 1956 symposium held in the US at Dartmouth by scholar John McCarthy. See Donahoe and Metzger, "Artificial Intelligence and Human Rights," 115.

22. Donahoe and Metzger, "Artificial Intelligence and Human Rights," 115.

23. Vijeyarasa and Bello y Villarino, "Lessons and Consequences of the Failure to Regulate AI for Women's Human Rights."

24. Kelan, *Patterns of Inclusion*, 7.

25. Santosh and Wall, "AI and Ethical Issues," 2.

26. United Nations Educational, Scientific and Cultural Organization, "Artificial Intelligence and Gender Equality," 4.

27. United Nations Educational, Scientific and Cultural Organization, 4.

28. Santosh and Wall, "AI and Ethical Issues," 4.

29. Gerards and Xenidis, *Algorithmic Discrimination in Europe*, 33.

30. For a detailed discussion of how DSS works and its potential use in the determination of applications for refugee status, see my co-authored article, Bello y Villarino and Vijeyarasa, "International Human Rights, Artificial Intelligence and the Challenge for the Pondering State: Time to Regulate?"

31. The person needs to have a "well-founded fear," according to article 1(A)(2) Convention relating to the Status of Refugees 1951.

32. Crawford, *The Atlas of AI*, 128.

33. Mayson, "Bias In, Bias Out," 2268; Hellman, "Measuring Algorithmic Fairness," 846.

34. Hovy and Prabhumoye, "Five Sources of Bias in Natural Language Processing," 2.

35. Hovy and Prabhumoye, 2.

36. Sun et al., "Mitigating Gender Bias in Natural Language Processing."

37. Sun et al., 1631.

38. Sun et al., 67. See also Susan Leavy, "Gender Bias in Artificial Intelligence," 16.

39. Hovy and Prabhumoye, "Five Sources of Bias in Natural Language Processing," 3.

40. Sun et al., "Mitigating Gender Bias in Natural Language Processing."

41. Hovy and Spruit, "The Social Impact of Natural Language Processing," 593.

42. Criado Perez, *Invisible Women*, 162.

43. Criado Perez, 162.

44. The UK Information Commissioner's Office, an independent body focused on information rights, offers a dual classification that focuses on the first two of these harms. See Information Commissioner's Office (ICO), https://ico.org.uk.

45. Chaudhuri et al., "Regulatory Frameworks Relating to Data Privacy and Algorithmic Decision Making in the Context of Emerging Standards on Algorithmic Bias," 2.

46. Lauret, "Amazon's Sexist AI Recruiting Tool."

47. Hellman, "Measuring Algorithmic Fairness," 813.

48. Mayson, "Bias In, Bias Out."

49. Manasi et al., "Mirroring the Bias," 298.

50. Brown, "Brilliance Knows No Gender."

51. Juquelier, Poncin, and Hazée, "Empathic Chatbots."

52. Ni Loideain, Adams, and Clifford, "Gender as Emotive AI and the Case of 'Nadia,'" 6.

53. Manasi et al., "Mirroring the Bias," 298.

54. Adams, "The Gendered Impact of Artificial Intelligence and the Fourth Industrial Revolution in South Africa," 373.

55. Adams, 373.

56. Manasi et al., "Mirroring the Bias," 299.

57. Toews, "Deepfakes Are Going to Wreak Havoc on Society. We Are Not Prepared."

58. Kirchengast, "Deepfakes and Image Manipulation."

59. Kirchengast, 308.

60. Ray, "Disinformation, Deepfakes and Democracies."

61. Paul, "California Makes 'Deepfake' Videos Illegal, but Law May Be Hard to Enforce."

62. Bouckaert, "License to Kill."

63. Vijeyarasa, *Sex, Slavery and the Trafficked Woman*, 155; Strossen, "Feminist Critique of the Feminist Critique of Pornography, an Essay."

64. MacKinnon, "Pornography as Trafficking."

65. See Kira, "When Non-Consensual Intimate Deepfakes Go Viral"; Ajder et al., *The State of Deepfakes: Landscape, Threats, and Impact*, 2; Wagner and Blewer, "'The Word Real Is No Longer Real.'" See similar reasoning in Khalid, "Deepfake Videos Are a Far, Far Bigger Problem for Women."

66. Dobbs v. Jackson Women's Health Organization.

67. Davis, "The State of Abortion Rights in the US"; Palacio, "Over the Precipice Into a Post-Roe World."

68. Kahn, "After Roe, Concerns Mount over A.I.-Enabled Surveillance."

69. Bhuiyan, "Facebook Gave Police Their Private Data."

70. Vijeyarasa, "Gendered Harms and the Regulation of Artificial Intelligence," 136–37.

71. Ragnedda, "New Digital Inequalities. Algorithms Divide," 61.

72. De Silva de Alwis, "Gendering the New International Convention on Cybercrimes and New Norms on Artificial Intelligence and Emerging Technologies," 10.

73. Lucero, "Artificial Intelligence Regulation and China's Future"; Roberts et al., "Governing Artificial Intelligence in China and the European Union"; "Full Translation."

74. National Artificial Intelligence Initiative Act 2021 (Public Law 116–283), Division E, United States; Trump, Executive Order 13859.

75. Gerards and Xenidis, *Algorithmic Discrimination in Europe.*

76. Pigola et al., "Artificial Intelligence-Driven Digital Technologies to the Implementation of the Sustainable Development Goals."

77. Basic Act on the Development of Artificial Intelligence, South Korea.

78. Department of Industry, Science and Resources, "Australia's Artificial Intelligence Ethics Framework."

79. Bello y Villarino et al., "Standardisation, Trust and Democratic Principles."

80. Council of Europe, Framework Convention on Artificial Intelligence and Human Rights, Democracy and the Rule of Law.

81. Council of Europe, art. 10.

82. Council of Europe, art. 17.

83. Council of Europe, art. 8.

84. Council of Europe, art. 8.

85. Council of Europe, Explanatory Report, para. 76.

86. Council of Europe, Explanatory Report, para. 77.

87. European Commission, Proposal for a Regulation of the European Parliament and the Council, 5.2.2.

88. European Commission, "Shaping Europe's Digital Future: AI Act."

89. European Commission.

90. New York City Department of Consumer and Worker Protection, Amendment to Title 6 of the Rules of the City of New York.

91. New York City Department of Consumer and Worker Protection.

92. Pacheco, Dispõe sobre o uso da Inteligência Artificial, sec. 4.

93. Pacheco, art. 12.

94. Pacheco, sec. 5.

95. Pacheco, art. 9, sec. 1.

96. Pacheco, 13–17.

97. Belli, Curzi, and Gaspar, "AI Regulation in Brazil," 13.

98. Treasury Board, Directive on Automated Decision-Making.

99. Algorithmic Impact Assessment Tool, Canada.

100. Treasury Board, Directive on Automated Decision-Making, art. 6.3.6.

101. Canadian Space Agency, "Evaluation of the Implementation of Gender-Based Analysis Plus at the Canadian Space Agency."

102. Women and Gender Equality Canada, "Gender-Based Analysis Plus (GBA Plus)"; Treasury Board, Directive on Automated Decision-Making, sec. Appendix C, 6.3.6.

103. Gunderson, "Intersectionality in HR Research," 1277.

104. Amani, "AI and 'Equality by Design,'" 18.

105. Hoogeveen et al., "Sex, Mines, and Pipelines."

106. Johnstone and Momani, "Gender Mainstreaming in the Canadian Armed Forces and the Department of National Defence."

107. Hankivsky and Mussell, "Gender-Based Analysis Plus in Canada."

108. Treasury Board of Canada Secretariat, "Using Artificial Intelligence (AI) to Automate Candidate Evaluations in the Staffing Process's Assessment Phase."

109. National Artificial Intelligence Initiative Act (Public Law 116–283), United States.

110. National Artificial Intelligence Initiative Act (Public Law 116–283), sec. 5101(a)(2).

111. Trump, Executive Order 13859. See also Vought, Memorandum: Driving Efficient Acquisition of Artificial Intelligence in Government.

112. Biden, Executive Order 14110.

113. Take It Down Act, United States.

114. Ajder et al., *The State of Deepfakes*, 1.

115. Take It Down Act, sec. 2(1), United States.

116. Take It Down Act, sec. 2(5).

117. Take It Down Act, sec. 3(3).

118. European Parliament and Council of the European Union, Regulation (EU) 2022/2065, paras. 61 and 62.

119. Criminal Code Amendment, Act No. 78, (Commonwealth) Australia.

120. European Parliament and Council of the European Union, Regulation (EU) 2022/2065, art. 6(1)(b).

121. Shattock, "Self-Regulation 2:0."

122. Appelman and Leerssen, "On 'Trusted' Flaggers," 472.

123. eSafety Commissioner, "The Global Online Safety Regulators Network."

124. Arnold, "Safe, but for Whom?"

125. Appelman and Leerssen, "On 'Trusted' Flaggers."

126. Hodge, "Don't Always Believe What You See," 61–62.

127. Association for Progressive Communications et al., "Feminist Principles of the Internet."

128. Association for Progressive Communications et al.

129. United Nations Educational, Scientific and Cultural Organization, "Artificial Intelligence and Gender Equality," 11.

130. AI for Good Global Summit, July 8–11, 2025, Geneva, Switzerland, https://aiforgood.itu.int/summit25/programme/.

131. Terms-We-Serve-With, https://termsweservewith.org.

132. Rakova, "A New Framework for Coming to Terms with Algorithms."

133. Rakova.

134. Rakova.

135. Crenshaw, "Race, Reform, and Retrenchment."

136. Crawford, *The Atlas of AI*, 144–45.

137. Crawford, 145.

138. Gerards and Xenidis, *Algorithmic Discrimination in Europe*, 65.

139. Schiek, "Broadening the Scope and the Norms of EU Gender Equality Law," 454; Sulmicelli, "Queer Responsive Regulation for Artificial Intelligence in Healthcare."

140. Schiek, 453.

141. For a brief discussion on this point, see Polli, "Fairness Optimized AI."

142. Sulmicelli, "Queer-Responsive Regulation for Artificial Intelligence in Healthcare."

143. Katyal and Jung, "The Gender Panopticon."

144. Katyal and Jung, 761.

145. Katyal and Jung, 761.

146. Henderson, Flood, and Scassa, "Artificial Intelligence in Canadian Healthcare," 483.

147. Katyal and Jung, "The Gender Panopticon," 762–63.

148. Murray, "Quotas for Men," 520.

149. Leavy, "Gender Bias in Artificial Intelligence," 14; Jackson, "Artificial Intelligence and Algorithmic Bias," 316.

150. Basic Act on the Development of Artificial Intelligence, art. 7, South Korea.

151. Office of the High Commissioner for Human Rights, *Working Paper—Gender-Sensitive Human Rights Due Diligence*.

152. European Commission, Proposal for a Regulation of the European Parliament and the Council, art. 3(56).

153. United Nations Educational, Scientific and Cultural Organization, "Measuring Digital Development," iii.

154. Vijeyarasa, "Realizing the Right to Development in the Context of Artificial Intelligence."

155. EQUALS and United Nations Educational, Scientific and Cultural Organization, "I'd Blush If I Could."

156. Collett, Neff, and Gouvea Gomes, *The Effects of AI on the Working Lives of Women*, 63.

157. Scassa, "Regulating AI in Canada," 29.

158. Scassa, 30.

159. Scassa, 29.

CONCLUSION: THE PRACTICALITIES OF REWRITING THE RULES

1. United Nations Women, Women Count, and UN Department of Economic and Social Affairs, "Progress on the Sustainable Development Goals," 2.

2. Cooper, "Crafting Prefigurative Law in Turbulent Times," 18.

3. Cooper, 24.

4. Cooper, 17.

5. Cleary, "Our Changing Institutions."

6. Hunter, "The Power of Feminist Judgments?," 143.

7. McFerran, Fos-Tuvera, and Acherhard-Hodges, "An Employment Right," 183.

8. Philippine Commission on Women, "Republic Act 9710: Magna Carta of Women."

9. Act Reinstituting Absolute Divorce as an Alternate Mode for Dissolution of Marriage.

10. McFerran Fos-Tuvera, and Acherhard-Hodges, "An Employment Right," 185.

11. McFerran Fos-Tuvera, and Acherhard-Hodges, 185.

12. Christopherson et al., *Tackling Legal Impediments to Women's Economic Empowerment.*

13. See, e.g., Goonesekere, *Violence, Law and Women's Rights in South Asia,* 10.

14. Htun, "Women and Democracy," 118.

15. Ping, "Rural Land Tenure Reforms in China," 59.

16. Bhattacharya and Daouk, "When No Law Is Better Than a Good Law."

17. Georgetown Institute for Women, Peace and Security and Peace Research Center Oslo, *Women, Peace and Security Index 2019/20,* 39.

18. Gouws, "Women's Activism around Gender-Based Violence in South Africa."

19. Kapur, "Gender, Sovereignty and the Rise of a Sexual Security Regime in International Law and Postcolonial India," 318, 319.

20. Gouws, "Women's Activism around Gender-Based Violence in South Africa," 412.

21. Vijeyarasa, "Women's Movements under Women Presidents."

22. Weldon and Htun, "Feminist Mobilisation and Progressive Policy Change."

23. Vijeyarasa, *The Woman President,* 222.

24. Lugones, "The Coloniality of Gender," 13.

25. Sheehy, *Adding Feminism to Law.*

26. McLachlin, "Foreword," 2.

27. Forrest, "Motion and Reading Speech."

28. Vijeyarasa, "Institutionalising Women's Experiences in Law."

29. Vijeyarasa.

30. Sawer, "Parliamentary Representation of Women"; Childs, "Feminist Institutional Change"; Holli and Harder, "Towards a Dual Approach."

31. Vijeyarasa, "Institutionalising Women's Experiences in Law."

32. Mulcahy and Seear, "On Tables, Doors and Listening Spaces."

33. Ailwood et al., "Beyond Women's Voices," 229–34.

34. Chacko, "Decolonial Feminism," 3.

35. Millbank, "Gender-Transformative Law Reform as Healthcare," 68.

36. Nesiah, "Lawfare, CVE, and International Conflict Feminism."

37. Liebeskind, "Preventing Gender-Based Violence," 645.

38. Klugman, *Gender Based Violence and the Law*, 20.

39. Nyhlén and Giritli Nygren, "'It's about Gender Equality and All That Stuff.'"

40. Engle, Nesiah, and Otto, "Feminist Approaches to International Law."

41. True, *The Political Economy of Violence Against Women*, 3.

BIBLIOGRAPHY

BOOKS, ARTICLES, REPORTS, AND OTHER SECONDARY SOURCES

Abdullah, Shamsul N., Ku Nor Izah Ku Ismail, and Lilac Nachum. "Does Having Women on Boards Create Value? The Impact of Societal Perceptions and Corporate Governance in Emerging Markets." *Strategic Management Journal* 37, no. 3 (2016): 466–76. https://doi.org/10.1002/smj.2352.

Adam, Alison. "Knowledge, Language and Rationality in AI." In *Artificial Knowing: Gender and the Thinking Machine*, 88–112. London: Routledge, 1998.

Adams, Rachel. "The Gendered Impact of Artificial Intelligence and the Fourth Industrial Revolution in South Africa: Inequality, Accessibility and Skills Development." In *Social Justice and Education in the 21st Century: Research from South Africa and the United States*, edited by Willie Pearson Jr. and Vijay Reddy, 365–79. Cham: Springer International Publishing, 2021.

Adams, Rachel, and Nóra Ní Loideáin. "Addressing Indirect Discrimination and Gender Stereotypes in AI Virtual Personal Assistants: The Role of International Human Rights Law." *Cambridge International Law Journal* 8, no. 2 (December 1, 2019): 241–57. https://doi.org/10.4337/cilj.2019.02.04.

African Development Bank. *Where Are the Women? Inclusive Boardrooms in Africa's Top Listed Companies?* African Development Bank, 2015. https://www.afdb.org/fileadmin/uploads/afdb/Documents/Publications/Where_are_the_Women_Inclusive_Boardrooms_in_Africa%E2%80%99s_top-listed_companies.pdf.

African Union. *Africa Mining Vision*. February 2009. https://au.int/en/documents/20100212/africa-mining-vision-amv.

Agarwal, Bina. "Gender and Land Rights Revisited: Exploring New Prospects via the State, Family and Market." *Journal of Agrarian Change* 3, no. 1–2 (2003): 184–224. https://doi.org/10.1111/1471-0366.00054.

Ahern, Kenneth, and Amy Dittmar. "The Changing of the Boards: The Impact on Firm Valuation of Mandated Female Board Representation." *Quarterly Journal of Economics* 127, no. 1 (2012): 137–97.

Ahmed, Salma, and David Fielding. "Changes in Maternity Leave Coverage: Implications for Fertility, Labour Force Participation and Child Mortality." *Social Science & Medicine* 241 (November 1, 2019): 112573. https://doi.org/10.1016/j.socscimed.2019.112573.

Ailwood, Sarah, Rachel Loney-Howes, Nan Seuffert, and Cassandra Sharp. "Beyond Women's Voices: Towards a Victim-Survivor-Centred Theory of Listening in Law Reform on Violence Against Women." *Feminist Legal Studies* 31, no. 2 (July 1, 2023): 217–41. https://doi.org/10.1007/s10691-022-09499-1.

Ajder, Henry, Giorgio Patrini, Francesco Cavalli, and Laurence Cullen. *The State of Deepfakes: Landscape, Threats, and Impact.* Deeptrace, September 2019. https://regmedia.co.uk/2019/10/08/deepfake_report.pdf.

Alaattinoğlu, Daniela, and Alice Margaria. "Trans Parents and the Gendered Law: Critical Reflections on the Swedish Regulation." *International Journal of Constitutional Law* 21, no. 2 (April 1, 2023): 603–24. https://doi.org/10.1093/icon/moad056.

Alam, Shahidul. "Majority World: Challenging the West's Rhetoric of Democracy." *Amerasia Journal* 34, no. 1 (January 1, 2008): 88–98. https://doi.org/10.17953/amer.34.1.l3176027k4q614v5.

Albagli, Pinjas, and Tomás Rau. "The Effects of a Maternity Leave Reform on Children's Abilities and Maternal Outcomes in Chile." *The Economic Journal* 129, no. 619 (April 1, 2019): 1015–47. https://doi.org/10.1111/ecoj.12586.

Albrecht, Clara, Anita Fichtl, Peter Redler, and Anita Dietrich. "Fathers in Charge? Parental Leave Policies for Fathers in Europe." *ifo DICE Report*, ifo Institut—Leibniz Institut für Wirtschaftsforschung an der Universität München, 15, no. 1 (April 2017): 49–51.

Algorithmic Impact Assessment Tool. Government of Canada, 2023. https://www.canada.ca/en/government/system/digital-government/digital-government-innovations/responsible-use-ai/algorithmic-impact-assessment.html.

Ali, Saleem H. "The Social Ecology of Artisanal Mining: Between Romanticisation and Anathema." In *Between the Plough and the Pick: Informal, Artisanal and Small-Scale Mining in the Contemporary World*, edited by Kuntala Lahiri-Dutt, 117–29. Canberra: ANU Press, 2018.

Allain, Jean. "White Slave Traffic in International Law." *Journal of Trafficking and Human Exploitation* 1, no. 1 (February 14, 2017): 1–40.

Álvarez, Paola D., and Paola G. Truffello. *Legislación comparada de protección a las trabajadoras víctimas de violencia de género: Argentina, Ecuador, España, Estados Unidos de América (Nueva York), Nueva Zelanda y Uruguay.* Santiago: Biblioteca del Congreso Nacional de Chile, March 2022. https://obtienearchivo.bcn.cl/obtienearchivo?id=repositorio/10221/33042/1/BCN_Proteccion_laboral_violencia_contra_la_mujer_VF_pdf.

Amani, Bita. "AI and 'Equality by Design.'" SSRN Scholarly Paper, February 1, 2021. In *Artificial Intelligence and the Law in Canada*, edited by Florian Martin-Bariteau and Teresa Scassa. Toronto: LexisNexis Canada, 2021. https://doi.org/10.2139/ssrn.3734665.

Amis, Lucy. *Building a Movement: Reflections on the History and Future of Business and Human Rights.* Eastbourne, East Sussex, UK: Institute for Human Rights and Business, December 2019. https://www.ihrb.org/uploads/reports/Building_a_Movement_Reflections_on_the_History_and_Future_of_Business_and_Human_Rights_-_IHRB.pdf.

Ammann, Odile. "Language Bias in International Legal Scholarship: Symptoms, Explanations, Implications and Remedies." *European Journal of International Law* 33, no. 3 (August 2022): 821–50.

Anam, Rumana Liza. "Inadequacies and Variations of Maternity Leave Policies throughout the World: Special Focus on Bangladesh." *BRAC University Journal* 5, no. 1 (2008): 93–98.

Andersen, Sara Helene. "Businesses and Human Rights: A Comparative Study of the United States, England and Denmark Using Third World Approaches to International Law." Thesis, European University Institute, 2018. https://cadmus.eui.eu/handle/1814/55904.

Appelman, Naomi, and Paddy Leerssen. "On 'Trusted' Flaggers," Special Issue: The Yale-Wikimedia Initiative on Intermediaries & Information and *Yale Journal of Law and Technology* White Paper Series. *Yale Journal of Law and Technology* 24, no. 1 (2022): 452–75.

Arnold, Bruce Baer. "Safe, but for Whom?: E-Safety Changes." *Precedent* (Sydney, N.S.W.), no. 166 (September 2021): 39–43.

Arrow, Michelle. *The Seventies: The Personal, the Political and the Making of Modern Australia*. Sydney, NSW: NewSouth Publishing, 2019.

Arthur-Holmes, Francis. "Gendered Division of Labour and 'Sympathy' in Artisanal and Small-Scale Gold Mining in Prestea-Huni Valley Municipality, Ghana." *Journal of Rural Studies* 81 (January 2021): 358–62. https://doi.org/10.1016/j.jrurstud.2020.11.001.

Arthur-Holmes, Francis, and Kwaku Abrefa Busia. "Household Dynamics and the Bargaining Power of Women in Artisanal and Small-Scale Mining in Sub-Saharan Africa: A Ghanaian Case Study." *Resources Policy* 69 (December 1, 2020): art. 101884. https://doi.org/10.1016/j.resourpol.2020.101884.

———. "Safety Concerns and Occupational Health Hazards of Women in Artisanal and Small-Scale Mining in Ghana." *The Extractive Industries and Society* 10 (June 2022): art. 101079. https://doi.org/10.1016/j.exis.2022.101079.

Arthur-Holmes, Francis, Thomas Yeboah, and Kwaku Abrefa Busia. "Dimensions of Women's Mobility, Livelihoods and Vulnerability in Artisanal and Small-Scale Mining-Induced Local Economy." *Journal of Rural Studies* 101 (July 2023): art. 103061. https://doi.org/10.1016/j.jrurstud.2023.103061.

Asian Development Bank. *Promoting Women's Economic Empowerment in Cambodia*. Metro Manila, Philippines: Asian Development Bank, 2015.

Association for Progressive Communications et al. "Feminist Principles of the Internet." n.d. Accessed September 14, 2022. https://feministinternet.org/.

Atrey, Shreya. "Women's Human Rights: From Progress to Transformation, an Intersectional Response to Martha Nussbaum." *Human Rights Quarterly* 40, no. 4 (November 20, 2017): 859–904.

Australian Council of Trade Unions. "Historic Day as Paid Family & Domestic Violence Leave to Come into Force," January 31, 2023. https://www.actu.org.au/actu-media/media-releases/2023/historic-day-as-paid-family-domestic-violence-leave-to-come-into-force.

Australian Federal Police. "Human Trafficking and Slavery," n.d. https://www.afp.gov.au/crimes/human-trafficking-and-people-smuggling/human-trafficking-and-slavery.

Australian Government, Office of Parliamentary Counsel. "Our Staff," 2023. https://www.opc.gov.au/about-opc/our-staff.

———. *Annual Report 2020–2021*, 2021. https://www.opc.gov.au/sites/default/files/annual_report_2021_final.pdf.

Badiee, Shaida, Eric Swanson, Lorenz Noe, Tawheeda Wahabzada, Amelia Pittman, and Deirdre Appel. *State of Gender Data Financing—2021*. Open Data Watch, May 2021. https://data2x.org/resource-center/state-of-gender-data-financing-2021/.

Baird, Marian. "Orientations to Paid Maternity Leave: Understanding the Australian Debate." *Journal of Industrial Relations* 46, no. 3 (September 1, 2004): 259–74. https://doi.org/10.1111/j.0022-1856.2004.00144.x.

Baird, Marian, Elizabeth Hill, and Lisa Gulesserian. "Expanding Paternity Leave in Southeast Asia." *East Asia Forum* (blog), June 14, 2019. https://eastasiaforum.org/2019/06/14/expanding-paternity-leave-in-southeast-asia/.

Baird, Marian, Ludo McFerran, and Ingrid Wright. "An Equality Bargaining Breakthrough: Paid Domestic Violence Leave." *Journal of Industrial Relations* 56, no. 2 (April 1, 2014): 190–207. https://doi.org/10.1177/0022185613517471.

Bakker, Isabella. *Gender Budget Initiatives: Why They Matter in Canada*. Alternative Federal Budget 2006, Technical Paper #1. Canadian Centre for Policy Alternatives, September 19, 2005. https://www.policyalternatives.ca/news-research/gender-budget-initiatives-why-they-matter-in-canada/.

Baldez, Lisa. *Defying Convention: US Resistance to the UN Treaty on Women's Rights*. Cambridge: Cambridge University Press, 2014.

Ban, Pamela, Justin Grimmer, Jaclyn Kaslovsky, and Emily West. *A Woman's Voice in the House: Gender Composition and Its Consequences in Committee Hearings*. December 10, 2018. https://scholar.harvard.edu/files/jaclynkaslovsky/files/draft_dec2018.pdf.

Banda, Fareda. "The Limits of Law: A Response to Martha C. Nussbaum." In *The Limits of Human Rights*, edited by Bardo Fassbender and Knut Traisbach, 267–79. Oxford: Oxford University Press, 2019.

Bankwest Curtin Economics Centre for the Australian Council of Trade Unions. *Family and Domestic Violence Leave Review*. Bankwest and Curtin University, July 30, 2021. https://bcec.edu.au/assets/2022/05/BCEC-Analysis-Costs-of-Family-Domestic-Violence-Leave-2021.pdf.

Bardzell, Shaowen. "Feminist HCI: Taking Stock and Outlining an Agenda for Design." In *Proceedings of the SIGCHI Conference on Human Factors in Computing Systems*, 1301–10. CHI '10. New York: Association for Computing Machinery, 2010. https://doi.org/10.1145/1753326.1753521.

Barnack-Tavlaris, Jessica L., Kristina Hansen, Rachel B. Levitt, and Michelle Reno. "Taking Leave to Bleed: Perceptions and Attitudes toward Menstrual Leave Policy." *Health Care for Women International* 40, no. 12 (December 2, 2019): 1355–73. https://doi.org/10.1080/07399332.2019.1639709.

Bartick, Melissa. "Losing Women, Losing Breastfeeding: A Crisis of Words." *Breastfeeding Medicine* 19, no. 5 (May 2024): 313–15. https://doi.org/10.1089/bfm.2024.0102.

Basu, Soumita. "The Global South Writes 1325 (Too)." *International Political Science Review* 37, no. 3 (June 1, 2016): 362–74. https://doi.org/10.1177/0192512116642616.

Batagol, Becky, and Ramona Vijeyarasa. "Lighting the Spark: Reimagining the Statutory Landscape through the Feminist Legislation Project." In *International Women's Rights Law and Gender Equality: Making the Law Work for Women*, edited by Ramona Vijeyarasa. Abingdon, Oxon; New York: Routledge, 2021.

Beall, Jo. "Trickle-down or Rising Tide? Lessons on Mainstreaming Gender Policy from Colombia and South Africa." *Social Policy & Administration* 32, no. 5 (1998): 513–34. https://doi.org/10.1111/1467-9515.00112.

Beckwith, Karen. "Numbers and Newness: The Descriptive and Substantive Representation of Women." *Canadian Journal of Political Science/Revue Canadienne de Science Politique* 40, no. 1 (March 2007): 27–49. https://doi.org/10.1017/S0008423907070059.

Belli, Luca, Yasmin Curzi, and Walter B. Gaspar. "AI Regulation in Brazil: Advancements, Flows, and Need to Learn from the Data Protection Experience." *Computer Law & Security Review* 48 (April 1, 2023): 105767. https://doi.org/10.1016/j.clsr.2022.105767.

Belliappa, Jyothsna Latha. "Menstrual Leave Debate: Opportunity to Address Inclusivity in Indian Organizations." *Indian Journal of Industrial Relations* 53, no. 4 (2018): 604–17.

Bello y Villarino, José-Miguel. "Middle Point, End of the Road or Just the Beginning? Anticorruption Efforts, Failures and Promises at the United Nations." *Max Planck Yearbook of United Nations Law Online* 25, no. 1 (September 22, 2022): 1–28. https://doi.org/10.1163/18757413_02501004.

———. "Women in Anticorruption Laws—The Case for More Gender-Responsive International Treaties." In *International Women's Rights Law and Gender Equality: Making the Law Work for Women*, edited by Ramona Vijeyarasa. Abingdon, Oxon; New York: Routledge, 2021.

Bello y Villarino, José-Miguel, David Hua, Barry Wang, and Melanie Trezise. "Standardisation, Trust and Democratic Principles: The Global Race to Regulate Artificial Intelligence." A report for the United States Studies Centre at the University of Sydney, July 31, 2023. https://www.ussc.edu.au/analysis/standardisation-trust-and-democratic-principles-the-global-race-to-regulate-artificial-intelligence.

Bello y Villarino, José-Miguel, and Ramona Vijeyarasa. "International Human Rights, Artificial Intelligence and the Challenge for the Pondering State: Time to Regulate?" *Nordic Journal of Human Rights* 40, no. 1 (2022): 194–215.

Bell-Williams, Melanie. "'Shop-Soiled' Women: Female Sexuality and the Figure of the Prostitute in 1950s British Cinema." *Journal of British Cinema and Television* 3, no. 2 (November 1, 2006): 266–83. https://doi.org/10.3366/JBCTV.2006.3.2.266.

Bergmann, Emily. "Parental Leave in the United States: Why the United States Should Follow France in Implementing Mandatory Paid Paternal Leave." *Barry Law Child and Family Law Journal* 9 (2021): 159–72.

Bertrand, Marianne, Sandra E. Black, Sissel Jensen, and Adriana Lleras-Muney. "Breaking the Glass Ceiling? The Effect of Board Quotas on Female Labour Market Outcomes in Norway." *The Review of Economic Studies* 86, no. 1 (January 1, 2019): 191–239. https://doi.org/10.1093/restud/rdy032.

Beveridge, Fiona, Kylie Stephen, and Susan M. Nott. *Making Women Count: Integrating Gender into Law and Policy-Making*. Aldershot: Ashgate/Dartmouth, 2000.

Bhattacharya, Utpal, and Hazem Daouk. "When No Law Is Better Than a Good Law." *Review of Finance* 13, no. 4 (October 1, 2009): 577–627. https://doi.org/10.1093/rof/rfp011.

Bhuiyan, Johana. "Facebook Gave Police Their Private Data. Now, This Duo Face Abortion Charges." *The Guardian*, August 10, 2022, sec. US news. https://www.theguardian.com/us-news/2022/aug/10/facebook-user-data-abortion-nebraska-police.

Bildhauer, Bettina, Camilla Røstvik, and Sharra Vostral, eds. *The Politics and History of Menstruation: Contextualising the Scottish Campaign to End Period Poverty.* Special Collection, Open Library of Humanities Journal. n.d. Accessed September 22, 2022. https://olh.openlibhums.org/collections/505/.

Bong, Sharon A. "Negotiating Resistance/Resilience through the Nexus of Spirituality-Sexuality of Same-Sex Partnerships in Malaysia and Singapore." *Marriage & Family Review* 47, no. 8 (2011): 648–65.

Bonnitcha, Jonathan, and Robert McCorquodale. "The Concept of 'Due Diligence' in the UN Guiding Principles on Business and Human Rights." *European Journal of International Law* 28, no. 3 (November 13, 2017): 899–919. https://doi.org/10.1093/ejil/chx042.

Bouckaert, Peter. "License to Kill." Human Rights Watch, March 2, 2017. https://www.hrw .org/report/2017/03/02/license-kill/philippine-police-killings-dutertes-war-drugs.

Boudewijn, Inge A. M., and Katy Jenkins. "Gender, Large-Scale Resource Extraction, and Environmental Inequality in Latin America." In *Handbook on Inequality and the Environment,* edited by Michael Long, Michael Lynch, and Paul Stretesky, 265–86. Cheltenham: Edward Elgar Publishing, 2023. https://www.elgaronline.com/edcollchap/book /9781800881136/book-part-9781800881136-27.xml.

Bourke-Martignoni, Joanna, and Elizabeth Umlas. *Gender-Responsive Due Diligence for Business Actors: Human Rights-Based Approaches.* Geneva, Switzerland: Geneva Academy of International Humanitarian Law and Human Rights, December 2018.

Bowleg, Lisa. "The Problem with the Phrase 'Women and Minorities': Intersectionality— An Important Theoretical Framework for Public Health." *American Journal of Public Health* 102, no. 7 (July 2012): 1267–73. https://doi.org/10.2105/AJPH.2012.300750.

Brandth, Berit, Brita Bungum, and Elin Kvande. "Fathers, Fathering and Parental Leaves." In *Research Handbook on Leave Policy,* edited by Ivana Dobrotić, Sonja Blum, and Alison Koslowski, 172–84. Cheltenham: Edward Elgar Publishing, 2022. https://www .elgaronline.com/edcollchap/book/9781800372214/book-part-9781800372214-23.xml.

Brown, Annie. "Brilliance Knows No Gender: Eliminating Bias In Chatbot Development." *Forbes,* April 30, 2021. https://www.forbes.com/sites/anniebrown/2021/04/30/brilliance -knows-no-gender-eliminating-bias-in-chatbot-development/.

Brown, Ira V. "'Am I Not a Woman and a Sister?' The Anti-Slavery Convention of American Women, 1837–1839." *Pennsylvania History: A Journal of Mid-Atlantic Studies* 50, no. 1 (1983): 1–19.

Budlender, Debbie. *The Political Economy of Women's Budgets in the South.* Cape Town, South Africa: Community Agency for Social Enquiry South Africa, 2000.

Burke, Thomas F. *Lawyers, Lawsuits, and Legal Rights: The Battle Over Litigation in American Society.* Berkeley: University of California Press, 2002.

Buss, Doris, Blair Rutherford, Cynthia Kumah, and Mary Spear. "Beyond the Rituals of Inclusion: The Environment for Women and Resource Governance in Africa's Artisanal and Small-Scale Mining Sector." *Environmental Science & Policy* 116 (February 1, 2021): 30–37. https://doi.org/10.1016/j.envsci.2020.10.019.

Buss, Doris, Blair Rutherford, Jennifer Stewart, Gisèle Eva Côté, Abby Sebina-Zziwa, Richard Kibombo, Jennifer Hinton, and Joanne Lebert. "A Mine of One's Own?: Gender Norms and Empowerment in Artisanal and Small-Scale Mining." In *Women's Economic Empowerment: Insights from Africa and South Asia,* edited by Kate Grantham, Gillian Dowie, and Arjan de Haan. Abingdon, Oxon: Routledge, 2021.

Bustelo, Mara. "The CEDAW Committee at the Crossroads." In *The Future of UN Human Rights Monitoring*, edited by Philip Alston and James Crawford, 79–112. Cambridge, UK: Cambridge University Press, 2000.

Butalia, Urvashi, and Nicky Falkof. "Making Feminist Sense in the Global South: A Conversation with Urvashi Butalia." *Feminist Theory*, January 5, 2022, 14647001211038887. https://doi.org/10.1177/14647001211038887.

Butler, Judith. "Performative Acts and Gender Constitution: An Essay in Phenomenology and Feminist Theory." *Theatre Journal* 40, no. 4 (December 1988): 519. https://doi.org/10.2307/3207893.

Buvinic, Mayra, and Shaida Badiee. "Gender Data Systems: Better Data for All." Center for Global Development (blog post). https://www.cgdev.org/blog/gender-data-systems-better-data-all.

Buxton, Abbi. "Responding to the Challenge of Artisanal and Small-Scale Mining. How Can Knowledge Networks Help?" London: International Institute for Environment and Development, 2013.

Byanyima, Winnie. "Strengthening Parliamentary Governance Through Gender Budgeting: The Experience of Three African Countries." Rome, Italy, 2000.

Cabrera Navarrete, Diana Elizabeth. "El trabajo que no existe, el dolor que no existe: mujeres jancheras, mineras artesanales de oro, en el cantón Camilo Ponce Enríquez." Master's thesis, Quito, Ecuador: Flacso Ecuador, 2023. http://repositorio.flacsoandes.edu.ec/handle/10469/19874.

Campbell, Meghan. "CEDAW and Women's Intersecting." *Revisita Direito* 11, no. 2 (2015): 479–504.

Canadian Space Agency. "Evaluation of the Implementation of Gender-Based Analysis Plus at the Canadian Space Agency." September 29, 2021. https://www.asc-csa.gc.ca/eng/publications/er-1920-0201.asp.

Cañero Ruiz, Julia, and Danislava Marinova. "¿Iguales e intransferibles?: preferencias por el sistema de permisos por nacimiento." *REIS: Revista Española de Investigaciones Sociológicas*, no. 190 (2025): 63–88.

Caparas, Victoria. "Work-Family Balance and Family Poverty in Asia: An Overview of Policy Contexts, Consequences and Challenges." New York: United Nations Expert Group Meeting "Assessing Family Policies: Confronting Family Poverty and Social Exclusion and Ensuring Work-Family Balance," June 1, 2011.

Caprioli, Mary, Valerie M. Hudson, Rose Mcdermott, Bonnie Ballif-Spanvill, Chad F. Emmett, and S. Matthew Stearmer. "The WomanStats Project Database: Advancing an Empirical Research Agenda." *Journal of Peace Research* 46, no. 6 (November 2009): 839–51. https://doi.org/10.1177/0022343309342947.

Carr, Marilyn, Martha Alter Chen, and Jane Tate. "Globalization and Home-Based Workers." *Feminist Economics* 6, no. 3 (January 1, 2000): 123–42. https://doi.org/10.1080/135457000750020164.

Catalyst. "The Bottom Line: Connecting Corporate Performance and Gender Diversity." March 26, 2014. https://women.govt.nz/inspiring-action-for-gender-balance/bottom-line-connecting-corporate-performance-and-gender.

Celis, Karen, and Sarah Childs. "The Substantive Representation of Women: What to Do with Conservative Claims?" *Political Studies* 60, no. 1 (March 1, 2012): 213–25. https://doi.org/10.1111/j.1467-9248.2011.00904.x.

Chacko, Shubha. "Decolonial Feminism: Charting a Path towards a Just and Liberatory Tomorrow." BRICS Feminist Watch, n.d. https://www.scribd.com/document/741264355/Shubha-Chacko-Decolonial-Feminism.

Chakraborty, Lekha S. "Fiscal and Regional Context of Gender Budgeting in Asia." In *Fiscal Policy for Sustainable Development in Asia-Pacific: Gender Budgeting in India*, edited by Lekha S. Chakraborty, 165–95. Singapore: Springer Nature, 2022. https://doi.org/10.1007/978-981-19-3281-6_7.

Chakraborty, Lekha, Veena Nayyar, and Komal Jain. "The Political Economy of Fiscal Interventions to Tackle Gender Inequalities: Empirical Evidences on 'Gender Budgeting' from India." *Policy Foundation*, July 2018.

Chandler, Andrea. "Women on Corporate Boards: A Comparison of Parliamentary Discourse in the United Kingdom and France." *Politics & Gender* 12, no. 3 (September 2016): 443–68. https://doi.org/10.1017/S1743923X15000574.

Chandra, Aparna, Jhuma Sen, and Rachna Chaudhary. "Righting Together: An Introduction to the Indian Feminist Judgments Project." *Verfassung in Recht und Übersee* 56, no. 1 (2023): 5–16. https://doi.org/10.5771/0506-7286-2023-1-5.

Chapkis, Wendy. "Trafficking, Migration, and the Law: Protecting Innocents, Punishing Immigrants." *Gender & Society* 17, no. 6 (December 1, 2003): 923–37. https://doi.org/10.1177/0891243203257477.

Charlesworth, Hilary. "Not Waving but Drowning: Gender Mainstreaming and Human Rights in the United Nations." *Harvard Human Rights Journal* 18 (2005): 1.

———. "Talking to Ourselves? Feminist Scholarship in International Law." In *Feminist Perspectives on Contemporary International Law*. Oxford: Hart Publishing, 2011. http://hdl.handle.net/1885/19995.

Chaudhuri, Abhik, Adam Smith, Allison Gardner, Linda Gu, Malek Salem, and Maroussia Lévesque. "Regulatory Frameworks Relating to Data Privacy and Algorithmic Decision Making in the Context of Emerging Standards on Algorithmic Bias." Paper presented at Neural Information Processing (NIPS) Conference, Montreal, Canada, 2018. https://www.researchgate.net/publication/329701534_Regulatory_frameworks_relating_to_data_privacy_and_algorithmic_decision_making_in_the_context_of_emerging_standards_on_algorithmic_bias.

Chauhan, Prashant, and Gagandeep Kaur. "Gender Bias and Artificial Intelligence: A Challenge within the Periphery of Human Rights." *Hasanuddin Law Review* 8, no. 1 (April 12, 2022): 46–59. https://doi.org/10.20956/halrev.v8i1.3569.

Chavez, Daniel. "The Watering Down of Participatory Budgeting and People Power in Porto Alegre, Brazil." *Participatory Learning and Action* 58 (June 1, 2008): 57–60.

Cheng, Sealing. "Sex Trafficking: Inside the Business of Modern Slavery (Review)." *Journal of World History* 21, no. 2 (August 1, 2010): 363–68. https://doi.org/10.1353/jwh.0.0120.

Chesler, Ellen. "Who Wrote CEDAW?" In *Women and the UN: A New History of Women's International Human Rights*, edited by Rebecca Adami and Dan Plesch, 104–24. London; New York: Routledge, 2021.

Childs, Sarah. "Feminist Institutional Change: The Case of the UK Women and Equalities Committee." *Parliamentary Affairs* 76, no. 3 (June 19, 2023): 507–31. https://doi.org/10.1093/pa/gsab066.

Childs, Sarah, and Mona Lena Krook. "Analysing Women's Substantive Representation: From Critical Mass to Critical Actors." *Government and Opposition* 44, no. 2 (2009): 125–45.

Chizema, Amon, Dzidziso S. Kamuriwo, and Yoshikatsu Shinozawa. "Women on Corporate Boards around the World: Triggers and Barriers." *The Leadership Quarterly* 26, no. 6 (December 1, 2015): 1051–65. https://doi.org/10.1016/j.leaqua.2015.07.005.

Christopherson, Katharine, Audrey Yiadom, Juliet Johnson, Francisca Fernando, Hanan Yazid, and Clara Thiemann. *Tackling Legal Impediments to Women's Economic Empowerment.* International Monetary Fund, 2022.

Chuang, Janie A. "Exploitation Creep and the Unmaking of Human Trafficking Law." *American Journal of International Law* 108, no. 4 (October 2014): 609–49. https://doi.org/10.5305/amerjintelaw.108.4.0609.

Cleary, Catherine Blanchard. "Our Changing Institutions: A Challenge to the Liberally Educated." Commencement address, Lawrence University, 1974. https://lux.lawrence.edu/addresses_commencement/32/.

Collett, Clementine, Gina Neff, and Livia Gouvea Gomes. *The Effects of AI on the Working Lives of Women.* Paris: United Nations Educational, Scientific and Cultural Organization, 2022.

Commission for Gender Equality. *Government's Gender Responsive Budgeting Framework: Commission for Gender Equality Review of Implementation Report*, 2021. South Africa. https://cge.org.za/wp-content/uploads/2021/07/CGE-Gender-Responsive-Budgeting-Framework.pdf.

Conklin, Michael. "Grandstanding or Gotcha: Asking Ketanji Brown Jackson 'Can You Provide a Definition for the Word "Woman"?'" SSRN Scholarly Paper. Rochester, NY: Social Science Research Network, April 2, 2022. https://doi.org/10.2139/ssrn.4074186.

Cools, Sara, Jon H. Fiva, and Lars J. Kirkebøen. "Causal Effects of Paternity Leave on Children and Parents." *The Scandinavian Journal of Economics* 117, no. 3 (2015): 801–28. https://doi.org/10.1111/sjoe.12113.

Coombs, Elizabeth, and Halefom Abraha. "Governance of AI and Gender: Building on International Human Rights Law and Relevant Regional Frameworks." In *Handbook on the Politics and Governance of Big Data and AI*, edited by Andrej Zwitter and Oskar J. Gstrein, 211–43. Cheltenham: Edward Elgar Publishing, 2022. https://papers.ssrn.com/sol3/papers.cfm?abstract_id=4221953.

Cooper, Davina. "Crafting Prefigurative Law in Turbulent Times: Decertification, DIY Law Reform, and the Dilemmas of Feminist Prototyping." *Feminist Legal Studies* 31, no. 1 (April 1, 2023): 17–42. https://doi.org/10.1007/s10691-022-09515-4.

———. "Towards an Adventurous Institutional Politics: The Prefigurative 'As If' and the Reposing of What's Real." *The Sociological Review* 68, no. 5 (September 1, 2020): 893–916. https://doi.org/10.1177/0038026120915148.

Costa, Monica, and Rhonda Sharp. "Gender-Responsive Budgeting." In *Handbook of Feminist Governance*, edited by Marian Sawer, Lee Banaszak, Jacqui True, and Johanna Kantola, 138–49. Cheltenham: Edward Elgar Publishing, 2023.

———. "Gender-Responsive Budgeting." Adelaide, Australia: University of South Australia, 2025. https://unisa.edu.au/research/social-relationships-communities/our-research/gender-responsive-budgeting/.

Cowan, Sharon, Chloë Kennedy, and Vanessa E. Munro. *Scottish Feminist Judgments: (Re)Creating Law from the Outside In.* London: Bloomsbury Publishing, 2019.

Crawford, Kate. *The Atlas of AI: Power, Politics, and the Planetary Costs of Artificial Intelligence.* New Haven, CT: Yale University Press, 2021. https://doi.org/10.2307/j.ctv1ghv45t.

Crenshaw, Kimberlé. "Race, Reform, and Retrenchment: Transformation and Legitimation in Antidiscrimination Law." *Harvard Law Review* 101, no. 7 (1988): 1331–87. https://doi.org/10.2307/1341398.

Criado Perez, Caroline. *Invisible Women: Data Bias in a World Designed for Men*. New York: Harry N. Abrams, 2019.

Dados, Nour, and Raewyn Connell. "The Global South." *Contexts* 11, no. 1 (February 1, 2012): 12–13. https://doi.org/10.1177/1536504212436479.

Daley, Elizabeth, Rachel Dore-Weeks, and Claudine Umuhoza. "Ahead of the Game: Land Tenure Reform in Rwanda and the Process of Securing Women's Land Rights." *Journal of Eastern African Studies* 4, no. 1 (2010): 131–52. https://doi.org/10.1080/17531050903556691.

Dancer, Helen, Bonnie Holligan, and Helena Howe, eds. *UK Earth Law Judgments Project: Reimaginging Law for People and Planet*. London: Bloomsbury Publishing, 2024. https://www.sussex.ac.uk/law/research/projects/earth_law.

Datta Gupta, Nabanita, Nina Smith, and Mette Verner. "Child Care and Parental Leave in the Nordic Countries: A Model to Aspire To?" SSRN Scholarly Paper. Rochester, NY, March 1, 2006. https://doi.org/10.2139/ssrn.890298.

Davies, Margaret. *Asking the Law Question*. Sydney: The Law Book Company, 1994. https://archive.org/details/askinglawquestiooooodavi/mode/2up.

Davis, Jarrett D., Glenn Michael Miles, and John H. Quinley III. "'Same Same, but Different': A Baseline Study on the Vulnerabilities of Transgender Sex Workers in the Sex Industry in Bangkok, Thailand." *International Journal of Sociology and Social Policy* 39, no. 7/8 (September 3, 2019): 550–73. https://doi.org/10.1108/IJSSP-01-2019-0022.

Davis, Martha F. "The State of Abortion Rights in the US." *International Journal of Gynecology & Obstetrics* 159, no. 1 (2022): 324–29. https://doi.org/10.1002/ijgo.14392.

De Silva de Alwis, Rangita. "Gendering the New International Convention on Cybercrimes and New Norms on Artificial Intelligence and Emerging Technologies." *Washington Journal of Law, Technology & Arts* 20, no. 2 (April 9, 2025). https://digitalcommons.law.uw.edu/wjlta/vol20/iss2/1.

Del Aguila, Alicia. *The Labour Situation of Indigenous Women in Peru—A Study*. Geneva, Switzerland: International Labour Organization, 2016.

Deininger, Klaus W., Aparajita Goyal, and Hari K. Nagarajan. "Women's Inheritance Rights and Intergenerational Transmission of Resources in India." *The Journal of Human Resources* 48, no. 1 (2013): 114–41. https://doi.org/10.1353/jhr.2013.0005.

Deloitte Global Boardroom Program. "Progress at a Snail's Pace: Women in the Boardroom—A Global Perspective," 7th ed. Deloitte Touche Tohmatsu, 2022. https://www2.deloitte.com/content/dam/Deloitte/global/Documents/gx-women-in-the-boardroom-seventh-edition.pdf.

———. "Women in the Boardroom: A Global Perspective," 8th ed. Deloitte Touche Tohmatsu, 2024. https://www2.deloitte.com/us/en/insights/topics/leadership/women-in-the-boardroom.html.

Denis, Emeline. "Enhancing Gender Diversity on Boards and in Senior Management of Listed Companies." OECD Corporate Governance Working Paper Series No. 28, September 20, 2022, https://www.oecd.org/en/publications/enhancing-gender-diversity-on-boards-and-in-senior-management-of-listed-companies_4f7ca695-en.html.

Department of Industry, Science and Resources. "Australia's Artificial Intelligence Ethics Framework." October 5, 2022. https://www.industry.gov.au/publications/australias -artificial-intelligence-ethics-framework/australias-ai-ethics-principles.

Devi, Bernadetta, Kuntala Lahiri-Dutt, Sara Beavis, and Aparna Lal. "Gendered Informal Gold Trading in Indonesia: Case Studies from Central Kalimantan." *The Extractive Industries and Society* 20 (December 1, 2024): 101553. https://doi.org/10.1016/j.exis.2024 .101553.

Dhir, Aaron. "Challenging Boardroom Homogeneity: Corporate Law, Governance and Diversity." *Books*, April 1, 2015. https://digitalcommons.osgoode.yorku.ca/faculty_books/269.

Dirlik, Arif. "Global South: Predicament and Promise." *The Global South* 1, no. 1 (2007): 12–23.

Dobson, John, and Mahdi Rastad. "Women on Boards: EU Board Gender Quotas, and Why the US Should Avoid Them." *Business & Professional Ethics Journal* 37, no. 1 (2018): 1–12. https://doi.org/10.5840/bpej201792964.

Doezema, Jo. "Loose Women or Lost Women? The Re-Emergence of the Myth of White Slavery in Contemporary Discourses of Trafficking in Women." *Gender Issues* 18, no. 1 (December 1, 1999): 23–50. https://doi.org/10.1007/s12147-999-0021-9.

———. "Now You See Her, Now You Don't: Sex Workers at the UN Trafficking Protocol Negotiation." *Social & Legal Studies* 14, no. 1 (March 1, 2005): 61–89. https://doi.org/10.1177 /0964663905049526.

Donahoe, Eileen, and Megan MacDuffee Metzger. "Artificial Intelligence and Human Rights." *Journal of Democracy* 30, no. 2 (2019): 115–26. https://doi.org/10.1353/jod .2019.0029.

Donovan, Brian. *White Slave Crusades: Race, Gender, and Anti-Vice Activism, 1887–1917.* Champaign-Urbana: University of Illinois Press, 2010.

Dorrough, Angela R., Monika Leszczyńska, Manuela Barreto, and Andreas Glöckner. "Revealing Side Effects of Quota Rules on Group Cooperation." *Journal of Economic Psychology* 57 (December 1, 2016): 136–52. https://doi.org/10.1016/j.joep.2016.09.007.

Douglas, Heather, Francesca Bartlett, Trish Luker, and Rosemary Hunter. *Australian Feminist Judgments: Righting and Rewriting Law.* Oxford: Hart Publishing, 2014.

Dowd, Nancy E. "Maternity Leave: Taking Sex Differences into Account." *Fordham Law Review* 54 (1986): 699.

Dowling, Michael, and Brian Lucey. "ChatGPT for (Finance) Research: The Bananarama Conjecture." *Finance Research Letters*, January 25, 2023, 103662. https://doi.org/10.1016/j .frl.2023.103662.

Dror, Yehezkel. "Law and Social Change." *Tulane Law Review* 33 (1959): 787–802.

Drozd, Breana. "Girls Just Wanna Have Equal Representation on Corporate Boards: A Comparative View of Female Directorships in Norway, France, and Japan." *Wisconsin International Law Journal* (blog), October 2020. https://wilj.law.wisc.edu/jus-gentium /girls-just-wanna-have-equal-representation-on-corporate-boards-a-comparative-view -of-female-directorships-in-norway-france-and-japan/.

Eftimie, Adriana, K. Heller, J. Strongman, J. Hinton, K. Lahiri-Dutt, and N. Mutemeri. "Gender Dimensions of Artisanal and Small-Scale Mining—A Rapid Assessment Toolkit." World Bank Group, 2012.

Eftimie, Adriana, Katherine Heller, John Strongman, Jennifer Hinton, Kuntala Lahiri-Dutt, Nellie Mutemeri, Chansouk Insouvanh, Michael Godet Sambo, and Susan Wagner. "Gender Dimensions of Artisanal and Small-Scale Mining: A Rapid Assessment Toolkit." World Bank and Gender Action Plan, 2012. https://womenandmining.org/wp-content /uploads/2019/04/Gender_and_ASM_Toolkit.pdf.

Einarsdóttir, Þorgerður J., Guðbjörg Linda Rafnsdóttir, and Margrét Valdimarsdóttir. "Structural Hindrances or Less Driven Women? Managers' Views on Corporate Quotas." *Politics & Gender* 16, no. 1 (2020): 285–313. https://doi.org/10.1017/S1743923X1800106X.

Eisenstein, Hester. "Femocrats, Official Feminism, and the Uses of Power: A Case Study of EEO Implementation in New South Wales, Australia." *Yale Journal of Law and Feminism* 2, no. 1 (1989): 51–73.

Elias, Juanita. *Gender Politics and the Pursuit of Competitiveness in Malaysia: Women on Board.* London: Routledge, 2020. https://doi.org/10.4324/9780429058691.

Elomäki, Anna. "Gender Quotas for Corporate Boards: Depoliticizing Gender and the Economy." *NORA: Nordic Journal of Women's Studies* 26, no. 1 (2018): 53–68. https://doi .org/10.1080/08038740.2017.1388282.

Elson, Diane. "Budgeting for Women's Rights: Monitoring Government Budgets for Compliance with CEDAW." New York: United Nations Development Fund for Women, December 12, 2006. https://gsdrcwebsite-pjp5ov869n.live-website.com/document-library /budgeting-for-womens-rights-monitoring-government-budgets-for-compliance-with -cedaw/.

Engle, Karen, Vasuki Nesiah, and Dianne Otto. "Feminist Approaches to International Law." SSRN Scholarly Paper. Rochester, NY, April 6, 2021. https://doi.org/10.2139/ssrn.3820771.

Enright, Máiréad, Julie McCandless, and Aoife O'Donoghue. *Northern / Irish Feminist Judgments: Judges' Troubles and the Gendered Politics of Identity.* London: Bloomsbury Publishing, 2017.

EQUALS and United Nations Educational, Scientific and Cultural Organization. "I'd Blush If I Could: Closing Gender Divides in Digital Skills through Education." Geneva: UNESCO, 2019. https://doi.org/10.54675/RAPC9356.

eSafety Commissioner. "The Global Online Safety Regulators Network." Australia. Accessed August 10, 2023. https://www.esafety.gov.au/about-us/who-we-are/international -engagement/the-global-online-safety-regulators-network.

Eydal, Guðný Björk, Ingólfur V. Gíslason, Tine Rostgaard, Berit Brandth, Ann-Zofie Duvander, and Johanna Lammi-Taskula. "Trends in Parental Leave in the Nordic Countries: Has the Forward March of Gender Equality Halted?" *Community, Work & Family* 18, no. 2 (April 3, 2015): 167–81. https://doi.org/10.1080/13668803.2014.1002754.

Eydal, Guðný, and Tine Rostgaard. "Policies Promoting Active Fatherhood in Five Nordic Countries." In *Contemporary Perspectives in Family Research,* 257–79, 2018. https://doi.org /10.1108/S1530-353520180000012011.

Farbenblum, Bassina, Laurie Berg, and Angela Kintominas. *Transformative Technology for Migrant Workers: Opportunities, Challenges, and Risks.* New York: Open Society Foundations, 2018.

Faur, Eleonor. "Contrasting Trends in Gender and Childcare in Argentina: Family Policies between LGBT Rights and Maternalism." *Current Sociology* 66, no. 4 (July 1, 2018): 617–28. https://doi.org/10.1177/0011392118765250.

Federo, Ryan. "The Rainbow Glass Ceiling: Breaking Barriers for LGBTQ+ Inclusion in Board Diversity." *Academy of Management Perspectives*, May 9, 2024, amp.2023.0186. https://doi.org/10.5465/amp.2023.0186.

Ferreira, Nuno, Maria Federica Moscati, and Senthorun Raj, eds. *Queer Judgments*. Coventry: CounterPress, 2025. https://counterpress.org.uk/publications/queer-judgments/#1637942607769-10714cdb-d9629f06-e96a.

Fineman, Martha. "Challenging Law, Establishing Differences: The Future of Feminist Legal Scholarship." *Florida Law Review* 42 (1990): 25–43.

Fischer, Judith D. "Framing Gender: Federal Appellate Judges' Choices about Gender-Neutral Language." *University of San Francisco Law Review* 43, no. 3 (2009): 473–506.

Fitz-Gibbon, Kate, Naomi Pfitzner, and Emma McNicol. "Domestic and Family Violence Leave across Australian Workplaces: Examining Victim-Survivor Experiences of Workplace Supports and the Importance of Cultural Change." *Journal of Criminology* 56, no. 2–3 (June 1, 2023): 294–312. https://doi.org/10.1177/26338076221148203.

Fitzsimmons, Stacey R. "Women on Boards of Directors: Why Skirts in Seats Aren't Enough." *Business Horizons*, Special Issue on Corporate Governance: Velocity and Visibility, 55, no. 6 (November 1, 2012): 557–66. https://doi.org/10.1016/j.bushor.2012.07.003.

Fontana, David, and Naomi Schoenbaum. "Unsexing Parenting." *Columbia Law Review* 119, no. 2 (2019): 309–68.

Forrest, Ruth, MP. "Motion and Reading Speech: Joint Sessional Gender and Equality Committee." Tasmanian Legislative Council, Tasmania, June 3, 2022. https://ruthforrest.com.au/parliament/speeches/motion/868-motion-joint-sessional-gender-and-equality-committee.

Fragoso, Lucía Pérez, and Corina Rodríguez Enríquez. "Gender Budgeting Efforts: Latin America and Canada." In *Fiscal Policies and Gender Equality*, ch. 5. International Monetary Fund. Accessed November 7, 2023. https://www.elibrary.imf.org/display/book/9781513590363/ch05.xml.

Franceschet, Susan. "Explaining Domestic Violence Policy Outcomes in Chile and Argentina." *Latin American Politics and Society* 52, no. 03 (2010): 1–29. https://doi.org/10.1111/j.1548-2456.2010.00088.x.

Franceschini, Ivan. "Outsourcing Exploitation: Chinese and Cambodian Garment Workers Compared." *Made in China Journal* (blog), September 24, 2017. https://madeinchinajournal.com/2017/09/24/outsourcing-exploitation-chinese-and-cambodian-garment-workers-compared/.

Frankenberg, Günter. "Critical Comparisons: Re-Thinking Comparative Law." *Harvard International Law Journal* 26, no. 2 (1985): 411–56.

Franzese, Paula A. "Reclaiming Our Noble Profession." *Seton Hall Law Review* 22 (1992): 307.

Fredman, Sandra. "Reversing Roles: Bringing Men into the Frame." *International Journal of Law in Context* 10, no. 4 (December 2014): 442–59.

Fudge, Judy. *Constructing Modern Slavery: Law, Capitalism, and Unfree Labour*. Cambridge: Cambridge University Press, 2025. https://doi.org/10.1017/9781108562058.

"Full Translation: China's 'New Generation Artificial Intelligence Development Plan' (2017)." *DigiChina* (blog). Published August 1, 2017. https://digichina.stanford.edu/work/full-translation-chinas-new-generation-artificial-intelligence-development-plan-2017/.

Galanter, Marc. "Reading the Landscape of Disputes—What We Know and Don't Know (and Think We Know) About Our Allegedly Contentious and Litigious Society." *UCLA Law Review* 31, no. 1 (n.d.): 4–72.

Gallagher, Anne T. "Two Cheers for the Trafficking Protocol." *Anti-Trafficking Review*, no. 4 (2015): 14.

Gay-Antaki, Miriam. "Feminist Geographies of Climate Change: Negotiating Gender at Climate Talks." *Geoforum* 115 (October 1, 2020): 1–10. https://doi.org/10.1016/j.geoforum .2020.06.012.

Geenen, Sara. "Relations and Regulations in Local Gold Trade Networks in South Kivu, Democratic Republic of Congo." *Journal of Eastern African Studies* 5, no. 3 (2011): 427–46.

Genna, Giulia. "Womenomics in Japan: Between Economic Miracle and Egalitarian Failure." *London School of Economics International Development Review* 2, no. 1 (2021): 1–12.

Genovese, Ann. "Goode v. Goode: The Practice of Feminist Judgment in Family Law." In *Australian Feminist Judgments: Righting and Rewriting Law*, edited by Heather Douglas, Francesca Bartlett, Trish Luker, and Rosemary Hunter. London: Bloomsbury Publishing, 2014.

Georgetown Institute for Women, Peace and Security (GIWPS) and Peace Research Institute Oslo (PRIO). *Women, Peace and Security Index 2019/20: Inclusion, Justice, Security.* Washington, DC: GIWPS and PRIO, 2019. https://giwps.georgetown.edu/wp-content /uploads/2019/12/WPS-Index-2019-20-Report.pdf.

Gerards, Janneke, and Raphaële Xenidis. *Algorithmic Discrimination in Europe: Challenges and Opportunities for Gender Equality and Non Discrimination Law.* Luxembourg City: Publications Office of the European Union, 2021. https://data.europa.eu/doi /10.2838/544956.

Gonzalez de la Vega Hernandez, Geraldina, Isabel Montoya Ramos, Laura Garcia Velasco, Pauline Capdevielle, Maria Jesus Medina Arellano, and Mildred del Rocio Carrillo Cartas. *Sentencias feministas: Reescribiendo la justicia con perspectiva de género. Proyecto México.* Mexico D.F.: Institute of Constitutional Studies of the State of Querétaro, 2022. https://biblioteca.corteidh.or.cr/documento/76526.

Goonesekere, Savitri, ed. *Violence, Law and Women's Rights in South Asia.* New Delhi and London: United Nations Development Fund for Women and SAGE Publications, 2004.

Gouws, Amanda. "Women's Activism around Gender-Based Violence in South Africa: Recognition, Redistribution and Representation." *Review of African Political Economy* 43, no. 149 (2016): 400–415. https://doi.org/10.1080/03056244.2016.1217838.

Govender, Pregs. "International Women's Day 2020: Economic Rights: From Words to Action." PregsGovender.com, March 8, 2020. https://www.pregsgovender.com/post /international-women-s-day-2020-economic-rights-from-words-to-action.

Grand Marín, Mónica. "La normatividad minera y el enfoque de género: Propuesta de un marco de acción para territorios de pequeña minería y minería de subsistencia en Colombia." Master's thesis, Planificación Territorial y Gestión Ambiental, Centro Universitario Internacional de Barcelona—UNIBA, 2021. https://diposit.ub.edu/dspace /handle/2445/176934.

Graycar, Reg, and Jenny Morgan. "Law Reform: What's in It for Women." *The Windsor Yearbook of Access to Justice* 23, no. 2 (2005): 393–419.

———. "On the Hidden Gender of Law: A Public Talk." *Australian Feminist Law Journal* 41, no. 1 (2015): 29–36. https://doi.org/10.1080/13200968.2015.1045110.

———. *The Hidden Gender of Law.* 2nd ed. Leichhardt, N.S.W: Federation Press, 2002.

Greif, Elisabeth. "Upward Translations—The Role of NGOs in Promoting LGBTI*-Human Rights under the Convention on the Elimination of All Forms of Discrimination Against Women (CEDAW)." *Peace Human Rights Governance* 4, no. 1 (2020): 9–34. https://doi.org/10.14658/pupj-phrg-2020-1-1.

Groeneveld, Sandra, Vincent Bakker, and Eduard Schmidt. "Breaking the Glass Ceiling, but Facing a Glass Cliff? The Role of Organizational Decline in Women's Representation in Leadership Positions in Dutch Civil Service Organizations." *Public Administration* 98, no. 2 (2020): 441–64. https://doi.org/10.1111/padm.12632.

Grovogu, Siba. "A Revolution Nonetheless: The Global South in International Relations." *The Global South* 5, no. 1 (2011): 175–90. https://doi.org/10.2979/globalsouth.5.1.175.

Guendelman, Sylvia, Jessica Lang Kosa, Michelle Pearl, Steve Graham, Julia Goodman, and Martin Kharrazi. "Juggling Work and Breastfeeding: Effects of Maternity Leave and Occupational Characteristics." *Pediatrics* 123, no. 1 (January 1, 2009): e38–46. https://doi.org/10.1542/peds.2008-2244.

Guerrero Salazar, Susana. "Repercusión mediática del informe de la RAE sobre el lenguaje inclusivo en la Constitución española." *Círculo de Lingüística Aplicada a la Comunicación* 89 (February 23, 2022): 1–18. https://doi.org/10.5209/clac.79497.

Güezmes García, Ana, and María-Noel Vaeza. *Advances in Care Policies in Latin America and the Caribbean: Towards a Care Society with Gender Equality.* United Nations Santiago: Division for Gender Affairs of the Economic Commission for Latin America and the Caribbean (ECLAC) and the Regional Office for the Americas and the Caribbean of UN-Women, 2022. https://lac.unwomen.org/sites/default/files/2023-03/S2201159_en.pdf.

Guibert-Lantoine, Catherine de, and Henri Leridon. "Contraception in France: An Assessment after 30 Years of Liberalization." *Population: An English Selection* 11 (1999): 89–113.

Gunderson, Morley. "Intersectionality in HR Research: Challenges and Opportunities." *International Journal of Manpower* 44, no. 7 (January 1, 2022): 1273–87. https://doi.org/10.1108/IJM-04-2022-0187.

Gupta, Indrani, Kanksha Barman, and Avantika Ranjan. "Are Gender Budgets Useful for Reducing Gender Inequalities? An Exploratory Study with a Focus on India." In *Transforming Unequal Gender Relations in India and Beyond: An Intersectional Perspective on Challenges and Opportunities*, edited by Saroj Pachauri and Ravi K. Verma, 149–67. Sustainable Development Goals Series. Singapore: Springer Nature, 2023. https://doi.org/10.1007/978-981-99-4086-8_9.

Halperin-Kaddari, Ruth, and Marsha A. Freeman. "Backlash Goes Global: Men's Groups, Patriarchal Family Policy, and the False Promise of Gender-Neutral Laws." *Canadian Journal of Women and the Law*, April 19, 2016. https://doi.org/10.3138/cjwl.28.1.182.

Hamplová, Eva, Václav Janeček, and Frank Lefley. "Board Gender Diversity and Women in Leadership Positions—Are Quotas the Solution?" *Corporate Communications* 27, no. 4 (2022): 742–59. https://doi.org/10.1108/CCIJ-02-2022-0022.

Hankivsky, Olena, and Linda Mussell. "Gender-Based Analysis Plus in Canada: Problems and Possibilities of Integrating Intersectionality." *Canadian Public Policy* 44, no. 4 (December 2018): 303–16. https://doi.org/10.3138/cpp.2017-058.

Harpur, Paul, Heather Douglas, and Jiwon Joo. "Submission to the Fair Work Commission: 4-Yearly Review of Modern Awards Family and Domestic Violence Leave (AM2015/1)," August 2017. https://law.uq.edu.au/files/57222/2017_harpurdouglas_fwc_140817.pdf.

Heathcote, Gina. "Naming and Shaming: Human Rights Accountability in Security Council Resolution 1960 (2010) on Women, Peace and Security." *Journal of Human Rights Practice* 4, no. 1 (2012): 82–105. https://doi.org/10.1093/jhuman/hus003.

Heidenreich, Vibeke. "Why Gender Quotas in Company Boards in Norway—and Not in Sweden?" In *Firms, Boards and Gender Quotas: Comparative Perspectives*, edited by Fredrik Engelstad and Mari Teigen, 29:147–83. Comparative Social Research. Emerald Group Publishing, 2012. https://doi.org/10.1108/S0195-6310(2012)0000029009.

Hellman, Deborah. "Measuring Algorithmic Fairness." *Virginia Law Review* 106, no. 4 (2020): 811–66.

Henderson, Bradley, Colleen Flood, and Teresa Scassa. "Artificial Intelligence in Canadian Healthcare: Will the Law Protect Us from Algorithmic Bias Resulting in Discrimination?" *Canadian Journal of Law and Technology* 19, no. 2 (January 1, 2022): 475.

Hevener Kaufman, Natalie, and Stephanie A. Lindquist. "Critiquing Gender-Neutral Treaty Language: The Convention on the Elimination of All Forms of Discrimination against Women." In *Women's Rights, Human Rights: International Feminist Perspectives*, edited by J. S. Peters and Andrea Wolper, 114–48. Routledge, 2018.

Hill, Elizabeth, Marian Baird, Ariadne Vromen, Rae Cooper, Zoe Meers, and Elspeth Probyn. "Young Women and Men: Imagined Futures of Work and Family Formation in Australia." *Journal of Sociology* 55, no. 4 (December 1, 2019): 778–98. https://doi.org/10.1177/1440783319877001.

Hillman, Ben. "The Limits of Gender Quotas: Women's Parliamentary Representation in Indonesia." *Journal of Contemporary Asia* 48, no. 2 (March 15, 2018): 322–38. https://doi.org/10.1080/00472336.2017.1368092.

Hilson, Gavin. "The 'Zambia Model': A Blueprint for Formalizing Artisanal and Small-Scale Mining in Sub-Saharan Africa?" *Resources Policy* 68 (October 1, 2020): 101765. https://doi.org/10.1016/j.resourpol.2020.101765.

Hilson, Gavin, Ekow Bartels, and Yanfei Hu. "Brick by Brick, Block by Block: Building a Sustainable Formalization Strategy for Small-Scale Gold Mining in Ghana." *Environmental Science & Policy* 135 (September 1, 2022): 207–25. https://doi.org/10.1016/j.envsci.2022.04.006.

Hilson, Gavin, Abigail Hilson, Agatha Siwale, and Roy Maconachie. "Female Faces in Informal 'Spaces': Women and Artisanal and Small-Scale Mining in Sub-Saharan Africa." *Africa Journal of Management* 4, no. 3 (July 3, 2018): 306–46. https://doi.org/10.1080/23322373.2018.1516940.

Hilson, Gavin, and Roy Maconachie. "Formalising Artisanal and Small-Scale Mining: Insights, Contestations and Clarifications." *Area* 49, no. 4 (2017): 443–51. https://doi.org/10.1111/area.12328.

Himmelweit, Susan. "The Experience of the UK Women's Budget Group." *International Workshop on Gender Auditing of Government Budgets*, 4–24. Rome, Italy, September 15–16, 2000.

Hinds, Róisín. *Increasing Financial Investment in Women and Girls through Gender Responsive Budgeting*. GSDRC Helpdesk Research Report 1081. Birmingham, UK: University of Birmingham, 2014. https://assets.publishing.service.gov.uk/media/57a089a3ed915d3cfd000356/hdq1081.pdf.

Hinton, Jennifer, Marcello Veiga, and Christian Beinhoff. "Women and Artisanal Mining: Gender Roles and the Road Ahead." In *The Socio-Economic Impacts of Artisanal and Small-Scale Mining in Developing Countries*, edited by Gavin Hilson, 1–29. Netherlands: Swets Publishers, 2003.

Hodge, Samuel. "Don't Always Believe What You See: Shallowfake and Deepfake Media Has Altered the Perception of Reality." *Hofstra Law Review* 50, no. 1 (September 1, 2021). https://scholarlycommons.law.hofstra.edu/hlr/vol50/iss1/4.

Hodson, Loveday, and Troy Lavers, eds. *Feminist Judgments in International Law*. Oxford: Hart Publishing, 2019. https://www.bloomsbury.com/au/feminist-judgments-in-international-law-9781509914425/.

Holli, Anne Maria, and Mette Marie Stæhr Harder. "Towards a Dual Approach: Comparing the Effects of Parliamentary Committees on Gender Equality in Denmark and Finland." *Parliamentary Affairs* 69, no. 4 (October 1, 2016): 794–811. https://doi.org/10.1093/pa/gsw006.

Holvoet, Nathalie, and Liesbeth Inberg. "Gender Mainstreaming in Sector Budget Support: The Case of the European Commission's Sector Support to Rwanda's Agriculture Sector." *Journal of International Women's Studies* 16, no. 2 (January 30, 2015): 155–69.

Hoogeveen, Dawn, Aleyah Williams, Alisha Hussey, Sally Western, and Maya K. Gislason. "Sex, Mines, and Pipelines: Examining 'Gender-Based Analysis Plus' in Canadian Impact Assessment Resource Extraction Policy." *The Extractive Industries and Society* 8, no. 3 (September 1, 2021): 100921. https://doi.org/10.1016/j.exis.2021.100921.

hooks, bell. *Ain't I a Woman: Black Women and Feminism*. Boston: South End Press, 1981.

Hosse, Zakir, Marufa Rahman, and Sajal Roy. "Paternity Leave: An Emerging Issue in Bangladesh." In *Connecting Asia: Understanding Foreign Relations, Organizations and Contemporary Issues*, edited by Debasish Nandy, 283–301. New Delhi: Kunal Books, 2020.

Hovy, Dirk, and Shrimai Prabhumoye. "Five Sources of Bias in Natural Language Processing." *Language and Linguistics Compass* 15, no. 8 (2021): e12432. https://doi.org/10.1111/lnc3.12432.

Hovy, Dirk, and Shannon L. Spruit. "The Social Impact of Natural Language Processing." In *Proceedings of the 54th Annual Meeting of the Association for Computational Linguistics* (Vol. 2: Short Papers), 591–98. Berlin: Association for Computational Linguistics, 2016. https://doi.org/10.18653/v1/P16-2096.

Htun, Mala. "Women and Democracy." In *Constructing Democratic Governance in Latin America*, edited by Jorge Domínguez and Michael Shifter, 118–36. Johns Hopkins University Press, 2003.

Huggins, Chris, Doris Buss, and Blair Rutherford. "A 'Cartography of Concern': Place-Making Practices and Gender in the Artisanal Mining Sector in Africa." *Geoforum* 83 (2017): 142–52.

Hull, Kathleen E. "The Cultural Power of Law and the Cultural Enactment of Legality: The Case of Same-Sex Marriage." *Law & Social Inquiry* 28, no. 3 (2003): 629–57. https://doi.org/10.1111/j.1747-4469.2003.tb00210.x.

Human Rights Law Centre. "Submission to Joint Standing Committee on Foreign Affairs, Defence and Trade on Establishing a Modern Slavery Act in Australia," Submission No. 27, April 2017. https://www.aph.gov.au/Parliamentary_Business/Committees/Joint/Foreign_Affairs_Defence_and_Trade/ModernSlavery/Submissions.

Human Rights Watch. *Hidden Chains: Rights Abuses and Forced Labor in Thailand's Fishing Industry*. Human Rights Watch, January 23, 2018. https://www.hrw.org/report/2018/01/23/hidden-chains/rights-abuses-and-forced-labor-thailands-fishing-industry.

Hunter, Rosemary. "The Power of Feminist Judgments?" *Feminist Legal Studies* 20, no. 2 (August 1, 2012): 135–48. https://doi.org/10.1007/s10691-012-9202-0.

Hunter, Rosemary, Clare McGlynn, and Erika Rackley. "Feminist Judgments: An Introduction." In *Feminist Judgments: From Theory to Practice*, edited by Rosemary Hunter, Clare McGlynn, and Erika Rackley, 3–29. Oxford: Hart Publishing, 2010. https://www.bloomsburyprofessional.com/uk/feminist-judgments-9781847317278/.

Hunter, Rosemary, and Erika Rackley. "Feminist Judgments on the UK Supreme Court." *Canadian Journal of Women and the Law* 32, no. 1 (March 2020): 85–113. https://doi.org/10.3138/cjwl.32.1.04.

Hyland, Marie, Simeon Djankov, and Pinelopi Koujianou Goldberg. "Do Gendered Laws Matter for Women's Economic Empowerment?" Working Paper 215. Peterson Institute for International Economics, March 2021. https://www.piie.com/sites/default/files/documents/wp21-5.pdf.

Hyland, Marie, Simeon Djankov, and Pinelopi Koujianou Goldberg. "Gendered Laws." Policy Research Working Paper. Washington, D.C.: World Bank, 2019. http://documents1.worldbank.org/curated/en/514981576015899984/pdf/Gendered-Laws.pdf.

Ikhide, Emily Edoisa. "The Political Economy of Gender-Responsive Budgeting in Nigeria." In *Gender-Responsive Budgeting in Africa: Access and Future Measures*, edited by Tinuade Adekunbi Ojo, 35–44. Cham: Springer Nature Switzerland, 2024. https://doi.org/10.1007/978-3-031-53333-4_4.

"ILO Welcomes Bangladesh's Plan to Introduce Paternity Leave." *The Financial Express*, March 7, 2022. https://thefinancialexpress.com.bd/national/ilo-welcomes-bangladeshs-plan-to-introduce-paternity-leave-1646655778.

International Institute for Democracy and Electoral Assistance, ed. *The Implementation of Quotas: Latin American Experiences: Workshop Report: Lima, Peru, 23–24 February 2003*. Quota Workshops Report Series, no. 2. Stockholm: International Institute for Democracy and Electoral Assistance, 2003.

Inter-Parliamentary Union. "Monthly Ranking of Women in National Parliaments," January 2, 2024. https://data.ipu.org/women-ranking/?date_month=1&date_year=2024.

"In the Gulf 99% of Kenyan Migrant Workers Are Abused, a Poll Finds." *The Economist*, September 15, 2022. https://www.economist.com/middle-east-and-africa/2022/09/15/in-the-gulf-99-of-kenyan-migrant-workers-are-abused-a-poll-finds.

Jackson, Emily. "Degendering Reproduction?" *Medical Law Review* 16, no. 3 (August 2008): 346–68. https://doi.org/10.1093/medlaw/fwn016.

Jackson, Maya C. "Artificial Intelligence and Algorithmic Bias: The Issues with Technology Reflecting History and Humans." *Journal of Business and Technology Law* 16, no. 2 (2021): 299–316.

Jahnsen, Synnøve Økland, and May-Len Skilbrei. "Debate—From Palermo to the Streets of Oslo: Pros and Cons of the Trafficking Framework." *Anti-Trafficking Review*, no. 4 (April 15, 2015). https://doi.org/10.14197/201215410.

Jenkins, Katy. "Unearthing Women's Anti-Mining Activism in the Andes: Pachamama and the 'Mad Old Women.'" *Antipode* 47, no. 2 (2015): 442–60.

———. "Women, Mining and Development: An Emerging Research Agenda." *The Extractive Industries and Society* 1, no. 2 (November 1, 2014): 329–39. https://doi.org/10.1016/j.exis.2014.08.004.

Jerneck, Anne. "What About Gender in Climate Change? Twelve Feminist Lessons from Development." *Sustainability* 10, no. 3 (March 2018), article 627. https://doi.org/10.3390/su10030627.

Jiraporn, Pornsit, Denise Potosky, and Sang Mook Lee. "Corporate Governance and Lesbian, Gay, Bisexual, and Transgender-Supportive Human Resource Policies from Corporate Social Responsibility, Resource-Based, and Agency Perspectives." *Human Resource Management* 58, no. 3 (2019): 317–36. https://doi.org/10.1002/hrm.21954.

Johnson, Katie N. *Sisters in Sin: Brothel Drama in America, 1900–1920.* Cambridge: Cambridge University Press, 2006.

Johnson, Pamela R., and Susan Gardner. "Domestic Violence and the Workplace: Developing a Company Response." *Journal of Management Development* 18, no. 7 (January 1, 1999): 590–97. https://doi.org/10.1108/02621719910284440.

Johnstone, Rachael, and Bessma Momani. "Gender Mainstreaming in the Canadian Armed Forces and the Department of National Defence: Lessons on the Implementation of Gender-Based Analysis Plus (GBA+)." *Armed Forces & Society* 48, no. 2 (April 1, 2022): 247–73. https://doi.org/10.1177/0095327X20956722.

Juquelier, Antoine, Ingrid Poncin, and Simon Hazée. "Empathic Chatbots: A Double-Edged Sword in Customer Experiences." *Journal of Business Research* 188 (February 1, 2025): 115074. https://doi.org/10.1016/j.jbusres.2024.115074.

Kahn, Jeremy. "After Roe, Concerns Mount over A.I.-Enabled Surveillance." *Fortune*, June 28, 2022. https://fortune.com/2022/06/28/after-roe-v-wade-fear-of-a-i-surveillance-abortion/.

Kamalnath, Akshaya. *The Corporate Diversity Jigsaw.* Cambridge: Cambridge University Press, 2022.

Kang, Wei, John K. Ashton, Ayan Orujov, and Yang Wang. "Realizing Gender Diversity on Corporate Boards." *International Journal of the Economics of Business* 30, no. 1 (October 18, 2022): 1–29. https://doi.org/10.1080/13571516.2022.2133337.

Kapur, Ratna. "Gender, Sovereignty and the Rise of a Sexual Security Regime in International Law and Postcolonial India." *Melbourne Journal of International Law* 14, no. 2 (November 1, 2013): 317–45. https://doi.org/10.3316/agis_archive.20150672.

———. "The (Im)possibility of Queering International Human Rights Law." In *Queering International Law: Possibilities, Alliances, Complicities, Risks,* edited by Dianne Otto, 134–147. New York: Routledge, 2017.

Katyal, Sonia K., and Jessica Y. Jung. "The Gender Panopticon: AI, Gender, and Design Justice." *UCLA Law Review* 68, no. 3 (2022 2021): 692–785.

Kelan, Elisabeth. *Patterns of Inclusion: How Gender Matters for Automation, Artificial Intelligence and the Future of Work.* Milton Park; New York: Routledge, 2025. https://www.routledge.com/Patterns-of-Inclusion-How-Gender-Matters-for-Automation-Artificial-Intelligence-and-the-Future-of-Work/Kelan/p/book/9781032669892.

Kemp, Deanna, Julia Keenan, and Jane Gronow. "Strategic Resource or Ideal Source? Discourse, Organizational Change and CSR." Edited by Christopher J. Rees and John Hassard. *Journal of Organizational Change Management* 23, no. 5 (January 1, 2010): 578–94. https://doi.org/10.1108/09534811011071298.

Khalid, Amrita. "Deepfake Videos Are a Far, Far Bigger Problem for Women." *Quartz*, October 9 2019. https://qz.com/1723476/deepfake-videos-feature-mostly-porn-according-to-new-study-from-deeptrace-labs/.

Khalifa, Rihab, and Simona Scarparo. "Gender Responsive Budgeting: A Tool for Gender Equality." *Critical Perspectives on Accounting*, SI: Accounting and Social Impact (Part I), 79 (September 1, 2021): 102183. https://doi.org/10.1016/j.cpa.2020.102183.

Kiberenge, Kenfrey. "Steady Rise of Kenyan Women in Hallowed Corporate Boardroom." *Daily Nation*, July 5, 2020. https://nation.africa/kenya/life-and-style/lifestyle/steady-rise-of-kenyan-women-in-hallowed-corporate-boardroom-1015160.

Kim, Nicky, and Giovanna Di Sauro. "Is Canada Closer to Enacting Modern Slavery Legislation? A Brief Update." Ontario Bar Association, March 31, 2022. https://oba.org/Is-Canada-Closer-to-Enacting-Modern-Slavery-Legislation-A-Brief-Update.

Kira, Beatriz. "When Non-Consensual Intimate Deepfakes Go Viral: The Insufficiency of the UK Online Safety Act." *Computer Law & Security Review* 54 (September 1, 2024): 106024. https://doi.org/10.1016/j.clsr.2024.106024.

Kirchengast, Tyrone. "Deepfakes and Image Manipulation: Criminalisation and Control." *Information & Communications Technology Law* 29, no. 3 (September 1, 2020): 308–23. https://doi.org/10.1080/13600834.2020.1794615.

Klick, Jonathan. "Market Response to Court Rejection of California's Board Diversity Laws." *Journal of Empirical Legal Studies* 22, no. 1 (2025): 4–26. https://doi.org/10.1111/jels.12405.

Klugman, Jeni. *Gender Based Violence and the Law*. World Development Report Background Paper. Washington, D.C.: World Bank, 2017. https://openknowledge.worldbank.org/handle/10986/26198.

Kotiranta, A., Anne Kovalainen, and P. Rouvinen. "Female Leadership and Firm Profitability," 2007. https://www.semanticscholar.org/paper/Female-Leadership-and-Firm-Profitability-Kotiranta-Kovalainen/73ca770a81de75124a303c66f7a9e48cc1e28081.

Kozuka, Souichirou. "A Governance Framework for the Development and Use of Artificial Intelligence: Lessons from the Comparison of Japanese and European Initiatives." *Uniform Law Review* 24, no. 2 (2019): 315–29.

Krause, Danielle. "The Domestic Violence Leave Act: The Need for Victim Workplace Leave on a Federal Level and in North Dakota." *North Dakota Law Review* 87, no. 1 (2011): 167–94.

Kreitzen, Nora. "Comparative Study on Greenwashing in the Cosmetics Industry: A Content Analysis." Bachelor in Arts thesis, Rhine-Waal University of Applied Sciences, 2022.

Krook, Mona Lena, and Pippa Norris. "Beyond Quotas: Strategies to Promote Gender Equality in Elected Office." *Political Studies* 62, no. 1 (March 1, 2014): 2–20. https://doi.org/10.1111/1467-9248.12116.

Kyaw, Khine, Sirimon Treepongkaruna, Pornsit Jiraporn, and Chaiyuth Padungsaksawasdi. "Does Board Gender Diversity Improve the Welfare of Lesbian, Gay, Bisexual, and Transgender Employees?" *Corporate Social Responsibility and Environmental Management* 29, no. 1 (2022): 200–210. https://doi.org/10.1002/csr.2196.

Laharnar, Naima, Nancy Perrin, Ginger Hanson, W. Kent Anger, and Nancy Glass. "Workplace Domestic Violence Leave Laws: Implementation, Use, Implications." *International Journal of Workplace Health Management* 8, no. 2 (January 1, 2015): 109–28. https://doi.org/10.1108/IJWHM-03-2014-0006.

Lahiri-Dutt, Kuntala, ed. *Between the Plough and the Pick: Informal, Artisanal and Small-Scale Mining in the Contemporary World*. Canberra: ANU Press, 2018. http://www.jstor.org/stable/j.ctt22h6r6o.

———. "Digging Women: Towards a New Agenda for Feminist Critiques of Mining." *Gender, Place & Culture* 19, no. 2 (2012): 193–212.

———. "Extractive Peasants: Reframing Informal Artisanal and Small-Scale Mining Debates." *Third World Quarterly* 39, no. 8 (2018): 1561–82.

———. "New Directions in Research on Women and Gender in Extractive Industries." *The Extractive Industries and Society* 9 (March 1, 2022): 101048. https://doi.org/10.1016/j.exis.2022.101048.

Lambert, Tarla. "Board Quotas for Women? EU Lawmakers Set New Rule for 2026." Women's Agenda, June 7, 2022. https://womensagenda.com.au/business/board-quotas-for-women-eu-lawmakers-set-new-rule-for-2026/.

Lambooy, Tineke. "Corporate Due Diligence as a Tool to Respect Human Rights." *Netherlands Quarterly of Human Rights* 28, no. 3 (September 1, 2010): 404–48. https://doi.org/10.1177/016934411002800304.

Langlois, Anthony J. "No Regional Pattern: LGBTIQ Rights and Politics in Asia." In *Routledge Handbook of Human Rights in Asia*. Milton Park; New York: Routledge, 2018.

Latorre Ruiz, Enrique, and Eulalia Pérez Sedeño. "Gender Bias in Artificial Intelligence." In *Gender in AI and Robotics: The Gender Challenges from an Interdisciplinary Perspective*, edited by Jordi Vallverdú, 61–75. Intelligent Systems Reference Library. Cham: Springer International Publishing, 2023. https://doi.org/10.1007/978-3-031-21606-0_4.

Lau, Chris. "Japan Wants 85% of Male Workers to Take Paternity Leave. But Fathers Are Too Afraid to Take It." CNN, March 26, 2023. https://www.cnn.com/2023/03/26/asia/japan-paternity-leave-policy-challenges-intl-hnk-dst/index.html.

Lau, Holning. "The Language of Westernization in Legal Commentary." *The American Journal of Comparative Law* 61, no. 3 (July 1, 2013): 507–38. https://doi.org/10.5131/AJCL.2012.0024.

Lauret, Julien. "Amazon's Sexist AI Recruiting Tool: How Did It Go So Wrong?" Medium, August 16, 2019. https://becominghuman.ai/amazons-sexist-ai-recruiting-tool-how-did-it-go-so-wrong-e3d14816d98e.

Lawson, Lynda. "Rice, Sapphires and Cattle: Work Lives of Women Artisanal and Small-Scale Miners in Madagascar." In *Between the Plough and the Pick: Informal, Artisanal and Small-Scale Mining in the Contemporary World*, edited by Kuntala Lahiri-Dutt, 171–92. Canberra: ANU Press, 2018. https://doi.org/10.22459/BPP.03.2018.

Leavy, Susan. "Gender Bias in Artificial Intelligence: The Need for Diversity and Gender Theory in Machine Learning." In *2018 IEEE/ACM 1st International Workshop on Gender Equality in Software Engineering (GE)*, 14–16, 2018.

Leavy, Susan, Barry O'Sullivan, and Eugenia Siapera. "Data, Power and Bias in Artificial Intelligence." arXiv, July 28, 2020. http://arxiv.org/abs/2008.07341.

Lee-Kuen, Irean Yap, Chan Sok-Gee, and Rozaimah Zainudin. "Gender Diversity and Firms' Financial Performance in Malaysia." *Asian Academy of Management Journal of Accounting and Finance* 13, no. 1 (2017): 41–62. https://doi.org/10.21315/aamjaf2017.13.1.2.

"Legistics: Gender-Neutral Language," December 2, 1999. Department of Justice Canada. https://canada.justice.gc.ca/eng/rp-pr/csj-sjc/legis-redact/legistics/p1p15.html.

Lepinard, Eleonore, and Marylene Lieber. *The Policy on Gender Equality in France*. European Parliament, Directorate General for Internal Policies, Policy Department C: Citizens' Rights and Constitutional Affairs, Women's Rights and Gender Equality, March 27, 2015. https://policycommons.net/artifacts/2100592/the-policy-on-gender-equality-in-france/2855890/.

Leppert, Rebecca, and Drew Desilver. "118th Congress Has a Record Number of Women." PEW Research Center, January 3, 2023. https://www.pewresearch.org/short-reads/2023/01/03/118th-congress-has-a-record-number-of-women/.

Leszczyńska, Monika. "Mandatory Quotas for Women on Boards of Directors in the European Union: Harmful to or Good for Company Performance?" *European Business Organization Law Review* 19, no. 1 (March 1, 2018): 35–61. https://doi.org/10.1007/s40804-017-0095-x.

LGBTIQ+ Health Australia. "Submission for the 2022/23 Federal Budget," March 2022. https://treasury.gov.au/sites/default/files/2022-03/258735_lgbtiq_health_australia.pdf.

Lichuma, Caroline Omari. "(Laws) Made in the 'First World': A TWAIL Critique of the Use of Domestic Legislation to Extraterritorially Regulate Global Value Chains." *ZaöRV: Zeitschrift für Ausländisches Öffentliches Recht und Völkerrecht* 81, no. 2 (2021). https://doi.org/10.17104/0044-2348-2021-2-497.

Liebeskind, Michelle Lewis. "Preventing Gender-Based Violence: From Marginalization to Mainstream in International Human Rights." *Revista Juridica Universidad de Puerto Rico* 63 (1994): 645.

Liebowitz, Debra J., and Susanne Zwingel. "Gender Equality Oversimplified: Using CEDAW to Counter the Measurement Obsession." *International Studies Review* 16, no. 3 (September 1, 2014): 362–89. https://doi.org/10.1111/misr.12139.

"List of Public Corporations by Market Capitalization." In *Wikipedia*, May 25, 2024. https://en.wikipedia.org/w/index.php?title=List_of_public_corporations_by_market_capitalization&oldid=1225552733#Trillion-dollar_companies.

Little, Ben, and Alison Winch. *The New Patriarchs of Digital Capitalism: Celebrity Tech Founders and Networks of Power*. Milton Park; New York: Routledge, 2021.

Lixinski, Lucas. "Regional Indigenous Rights and the (Dis)Contents of Translation: A View from Latin America." *Research Handbook on the International Law of Indigenous Rights*, April 12, 2022, 10–24.

Lomaz Jørgensen, Freja, and Ea Høg Utoft. "Maternity Leave as Upskilling: A Danish (Neoliberal) Feminist Movement on LinkedIn?" *NORA: Nordic Journal of Feminist and Gender Research* 32, no. 4 (2024): 1–15. https://doi.org/10.1080/08038740.2024.2307406.

Loong, Lee Hsien, Prime Minister. "National Day Rally 2015." Speech, August 23, 2015. https://www.pmo.gov.sg/Newsroom/national-day-rally-2015.

López Belloso, María. "Women's Rights Under AI Regulation: Fighting AI Gender Bias Through a Feminist and Intersectional Approach." In *Law and Artificial Intelligence: Regulating AI and Applying AI in Legal Practice*, edited by Bart Custers and Eduard Fosch-Villaronga, 87–107. Information Technology and Law Series. The Hague: T.M.C. Asser Press, 2022. https://doi.org/10.1007/978-94-6265-523-2_5.

Lucero, Karman. "Artificial Intelligence Regulation and China's Future." *Columbia Journal of Asian Law* 33, no. 1 (2019): 94–171.

Lugones, Maria. "The Coloniality of Gender." In *The Palgrave Handbook of Gender and Development: Critical Engagements in Feminist Theory and Practice*, edited by Wendy Harcourt, 13–33. London: Palgrave Macmillan UK, 2016. https://doi.org/10.1007/978-1-137-38273-3_2.

Luna, Jessie K., Becca Chalit Hernandez, and Abdoulaye Sawadogo. "The Paradoxes of Purity in Organic Agriculture in Burkina Faso." *Geoforum* 127 (December 1, 2021): 46–56. https://doi.org/10.1016/j.geoforum.2021.09.014.

Lungu, Gatian F. "Women and Representative Bureaucracy in Zambia: The Case of Gender-Balancing in the Civil Service and Para-Statal Organizations." *Women's Studies International Forum* 12, no. 2 (January 1, 1989): 175–82. https://doi.org/10.1016/0277-5395(89)90021-6.

Lutz, Christoph. "Digital Inequalities in the Age of Artificial Intelligence and Big Data." *Human Behavior and Emerging Technologies* 1, no. 2 (2019): 141–48. https://doi.org/10.1002/hbe2.140.

Lynas, Danellie. "A Good Business or a Risky Business: Health, Safety and Quality of Life for Women Smallscale Miners in PNG." In *Between the Plough and the Pick: Informal, Artisanal and Small-Scale Mining in the Contemporary World*, edited by Kuntala Lahiri-Dutt, 151–70. Canberra: ANU Press, 2018. https://doi.org/10.22459/BPP.03.2018.

MacGregor, Sherilyn. "'Gender and Climate Change': From Impacts to Discourses." *Journal of the Indian Ocean Region* 6, no. 2 (December 1, 2010): 223–38. https://doi.org/10.1080/19480881.2010.536669.

Mack, Jessica. "One Feminist Asks, 'Is Polygamy Inherently Bad for Women?'" *Ms. Magazine*, January 5, 2011. https://msmagazine.com/2011/01/05/one-feminist-asks-is-polygamy-inherently-bad-for-women/.

MacKinnon, Catharine A. "Pornography as Trafficking." *Michigan Journal of International Law* 26 (2005): 993.

———. *Toward a Feminist Theory of the State*. Harvard University Press, 1989.

Maglaty, Jeanne. "When Did Girls Start Wearing Pink?" *Smithsonian Magazine*, April 7, 2011. https://www.smithsonianmag.com/arts-culture/when-did-girls-start-wearing-pink-1370097/.

Magnier, Véronique, and Darren Rosenblum. "Quotas and the Transatlantic Divergence of Corporate Governance." *Northwestern Journal of International Law & Business* 34, no. 2 (2014): 249–298.

Majury, Diana. "Introducing the Women's Court of Canada." *Canadian Journal of Women and the Law* 18, no. 1 (2006): 1–12.

Malone, Aaron, and Gerardo Martínez. *Realities and Expectations of ASM in Peru*. Lima: Solidaridad, August 2022. https://www.solidaridadnetwork.org/wp-content/uploads/2022/12/Full-Report-Realities-and-expectations-ASM-Peru-2022.pdf.

Manasi, Ardra, Subadra Panchanadeswaran, Emily Sours, and Seung Ju Lee. "Mirroring the Bias: Gender and Artificial Intelligence." *Gender, Technology and Development* 26, no. 3 (December 1, 2022): 295–305. https://doi.org/10.1080/09718524.2022.2128254.

Manji, Ambreena. "Taking on the State: An African Perspective." *Feminists@law* 10, no. 2 (November 8, 2020). https://doi.org/10.22024/UniKent/03/fal.940.

Mansbridge, Jane. "Quota Problems: Combating the Dangers of Essentialism." *Politics & Gender* 1, no. 4 (December 2005): 622–38. https://doi.org/10.1017/S1743923X05220196.

———. "Should Blacks Represent Blacks and Women Represent Women? A Contingent 'Yes.'" *The Journal of Politics* 61, no. 3 (1999): 628–57. https://doi.org/10.2307/2647821.

Månsdotter, Anna, Lars Lindholm, and Anna Winkvist. "Paternity Leave in Sweden—Costs, Savings and Health Gains." *Health Policy* 82, no. 1 (June 1, 2007): 102–15. https://doi.org/10.1016/j.healthpol.2006.09.006.

Mantouvalou, Virginia. "The UK Modern Slavery Act 2015 Three Years On." *The Modern Law Review* 81, no. 6 (2018): 1017–45. https://doi.org/10.1111/1468-2230.12377.

Marchal, Léa. "Reducing Gender Inequalities through Gender Budgeting: A Huge Challenge for Public Institutions?" *EqualTimes* (blog), July 15, 2020. https://www.equaltimes.org/reducing-gender-inequalities.

Marecek, Jeanne, and Udeni M. H. Appuhamilage. "Present but Unnamed: Feminisms and Psychologies in Sri Lanka." In *Handbook of International Feminisms: Perspectives on Psychology, Women, Culture, and Rights*, edited by Alexandra Rutherford, Rose Capdevila, Vindhya Undurti, and Ingrid Palmary, 315–33. New York: Springer, 2011. https://doi.org/10.1007/978-1-4419-9869-9_15.

Marrades, Ana. "Language and Gender: The Importance of Including a Gender Perspective in the Language of the Constitutional Reform in Spain." *European Journal of Law Reform* 22 (2020): 61.

Marschke, Melissa, and Peter Vandergeest. "Slavery Scandals: Unpacking Labour Challenges and Policy Responses within the off-Shore Fisheries Sector." *Marine Policy* 68 (June 1, 2016): 39–46. https://doi.org/10.1016/j.marpol.2016.02.009.

Martinez, Gerardo, Nicole M. Smith, and Aaron Malone. "Formalization Is Just the Beginning: Analyzing Post-Formalization Successes and Challenges in Peru's Small-Scale Gold Mining Sector." *Resources Policy* 74 (December 1, 2021): 102390. https://doi.org/10.1016/j.resourpol.2021.102390.

Masson, Dominique. "Changing State Forms, Competing State Projects: Funding Women's Organizations in Quebec." *Studies in Political Economy* 89, no. 1 (March 2012): 79–103. https://doi.org/10.1080/19187033.2012.11675002.

Mastrangelo, Andrea. "Miserias preciosas. Trabajo infantil y género en minería artesanal (Misiones, Argentina)." In *Gênero e trabalho infantil na pequena mineração: Brasil, Peru, Argentina, Bolivia*, 135–51. Centro de Tecnologia Mineral and Conselho Nacional de Desenvolvimento Científico e Tecnológico, 2006.

Mateos de Cabo, Ruth, Siri Terjesen, Lorenzo Escot, and Ricardo Gimeno. "Do 'Soft Law' Board Gender Quotas Work? Evidence from a Natural Experiment." *European Management Journal* 37, no. 5 (October 1, 2019): 611–24. https://doi.org/10.1016/j.emj.2019.01.004.

Mathen, Carissima. "Equality before the Charter: Reflections on Fraser v. Canada (Attorney General)." *The Supreme Court Law Review: Osgoode's Annual Constitutional Cases Conference* 104, no. 1 (January 1, 2022). https://doi.org/10.60082/2563-8505.1428.

Matsuda, Mari J. "When the First Quail Calls: Multiple Consciousness as Jurisprudential Method." *Women's Rights Law Reporter* 11 (1989): 297–300.

Maynard, Douglas H. "The World's Anti-Slavery Convention of 1840." *The Mississippi Valley Historical Review* 47, no. 3 (1960): 452–71. https://doi.org/10.2307/1888877.

Mayson, Sandra G. "Bias In, Bias Out." *Yale Law Journal* 128, no. 8 (2019): 2122–2473.

McCall, Leslie. "The Complexity of Intersectionality." *Signs: Journal of Women in Culture and Society* 30, no. 3 (March 1, 2005): 1771–1800. https://doi.org/10.1086/426800.

McCarthy, J, M.L. Minsky, N. Rochester, and C.E. Shannon. "Dartmouth Summer Research Project on Artificial Intelligence." Dartmouth College, New Hampshire, 1956. https://home.dartmouth.edu/about/artificial-intelligence-ai-coined-dartmouth.

McClane, Jeremy, and Darren Rosenblum. "Why Corporate Boards Should Include LGBTQ People." *Seattle University Law Review* 46 (2023): 255.

McDonald, Elisabeth, Rhonda Powell, Mamari Stephens, and Rosemary Hunter. *Feminist Judgments of Aotearoa New Zealand: Te Rino: A Two-Stranded Rope*. London: Bloomsbury Publishing, 2017.

McFerran, Ludo, Anna Lee Fos-Tuvera, and Jane Aeberhard-Hodges. "An Employment Right—Standard Provisions for Working Women Experiencing Domestic Violence." *University of Oxford Human Rights Hub Journal* 1 (2018): 167–98.

McLachlin, Beverley, Chief Justice. "Foreword." In *Adding Feminism to Law: The Contributions of Justice Claire L'Heureux-Dubé*, edited by Elizabeth Sheehy. Toronto: Irwin Law, 2004.

Meil, Gerado, Karin Wall, Susana Atalaia, and Anna Escobedo. "Trends towards De-gendering Leave Use in Spain and Portugal." In *Research Handbook on Leave Policy Parenting and Social Inequalities in a Global Perspective*, edited by Ivana Dobrotić, Sonja Blum, and Alison Koslowski, 218–30. Cheltenham: Edward Elgar Publishing, 2022. https://www.elgaronline.com/edcollchap/book/9781800372214/book-part-9781800372214-27.xml.

Merry, Sally Engle. *Human Rights and Gender Violence: Translating International Law into Local Justice*. University of Chicago Press, 2009.

Meyer, Mary K. "Negotiating International Norms: The Inter-American Commission of Women and the Convention on Violence Against Women." *Aggressive Behavior* 24, no. 2 (1998): 135–46. https://doi.org/10.1002/(SICI)1098–2337(1998)24:2<135::AID-AB4>3.0.CO;2-L.

Millbank, Jenni. "Gender-Transformative Law Reform as Healthcare." In *International Women's Rights Law and Gender Equality: Making the Law Work for Women*, edited by Ramona Vijeyarasa. London: Routledge, 2021.

Miller, Vernon D., Fredric M. Jablin, Mary K. Casey, Martha Lamphear-Van Horn, and Caroline Ethington. "The Maternity Leave as a Role Negotiation Process." *Journal of Managerial Issues* 8, no. 3 (1996): 286–309.

Millones, Jorge. "Conga Mines: Development as Conflict in Peru." *South Atlantic Quarterly* 115, no. 3 (July 1, 2016): 640–47. https://doi.org/10.1215/00382876-3608708.

Milner, Alan. "Legal Education and Training in Nigeria." *International and Comparative Law Quarterly Supplementary Publication* 10 (1965): 110.

Ministerio del Ambiente and Proyecto planetGOLD Perú. *Estudio desde una perspectiva de género sobre la minería aurífera artesanal y de pequeña escala en el Perú*. Lima: Programa de las Naciones Unidas para el Desarrollo, 2022.

Ministry of Education. "Rashtriya Madhyamik Shiksha Abhiyaan." Last updated February 19, 2021. India. https://rmsa.jk.gov.in/girlshostel.html.

Ministry of Social and Family Development, Government of Singapore. "Council for Board Diversity." Accessed January 10, 2023. https://www.councilforboarddiversity.sg/resources/latest-statistics/.

Ministry of Women, Family and Community Development. Women Directors' Programme, 2011. Malaysia. https://www.kpwkm.gov.my/kpwkm/uploads/files/Dokumen/Dasar/Women-Directors-Programme.pdf.

Mohanty, Chandra Talpade. *Feminism Without Borders: Decolonizing Theory, Practicing Solidarity*. Durham: Duke University Press, 2003.

———. "Under Western Eyes: Feminist Scholarship and Colonial Discourses." *Boundary 2* 12, no. 3 and 13, no. 1 (Spring–Autumn 1984): 333–58. https://doi.org/10.2307/302821.

Monfort, Marie Christine. "The Role of Women in the Seafood Industry." Food and Agricultural Organization of the United Nations, May 2015.

Mooney, Annabelle. "When a Woman Needs to Be Seen, Heard and Written as a Woman: Rape, Law and an Argument against Gender Neutral Language." *International Journal for the Semiotics of Law* 19, no. 1 (March 1, 2006): 39–68. https://doi.org/10.1007/s11196-005-9010-9.

Moretti, Daniele. "The Gender of the Gold: An Ethnographic and Historical Account of Women's Involvement in Artisanal and Small-Scale Mining in Mount Kaindi, Papua New Guinea." *Oceania* 76, no. 2 (2006): 133–49. https://doi.org/10.1002/j.1834-4461.2006.tb03041.x.

Mudimbe-Boyi, Elisabeth. *Beyond Dichotomies: Histories, Identities, Cultures, and the Challenge of Globalization.* New York: SUNY Press, 2002. https://sunypress.edu/Books/B/Beyond-Dichotomies2.

Mulcahy, Sean, and Kate Seear. "On Tables, Doors and Listening Spaces: Parliamentary Human Rights Scrutiny Processes and Engagement of Others." *Australian Journal of Human Rights* 28, no. 2–3 (September 2, 2022): 286–307. https://doi.org/10.1080/1323238X.2022.2135677.

Mulyaningrum, Lella NQ. Irwan, and Ruslina Lisda Mujibah. "Gender Mainstreaming in the Budget System of Indonesian Governance." In *International Conference Asia – America – Africa – Australia Public Finance Management Conference. "Evaluating and Improving Good Public Governance."* Bandung: Universitas Pasundan, 2015.

Mun, Eunmi, and Mary C. Brinton. "Workplace Matters: The Use of Parental Leave Policy in Japan." *Work and Occupations* 42, no. 3 (August 2015): 335–69. https://doi.org/10.1177/0730888415574781.

Murciano-Goroff, Raviv. "Missing Women in Tech: The Labor Market for Highly Skilled Software Engineers." *Management Science* 68, no. 5 (May 2022): 3262–81. https://doi.org/10.1287/mnsc.2021.4077.

Murray, Jill. "The International Regulation of Maternity: Still Waiting for the Reconciliation of Work and Family Life." *International Journal of Comparative Labour Law and Industrial Relations* 17, no. 1 (March 1, 2001). https://kluwerlawonline.com/api/Product/CitationPDFURL?file=Journals\IJCL\337848.pdf.

Murray, Rainbow. "Quotas for Men: Reframing Gender Quotas as a Means of Improving Representation for All." *American Political Science Review* 108, no. 3 (August 2014): 520–32. https://doi.org/10.1017/S0003055414000239.

Nakazato, Hideki. "Culture, Policies and Practices on Fathers' Work and Childcare in Japan: A New Departure from Old Persistence?" In *Contemporary Perspectives in Family Research*, 235–55, 2018. https://doi.org/10.1108/S1530-353520180000012010.

———. "Has 'Nordic Turn' in Japan Crystalized?: Politics of Promoting Parental Leave Take-up among Fathers and the Divergence from the Nordic System." *Journal of Family Studies* 29, no. 6 (February 21, 2023): 2615–30. https://doi.org/10.1080/13229400.2023.2179533.

Nesiah, Vasuki. "Lawfare, CVE, and International Conflict Feminism." In *The Cunning of Gender Violence: Geopolitics and Feminism*, edited by Lila Abu-Lughod, Rema Hammami, and Nadera Shalhoub-Kevorkian, 55–87. Next Wave: New Directions in Women's Studies. Durham: Duke University Press, 2023.

———. "Missionary Zeal for a Secular Mission: Bringing Gender to Transitional Justice and Redemption to Feminism." In *Feminist Perspectives on Contemporary International Law: Between Resistance and Compliance?*, edited by Sari Kouvo and Zoe Pearson, 137–57. Oñati International Series in Law and Society. Oxford: Hart Publishing, 2011. https://www.bloomsburyprofessional.com/uk/feminist-perspectives-on-contemporary-international-law-9781782255857/.

Ni Loideain, Nora, Rachel Adams, and Damian Clifford. "Gender as Emotive AI and the Case of 'Nadia': Regulatory and Ethical Implications." SSRN Scholarly Paper. Rochester, NY: Social Science Research Network, June 2, 2021. https://doi.org/10.2139/ssrn.3858431.

Nolan, Justine, and Martijn Boersma. "Regulating the Business of Modern Slavery: Law, What Is It Good For?" In *Addressing Modern Slavery*, 113–64. Sydney: NewSouth Publishing, 2019. http://ebookcentral.proquest.com/lib/uts/detail.action?docID=5891283.

Norwegian Ministry of Foreign Affairs. "Born to Live in Freedom: Strategy to Strengthen Development Efforts to Combat Modern Slavery (2021–2025)." Oslo, Norway, July 1, 2021. https://www.regjeringen.no/en/historical-archive/solbergs-government/ud/tema-og -redaksjonelt-innhold/redaksjonelle-artikler/2021/strategy-to-combat-modern-slavery -2021-2025/id2864979/.

Nur Janti (The Jakarta Post). "New House Bill Spells Progress for Working Mothers." *The Jakarta Post*, June 18, 2022. https://www.thejakartapost.com/paper/2022/06/17/new-house -bill-spells-progress-for-working-mothers.html.

Nussbaum, Martha C. "Women's Progress and Women's Human Rights." *Human Rights Quarterly* 38, no. 3 (August 3, 2016): 589–622. https://doi.org/10.1353/hrq.2016.0043.

———. "Women's Progress and Women's Human Rights." In *The Limits of Human Rights*, edited by Bardo Fassbender and Knut Traisbach. Oxford University Press, 2019. https:// oxford-universitypressscholarship-com.ezproxy1.library.usyd.edu.au/view/10.1093 /oso/9780198824756.001.0001/oso-9780198824756-chapter-17.

Nygård, Mikael, and Ann-Zofie Duvander. "Social Inclusion or Gender Equality? Political Discourses on Parental Leave in Finland and Sweden." *Social Inclusion* 9, no. 2 (June 11, 2021): 300–312. https://doi.org/10.17645/si.v9i2.3844.

Nyhlén, Sara, and Katarina Giritli Nygren. "'It's about Gender Equality and All That Stuff . . .': Enacting Policies on Gender-Based Violence into Everyday Preventive Work in Rural Sweden." *Journal of Gender-Based Violence* 3, no. 3 (October 1, 2019): 355–71. https://doi.org/10.1332/239868019X15627570242841.

Obama, Barack. "Statement by the President on the Easing of Sanctions on Burma." July 11, 2012. https://obamawhitehouse.archives.gov/the-press-office/2012/07/11/statement -president-easing-sanctions-burma.

OECD. "France—Restricted Civil Liberties." Social Institutions & Gender Index Dashboard. Accessed February 19, 2025. https://www.oecd.org/en/data/dashboards/social -institutions-gender-index/restricted-civil-liberties.html.

———. "OECD Best Practices for Gender Budgeting." *OECD Journal on Budgeting* 23, no. 1 (March 8, 2023). https://doi.org/10.1787/9574ed6f-en.

OECD.stat. "Employment: Female Share of Seats on Boards of the Largest Publicly Listed Companies." Accessed June 20, 2025. https://stats.oecd.org/index.aspx?queryid=54753.

O'Faircheallaigh, Ciaran, and Tony Corbett. "Understanding and Improving Policy and Regulatory Responses to Artisanal and Small Scale Mining." *The Extractive Industries and Society* 3, no. 4 (November 1, 2016): 961–71. https://doi.org/10.1016/j.exis.2016.11.002.

Office of the High Commissioner for Human Rights. *Guiding Principles on Business and Human Rights: Implementing the United Nations "Protect, Respect and Remedy" Framework*. New York and Geneva: United Nations, 2011. https://www.ohchr.org/sites/default /files/documents/publications/guidingprinciplesbusinesshr_en.pdf.

———. *Working Paper—Gender-Sensitive Human Rights Due Diligence*. Geneva: 7th UN Forum on Business and Human Rights, 2018.

Ofosu, Eugene K., Michelle K. Chambers, Jacqueline M. Chen, and Eric Hehman. "Same-Sex Marriage Legalization Associated with Reduced Implicit and Explicit Antigay Bias." *Proceedings of the National Academy of Sciences* 116, no. 18 (April 30, 2019): 8846–51. https://doi.org/10.1073/pnas.1806000116.

Okafor, Obiora Chinedu. "Newness, Imperialism, and International Legal Reform in Our Time: A Twail Perspective." *Osgoode Hall Law Journal* 43, no. 1 (January 1, 2005): 171–91. https://doi.org/10.60082/2817-5069.1348.

Oko, Okechukwu. "Legal Education and Training in Nigeria." *African Journal of International and Comparative Law* 6, no. 2 (1994): 271–92.

Oliver, Rhys, Barnaby Alexander, Stephen Roe, and Miriam Wlasny. *The Economic and Social Costs of Domestic Abuse.* Home Office Research Report 107, January 2019. https://assets .publishing.service.gov.uk/government/uploads/system/uploads/attachment_data /file/918897/horr107.pdf.

"On Its Tenth Birthday, Gay Marriage in America Is Under Attack." *The Economist*, June 26, 2025.

Ondieki, Elvis. "Woman of Many Firsts about to Call It Quits from Corporation Board." *Daily Nation*, July 5, 2020. https://nation.africa/kenya/life-and-style/lifestyle/woman-of -many-firsts-about-to-call-it-quits-from-corporation-board-1104582.

Orellana, Marcos A. "Indigenous Peoples, Energy and Environmental Justice: The Pangue/ Ralco Hydroelectric Project in Chile's Alto BíoBío." *Journal of Energy & Natural Resources Law* 23, no. 4 (2005): 511–28. https://doi.org/10.1080/02646811.2005.11433418.

Otto, Dianne. "Afterword: The Future(s) of Feminist Engagement with International Law." In *Research Handbook on Feminist Engagement with International Law.* Cheltenham: Edward Elgar Publishing, 2019. https://www-elgaronline-com.ezproxy1.library.usyd .edu.au/view/edcoll/9781785363917/9781785363917.00041.xml.

———. "Introduction: Embracing Queer Curiosity." In *Queering International Law: Possibilities, Alliances, Complicities, Risks*, edited by Dianne Otto, 1–11. Routledge Research in International Law. London: Taylor and Francis, 2017.

Pahuja, Sundhya. *Decolonising International Law: Development, Economic Growth and the Politics of Universality.* Cambridge: Cambridge University Press, 2011.

Paige, Tamsin Phillipa. "The Maintenance of (International Peace and Security) Heteronormativity." In *Queering International Law: Possibilities, Alliances, Complicities, Risks*, edited by Dianne Otto, 91–109. Routledge Research in International Law. London: Taylor and Francis, 2017.

Pailey, Robtel Neajai. "De-Centring the 'White Gaze' of Development." *Development and Change* 51, no. 3 (2020): 729–45. https://doi.org/10.1111/dech.12550.

Palacio, Herminia. "Over the Precipice Into a Post-Roe World—A Look at Abortion Rights and Access in the United States." *American Journal of Public Health* 112, no. 9 (September 2022): 1273–75. https://doi.org/10.2105/AJPH.2022.307016.

Paul, Eitan. "Raising Representation? Gender and Village Budgeting Reforms in Indonesia." Thesis, University of Michigan, 2022. https://doi.org/10.7302/6196.

Paul, Kari. "California Makes 'Deepfake' Videos Illegal, but Law May Be Hard to Enforce." *The Guardian*, October 7, 2019. https://www.theguardian.com/us-news/2019/oct/07 /california-makes-deepfake-videos-illegal-but-law-may-be-hard-to-enforce.

Pennington, Alison. "Workplace Policy Reform in New Zealand: What Are the Lessons for Australia?" Canberra: The Centre for Future Work at the Australia Institute, March 2019.

Pérez-Hernández, Cándido, and Anna Escobedo. "Mexico: Leave Policy, Co-Responsibility in Childcare and Informal Employment." In *Parental Leave and Beyond*, edited by Peter Moss, Ann-Zofie Duvander, and Alison Koslowski, 129–46. Bristol: Policy Press, 2019. https://bristoluniversitypressdigital.com/display/book/9781447338796/ch008.xml.

Perkins, Roberta. "Wicked Women or Working Girls: The Prostitute on the Silver Screen." *Medial International Australia* 51, no. 1 (1981): 28–34.

Perks, Rachel, Jocelyn Kelly, Stacie Constantian, and Phuong Pham. "Resources and Resourcefulness: Gender, Human Rights and Resilience in Artisanal Mining Towns of Eastern Congo." In *Between the Plough and the Pick: Informal, Artisanal and Small-Scale Mining in the Contemporary World*, edited by Kuntala Lahiri-Dutt, 209–31. Canberra: ANU Press, 2018. https://doi.org/10.22459/BPP.03.2018.

Permanyer, Iñaki. "A Critical Assessment of the UNDP's Gender Inequality Index." *Feminist Economics* 19, no. 2 (April 2013): 1–32. https://doi.org/10.1080/13545701.2013.769687.

Petts, Richard J., and Chris Knoester. "Paternity Leave-Taking and Father Engagement." *Journal of Marriage and Family* 80, no. 5 (2018): 1144–62. https://doi.org/10.1111/jomf.12494.

Phalen, Anthony. "Bolivian Tin Miners' Wives Fast, Win Amnesty, Jobs, Freedom, 1977–1978." *Global Nonviolence Action Database* (blog), November 11, 2009. https://nvdatabase .swarthmore.edu/content/bolivian-tin-miners-wives-fast-win-amnesty-jobs-free dom-1977-1978.

Philipps, Lisa. "Gender Budgets and Tax Policy-Making: Contrasting Canadian and Australian Experiences." *Law in Context* 24, no. 2 (December 23, 2020): 143–68. https://doi.org /10.3316/ielapa.002639602941695.

Pigola, Angélica, Priscila Rezende Da Costa, Luísa Cagica Carvalho, Luciano Ferreira Da Silva, Cláudia Terezinha Kniess, and Emerson Antonio Maccari. "Artificial Intelligence-Driven Digital Technologies to the Implementation of the Sustainable Development Goals: A Perspective from Brazil and Portugal." *Sustainability* 13, no. 24 (December 10, 2021): 13669. https://doi.org/10.3390/su132413669.

Pilau Sobrinho, Liton Lanes, Cleide Calgaro, and Thiago dos Santos da Silva. "Public Policies, Neoextractivist Development and Indian Cosmovision: The Political Project of the Highway Cutting TIPNIC in Bolivia." *Revista eletrônica do Curso de Direito da UFSM* 14, no. 2 (2019): e38606–e38606. https://doi.org/10.5902/1981369438606.

Ping, Li. "Rural Land Tenure Reforms in China: Issues, Regulations and Prospects for Additional Reform." *Land Reform, Land Settlement, and Cooperatives*, no. 3 (2003): 59–72.

Piscopo, Jennifer M., and Susan Clark Muntean. "Corporate Quotas and Symbolic Politics in Advanced Democracies." *Journal of Women, Politics & Policy* 39, no. 3 (July 3, 2018): 285–309. https://doi.org/10.1080/1554477X.2018.1477396.

Poirot, Stéphanie. "Devoir de vigilance des entreprises: Entre hard et soft law, une réponse au «social washing»?" *The Conversation* (blog), May 24, 2018. http://theconversation .com/devoir-de-vigilance-des-entreprises-entre-hard-et-soft-law-une-reponse-au -social-washing-96451.

Polischuk, Luciana, and Daniel L. Fay. "Administrative Response to Consequences of COVID-19 Emergency Responses: Observations and Implications From Gender-Based Violence in Argentina." *The American Review of Public Administration* 50, no. 6–7 (August 1, 2020): 675–84. https://doi.org/10.1177/0275074020942081.

Polli, Frida, "Fairness Optimized AI." In *Gender and AI: Promise and Perils: Session 2—Outputs*, Radcliffe Institute for Advanced Study, Harvard University, April 11, 2025. https://www.radcliffe.harvard.edu/event/2025-gender-and-ai-conference.

Porter, Monica. "Combating Gender Inequality at Home and at Work: Why the International Labour Organization Should Provide for Mandatory Paid Paternity Leave Notes." *George Washington International Law Review* 48, no. 1 (2015): 203–32.

Ragnedda, Massimo. "New Digital Inequalities. Algorithms Divide." In *Enhancing Digital Equity: Connecting the Digital Underclass*, edited by Massimo Ragnedda, 61–83. Cham: Springer International Publishing, 2020. https://doi.org/10.1007/978-3-030-49079-9_4.

Raibaud, Yves. *La ville, faite par et pour les hommes: dans l'espace urbain, une mixité en trompe-l'oeil*. Paris: Belin, 2015.

Raj, Senthorun. *Feeling Queer Jurisprudence: Injury, Intimacy, Identity*. London: Routledge, 2020. https://doi.org/10.4324/9781351128063.

Rakova, Bogdana. "A New Framework for Coming to Terms with Algorithms." *Medium*, May 24, 2023. https://points.datasociety.net/a-new-framework-for-coming-to-terms-with-algorithms-97c74d9667d0.

Ramalekana, Nomfundo. "A Critique of the Stigma Argument Against Affirmative Action in South Africa." *University of Oxford Human Rights Hub Journal* 4 (April 5, 2022): 1–32.

Ramji-Nogales, Jaya. "Revisiting the Category 'Women': Research Handbook on Feminist Engagement with International Law." In *Research Handbook on Feminist Engagement with International Law*, 240–52. Cheltenham: Edward Elgar Publishing, 2019. https://www.elgaronline.com/view/edcoll/9781785363917/9781785363917.00022.xml.

Raney, Catherine A. "From Housewife to Household Weapon: Women from the Bolivian Mines Organize Against Economic Exploitation and Political Oppression." Senior thesis, Claremont McKenna College, 2013. https://scholarship.claremont.edu/cmc_theses/591/.

Ransil, Talley Timms. "Corporations without Representation: The Constitutionality of Gender Diversity Mandates." *Utah Law Review* 2021, no. 5 (2021): 1269–92.

Ray, Andrew. "Disinformation, Deepfakes and Democracies: The Need for Legislative Reform." *UNSW Law Journal* 44 (2021): 983–1013.

Ray, Rebecca, Janet C. Gornick, and John Schmitt. *Parental Leave Policies in 21 Countries: Assessing Generosity and Gender Equality*. Washington, D.C.: Center for Economic and Policy Research, September 2008. https://cepr.net/publications/parental-leave-policies-in-21-countries-assessing-generosity-and-gender-equality/.

Rende Taylor, Lisa, and Elena Shih. "Worker Feedback Technologies and Combatting Modern Slavery in Global Supply Chains: Examining the Effectiveness of Remediation-Oriented and Due-Diligence-Oriented Technologies in Identifying and Addressing Forced Labour and Human Trafficking." *Journal of the British Academy* 7 (s1) (2019): 131–65. https://doi.org/10.5871/jba/007s1.131.

Resurreccion, Bernadette P., and Rebecca Elmhirst. *Gender and Natural Resource Management: Livelihoods, Mobility and Interventions*. London: Routledge, 2012.

Ripoll, Hazel. "Australia to Introduce Paid Domestic Violence Leave." *Public Services International* (blog), August 18, 2022. https://publicservices.international/resources/news/australia-to-introduce-paid-domestic-violence-leave?id=13212&lang=en.

Roberts, Adrienne. "The Political Economy of 'Transnational Business Feminism.'" *International Feminist Journal of Politics* 17, no. 2 (April 3, 2015): 209–31. https://doi.org/10.1080/14616742.2013.849968.

Roberts, Anthea. *Is International Law International?* Oxford: Oxford University Press, 2017.

Roberts, Huw, Josh Cowls, Emmie Hine, Jessica Morley, Vincent Wang, Mariarosaria Taddeo, and Luciano Floridi. "Governing Artificial Intelligence in China and the European Union: Comparing Aims and Promoting Ethical Outcomes." *The Information Society* 39, no. 2 (March 15, 2023): 79–97. https://doi.org/10.1080/01972243.2022.2124565.

Robles, Maria Eugenia, Boris Verbrugge, and Sara Geenen. "Does Formalization Make a Difference in Artisanal and Small-Scale Gold Mining? Insights from the Philippines." *The Extractive Industries and Society* 10 (June 1, 2022): 101078. https://doi.org/10.1016/j.exis.2022.101078.

Rocha, Miriam. "Promoting Gender Equality through Regulation: The Case of Parental Leave." *The Theory and Practice of Legislation* 9, no. 1 (January 2, 2021): 35–57. https://doi.org/10.1080/20508840.2020.1830565.

Rodriguez Fernandez, Gisela Victoria. "Reproduciendo Otros Mundos: Indigenous Women's Struggles Against Neo-Extractivism and the Bolivian State." PhD dissertation, Sociology, Portland State University, 2019.

Rogers, Nicole, and Michelle Maloney, eds. *Law as If Earth Really Mattered: The Wild Law Judgment Project*. London: Routledge, 2017. https://www.routledge.com/Law-as-if-Earth-Really-Mattered-The-Wild-Law-Judgment-Project-1st-Edition/Rogers-Maloney/p/book/9781138669086.

Rogner, Isabella. "From 'Golden Suits' to 'Golden Skirts': An Evaluation of the Norwegian Gender Quota for Corporate Boards." In *Gender Equality in Eastern Europe (and beyond)—Laws and Practices*, edited by Justyna Stypinska. Berlin: Sociology Working Papers, 2017.

Rosenblum, Darren. "Feminizing Capital: A Corporate Imperative." *Elisabeth Haub School of Law Faculty Publications*, January 1, 2009. https://digitalcommons.pace.edu/lawfaculty/399.

———. "Internalizing Gender: Why International Law Theory Should Adopt Comparative Methods." *Columbia Journal of Transnational Law* 45, no. 3 (2007): 759–828.

———. "Unsex Cedaw, or What's Wrong with Women's Rights." *Columbia Journal of Gender and Law* 20, no. 2 (July 31, 2011): 98–194.

———. "Unsex Mothering: Toward a New Culture of Parenting." *Harvard Journal of Law & Gender* 35 (2012): 57–116.

Roy, Eleanor Ainge, and Eleanor de Jong. "'A Huge Win': New Zealand Brings in Paid Domestic Violence Leave." *The Guardian*, July 26, 2018, World News. https://www.theguardian.com/world/2018/jul/26/new-zealand-paid-domestic-violence-leave-jan-logie.

Rubiano, María Juliana, María Alejandra Vélez, and Ximena Rueda. "Minería de oro artesanal y de pequeña escala: Estrategias para su formalización y diferenciación de la minería ilegal." Universidad de los Andes, 2020. https://hdl.handle.net/1992/69581.

Rubin, Marilyn Marks, and John R. Bartle. "Gender-Responsive Budgeting: A Budget Reform to Address Gender Inequity." *Public Administration* 101, no. 2 (2023): 391–405. https://doi.org/10.1111/padm.12802.

Rubio-Marín, Ruth, ed. ""Transformative Gender Constitutionalism: Towards an Egalitarian Family Structure and Sexual and Reproductive Order," In *Global Gender Constitutionalism and Women's Citizenship: A Struggle for Transformative Inclusion*, 249–311. Cambridge: Cambridge University Press, 2022.

———. "On Constitutionalism and Women's Citizenship." *Current Legal Problems* 74, no. 1 (December 1, 2021): 361–402. https://doi.org/10.1093/clp/cuab013.

Ruggie, John Gerard. "Protect, Respect, and Remedy: The UN Framework for Business and Human Rights." In Mashood A. Baderin and Manisuli Ssenyonjo, *International Human Rights Law: Six Decades after the UDHR and Beyond*, 519–38. London: Routledge, 2010.

Sagafi-nejad, Tagi, and John H. Dunning. *The UN and Transnational Corporations: From Code of Conduct to Global Compact*. Indianapolis: Indiana University Press, 2008.

Sahan, Erinch. *The Journey to Sustainable Food: A Three-Year Update on the Behind the Brands Campaign*. Oxfam Briefing Paper, April 19, 2016.

———. "Women in Global Supply Chains: Campaigning for Change." In *Gender Equality and Responsible Business: Expanding CSR Horizons*, edited by Kate Grosser, Maureen A. Kilgour, and Lauren McCarthy. London: Taylor and Francis, 2017.

Salcedo, Emily Sanchez. "The Dilemma on 'Daddy Days.'" SSRN Scholarly Paper, January 29, 2013. https://doi.org/10.2139/ssrn.2208645.

Salmivaara, Anna. "New Governance of Labour Rights: The Perspective of Cambodian Garment Workers' Struggles." *Globalizations* 15, no. 3 (2018): 329–46. https://doi.org/10.1080/14747731.2017.1394069.

Samaddar, Ranabir. "Theorising Transit Labour in Informal Mineral Extraction Processes." In *Between the Plough and the Pick: Informal, Artisanal and Small-Scale Mining in the Contemporary World*, edited by Kuntala Lahiri-Dutt, 133–50. Canberra: ANU Press, 2018. https://doi.org/10.22459/BPP.03.2018.

Santosh, KC, and Casey Wall. "AI and Ethical Issues." In *AI, Ethical Issues and Explainability—Applied Biometrics*, 1–20. SpringerBriefs in Applied Sciences and Technology. Springer Nature Singapore, 2022. https://doi.org/10.1007/978-981-19-3935-8_1.

Sardar Ali, Shaheen. "Women's Rights, CEDAW and International Human Rights Debates." In *Rethinking Empowerment: Gender and Development in a Global/Local World*, edited by Jane L. Parpart, Shirin M. Rai, and Kathleen A. Staudt. London: Routledge, 2003.

Sarkar, Mahua. "Constrained Labour as Instituted Process: Transnational Contract Work and Circular Migration in Late Capitalism." *European Journal of Sociology / Archives Européennes de Sociologie* 58, no. 1 (April 2017): 171–204. https://doi.org/10.1017/S0003975617000054.

Sawer, Marian. "Parliamentary Representation of Women: From Discourses of Justice to Strategies of Accountability." *International Political Science Review* 21, no. 4 (October 1, 2000): 361–80. https://doi.org/10.1177/0192512100214003.

Sawer, Marian, and Miranda Stewart. "Gender Budgeting." In *How Gender Can Transform the Social Sciences: Innovation and Impact*, edited by Fiona Jenkins and Karen Downing, 117–26. Cham: Springer International Publishing, 2020. https://doi.org/10.1007/978-3-030-43236-2_12.

Saypoff, Talia. "Breeding Incentives: Parental Leave in Japan and the United States." *Hastings Women's Law Journal* 23, no. 2 (2012): 275–94.

Scassa, Teresa. "Regulating AI in Canada: A Critical Look at the Proposed Artificial Intelligence and Data Act." *The Canadian Bar Review* 101, no. 1 (May 25, 2023). https://cbr.cba.org/index.php/cbr/article/view/4817.

Schank, Hana, and Elizabeth Wallace. "When Women Choose Children Over a Career." *The Atlantic*, December 19, 2016. https://www.theatlantic.com/business/archive/2016/12/opting-out/500018/.

Schaper, Stefan, and Irene Pollach. "Modern Slavery Statements: From Regulation to Substantive Supply Chain Reporting." *Journal of Cleaner Production* 313 (September 1, 2021): 127872. https://doi.org/10.1016/j.jclepro.2021.127872.

Schiek, Dagmar. "Broadening the Scope and the Norms of EU Gender Equality Law: Towards a Multidimensional Conception of Equality Law." *Maastricht Journal of European and Comparative Law* 12, no. 4 (December 1, 2005): 427–66. https://doi.org/10.1177/1023263X0501200405.

Schweikart, Debora. "The Gender Neutral Pronoun Redefined." *Women's Rights Law Reporter* 20 (1998): 1.

Seck, Sara L., and Penelope Simons. "Resource Extraction and the Human Rights of Women and Girls." *Canadian Journal of Women and the Law* 31, no. 1 (2019): i–vii.

Seierstad, Cathrine, Geraldine Healy, Eskil Sønju Le Bruyn Goldeng, and Hilde Fjellvær. "A 'Quota Silo' or Positive Equality Reach? The Equality Impact of Gender Quotas on Corporate Boards in Norway." *Human Resource Management Journal* 31, no. 1 (2021): 165–86. https://doi.org/10.1111/1748-8583.12288.

Seierstad, Cathrine, and Tore Opsahl. "For the Few Not the Many? The Effects of Affirmative Action on Presence, Prominence, and Social Capital of Women Directors in Norway." *Scandinavian Journal of Management* 27, no. 1 (2011): 44–54.

Senate of the Philippines. "Legislative Process," 2001. Accessed January 7, 2018. https://www.senate.gov.ph/about/legpro.asp.

Sharp, Rhonda. *The Economics and Politics of Auditing Government Budgets for Their Gender Impacts.* Hawke Research Institute, January 1, 2000. https://apo.org.au/node/8490.

Sharp, Rhonda, and Ray Broomhill. "Women and Government Budgets." *Australian Journal of Social Issues* 25, no. 1 (1990): 1–14. https://doi.org/10.1002/j.1839-4655.1990.tb00872.x.

Shattock, Ethan. "Self-Regulation 2:0? A Critical Reflection of the European Fight against Disinformation." *Harvard Kennedy School Misinformation Review,* May 31, 2021. https://doi.org/10.37016/mr-2020-73.

Sheehy, Elizabeth, ed. *Adding Feminism to Law: The Contributions of Justice Claire L'Heureux-Dubé.* Toronto: Irwin Law, 2004.

Shrivastava, Nidhi. "The Power of Celebrity Culture and Its Response to Rape and Sexual Violence against Women in Post-2012 India." In *Building Bridges in Celebrity Studies,* edited by J. Raphael, B. Deb, and N. Shrivastava, 96–106. Waterhill Publishing, 2016.

Sikand, Nandini. "India's Daughter: It Is Time to Retire the Realist Rape Documentary." *Camera Obscura: Feminism, Culture, and Media Studies* 38, no. 2 (113) (September 1, 2023): 119–43. https://doi.org/10.1215/02705346-10654927.

Sikhosana, Nqobile, Ogochukwu Nzewi, Mpumelelo Ndlovu, and Wayne Malinga. "Gender-Responsive Budgeting in Climate Change Financing: A Panacea for Confronting Climate Change Vulnerability in South Africa?" In *Gender-Responsive Budgeting in Africa: Access and Future Measures,* edited by Tinuade Adekunbi Ojo, 21–34. Springer Nature Switzerland, 2020.

Sinclair, Amy, and Freya Dinshaw. *Paper Promises? Evaluating the Early Impact of Australia's Modern Slavery Act.* Human Rights Law Centre, 2022. https://www.hrlc.org.au/reports/2022-2-3-paper-promises-evaluating-the-early-impact-of-australias-modern-slavery-act/.

Singh, Amit, Shubham Singhania, and Varda Sardana. "Do Women on Boards Affect Firm's Financial Performance? Evidence from Indian IPO Firms." *Australasian Accounting, Business and Finance Journal* 13, no. 2 (September 22, 2019): 53–68. https://doi.org/10.14453/aabfj.v13i2.4.

Singh, Val, and Susan Vinnicombe. "Why So Few Women Directors in Top UK Boardrooms? Evidence and Theoretical Explanations." *Corporate Governance: An International Review* 12, no. 4 (2004): 479–88. https://doi.org/10.1111/j.1467-8683.2004.00388.x.

Smart, Carol. *Feminism and the Power of Law.* London: Routledge, 1989.

———. "The Woman of Legal Discourse." *Social & Legal Studies* 1, no. 1 (March 1992): 29–44.

Smith, Nina, Valdemar Smith, and Mette Verner. "Do Women in Top Management Affect Firm Performance? A Panel Study of 2,500 Danish Firms." *International Journal of Productivity and Performance Management* 55, no. 7 (January 1, 2006): 569–93. https://doi .org/10.1108/17410400610702160.

Smith, Tyson, and Michael Kimmel. "The Hidden Discourse of Masculinity in Gender Discrimination Law." *Signs: Journal of Women in Culture and Society* 30, no. 3 (March 1, 2005): 1827–49. https://doi.org/10.1086/427524.

Son, Keonhi. "The Origin of Social Policy for Women Workers: The Emergence of Paid Maternity Leave in Western Countries." *Comparative Political Studies* 57, no. 1 (January 1, 2024): 69–100. https://doi.org/10.1177/00104140231169024.

Souza, Luísa Cardoso Guedes de. "Parenting Intentions of Same-Sex Couples: A Case Study in Brasília, Brazil." Thesis, Universidade Federal de Minas Gerais, March 13, 2020. https://repositorio.ufmg.br/handle/1843/34419.

Spivak, Gayatri Chakravorty. "Can the Subaltern Speak?" In *Can the Subaltern Speak?: Reflections on the History of an Idea*, edited by Rosalind C Morris, 21–78. New York: Columbia University Press, 2010. http://www.jstor.org/stable/10.7312/morr14384.

Srinivasan, Vasanthi, and Rejie George. "Building the Women Directorship Pipeline in India: An Exploratory Study." *SSRN Electronic Journal*, 2013. https://doi.org/10.2139/ssrn .2346109.

Stanchi, Kathryn M., Linda L. Berger, and Bridget J. Crawford. *Feminist Judgments: Rewritten Opinions of the United States Supreme Court.* Cambridge: Cambridge University Press, 2016.

Stanford, Jim. *Economic Aspects of Paid Domestic Violence Leave Provisions.* Canberra: Centre for Future Work at the Australia Institute, December 2016.

Statement by NSW Anti-Slavery Commissioner Dr. James Cockayne on the Review of the Modern Slavery Act 2018 (NSW). Legal and Constitutional Affairs Legislation Committee, Parliament of Australia, March 21, 2025. https://dcj.nsw.gov.au/legal-and-justice /our-commissioners/anti-slavery-commissioner/news-and-media/statement-by-nsw -anti-slavery-commissioner-dr-james-cockayne-on-.html.

Statista. "Japan: Share of Women on Boards of Publicly Listed Companies 2021." Accessed January 10, 2023. https://www.statista.com/statistics/1311751/japan-share-women-boards -largest-publicly-listed-companies/.

Stevenson, Mark, and Rosanna Cole. "Modern Slavery in Supply Chains: A Secondary Data Analysis of Detection, Remediation and Disclosure." *Supply Chain Management: An International Journal* 12, no. 3 (January 1, 2018): 81–99. https://doi.org/10.1108/SCM-11 -2017-0382.

Stone, Elissa. "How the Family and Medical Leave Act Can Offer Protection to Domestic Violence Victims in the Workplace Comment." *University of San Francisco Law Review* 44, no. 3 (2010): 729–54.

Strossen, Nadine. "Feminist Critique of the Feminist Critique of Pornography, an Essay." *Virginia Law Review* 79, no. 5 (1993): 1099–1190.

Suk, Julie C. "From Antidiscrimination to Equality: Stereotypes and the Life Cycle in the United States and Europe Evolutions in Antidiscrimination Law in Europe and North America." *American Journal of Comparative Law* 60, no. 1 (2012): 75–98.

———. "Work-Family Conflict and the Pipeline to Power: Lessons from European Gender Quotas." *Michigan State Law Review* 2012, no. 5 (2012): 1797–1816.

Sukadana, I. Ketut, Ni Made Sukaryati Karma, and Ni Made Puspasutari Ujianti. "Can Local Law Prevent Polygamy? A Case of Local Law Implementation in Bali," 6–9. *Advances in Social Science, Education and Humanities Research* 282 (2018). https://www.researchgate.net/publication/329938010_Can_Local_Law_Prevent_Polygamy_A_Case_of_Local_Law_Implementation_in_Bali.

Sulmicelli, Sergio. "Queer-Responsive Regulation for Artificial Intelligence in Healthcare: A Comparative Study." *UNSW Law Journal* 48, no. 4 (2025, forthcoming).

Sun, Tony, Andrew Gaut, Shirlyn Tang, Yuxin Huang, Mai ElSherief, Jieyu Zhao, Diba Mirza, Elizabeth Belding, Kai-Wei Chang, and William Yang Wang. "Mitigating Gender Bias in Natural Language Processing: Literature Review." In *Proceedings of the 57th Annual Meeting of the Association for Computational Linguistics*, edited by Anna Korhonen, David Traum, and Lluis Márquez, 163040. Association for Computational Linguistics, June 21, 2019. https://doi.org/10.48550/arXiv.1906.08976.

Sushant, and Moumita Laha. "Game Changer or Accounting Practice? Gender Responsive Budgeting in India." *Public Money & Management* 41, no. 7 (October 3, 2021): 539–47. https://doi.org/10.1080/09540962.2021.1965401.

Swanberg, Jennifer, Mamta Ojha, and Caroline Macke. "State Employment Protection Statutes for Victims of Domestic Violence: Public Policy's Response to Domestic Violence as an Employment Matter." *Journal of Interpersonal Violence* 27, no. 3 (2012): 587–619.

Szydło, Marek. "Constitutional Values Underlying Gender Equality on Boards of Companies: How Should the EU Put These Values into Practice?" *International & Comparative Law Quarterly* 63, no. 1 (January 2014): 167–96. https://doi.org/10.1017/S002058931300050X.

Tamale, Sylvie, and Jane Bennett. "Legal Voice: Challenges and Prospects in the Documentation of African Legal Feminism." *Feminist Africa*, no. 15 (2011). https://www.africabib.org/rec.php?RID=343319624.

Tatonetti, Lisa. *Written by the Body: Gender Expansiveness and Indigenous Non-Cis Masculinities*. Minneapolis: University of Minnesota Press, 2021.

Taylor, Alexis M. "The UN and the Global Compact." *New York Law School Journal of Human Rights* 17, no. 3 (2001): 975–84.

Tellier, Geneviève. "Canadian Economic and Fiscal Policy: Questioning Markets' Neutrality." In *The Palgrave Handbook of Gender, Sexuality, and Canadian Politics*, edited by Manon Tremblay and Joanna Everitt, 459–83. Cham: Springer International Publishing, 2020. https://doi.org/10.1007/978-3-030-49240-3_23.

Terjesen, Siri, Ruth Sealy, and Val Singh. "Women Directors on Corporate Boards: A Review and Research Agenda." *Corporate Governance: An International Review* 17, no. 3 (2009): 320–37. https://doi.org/10.1111/j.1467-8683.2009.00742.x.

Theumer, Emmanuel. "The Self-Perceived Gender Identity." *Interventions* 22, no. 4 (May 18, 2020): 498–513. https://doi.org/10.1080/1369801X.2020.1749708.

Thomson, Michael. "The Foetal Subject: Law, Gender and Embodiment." In *The Cambridge Companion to Gender and the Law*, edited by Stéphanie Hennette Vauchez and Ruth Rubio-Marín. Cambridge: Cambridge University Press, 2023. https://doi.org/10.1017/9781108634069.

Thornton, Margaret. *The Liberal Promise: Anti-Discrimination Legislation in Australia*. New York: Oxford University Press, 1990.

Tickler, David, Jessica J. Meeuwig, Katharine Bryant, Fiona David, John A. H. Forrest, Elise Gordon, Jacqueline Joudo Larsen, et al. "Modern Slavery and the Race to Fish." *Nature Communications* 9, no. 1 (November 7, 2018): 4643. https://doi.org/10.1038/s41467-018-07118-9.

Tobalagba, Anais, and Ramona Vijeyarasa. "Engendering Regulation of Artisanal and Small-Scale Mining: Participation, Protection and Access to Justice." *Third World Quarterly* 41, no. 10 (2020): 1635–52.

Toews, Rob. "Deepfakes Are Going to Wreak Havoc on Society. We Are Not Prepared." *Forbes*, May 25, 2020. https://www.forbes.com/sites/robtoews/2020/05/25/deepfakes-are-going-to-wreak-havoc-on-society-we-are-not-prepared/.

Toledo Orozco, Zaraí. "(Under)Mining State Authority: The Politics of Informal Gold Mining in Bolivia and Peru (2000–2017)." Dissertation, University of British Columbia, 2020. https://doi.org/10.14288/1.0395179.

Toupin, Sophie. "Shaping Feminist Artificial Intelligence." *New Media & Society* 26, no. 1 (January 1, 2024): 580–95. https://doi.org/10.1177/14614448221150776.

Treasury Board of Canada Secretariat. "Using Artificial Intelligence (AI) to Automate Candidate Evaluations in the Staffing Process's Assessment Phase." February 28, 2024. https://open.canada.ca/data/en/dataset/52b8574d-5c95-463b-b375-8edd092cea30.

True, Jacqui. *The Political Economy of Violence Against Women*. New York: Oxford University Press, 2012.

UN Secretary-General. "Report of the Secretary-General: Development in Small-Scale Mining." Committee on Natural Resources, 3rd session. United Nations Economic and Social Council, United Nations, April 1, 1996. https://digitallibrary.un.org/record/212330.

UN Women. "Facts and Figures: Women's Leadership and Political Participation," October 2024. ttps://www.unwomen.org/en/what-we-do/leadership-and-political-participation/facts-and-figures.

———. "In the Biggest Electoral Year in History, 113 Countries Have Never Had a Woman Head of State, New UN Women Data Shows," June 24, 2024. https://www.unwomen.org/en/news-stories/press-release/2024/06/in-the-biggest-electoral-year-in-history-113-countries-have-never-had-a-woman-head-of-state-new-un-women-data-shows.

UN Women Australia. "Explainer: What Is Gender-Responsive Budgeting?" *UN Women Australia* (blog), November 13, 2023. https://unwomen.org.au/explainer-what-is-gender-responsive-budgeting/.

UN Women and Inter-Parliamentary Union. *Gender-Responsive Law-Making*. Handbook for Parliamentarians No. 33. Geneva; New York: UN Women and IPU, November 2021. https://www.unwomen.org/sites/default/files/2021-11/Handbook-on-gender-responsive-law-making-en.pdf.

UNICEF. "2 in 3 Infants Live in Countries Where Dads Are Not Entitled to a Single Day of Paid Paternity Leave," June 13, 2018. https://www.unicef.org/press-releases/2-3-infants-live-countries-where-dads-are-not-entitled-single-day-paid-paternity.

UNIFEM. *Gender Responsive Budgeting and Women's Reproductive Rights: A Resource Pack*. New York: United Nations Development Fund for Women (UNIFEM), 2006. https://www.unfpa.org/sites/default/files/pub-pdf/gender_responsive_eng.pdf.

———. Report of the Ad Hoc Committee of the Whole of the Twenty-Third Special Session of the General Assembly (Beijing + 5), A/S-23/10/Rev.1 (2000). https://documents-dds-ny.un.org/doc/UNDOC/GEN/N00/546/61/PDF/N0054661.pdf?OpenElement.

United Nations Educational, Scientific and Cultural Organization. "Artificial Intelligence and Gender Equality: Key Findings of UNESCO's Global Dialogue—UNESCO Digital Library." Paris: UNESCO, 2020. https://unesdoc.unesco.org/ark:/48223/pf0000374174.

———. "Measuring Digital Development: Facts and Figures 2022," 2022. https://www.itu.int/hub/publication/d-ind-ict_mdd-2022/.

United Nations Environment Programme and United Nations Institute for Training and Research. *Handbook: Developing National ASGM Formalization Strategies within National Action Plans*, 2018. https://wedocs.unep.org/xmlui/handle/20.500.11822/26437.

United Nations Women, Women Count, and UN Department of Economic and Social Affairs. "Progress on the Sustainable Development Goals: The Gender Snapshot 2024." New York: United Nations, 2024. https://www.unwomen.org/en/resources/gender-snapshot.

United States Department of State. "What Is Modern Slavery?" Archived content. Accessed November 7, 2023. https://www.state.gov/what-is-modern-slavery/.

Vandenbeld, Anita, and Ha Hoa Ly. "Women's Representation in the National Assembly of Viet Nam—The Way Forward." Vietnam: United Nations Development Programme, 2012. https://www.undp.org/sites/g/files/zskgke326/files/migration/vn/31211_Women_s_Representation_in_Leadership_in_the_National_Assembly_-_the_way_forward_final.pdf.

Vandergeest, Peter, and Melissa Marschke. "Modern Slavery and Freedom: Exploring Contradictions through Labour Scandals in the Thai Fisheries." *Antipode* 52, no. 1 (2020): 291–315. https://doi.org/10.1111/anti.12575.

van Staveren, Irene. "To Measure Is to Know? A Comparative Analysis of Gender Indices." *Review of Social Economy* 71, no. 3 (September 1, 2013): 339–72. https://doi.org/10.1080/00346764.2012.707398.

Velkova, Irina. "Quotas for Women on Corporate Boards: The Call for Change in Europe." In *SSRN Electronic Journal*, 2015. https://doi.org/10.2139/ssrn.1947701.

Verbrugge, Boris, and Beverly Besmanos. "Formalizing Artisanal and Small-Scale Mining: Whither the Workforce?" *Resources Policy* 47 (March 1, 2016): 134–41. https://doi.org/10.1016/j.resourpol.2016.01.008.

Veronelli, Gabriela A. "The Coloniality of Language: Race, Expressivity, Power, and the Darker Side of Modernity." *Wagadu* 13 (2015): 108–34.

Vijeyarasa, Ramona. "Between Equality and Stagnation: A Comparative Evaluation of Paid Parental Leave Policies in Latin America." *International Journal of Law in Context*, forthcoming in 2025.

———. "Comparing Whose Laws? Interrogating Biases in Comparative Law and Scholarship through the Lens of Domestic Violence Workplace Leave." *International Journal of Comparative Labour Law and Industrial Relations* 40, no. 3 (2024).

———. "Does Law Matter?: Defending the Value of Gender-Responsive Legislation to Advance Gender Equality." *NYU Journal of Legislation and Public Policy* 24, no. 3 (2022): 671–723.

———. "Flamer-Caldera v Sri Lanka: Asia-Wide Implications of an Essential Evolution in CEDAW's Jurisprudence." *Asian Journal of International Law*, (2022), 1–11. https://doi.org/10.1017/S2044251322000583.

———. "Gendered Harms and the Regulation of Artificial Intelligence: A Comparative Assessment of Emerging Legislative Practice." *Notre Dame Journal of Emerging Technologies* 5, no. 1 (2023): 114–61.

———. "Institutionalising Women's Experiences in Law: Possibilities and Pitfalls of Parliamentary Gender Audit Committees." *Alternative Law Journal* 49, no. 2 (2024): 1–12. https://doi.org/10.1177/1037969X241253001.

———. "In Pursuit of Gender-Responsive Legislation: Transforming Women's Lives through the Law." In *International Women's Rights Law and Gender Equality: Making the Law Work for Women*, edited by Ramona Vijeyarasa. Abingdon; New York: Routledge, 2021.

———. "Making the Law Work for Women: Standard-Setting through a New Gender Legislative Index." *Alternative Law Journal* 44, no. 4 (2019): 275–80. https://doi.org/10.1177/1037969X19861751

———. "Misdirected by the 'Daddy Quota': A Comparative Study of Paid Parental Leave across Twenty-One Asian Nations." *Asian Journal of Comparative Law*, first published online March 12, 2025. https://doi.org/10.1017/asjcl.2025.5.

———. "A Missed Opportunity: How Australia Failed to Make Its Modern Slavery Act a Good Practice Global Example." *Adelaide Law Review* 40, no. 3 (2019): 857–65.

———. "A Move in the Right Direction? The Model Law against Trafficking in Persons and the ILO Operational Indicators." *International Migration* 57, no. 1 (2019): 177–91. https://doi.org/10.1111/imig.12504.

———. "'Proposing a Gender-Responsive Reform of the Australian 'Modern Slavery' Act: Voice, Disaggregation and Accountability." In *The Feminist Legislation Project: Rewriting Laws for Gender-Based Justice*, edited by Becky Batagol, Kate Seear, Heli Askola, and James Walvisch. London: Routledge, Taylor and Francis, 2025.

———. "Quantifying CEDAW: Concrete Tools for Enhancing Accountability for Women's Human Rights." *Harvard Human Rights Journal* 34, no. 1 (2021): 37–80.

———. "Realizing the Right to Development in the Context of Artificial Intelligence: A Dual Opportunity." Forthcoming.

———. *Sex, Slavery and the Trafficked Woman: Myths and Misconceptions about Trafficking and Its Victims*. London: Routledge, 2016.

———. "Three Decades of CEDAW Committee General Recommendations: A Roadmap for Domestication, Reporting and Stronger Accountability for Women's Rights." *Max Planck Yearbook of United Nations Law* 19, no. 2 (2020): 797–829.

———. *The Woman President: Leadership, Law and Legacy for Women Based on Experiences from South and Southeast Asia*. Oxford: Oxford University Press, 2022.

———. "Women's Absence in Sri Lankan Politics: Lessons on the Effectiveness and Limitations of Quotas to Address Under-representation." *Women Studies International Forum* 81, no. 102371 (July/August 2020).

———. "Women's Movements under Women Presidents: Bringing a Gender Perspective to the Legal System." *Gender & Development* 29, no. 2–3 (September 2, 2021): 569–91. https://doi.org/10.1080/13552074.2021.1978736.

Vijeyarasa, Ramona, and José-Miguel Bello y Villarino. "Lessons and Consequences of the Failure to Regulate AI for Women's Human Rights." OpenGlobalRights, July 14, 2022. https://www.openglobalrights.org/lessons-and-consequences-of-failure-to-regulate-ai/.

————. "Modern-Day Slavery—A Judicial Catchall for Trafficking, Slavery and Labour Exploitation: A Critique of Tang and Rantsev." *Journal of International Law and International Relations* 9 (2013): 38–76.

Vijeyarasa, Ramona, and Mark Liu. "Fast Fashion for 2030: Using the Pattern of the Sustainable Development Goals (SDGs) to Cut a More Gender-Just Fashion Sector." *Business and Human Rights Journal* 7 (2022): 45–66. https://doi.org/10.1017/bhj.2021.29.

Viscidi, Lisa. "Turmoil in South America and the Impact on Energy Markets." *Istituto Affari Internazionali (IAI) Papers* 19 (December 26, 2019). https://www.jstor.org/stable/resrep23661.

Voss, H., M. Davis, M. Sumner, L. Waite, I. A. Ras, D. Singhal, and D. Jog. "International Supply Chains: Compliance and Engagement with the Modern Slavery Act." *Journal of the British Academy* 7, no. s1 (June 18, 2019): 61–76.

Wagner, Travis L., and Ashley Blewer. "'The Word Real Is No Longer Real': Deepfakes, Gender, and the Challenges of AI-Altered Video." *Open Information Science* 3, no. 1 (January 1, 2019): 32–46. https://doi.org/10.1515/opis-2019-0003.

Wang, Jenny Jing. "How Managers Use Culture and Controls to Impose a '996' Work Regime in China That Constitutes Modern Slavery." *Accounting & Finance* 60, no. 4 (2020): 4331–59. https://doi.org/10.1111/acfi.12682.

Wang, Mingzhu, and Elisabeth Kelan. "The Gender Quota and Female Leadership: Effects of the Norwegian Gender Quota on Board Chairs and CEOs." *Journal of Business Ethics* 117, no. 3 (2013): 449–66. https://doi.org/10.1007/s10551-012-1546-5.

Ward, Kristy. "Gender Regimes and Cambodian Labor Unions." *Gender & Society* 36, no. 4 (August 1, 2022): 578–601. https://doi.org/10.1177/08912432221102155.

Warren, Elizabeth. "What Is a Women's Issue—Bankruptcy, Commercial Law, and Other Gender-Neutral Topics Essay Written for the Occasion of the 25th Anniversary of the Harvard Women's Law Journal." *Harvard Women's Law Journal* 25 (2002): 19–56.

Watson, Nicole, and Heather Douglas, eds. *Indigenous Legal Judgments: Bringing Indigenous Voices into Judicial Decision Making.* London: Routledge, 2021. https://www.routledge.com/Indigenous-Legal-Judgments-Bringing-Indigenous-Voices-into-Judicial-Decision/Watson-Douglas/p/book/9780367467456.

Weatherall, Ruth, Mihajla Gavin, and Natalie Thorburn. "Safeguarding Women at Work? Lessons from Aotearoa New Zealand on Effectively Implementing Domestic Violence Policies." *Journal of Industrial Relations* 63, no. 4 (September 1, 2021): 568–90. https://doi.org/10.1177/0022185621996766.

Webb, Meg, MP. "Motion—Gender Responsive Budgeting." Presented at the Tasmania Legislative Council, Hobart, Tasmania, March 8, 2022. https://megwebb.com.au/motion-gender-responsive-budgeting/.

Weiss, Sabrina Rojas. "Celebrity Dads Raising Awareness About Paternity Leave," Motherly, June 11, 2021. https://www.mother.ly/news/celebrity-news/celebrity-fathers-paternity-leave/.

Weissbrodt, David, and Muria Kruger. "Norms on the Responsibilities of Transnational Corporations and Other Business Enterprises with regard to Human Rights." *American Journal of International Law* 97, no. 4 (October 2003): 901–22. https://doi.org/10.2307/3133689.

Weldon, S. Laurel, and Mala Htun. "Feminist Mobilisation and Progressive Policy Change: Why Governments Take Action to Combat Violence against Women." *Gender & Development* 21, no. 2 (July 1, 2013): 231–47. https://doi.org/10.1080/13552074.2013.802158.

Wettstein, Florian. "CSR and the Debate on Business and Human Rights: Bridging the Great Divide." *Business Ethics Quarterly* 22, no. 4 (October 2012): 739–70. https://doi.org/10.5840/beq201222446.

Widiss, Deborah A. "Domestic Violence and the Workplace: The Explosion of State Legislation and the Need for a Comprehensive Strategy." *Florida State University Law Review* 35, no. 3 (2008): 669–728.

———. "Pregnancy and Work—50 Years of Legal Theory, Litigation, and Legislation." SSRN Scholarly Paper. Rochester, NY: Social Science Research Network, 2021. https://papers.ssrn.com/abstract=3800211.

Wilhelm, Miriam, Alin Kadfak, Vikram Bhakoo, and Kate Skattang. "Private Governance of Human and Labor Rights in Seafood Supply Chains—The Case of the Modern Slavery Crisis in Thailand." *Marine Policy* 115 (May 1, 2020): 103833. https://doi.org/10.1016/j.marpol.2020.103833.

Williams, Christopher. "The End of the 'Masculine Rule'? Gender-Neutral Legislative Drafting in the United Kingdom and Ireland." *Statute Law Review* 29, no. 3 (October 1, 2008): 139–53. https://doi.org/10.1093/slr/hmn015.

Wiryawan, I. Wayan Gde. "The Rights of Paternity Leave for Husbands in Indonesian Legal Renewal." *International Journal of Criminal Justice Sciences* 18, no. 1 (May 30, 2023): 132–47.

Women and Gender Equality Canada. "Gender-Based Analysis Plus (GBA Plus)," March 31, 2021. https://women-gender-equality.canada.ca/en/gender-based-analysis-plus.html.

Wong, Elizabeth, Judy Jou, Amy Raub, and Jody Heymann. "Comparing the Availability of Paid Parental Leave for Same-Sex and Different-Sex Couples in 34 OECD Countries." *Journal of Social Policy* 49, no. 3 (July 2020): 525–45. https://doi.org/10.1017/S0047279419000643.

Wood, Stepan. "Rights of Nature: What Are They?" Centre for Law and the Environment, September 1, 2023. https://commons.allard.ubc.ca/cle/10.

World Bank. *Mining Together: Large-Scale Mining Meets Artisanal Mining.* Washington, D.C.: World Bank, March 2009. https://documents1.worldbank.org/curated/pt/148081468163163514/pdf/686190ESW0P1120ngoTogether0HD0final.pdf.

———. *Women, Business and the Law 2022.* World Bank Group, 2022. https://openknowledge.worldbank.org/entities/publication/b187725b-29ff-5c61-91e7-5110ab3c4a71.

———. "World Bank Urges Action for Gender Equality in Artisanal and Small-Scale Mining." Press release, February 5, 2024. https://www.worldbank.org/en/news/press-release/2024/02/05/world-bank-urges-action-for-gender-equality-in-artisanal-and-small-scale-mining.

World Economic Forum. "The 'AI Divide' between the Global North and Global South," January 16, 2023. https://www.weforum.org/agenda/2023/01/davos23-ai-divide-global-north-global-south/.

———. *The Global Gender Gap Report 2021.* Geneva: World Economic Forum, March 30, 2021. https://www.weforum.org/reports/global-gender-gap-report-2021.

———. *The Global Gender Gap Report 2024*. Geneva: World Economic Forum, June 20, 2024. https://www3.weforum.org/docs/WEF_GGGR_2023.pdf.

———. "Only 14 Countries Have Full Equal Rights for Women," March 10, 2023. https://www.weforum.org/agenda/2023/03/only-14-countries-have-full-equal-rights-for-women/.

———. "Why We Must Act Now to Close the Digital Gender Gap in AI," August 22, 2022. https://www.weforum.org/agenda/2022/08/why-we-must-act-now-to-close-the-gender-gap-in-ai/.

Yakovleva, Natalia. "Perspectives on Female Participation in Artisanal and Small-Scale Mining: A Case Study of Birim North District of Ghana." *Resources Policy* 32, no. 1 (March 1, 2007): 29–41. https://doi.org/10.1016/j.resourpol.2007.03.002.

Yoon, Lina. "South Korea Court Recognizes Equal Benefits for Same-Sex Couple." Human Rights watch, February 22, 2023. https://www.hrw.org/news/2023/02/22/south-korea-court-recognizes-equal-benefits-same-sex-couple.

Zachary, M. "Precautionary Measures Curb Workplace Violence Liability." *Supervision* 59, no. 9 (1998): 20–21.

Zwingel, Susanne. "Women's Rights Norms as Content-in-Motion and Incomplete Practice." *Third World Thematics: A TWQ Journal* 2, no. 5 (2017): 675–90. https://doi.org/10.1080/23802014.2017.1365625.

LEGAL MATERIALS

International

CEDAW Committee. General Recommendation No. 9: Statistical Data Concerning the Situation of Women (1989). http://hrlibrary.umn.edu/gencomm/generl19.htm.

———. General Recommendation No. 12: Violence against Women (Eighth Session, 1989). https://www.refworld.org/legal/general/cedaw/1989/en/53527.

———. General Recommendation No. 19: Violence against Women (Eleventh Session, 1992), UN Doc. CEDAW/C/1992/L.1/Add.15 (1992) § (1992). http://hrlibrary.umn.edu/gencomm/generl19.htm.

———. General Recommendation No. 21: Equality in Marriage and Family Relations (Thirteenth Session, 1992), UN Doc. A/49/38 at 1 (1994) § (1994). http://www.refworld.org/docid/48abd52c0.html.

———. General Recommendation No. 35: Gender-Based Violence against Women, Updating General Recommendation No. 19, UN Doc. CEDAW/C/GC/35 (2017). https://digitallibrary.un.org/record/1305057?ln=en&v=pdf.

———. General Recommendation No. 40: Equal and Inclusive Representation of Women in Decision-Making Systems, UN Doc. CEDAW/C/GC/40 § (2024). https://digitallibrary.un.org/record/4067705?ln=en&v=pdf.

Council of Europe. Explanatory Report to the Council of Europe Framework Convention on Artificial Intelligence and Human Rights, Democracy and the Rule of Law. Council of Europe Treaty Series no. 225 (2024). https://rm.coe.int/1680afae67.

———. Framework Convention on Artificial Intelligence and Human Rights, Democracy and the Rule of Law. Council of Europe Treaty Series no. 225. Vilnius, September 5, 2024. http://rm.coe.int/1680afae3c.

European Commission. "Shaping Europe's Digital Future: AI Act," April 30, 2024. https:// digital-strategy.ec.europa.eu/en/policies/regulatory-framework-ai.

European Court of Human Rights. Hallier and Others v. France, Application No. 46386/10, (2017) (January 18, 2018).

European Parliament and the Council of the European Union. Directive (EU) 2014/95/EU of the European Parliament and of the Council as regards disclosure of non-financial and diversity information by certain large undertakings and groups (2014). http://data .europa.eu/eli/dir/2014/95/oj.

———. Directive (EU) 2019/1158 on Work-Life Balance for Parents and Carers and Repealing Council Directive 2010/18/EU (2019). http://data.europa.eu/eli/dir/2019/1158/oj.

———. Directive (EU) 2022/2381 of 23 November 2022 on Improving the Gender Balance among Directors of Listed Companies and Related Measures (2022). http://data.europa .eu/eli/dir/2022/2381/oj.

———. Directive (EU) 2024/1760 on Corporate Sustainability Due Diligence (2024). http:// data.europa.eu/eli/dir/2024/1760/oj.

———. Regulation (EU) 2017/821 of the European Parliament and of the Council laying down supply chain due diligence obligations for Union importers of tin, tantalum and tungsten, their ores, and gold originating from conflict-affected and high-risk areas (2017). http://data.europa.eu/eli/reg/2017/821/oj

———. Regulation (EU) 2022/2065 of the European Parliament and of the Council on a Single Market for Digital Services (2022). http://data.europa.eu/eli/reg/2022/2065/oj.

———. Regulation (EU) 2024/1689 of the European Parliament and the Council Laying Down Harmonised Rules on Artificial Intelligence (Artificial Intelligence Act), Regulation (EU) 2024/1689 (2024). http://data.europa.eu/eli/reg/2024/1689/oj.

International Agreement for the Suppression of the White Slave Traffic (1904; entered into force July 18, 1905). https://treaties.un.org/pages/ViewDetails.aspx?src=TREATY &mtdsg_no=VII-8&chapter=7&clang=_en.

International Commission of Jurists. Yogyakarta Principles on the Application of International Human Rights Law in Relation to Sexual Orientation and Gender Identity (2016). http://yogyakartaprinciples.org/wp-content/uploads/2016/08/principles_en.pdf.

International Convention for the Suppression of the White Slave Traffic, 3 LNTS 278 (1910). https://treaties.un.org/pages/ViewDetails.aspx?src=TREATY&mtdsg_no=VII-9& chapter=7&clang=_en.

International Labour Organization. Abrogation of Convention C045—Underground Work (Women) Convention, 1935 (No. 45) (2024). https://normlex.ilo.org/dyn/normlex/en/f? p=NORMLEXPUB:12100:0::NO::P12100_INSTRUMENT_ID:312190.

———. Convention Concerning Equal Opportunities and Equal Treatment for Men and Women Workers: Workers with Family Responsibilities, 156 (1981). https://normlex.ilo .org/dyn/nrmlx_en/f?p=NORMLEXPUB:12100:0::NO::P12100_ILO_CODE:C156.

———. Maternity Protection Convention, C003 (1919). https://www.ilo.org/dyn/normlex /en/f?p=NORMLEXPUB:12100:0::NO::P12100_INSTRUMENT_ID:312148.

———. Maternity Protection Convention, C183 (2000). https://normlex.ilo.org/dyn/nrmlx _en/f?p=NORMLEXPUB:12100:0::NO::P12100_ILO_CODE:C183.

———. Maternity Protection Convention (Revised), C103 (1952). https://www.ilo.org/dyn /normlex/en/f?p=NORMLEXPUB:12100:0::NO::P12100_ILO_CODE:C103.

———. Maternity Protection Recommendation, R191 (2000). https://normlex.ilo.org/dyn/nrm
    lx_en/f?p=NORMLEXPUB:12100:0::NO:12100:P12100_INSTRUMENT_ID:312529:NO.
———. Work in Fishing Convention, C188 (2007). https://normlex.ilo.org/dyn/nrmlx_en
    /f?p=NORMLEXPUB:12100:0::NO::P12100_ILO_CODE:C188.
———. Violence and Harassment Convention, C190 (2019). https://normlex.ilo.org/dyn
    /nrmlx_en/f?p=NORMLEXPUB:12100:0::NO::P12100_ILO_CODE:C190.
League of Nations. Convention to Suppress the Slave Trade and Slavery. 60 LNTS 253, Can
    TS 1928 No 5 § (1926).
Organization of American States. Inter-American Convention on the Prevention, Punish-
    ment, and Eradication of Violence against Women (Belém do Pará Convention), 1438
    UNTS 63 (1995). https://www.oas.org/juridico/english/treaties/a-61.html.
United Nations. Beijing Declaration and Platform for Action. Fourth World Conference for
    Women, September 1995. UN Doc. A/CONF. 177/20 (1995) and A/CONF. 177/20/Add. 1
    (1995). https://www.un.org/en/conferences/women/beijing1995.
———. Protocol against the Illicit Manufacturing of and Trafficking in Firearms, Their Parts
    and Components and Ammunition, supplementing the United Nations Convention against
    Transnational Organized Crime (2001; entered into force July 3, 2005). https://treaties.un
    .org/pages/viewdetails.aspx?src=treaty&mtdsg_no=xviii-12-c&chapter=18&clang=_en.
———. Protocol against the Smuggling of Migrants by Land, Sea and Air, supplement-
    ing the United Nations Convention against Transnational Organized Crime (2000;
    entered into force January 28, 2004). https://treaties.un.org/pages/ViewDetails.aspx?
    src=TREATY&mtdsg_no=XVIII-12-b&chapter=18&clang=_en.
———. Protocol to Prevent, Suppress and Punish Trafficking in Persons, Especially Women
    and Children, supplementing the United Nations Convention against Transnational Or-
    ganized Crime (2000; entered into force December 25, 2003). https://treaties.un.org/pages
    /ViewDetails.aspx?src=TREATY&mtdsg_no=XVIII-12-a&chapter=18.
United Nations Conference of Plenipotentiaries on a Supplementary Convention on the
    Abolition of Slavery, the Slave Trade, and Institutions and Practices Similar to Slavery.
    Supplementary Convention on the Abolition of Slavery, the Slave Trade, and Institutions
    and Practices Similar to Slavery. Geneva, September 7, 1956. https://treaties.un.org/doc
    /Treaties/1957/04/19570430%2001-00%20AM/Ch_XVIII_4p.pdf
United Nations Conference of Plenipotentiaries on the Status of Refugees and Stateless
    Persons. Convention Relating to the Status of Refugees, 1951. https://www.refworld.org
    /legal/agreements/unga/1951/en/39821.
United Nations Environment Programme. Minamata Convention on Mercury, 2013.
    https://www.unep.org/globalmercurypartnership/resources/policy-and-strategy
    /minamata-convention-mercury.
United Nations General Assembly. Convention on the Elimination of All Forms of Dis-
    crimination against Women. G.A. Res. 34/180, 34 U.N. GAOR Supp. (No. 46) at 194,
    U.N. Doc. A/34/46 (1979; entered into force September 3, 1981).
———. Convention against Transnational Organized Crime, A/RES/55/25 (2000). https://
    www.refworld.org/docid/3b00f55b0.html.
———. Optional Protocol to the Convention on the Elimination of All Forms of Discrimi-
    nation against Women, G.A. Res. 54/4, December 22, 2000.
United Nations Global Compact. United Nations, 2000. https://unglobalcompact.org/.

Domestic

Act on Equal Status and Equal Rights of Women and Men, No. 10/2008 (2008). Iceland. https://natlex.ilo.org/dyn/natlex2/natlex2/files/download/82800/ISL82800%202015 .pdf.

Act on Maternity and Parental Leave, No. 144/2020 (2020). Iceland. https://www.government .is/library/04-Legislation/Act_on_Maternity_Paternity_Leave_and%20Parental _Leave_No_144_2020.pdf.

Act Reinstituting Absolute Divorce as an Alternate Mode for Dissolution of Marriage, Congress of the Philippines (19th Congress), H. No. 9349 (2024). https://legacy.senate.gov .ph/lisdata/4421540192!.pdf.

Act respecting Amendment to Act on Public Limited Companies and Act on Private Limited Companies (Ownership, Sex Ratios and Acting Chairmen of Boards of Directors), No. 13/2010 (8 March 2010). Iceland. https://www.government.is/publications/legislation /lex/2018/02/06/TRANSLATION-OF-RECENT-AMENDMENTS-OF-ICELANDIC -PUBLIC-AND-PRIVATE-LIMITED-COMPANIES-LEGISLATION-2008-2010-in cluding-Acts-13-2010-sex-ratios-and-68-2010-minority-protection-remuneration/.

Advisory Committee of the Modern Slavery Registry (Business & Human Rights Resource Centre, Humanity United, Freedom Fund, Anti-Slavery International, Ethical Trading Initiative, UNICEF UK, Focus on Labour Exploitation [FLEX], Freedom United, and CORE Coalition). Submission No. 9 to Joint Standing Committee on Foreign Affairs, Defence and Trade, 2017. Australia. https://www.aph.gov.au/Parliamentary _Business/Committees/Joint/Foreign_Affairs_Defence_and_Trade/DefenceAR 2021-22/Submissions.

Approval of the emerging obligations of international human rights law, in relation to equality and non-discrimination between women and men, including formal, substantial and recognition equality, Ley No. 19846 (2019). Uruguay. https://www.impo.com.uy /bases/leyes/19846-2019.

Asamblea Nacional de Venezuela. "Exposición de motivos: Ley organica sobre el derecho de las mujeres a una vida libre de violencia." Gaceta Oficial No. 40.548, November 25, 2014. https://www.refworld.org/es/leg/legis/pleg/2014/es/134653.

Bangladesh Labour Act (Amendment) 2023, Act No. 41 of 2023 (2023).

Basic Act on the Development of Artificial Intelligence and Establishment of Trust (Basic Act on Artificial Intelligence), Act No. 044-202-6275 (2025; enters into force January 2026). Ministry of Science and ICT (Artificial Intelligence-Based Policy Division), South Korea. https://cset.georgetown.edu/publication/south-korea-ai-law-2025/.

Basic Policy on Economic and Fiscal Management and Reform 2023 (English ver.). Cabinet decision, June 16, 2023. Japan. https://www5.cao.go.jp/keizai-shimon/kaigi/cabinet /honebuto/2023/decision0616.html.

Biden, Joseph. Executive Order 14110, Safe, Secure, and Trustworthy Development and Use of Artificial Intelligence, October 30, 2023. https://www.federalregister.gov/documents /2023/11/01/2023-24283/safe-secure-and-trustworthy-development-and-use-of -artificial-intelligence.

California Transparency in Supply Chains Act, an Act to add Section 1714.43 to the Civil Code, and to add Section 19547.5 to the Revenue and Taxation Code, relating to human trafficking, California Senate Bill 657 (2012). https://oag.ca.gov/sites/all/files/agweb/pdfs /cybersafety/sb_657_bill_ch556.pdf.

Canadian Gender Budgeting Act, S.C. 2018, c. 27, s. 314 (2018). https://laws-lois.justice.gc.ca/eng/acts/C-17.2/FullText.html.

Childcare and Family Care Leave Act, No. 76 (1991). Japan. https://www.japaneselawtranslation.go.jp/en/laws/view/3543.

Child Development Co-Savings Act (2001). Singapore Statutes Online. https://sso.agc.gov.sg/Act/CDCSA2001.

Código del Trabajo (Chile), Ley 21592 (2002). https://www.bcn.cl/leychile/navegar?idNorma=207436.

Código del Trabajo (Colombia), Ley 2141 de 2021 (2021). Por medio de la cual se modifican los artículos 239 y 240 del cst, con el fin de establecer el fuero de paternidad. https://www.funcionpublica.gov.co/eva/gestornormativo/norma.php?i=168351.

Código de Trabajo de Costa Rica, Ley 2 (1943). https://www.mtss.go.cr/elministerio/marco-legal/documentos/Codigo_Trabajo_RPL.pdf.

Código del Trabajo (Dominican Republic), Law No. 16–92 § (1992). https://natlex.ilo.org/dyn/natlex2/natlex2/files/download/29744/DOM29744.pdf.

Código del Trabajo (Ecuador), No. 2005–017 (2005). https://bicade.com.ec/codigo-del-trabajo-actualizado-al-14-de-mayo-de-2025/.

Código de Trabajo de la República de El Salvador (2021). https://www.colsiba.org/wp-content/uploads/2021/09/Cod_Trab_ElSalv1.pdf.

Código de Trabajo (Guatemala), Decreto No. 1441 (2011). https://www.leyestributariasguatemala.com/leyes/codigo-de-trabajo-decreto-no.-1441-titulo-i-y-ii.

Código del Trabajo (Honduras), Decreto No. 189–59 (1959). https://www.tsc.gob.hn/web/leyes/codigo_de_trabajo.pdf.

Código del Trabajo (Nicaragua), Ley No. 185 (1996). http://legislacion.asamblea.gob.ni/Normaweb.nsf/(All)/FA251B3C54F5BAEF062571C40055736C?opendocument.

Constitución de la República del Ecuador (2008). Registro Oficial No. 449. https://www.gob.ec/sites/default/files/regulations/2018-11/constitucion_de_bolsillo.pdf.

Constitution of Austria (Bundes-Verfassungsgesetz), (version as of 21 August 2024), https://www.ris.bka.gv.at/Dokumente/Erv/ERV_1930_1/ERV_1930_1.pdf.

Constitutional Court of Colombia. Parejas Adoptantes del Mismo Sexo, Sentencia No. C-415/22 (November 23, 2022). Colombia. https://www.corteconstitucional.gov.co/relatoria/2022/c-415-22.htm.

Corporations: Boards of Directors, California Senate Bill 826 (2018). https://leginfo.legislature.ca.gov/faces/billTextClient.xhtml?bill_id=201720180SB826.

Criminal Code Amendment (Deepfake Sexual Material) Bill 2024, Act No. 78 (2024). Parliament of the Commonwealth of Australia. https://www.aph.gov.au/Parliamentary_Business/Bills_LEGislation/Bills_Search_Results/Result?bId=r7205.

Décision no 2017–750 DC du 23 mars 2017 (2017). Conseil Constitutionnel (France). https://www.conseil-constitutionnel.fr/decision/2017/2017750DC.htm.

Décret no 2021–574 du 10 mai 2021 relatif à allongement et à l'obligation de prise d'une partie du congé de paternité et d'accueil de l'enfant [Decree 2021–574 of May 10, 2021, relating to the extension and the obligation to take part of paternity and childcare leave]. *Journal Officiel de la République Francaise* no 0110 (2021). France. https://www.legifrance.gouv.fr/jorf/id/JORFTEXT000043492531.

Denisse Patricia Muñoz Tempio contra Suseso, Compin y Consalud, No. 37322–2021 (September 1, 2021). Court of Appeals of Santiago (Chile).

Dobbs, State Health Officer of the Mississippi Department of Health, et al. v. Jackson Women's Health Organization et al. 597 (US Supreme Court 2022). https://www.supremecourt.gov/opinions/21pdf/19-1392_6j37.pdf.

Dodd–Frank Wall Street Reform and Consumer Protection Act, Public Law No. 111–203, 124 Stat. 1376 (2010). 111th US Congress. https://www.govinfo.gov/content/pkg/PLAW-111publ203/html/PLAW-111publ203.htm.

Domestic Abuse (Safe Leave) Act (Northern Ireland) 2022 (2022). https://www.legislation.gov.uk/nia/2022/27/section/1/enacted.

Domestic Violence—Victims' Protection Act 2018, No. 21 (2018). New Zealand. https://www.legislation.govt.nz/act/public/2018/0021/latest/DLM7054315.html.

Employment Standards Code, C.C.S.M. c. E110 (2016). Manitoba, Canada. https://web2.gov.mb.ca/laws/statutes/ccsm/e110.php.

Establece normas sobre accidentes del trabajo y enfermedades profesionales, Ley 16744 (1968). Chile. https://www.bcn.cl/leychile/navegar?i=28650.

Fair Work Amendment (Paid Family and Domestic Violence Leave) Act 2022, No. 47 (2022). Australia. https://www.aph.gov.au/Parliamentary_Business/Bills_Legislation/Bills_Search_Results/Result?bId=r6882.

Federal law supplementing the Swiss Civil Code, No. 220 (1911). Switzerland.

Financial Management Amendment (Gender Responsive Budgeting) Act 2024. Victoria, Australia. https://www.legislation.vic.gov.au/bills/financial-management-amendment-gender-responsive-budgeting-bill-2024.

Föräldrabalk (Children and Parents Code) 1949:381 (1949). Sweden. https://lagen.nu/1949:381.

Gobierno de El Salvador. *Plan Quinquenal de Desarrollo: 2010–2014*, November 2010. https://faolex.fao.org/docs/pdf/els140953.pdf.

Hindu Succession Act 2005 (Amending the Hindu Succession Act 1956), No. 39 (2005). India. https://www.indiacode.nic.in/repealedfileopen?rfilename=A2005-39.pdf.

Initiatiefvoorstel Wet Zorgplicht Kinderarbeid [Child Labor Due Diligence Act], Law No. 34506 (2016). Netherlands. https://www.parlementairemonitor.nl/9353000/1/j9vvij5epmj1ey0/vk57guit62wn.

Labor Standards Act, No. 49 (1947). Japan. https://www.japaneselawtranslation.go.jp/en/laws/view/3567/en.

Labour Code (2007). Afghanistan. https://natlex.ilo.org/dyn/natlex2/r/natlex/fe/details?p3_isn=78309.

Ley de Licencia Especial para empleados con situaciones de violencia doméstica o de género, maltrato de menores, hostigamiento sexual en el empleo, agresión sexual, actos lascivos o de acecho en su modalidad grave, Ley N.º 83–2019 (2019). Puerto Rico. https://bvirtualogp.pr.gov/ogp/Bvirtual/leyesreferencia/PDF/83-2019.pdf.

Ley de Municipios Autónomos del Estado Libre Asociado de Puerto Rico (Council Act), Ley N.º 107–2005 (2005).

Ley de violencia hacia las mujeres basadas en genero: Modificacion a Disposiciones Del Codigo Civil y Codigo Penal. Derogacion de Los Arts 24 A 29 de Ley 17,514, Ley N.º 19580 (2018). Uruguay. https://www.impo.com.uy/bases/leyes/19580-2017.

Ley especial para una vida libre de violencia para las mujeres, Ley N.º 520 de 2011 (2011). El Salvador. https://www.refworld.org/es/leg/decre/pleg/2011/es/133211.

Ley Federal del Trabajo: Nueva Ley publicada en el Diario Oficial de la Federación el 10 de abril de 1970; última reforma publicada DOF June 12, 2015 (2015). Mexico. https://www.gob.mx/cms/uploads/attachment/file/156203/1044_Ley_Federal_del_Trabajo.pdf.

Ley General del Trabajo (1939). Bolivia. https://www.lexivox.org/norms/BO-L-19390524.html.

Ley Orgánica 1/2004, de 28 de diciembre, de Medidas de Protección Integral contra la Violencia de Género, 21760 (2004). Spain. https://www.boe.es/boe/dias/2004/12/29/pdfs/A42166-42197.pdf.

Ley Orgánica Integral para prevenir y erradicar la violencia contra las mujeres, Oficio no. SAN-2018-0395 (2018). Ecuador. https://www.igualdad.gob.ec/wp-content/uploads/downloads/2018/05/ley_prevenir_y_erradicar_violencia_mujeres.pdf.

Ley Orgánica sobre el derecho de las mujeres a una vida libre de violencia, N.º 38.668 (2007). Venezuela. https://www.acnur.org/fileadmin/Documentos/BDL/2008/6604.pdf.

Ley para la administración y transformación de los recursos humanos en el Gobierno de Puerto Rico, Ley N.º 83–2017 (2017).

Ley para prevenir, sancionar y erradicar la violencia contra las mujeres y los integrantes del grupo familiar, Ley N.º 30364 (2015). Peru. https://www.gob.pe/74905-ley-n-30364-ley-para-prevenir-sancionar-y-erradicar-la-violencia-contra-las-mujeres-y-los-integrantes-del-grupo-familiar.

Loi des Belges N.º 2007002011. Loi visant au contrôle de l'application des résolutions de la conférence mondiale sur les femmes réunie à Pékin en septembre 1995 et intégrant la dimension du genre dans l'ensemble des politiques fédérales (Law aimed at monitoring the implementation of the resolutions of the World Conference on Women held in Beijing in September 1995 and integrating the gender dimension into all federal policies), promulgated January 12, 2007, published February 13, 2007. Belgium.

Maternity Act (Act on the Right to Leave and Unemployment Benefits in Case of Maternity of 30/09/2022), LBK No. 1391. Denmark.

Maternity Protection Act, 1994, No. 34 (1994). Ireland. https://www.irishstatutebook.ie/eli/1994/act/34/enacted/en/html.

McIntyre, Alex. Motion for Leave to Bring in a Bill (Standing Order No. 23): Domestic Abuse (Safe Leave) (2025). United Kingdom. https://hansard.parliament.uk/commons/2025-01-07/debates/B6EBA9A0-49AD-4A5E-AD54-B5D0855247CE/DomesticAbuse(SafeLeave).

Minerals and Mining (Amendment) Act, No. 995 (2019). Ghana. https://www.mincom.gov.gh/wp-content/uploads/2021/06/Minerals-and-Mining-Amendment-Act-2019-Act-995.pdf.

Ministerio de la Mujer y Desarrollo Social. *Plan Nacional contra la Violencia hacia la Mujer 2009–2015* (2009). Peru. https://www.mimp.gob.pe/files/direcciones/dgfc/diff/politicas_nacionales/9_PlanNacional_contra_la_Violencia_hacia_la_Mujer.pdf.

Modern Slavery Act, No. 153 (2018). Commonwealth, Australia. https://www.aph.gov.au/Parliamentary_Business/Bills_Legislation/Bills_Search_Results/Result?bId=r6148.

Modern Slavery Act (2015). United Kingdom. http://www.legislation.gov.uk/ukpga/2015/30/contents/enacted.

Modifícanse las Leyes 19.121, 20 de agosto de 2013, y 19.161, 1 de noviembre de 2013 (Licencia por Paternidad), Ley N.º 20312 (2024). Uruguay. https://www.impo.com.uy/bases/leyes-originales/20312–2024.

National Artificial Intelligence Initiative Act. Public Law 116–283, Division E, January 1, 2021. United States.

National Finance Act, Act No. 12698 (2014). South Korea.

New York City Department of Consumer and Worker Protection. Amendment to Title 6 of the Rules of the City of New York, Local Law 144 of 2021 (2023). https://rules .cityofnewyork.us/wp-content/uploads/2023/04/DCWP-NOA-for-Use-of-Automated -Employment-Decisionmaking-Tools-2.pdf.

Norwegian Public Limited Liability Companies Act, Act of 13 June 1997, No. 45 (1997). https://www.euronext.com/en/media/7189/download?attachment.

Obama, Barack. Executive Order—Strengthening Protections Against Trafficking in Persons in Federal Contracts, September 25, 2012. https://obamawhitehouse.archives.gov /the-press-office/2012/09/25/executive-order-strengthening-protections-against-traf ficking-persons-fe.

———. Presidential Memorandum—Establishing Policies for Addressing Domestic Violence in the Federal Workforce, April 18, 2012. https://obamawhitehouse.archives.gov /the-press-office/2012/04/18/presidential-memorandum-establishing-policies-address ing-domestic-violen.

Office of the Attorney General, State of California. "The California Transparency in Supply Chains Act." March 31, 2015. https://oag.ca.gov/SB657.

Pacheco, Rodrigo, Senador. Dispõe sobre o uso da Inteligência Artificial. Projeto de Lei N.º 2338 (2023). Brazil. https://www25.senado.leg.br/web/atividade/materias/-/materia /157233.

Paternity Leave and Benefit Act 2016, No. 11 (2016). Ireland. https://www.oireachtas.ie/en /bills/bill/2016/43/.

Philippine Commission on Women. "Republic Act 9710: Magna Carta of Women," August 14, 2009. https://pcw.gov.ph/magna-carta-of-women/.

Precious Minerals Marketing Corporation Act, P.N.D.C.L. 219 (1989). Ghana. https://www .brr.gov.gh/reg_details?id=NDI5.

Proyecto de Ley No. 29409, que concede el derecho de licencia por paternidad a los trabajadores de la actividad pública y privada (Bill to Grant Paternity Leave to Workers in the Public and Private Sector). Congreso de la República de Peru, 24 August 2022. https://www.congreso.gob.pe/Docs/comisiones2022/Trabajo/files/exposiciones/susten tacion_pl_2890.pdf.

Real Decreto 1917/2008, de 21 de noviembre, por el que se aprueba el programa de inserción sociolaboral para mujeres víctimas de violencia de género, BOE-A-2008–19918 (2008). Spain. https://www.boe.es/buscar/doc.php?id=BOE-A-2008-19918.

Real Decreto Legislativo 2/2015, de 23 de octubre, por el que se aprueba el texto refundido de la Ley del Estatuto de los Trabajadores, BOE-A-2015–11430 (2015). Spain. https:// www.boe.es/buscar/doc.php?id=BOE-A-2015-11430.

Real Decreto Ley sobre el Seguro de Maternidad (22 de marzo de 1929). Spain. http://www .ub.edu/ciudadania/hipertexto/evolucion/textos/social1929.htm.

Regimen de Contrato de Trabajo, Ley No 20.744 (1976). Argentina. https://www.argentina .gob.ar/normativa/nacional/ley-20744-25552/actualizacion.

Régimen de Licencia Especial con goce de haberes para agentes públicos del género femenino, que se desempeñan en el ámbito del sector público provincial que sean víctimas de hechos de violencia de género, Ley Provincial L No. 5086 (2015). Río Negro, Argentina. https://web.legisrn.gov.ar/digesto/normas/ver?id=2016010004.

Relative au devoir de vigilance des sociétés mères et des entreprises donneuses d'ordre, Loi no 2017–399 (2017). France. https://www.legifrance.gouv.fr/eli/loi/2017/3/27/2017-399 /jo/texte.

Republic Act No. 7192: Women in Development and Nation Building Act: An Act promoting the integration of women as full and equal partners of men in development and nation building and for other purposes, (1992). Philippines. https://pcw.gov.ph/republic -act-7192-women-in-development-and-nation-building-act/.

Republic Act No. 7845: General Appropriations Act (1995), an Act appropriating funds for the operation of the Government of the Republic of the Philippines from January 1 to December 31. https://pcw.gov.ph/republic-act-7845-general-appropriations -act-of-1995/.

Republic Act No. 9262: Anti-Violence Against Women and Their Children Act of 2004, An act defining violence against women and their children, providing for protective measures for victims, prescribing penalties therefor, and for other purposes (2004). Philippines. https://pcw.gov.ph/republic-act-9262-anti-violence-against-women-and-their -children-act-of-2004/.

Small-Scale Gold Mining Act, P.N.D.C.L. 218 (1989). Ghana. https://lawsghana.com/pre _1992_legislation/PNDC%20Law/SMALL-SCALE%20GOLD%20MINING%20 LAW,%201989%20(PNDCL%20218)/83.

"Supplementary Information Tables: Gender-Based Analysis Plus (GBA Plus)." *2020–21 Departmental Results Report.* Ottawa: Department of Justice Canada, October 13, 2021. https://www.justice.gc.ca/eng/rp-pr/cp-pm/dpr-rr/2020_2021/supp/gba-acs.html#s1–2.

Take It Down Act (Public Law No. 119-12), May 19, 2025. United States. https://www .congress.gov/bill/119th-congress/senate-bill/146/text.

Treasury Board. Directive on Automated Decision-Making (2019). Canada. https://www .tbs-sct.canada.ca/pol/doc-eng.aspx?id=32592.

Trump, Donald. Executive Order 13859, Maintaining American Leadership in Artificial Intelligence, February 11, 2019. https://www.federalregister.gov/documents/2019/02/14/2019 –02544/maintaining-american-leadership-in-artificial-intelligence.

Vought, Russell. Memorandum: Driving Efficient Acquisition of Artificial Intelligence in Government. Executive Office of the President, April 3, 2025. https://www.white house.gov/wp-content/uploads/2025/02/M-25-22-Driving-Efficient-Acquisition-of -Artificial-Intelligence-in-Government.pdf.

Work Life Balance and Miscellaneous Provisions Act 2023, No. 8 (2023). Ireland. https:// www.irishstatutebook.ie/eli/2023/act/8/enacted/en/pdf.

Founded in 1893,
UNIVERSITY OF CALIFORNIA PRESS
publishes bold, progressive books and journals
on topics in the arts, humanities, social sciences,
and natural sciences—with a focus on social
justice issues—that inspire thought and action
among readers worldwide.

The UC PRESS FOUNDATION
raises funds to uphold the press's vital role
as an independent, nonprofit publisher, and
receives philanthropic support from a wide
range of individuals and institutions—and from
committed readers like you. To learn more, visit
ucpress.edu/supportus.

www.ingramcontent.com/pod-product-compliance
Ingram Content Group UK Ltd.
Pitfield, Milton Keynes, MK11 3LW, UK
UKHW011449101225
465928UK00004B/16